Strategic Analytics

Strategic Analytics

Integrating Management Science and Strategy

Martin Kunc, Ph.D.

This edition first published 2019
© 2019 John Wiley & Sons Ltd

The right of Martin Kunc to be identified as the author of this work has been asserted in accordance with law.

Registered Offices
John Wiley & Sons, Inc., 111 River Street, Hoboken, NJ 07030, USA
John Wiley & Sons Ltd, The Atrium, Southern Gate, Chichester, West Sussex, PO19 8SQ, UK

Editorial Office
9600 Garsington Road, Oxford, OX4 2DQ, UK

For details of our global editorial offices, customer services, and more information about Wiley products visit us at www.wiley.com.

Wiley also publishes its books in a variety of electronic formats and by print-on-demand. Some content that appears in standard print versions of this book may not be available in other formats.

Library of Congress Cataloging-in-Publication Data
Names: Kunc, Martin, author.
Title: Strategic analytics : integrating management science and strategy /
    Martin Kunc, University of Warwick.
Description: Hoboken, NJ : John Wiley & Sons, [2019] | Includes
    bibliographical references and index. |
Identifiers: LCCN 2018025510 (print) | LCCN 2018028470 (ebook) | ISBN
    9781118943694 (Adobe PDF) | ISBN 9781118943687 (ePub) | ISBN 9781118907184
    (hardcover)
Subjects: LCSH: Management science. | Decision making. | Strategic planning.
Classification: LCC HD30.25 (ebook) | LCC HD30.25 .K8165 2018 (print) | DDC
    658.4/012–dc23
LC record available at https://lccn.loc.gov/2018025510

Cover design by Wiley
Cover image: © Michel Leynaud/Getty Images

Set in 10/12pt WarnockPro by SPi Global, Chennai, India
Printed in Singapore by C.O.S. Printers Pte Ltd

10 9 8 7 6 5 4 3 2 1

Contents

About the Companion website

This book is accompanied by a companion website:

www.wiley.com/go/kunc/strategic-analytics

The website includes:

- Power points
- Excels
- Models

1

Introduction to Strategic Analytics

Objectives

1) To explain Strategic Analytics
2) To introduce the main pillars of the book: the fields of analytics, management science, information technology, statistics and strategic management
3) To explain the fields of analytics, management science, information technology, big data analytics and strategic management

Learning outcomes and managerial capabilities developed

1) Managers can learn to tackle complex problems in strategy through the integration of analytics within strategic management processes
2) Principles of Analytics: tools, support systems and methods
3) Identification of strategic problems

In today's environment, managers face turbulence and crisis. More information than ever is generated continuously: social media, financial performance management systems, customer relationship management systems, and internal and external reports. There are powerful trends: measuring and quantifying everything and skills in quantitative subjects are widely available. The problem for managers is not only to make sense of abundant quantitative information but also to engage with staff possessing analytical skills. Simultaneously managing multiple factors under pressure requires new managerial capabilities. Managers need to develop their strategies using clear strategy processes supported by the increasing availability of data. This situation calls for a different approach to strategy, such as an integration with analytics, as the science of extracting value from data and structuring complex problems.

Managers' decision processes can fall into a continuum which has on one hand pure analysis, which relies on established processes, and pure synthesis that involves identification of patterns and new ideas (Pidd, 2009). Strategic

Strategic Analytics: Integrating Management Science and Strategy, First Edition. Martin Kunc.
© 2019 John Wiley & Sons Ltd. Published 2019 by John Wiley & Sons Ltd.
Companion website: www.wiley.com/go/kunc/strategic-analytics

planning involves a mix between both extremes: analysis to identify problems and synthesis to observe trends and emerging situations before competitors. However, there is not a clear process when combining the two. Sometimes, emerging situations are discovered and then analysis is employed to confirm their impact while transforming them into new emergent strategies. In other circumstances, there is a careful planning process involving extensive data gathering and the construction of complex financial, operational and other type models to validate the new strategies.

The idea behind "Strategic Analytics" is to answer a simple question: how can quantitative and qualitative information be used to make strategic decisions? Strategic Analytics does not imply turning managers into quantitative analysts or quantitative analysts into expert strategists. Organizations need interdisciplinary teams comprised by members who can talk to each other sharing a common language. Thus, Strategic Analytics works on the basis of providing a reasonable understanding of how a variety of quantitative methods, in conjunction with structured and unstructured data, can be used to help strategic decision making in any organization. There is also the intent to show the real and practical benefit of Strategic Analytics. Strategic Analytics does not pretend to offer easy solutions to strategic problems but different ways of analyzing and solving strategic problems beyond the traditional qualitative approach to strategic management. Strategic Analytics is also an understanding of the context and processes in which analytics skills can be applied to support strategic management.

Future managers are taught a wide variety of concepts in strategy subjects but they are not taught how to apply them or even to connect them to related problems. Future managers need to develop capabilities to tackle problems that are not structured in a neat way like case studies are. In that sense, each chapter focuses on a case study with limited information that has to be solved applying a combination of theoretical concepts and analytical methods (quantitative and qualitative). The aim of this founding principle is to integrate strategic concepts with analytical tools in a unique set of capabilities (skills) to help future managers to tackle strategic problem using multiple sources of information. The main benefit is that quantitative methods, which are usually seen as a difficult experience for managers, are connected with a hands-on subject like strategy. Therefore, managers can learn capabilities to tackle complex problems in strategy through the integration of analytics (quantitative/qualitative methods to extract value from data) within strategic management processes. Therefore, the book will provide a bridge to integrate quantitative methods with their application in strategy adding rigorous methods to solve real issues in strategy.

The rest of the chapter introduces the main pillars of the book: the fields of analytics, management science, information technology, statistics and strategic management.

1.1 What is Analytics?

Organizations are competing using analytics because there is an increasing amount of data, people with capabilities to use data and, in a highly competitive environment, it is more difficult to compete effectively. While organizations can use basic descriptive statistics from any of their existing data, organizations using analytics apply modeling to understand their environments, predict the behavior of key actors, e.g. customers and suppliers, and optimize operations. Organizations can obtain competitive advantage using multiples analytics applications but it requires a new type of organization and management (Davenport, 2006):

> a companywide embrace of analytics impels changes in culture, processes, behavior and skills for many employees. And so, like any major transition, it requires leadership from executives at the very top who have a passion for the quantitative approach... CEOs leading the analytics charge require both an appreciation of and a familiarity with the subject. A background in statistics isn't necessary, but those leaders must understand the theory behind various quantitative methods so that they recognize those methods' limitations-which factors are weighed and which ones aren't... Of course, not all decision should be grounded in analytics... For analytics-minded leaders, then, the challenge boils down to knowing when to run with the numbers and when to run with their guts (Davenport, 2006: pages 102–103)

An analytical perspective is important, when data has become a key strategic asset of organizations in recent years, and analytics creates value by delivering systematic decision support in a well-timed way (Laursen and Thorlund, 2010; Holsapple et al., 2014). Business analytics, one of the multiple branches in Analytics, comprises three key elements: Information Systems, Human Competencies, and Business Processes (Laursen and Thorlund, 2010). Business analytics reflects the convergence of three disciplines: statistics, information systems, and management science (Laursen and Thorlund, 2010). While the supporting disciplines are traditional, the innovation lies in their intersections. For example, data mining aims to understand characteristics and patterns among variables in large databases using a variety of statistical analysis, e.g. correlation and regression analysis. Information technology provides data and supports decision support systems, which are sustained by management science tools together with statistical analysis, for the development of analytics. Business analytics is rooted in advances of information technology systems, which involve the acquisition, generation, assimilation, selection and presentation of data, together with tools, statistics and management science, to develop the data into knowledge to support decision making. In a similar definition, Mortenson et al. (2015) suggest analytics is the intersection of basic disciplines: technologies (electrical engineering and computer science), decision making (psychology and behavioral science) and quantitative methods (mathematics, statistics and economics); and their applications: information systems, artificial intelligence and operational research. Figure 1.1 shows Mortenson et al.'s (2015) representation of the concept of analytics.

In terms of types of analytics, Davenport proposes three types: descriptive, predictive, and prescriptive (Davenport, 2013), which are described below.

- **Descriptive Analytics.** It employs traditional statistical skills to present data collected from internal organizational activities and external data. It is utilized to understand what happened during their past business activities in order to disclose whether the current business objectives have been obtained. Then the next step is to investigate the reasons behind the results by drilling down into more detailed data and explore scientifically, e.g. test and validate or reject hypotheses. It is characterized traditionally as data mining, business intelligence and dashboards.
- **Predictive Analytics.** It involves statistical and mathematic techniques to predict future unknown events or behaviors based on historical data to

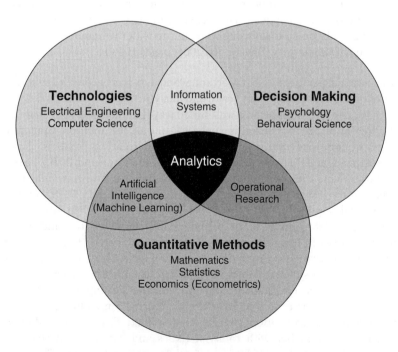

Figure 1.1 The analytics field. *Source:* Mortenson et al. (2015: figure 1, page 586). Reproduced with permission of Elsevier.

support operations. Some of the popular techniques in this area cover decision tree, text analytics, neural networks, regression modeling, and time-series forecasting. Predictive analytics also relies on data mining and other machine learning algorithms to identify trends, patterns, or relationships as volume, variety, and velocity of data increases.

- **Prescriptive Analytics.** It uses optimization and/or simulation to identify the best alternatives to improve performance. Prescriptive analytics is used in many areas of business, including operations, marketing, and finance. For example, finding the best pricing or portfolio of new product investments strategy to maximize revenue. Prescriptive analytics can address questions such as: How much should we produce to maximize profit? Should we change our plans if a natural disaster closes a supplier's factory and if so, by how much?

In terms of analytics, there is a wide variety of tools so an exhaustive list of tools will be beyond the scope of this book. Table 1.1 shows a list of the most common tools extracted from Gandomi and Haider (2015) and Chen et al. (2012).

From a process perspective, Liberatore and Luo (2010) suggest analytics follows a four-step process. First, data is collected from diverse systems. Then data extraction and manipulation are two tasks performed together with the objective to obtain and organize the data for analysis. The second step is data analysis comprising three activities: analysis; predictive modeling; and optimization. Analysis can involve presenting and analyzing data using interactive tables, charts and dashboards. Predictive modeling is employed to estimate trends, classify data and validate relationships. Optimization attempts to obtain the optimal solution. The methods employed in this stage are discussed in the next section. The third step is the interpretation of the analysis into insights. Data visualization offers insights into what happened in the past. The purpose of predictive modeling is to help to foresee future issues if the current trends continue. Optimization gives potential solutions under certain situations. The fourth step involves translating the insights into actions related to operational aspects, redefining processes or defining/adjusting strategies.

It is important to remember that big data and data science terms are different: big data refers to the data in large volume; and data science to the methods to analyze this data. One of the recent fields emerging from the rise of big data and analytics is data science. Data science is as an interdisciplinary field that combines statistics, data mining and other tools to generate analytical insights and prediction models from structured and unstructured big data (George et al., 2016). Data science focuses on the systematic study of the organization, properties, and analysis of data and the process of inference together with confidence in the inference (Dhar, 2013). Big data, as the raw material for data science, has a set of characteristics: volume, variety and velocity. Building on

Table 1.1 A selection of Analytics tools.

Method	Brief description	Suggested further reading
Text analytics	Text analytics is employed to extract information from textual data such as social network, blogs, online forums, survey responses, documents, news and any logs from interactions with customers.	Aggarwal and Zhai (2012)
	The basic tools to perform the analysis are statistical analysis, computational linguistics and machine learning. Some of the outcomes from their use are:	
	• Information extraction generates structured data from unstructured text	
	• Text summarization provides summaries from multiple documents to present the key information existing in the original text considering location and frequency of text units	
	• Sentiment analysis analyze text, which contains opinions, to infer positive or negative sentiment. The analysis can be performed at document, sentence and aspect levels	
Data analytics	Data analytics comprises technologies based on data mining and statistical analysis. More specifically, data mining algorithms, such as statistical machine learning (Bayesian networks, Hidden Markov models), sequential and temporal mining, spatial mining, process mining and network mining, are the key tools. Data mining algorithms perform classifications, clustering, regression, association analysis and network analysis.	Berry and Linoff (1997) Hand et al. (2001)
Network analytics	It evolved from bibliometric analysis, citation networks and co-authorship networks tools. The current focus is on link mining, which is the prediction of links – social relationships, collaboration – between end users, customers, etc., and community detection, which involves representing networks as graphs and applying graph theory to identify communities	Aggarwal (2011)
	Another focus is on the dynamics of social networks using agent-based models, social influence and information diffusion models	

Table 1.1 (Continued)

Method	Brief description	Suggested further reading
Visual analytics	The objective is to facilitate analytical reasoning through interactive visual interfaces that synthesize information from big, ambiguous and dynamic data. It integrates information visualization with data management and data analysis together with human perception and cognition fields. Some applications are in: • Spatial data such as geographic measurements, GPS data, and remote sensing • Temporal data such as patterns, trends and correlations of data over time • Network data related to different real networks such as transportation, electric power grids, communities, etc.	Andrienko and Andrienko (2005) Dykes et al. (2005) Simoff et al. (2008)

the notion of volume, "data scope" refers to the level of completeness of data describing events (George et al., 2016). Scope implies a wide range of variables, whole populations rather than samples, and numerous observations on each participant. A higher number of observations shifts the analysis from samples to populations (McAfee and Brynjolfsson, 2012). Variety relates to the extreme diversity in the type of data provided from internal and external sources from numeric to textual data. In terms of velocity, data is streaming in at unprecedented speed and must be dealt with in a timely manner. Another characteristic in addition to increasing velocity and variety of data is variability since data flows can be highly inconsistent with periodic peaks occurring in different units of time, e.g. minutes, days, months.

For the analysis of big data, there are a number of challenges because traditional statistical concepts apply to situations where a sample of the population is analyzed; however big data can capture the entire population (George et al., 2016). First, there is a (very) large number of potential explanatory variables available. Secondly, the data are too large to be processed by conventional personal computers. Thirdly, a model that shows a strong relationship between independent variables and the dependent variable together with strong predictive validity, may not demonstrate a causal relationship between variables. Causality needs a field experiment in which an independent variable is manipulated for a random sample of the target population. Fourthly, statistical significance becomes less meaningful when working with big data. Variables that have a small effect on the dependent variable will be significant if the sample size is large enough and spurious correlations will appear when using a large number of variables (George et al., 2016).

Laursen and Thorlund (2010) offer a useful guide to connect questions, type of analysis and competencies required to perform analytics, see Table 1.2.

Table 1.2 Approaches to analyze big data.

Type of question	Type of analysis	Competencies required
Is there any relation between an action and the results obtained?	The most basic analysis is to retrieve a set of data that provides evidence of the actions, e.g. price changes, and results, e.g. sales changes. Then, the data is presented in a certain format, e.g. a contingency table, bar charts, etc., leaving the interpretation to the users. This is usually the realm of visual analytics (Reference) or descriptive analytics	Data manager or report developer to retrieve data and organize in a visual format. No knowledge of the business is required
What is the behavior of a certain customer/ performance?	Sometimes, there is no knowledge about the performance of a certain variable so the result of this analysis is simple descriptive statistics such as sums, average, range and standard deviations. This is usually the realm of descriptive analytics (Keim et al., 2008)	Data manager or report developer to retrieve data and organize in a visual format. No knowledge of the business is required
What is the correlation between a certain event and the results? Is the action causing any effect on the results?	Hypothesis-driven analytics employs statistical analysis and the intention is to validate the correlations between events and results. Interestingly, the use of traditional statistical tests to validate correlations, e.g. 95% confidence interval, may not be relevant in the context of big data since the data contains the whole population (so a comparison of the average between variables may be enough) (George et al., 2016). In terms of analysis, they can be cross-sectional, e.g. regression analysis, or longitudinal, e.g. time series analysis	Analytics to execute appropriate statistical tests and business knowledge to ensure the quality of the selection of the variables, e.g. variables clearly describe the business

Table 1.2 (Continued)

Type of question	Type of analysis	Competencies required
What can be learnt from the events that occurred/actions taken?	Data-driven analytics, e.g. data mining and explorative analytics, attempts to create models for specific decision support. This is not theory driven but data driven. In other words, the algorithms will find the optimal model without restrictions. The quality of the findings depends on the performance in the data set not the theoretical significance. However, there are validation procedures such as testing the model in a different subset of data than the one employed to develop it (Lismont et al. 2017) Data-driven is best suited for complex tasks due to changes in data, large amounts of data and variables, and limited initial knowledge	Computer science to develop algorithms, e.g. neural network, decision trees, binary regression, and machine learning that search across the data and creates models explaining the relationships in the data Business is also required to evaluate the reasonability of the model
What is the best model to describe the factors driving the results with and without a clear variable in mind?	Data-driven analytics can also be performed with a specific variable in mind but no knowledge about the drivers of the variable. Then, the model is employed in predictive mode to find out future events (predictive analytics). In this case, data mining has a target variable and a lot of input variables without knowing their impact on the target variable Another analysis is just simply looking for patterns in data. This is employed when there is a large set of variables that do not generate sufficient information so there is a need to reduce, or group, them into a smaller, and more meaningful, set of variables. This is usually performed through cluster analysis (Kaufman and Rousseeuw, 2009), cross-sell or basket analysis models (Berry and Linoff, 1997) and up-sell models (Cohen, 2004)	Computer science to develop algorithms to search for variables to create a model

1.2   What is Management Science?

While analytics provide the context for the use of data for decision making, management science, together with statistics, is one of the engines behind analytics. According to Mayer et al. (2004), the six purposes of management science in the area of supporting strategy making are:

- **Research and analyze:** Management science can generate knowledge in a specific domain, and specific issues, to develop deeper understanding of the impact of issues on the performance of organizations or society.
- **Design and recommend:** This activity focuses on translating available knowledge into new strategies by making recommendations or designing the strategies.
- **Provide strategic advice:** Its role is to provide advice to a client on a strategy for achieving certain goals given a certain context (e.g. environment, responses of other actors, etc.). It involves understanding the requirements of the decision makers and the organization.
- **Clarify arguments and values:** In this role, management science practitioners analyze the values and argumentation systems that underpin the organizational debate. Given this purpose, analysts seek to improve the quality of the discussion detecting biases or limitations in the arguments
- **Democratize:** Analysis activities can have normative and ethical objectives related to the stakeholders. Powerful interests can be involved affecting the discussion so management science analysts can support views and opinions overlooked due to the lack of power. For example, simulation models may be useful to support claims over environmental impact.
- **Mediate:** In this role, management science designs the rules and procedures for the strategic making process and manages the interactions and progress of the process, especially facilitating meetings with different stakeholders and strategic decision makers.

The top part of Figure 1.2 shows management science mostly oriented towards objects and focused on systems, strategies, and models, while the bottom part indicates its orientation to subjects, which comprises working with people (decision makers, stakeholders, experts) and their interactions during the strategic management process. The arrows point to "styles" of analysis. When management science encompasses systems and strategies, the styles are rational, argumentative and client-advisory as it provides reasons and arguments to support the decision-making process. When management science approaches the subjective part of strategic management processes, the styles will be participative, interactive and process-oriented since their role is to generate forums for discussions where modes are "transitional objects" (Mayer et al., 2004).

In practical terms, the translation of a strategic problem to the analytical world is accomplished through the process of finding meaning and structure to

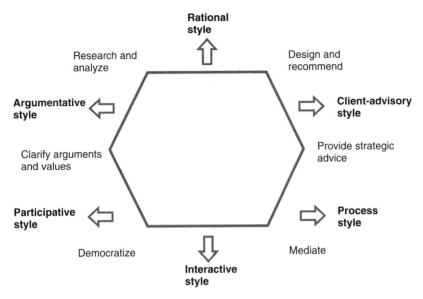

Figure 1.2 Management science styles. *Source:* Walker (2009). Reproduced with permission of Elsevier.

the strategic problem through the development of a model (Mayer et al., 2004). The model helps to visualize the data required together with precise definitions reducing ambiguity and confusion. The structure of the model can be validated to identify incoherent statements and spurious assumptions. The results of the model reflect the current and future behavior of the strategic problem given the assumptions about the problem. Finally, experiments on solutions and selection of strategic choices can illuminate a satisficing solution. The importance of each of the previous steps, translation, visualization, validation, simulation and experimentation, depends on the emphasis of the use of the model as indicated in Figure 1.2. A key aspect to highlight is the model cannot be only one solution but part of multiple models or methodologies to triangulate the strategic insights obtained. Figure 1.3 shows a categorization of modeling methods in management science reflecting the richness of the field.

From a management science perspective, **qualitative methods** are predominantly employed to structure problems that are ill-structured (not clearly visualized in the minds of the strategic decision makers) or parameters difficult to quantify (Williams, 2008). The methods cover multiple set of issues. For example, one strategic problem may consist of understanding interconnectedness inside the organization and across industry (see Soft Systems Methodology, Cognitive mapping and Causal loop diagrams in Table 1.3) or the need to manage interactions with other actors/stakeholders (see Drama theory in Table 1.3). Other strategic problems addressed are uncertain futures (see Scenario

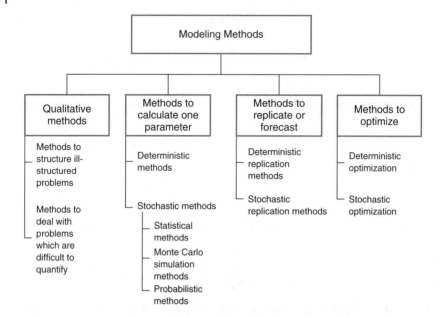

Figure 1.3 Basic categorization of modeling methods in management science.
Source: Adapted from Williams (2008). Reproduced with permission of John Wiley & Sons.

Table 1.3 Qualitative methods in Management Science.

Method	Brief description	Suggested further reading
Soft Systems Methodology	Approach used to understand and model human activity systems. The process involves appreciating the problem situation, uncovering different views from the key stakeholders, defining human activity systems and identifying desirable and feasible changes to improve the problem situation	Checkland and Scholes (1990)
Cognitive mapping	Group-based process to make sense of complex problems developing shared understanding using individual decision makers' construction of reality	Eden and Ackermann (2013)
Causal loop diagrams	It is a method to represent the feedback structures responsible for the behavior of systems. It involves identifying causal relationships among concepts as well as the type of linkage (positive or negative). It can be a group- or individual-based method	Sterman (2000)

Table 1.3 (Continued)

Method	Brief description	Suggested further reading
Drama theory	A modeling method to understand activities between two or more competing or co-operating entities considering that humans, as decision makers, may be irrational so employing drama can be a useful framework of analysis. It involves the use of role play	Bryant (2003)
Scenario analysis	It is a group process to help organizations to learn about future events by considering alternative possible outcomes and how the future will affect them through stories	van der Heijden (2005)
Robustness analysis	It supports decision making when there is radical uncertainty about the future, so it attempts to support rational decisions today given unknowable future conditions. It resolves the paradox by assessing decisions in terms of the attractive future options that they may keep open. It involves the use of decision trees to evaluate the diverse configurations to be faced at the end of the decision	Rosenhead and Mingers (2001)
Decision trees	It basically consists of a simple diagram of decisions and consequences considering the uncertainty of their outcome through their probabilities. The decisions and outcomes are represented as branches and nodes, so the tree represents a sequential path of the set of decisions and their outcomes. Then decision makers choose the optimal decision, which reflects the maximum expected values	No specific reading is suggested since it is a fairly standard technique available in quantitative methods books
Analytic hierarchy process	It implies selecting between different options considering the multiple goals a decision maker has. The idea is to structure the criteria set hierarchically, with the overall goal of the decision at the top of the model, and then comparing between pairs of criteria while maintaining consistency using decision-weights	Saaty (1980)
Multi-criteria decision analysis	It is similar to the analytic hierarchy process but the main focus is on the use of diverse methods for evaluating the weights on the criteria and then applying the weights to the criteria scores for each individual option	Belton and Stewart (2001)

analysis in Table 1.3) or uncertainty in the strategic choices existing (see Robustness analysis in Table 1.3). Qualitative methods can also work in situations where parameters are difficult to quantify (Williams, 2008) so the aim of these methods is to support decision makers to quantify parameters leading to an initial quantitative evaluation of the strategic problem. For example, decision trees can evaluate strategic actions considering subjective probabilities (see Decision trees in Table 1.3), and analytic hierarchy process and multi-criteria decision analysis (see Analytic hierarchy process and Multi-criteria decision analysis in Table 1.3) focus on the quantification of preferences in order to evaluate strategic options and choices.

Methods to calculate one parameter or a certain attribute of a system involve two types: deterministic; and stochastic. Deterministic methods can include a simple profits statement analysis, where the attribute is profit, to the evaluation of the relative efficiency across multiple decision-making units, considering one dimension. Stochastic models assume that there is not one unique result of a certain attribute but a range of values. Depending on the purpose of the analysis, they can be evaluated as Statistical, Monte Carlo or Probabilistic (Table 1.4).

Methods to replicate are utilized to understand how a system behaved in the past, behaves currently or how it will behave in the future based on models reflecting the interactions between the different components of the systems. The aim of the methods is to achieve a representation of the system that is accepted by the users (validation) while simple enough to

Table 1.4 Quantitative methods to calculate one attribute in Management Science.

Method	Brief description	Suggested further reading
Data Envelopment Analysis	This method evaluates the relative efficiency of similar decision-making units in terms of inputs and outputs. The graphical nature of the tool allows the decision maker to see the optimum units at the frontier and highlight the inefficient units	Cooper et al. (2006)
Statistics	There is a large range of methods for analyzing data but the methods attempt to basically evaluate relationships between variables (correlation), independence between groups (factor analysis), differences between groups and treatments (analysis of variance), grouping items (clustering) and finding explanatory factors (regressions)	Cortinhas and Black (2012)

Table 1.4 (Continued)

Method	Brief description	Suggested further reading
Monte Carlo	It is a broad class of computational algorithms that rely on repeated random sampling to obtain a range of possible outcomes and the probabilities they will occur for any choice of action. It allows considering risk in quantitative analysis and decision making	No specific reading is suggested since it is a fairly standard technique available in quantitative methods books
Probabilistic	It involves the use of probabilities to evaluate the future result of a certain event based on judgmental, historical or experimental information. There are many different methods among them Bayesian methods, Fuzzy methods, Stochastic/Markov processes and Risk analysis	Cortinhas and Black (2012)

understand how it works (conceptualization). The methods can be classified as deterministic and stochastic. The main deterministic method is System Dynamics, a methodology developed at MIT in the late 1950s (Table 1.5). Stochastic methods consider the existence of uncertainty in the system and its impact on the performance of the system. The uncertainty may be generated by randomness (discrete event simulation) or aggregation of multiple individual agents (agent-based simulation) (Table 1.5). Modeling can be very useful when the organization is facing up to complex issues as an interpretative approach to solve them. However, it is impossible to provide a comprehensive validation that a model is completely correct because of the interpretative approach to the complex problem. The key is the process of modeling, especially problem and model formulation (Robinson, 2004).

Simulation models can be used in different modes. The evaluation of their use is discussed in Pidd (2009) and it is based on Lane's folding star (Lane, 1995). For example, *ardent modeling* consists of the development of a formal mathematical model, which is able to run simulations, in order to develop a set of recommendations for changes in the real world. In *qualitative modeling*, the development of the model provides common language for managers or stakeholders to discuss their views of the system/problem under consideration. The model is mainly used to facilitate interpretation of the problem so there is no need to generate equations and gather data to run simulations. The main objective is to appreciate the situation. When the model use is *discursive modeling*, a formal mathematical model is developed with the objective to support

Table 1.5 Quantitative methods to replicate in Management Science.

Method	Brief description	Suggested further reading
System Dynamics	It represents organizations as a set of stocks and flows, which reflect accumulation processes, and feedback loops representing information flows and causal relations between the components of the organization. The representation of the behavior is mainly developed through time series of variables. Models are developed in either group- or individual-based processes	Morecroft (2015)
Discrete Event Simulation	This method evaluates the impact of randomness in the behavior of people or materials as they move through business processes considering resources available. People or materials form queues until they are served in the case of scarce resources. The behavior is represented using rules and logical relationships between the components of the system. The main outcome of the analysis is a probability distribution of selected parameters	Robinson (2004)
Agent-based simulation	This method focuses on the decision-making processes of individual entities and their emergent behavior over time. It usually involves evaluating the emerging behaviors resulting from the interaction of multiple individual entities. The focus is on understanding how individuals behaving in a certain manner and interacting with other individuals generate macro-level behavior	Macal and North (2005)

training through experimentation. Its aim is to foster learning and appreciation of the complexity involved in certain situations.

The model acts as a practice or training ground for managers (Lane, 1995). The model is generated to convey important theoretical elements, e.g. feedback processes, and includes guidelines to structure user's experience (Lane, 1995). However, the interaction between the model and the users cannot be completely structured so interpretation of the situation will also arise. Finally, *theoretical modeling* implies the development of a formal mathematical model, which does not represent a specific problem or situation, to offer policy insights and communicate the conceptualization of a problem in general terms without specific users and with the intention to raise awareness.

Optimization methods develop models to find the "best" or "optimal" solution from a set of possible solutions. These models have generally two elements: the objective function, which represents the set of decision variables whose optimal value needs to be found; and a set of constraints, which limit the values that the decision variables can take. There are two major types of models: deterministic; and stochastic (Table 1.6).

Table 1.6 Quantitative methods to optimize in Management Science.

Method	Brief description	Suggested further reading
Deterministic optimization	There are different techniques under this method: linear programming (single objective function, linear combination of decision variables and the decision variables can have any value except non-negative); integer and mixed programming (the only difference with linear programming is that all or some of the decision variables can only have integer values); non-linear programming (the objective function and the constraints are related non-linearly); goal programming (there are multiple competing objectives but if the objectives can be weighted, then the problem will be presented as single-objective linear programming); and dynamic programming (the problem is divided into stages with a decision at each stage subject to the state to move in the next stage and the objective function has to satisfy a recursive requirement such as cost or distance)	Winston and Goldberg (2004)
Stochastic optimization	It is the process of maximizing or minimizing a mathematical or statistical function when one or more of the input parameters are subject to randomness. Stochastic processes always involve probability The objective is to maximize the function's output value in the face of numerous random input variables	Heyman and Sobel (2003)

Given strategic management processes are complex and uncertain, it is important to explore the consequences of strategic decisions and plans before implementing them. Often the process of exploring the consequences is performed intuitively by highly experienced managers based on their long experience. While it is definitively important to have experience, as well as deep knowledge, in crafting strategy (Pidd, 2009), managers also have limited rationality and are subject to biases and heuristics. Biases and heuristics are useful in detecting patterns that resemble previous experience but strategies tend to be forward looking and uncertain, so previous experience may hinder rather than help managers.

Consequently, the role of external and explicit models, as the main outcome of management science processes (an integral discipline in Analytics) is to provide the platform to capture the critical aspect of the issues the decisions and plans are addressing. Management science models will not replace strategic decision makers but they can be valuable tools to direct their thinking and articulate existing knowledge. Models can account for conditions where decision makers are unsure about the result of a choice, so a formal model can provide optimized options for the set of choices under consideration (prescriptive analytics). In other circumstances, the model may help to understand the current situation to identify opportunities or threats using either existing big data or eliciting assumptions (descriptive analytics). Models are also able to present evidence of future issues when certain strategic decisions are implemented (predictive analytics). In other words, models facilitate "procedural rationality" (Pidd, 2009). Thus, models are concerned with the nature of strategy processes (search, design and evaluation) rather than the outcome of the strategy process (e.g. differentiation or low costs, diversification or integration). In that way, models and modeling can be considered systematic procedures to support decision making of bounded rational decision makers (Pidd, 2009).

Strategy Analytics requires formal, illustrative and metaphorical models as they are the most suitable for the issues faced during the strategy process. Realistic management science models involving more operational detail, big data and process dimensions can become a competitive advantage. This is usually the realm of strategic operational research (Bell, 1998) and this is a useful description for many traditional big data analytics tools used currently in organizations. In other words, big data analytics is a source of "competitive advantage" but it does not directly support strategy design processes. Thus, strategic analytics differs from operational analytics.

1.3 What is Information Technology: New Challenges?

Currently, information technology needs to consider two key sources of data for decision making: digital data streams flowing from a multitude of sources most of them without being controlled by the companies; and traditional data warehouses, which store the data generated mostly by transactional and internal systems. In any case, the key function of information technology is to deliver information to the strategy development process. One of the issues is the lack of a specific type of information that is going to be required and the timing for its use, especially to discuss emergent issues, e.g. high customer churn rate. Emergent issues can lead to the establishment of new strategies based on the knowledge generated from the analysis of the information, e.g. new pricing strategies to keep customers. In the case of designed strategies, they start defining objectives and performance measures, e.g. customer satisfaction, so the requirements for the type of information are clear and lead to purposeful creation of the data management processes, e.g. automatic capture of customer feedback. Some of the information acts as leads for future events so it helps to predict future results, e.g. level of customer satisfaction can predict the future churn rate. Other information reflects past behavior and supports monitoring processes related to the achievement of objectives and learning from the effectiveness of actions. The past information can be employed in optimization processes through learning the impact of actions to improve performance.

The revolution in the digital world is relentless and it is creating digital streams of structure and unstructured data which offer opportunities for existing and new firms to leverage decision making (Pigni et al., 2016). One of the incredible paradoxes of this revolution is that organizations may be data rich but information poor due to the limited competencies for exploiting data and transforming it into information and knowledge (Pigni et al., 2016). Digital data streams promise to start an era beyond Business Intelligence (BI) because BI exploits a large volume of data that has changed slowly, e.g. transactional data, and is created internally in the company. Digital data streams change fast, are generated by multiple sources (humans or machines), and there is a need to harvest from external environments or non-traditional sources so the challenges are different.

Pigni et al. (2016) suggest that digital data streams can provide multiple views on a transaction such as pre- and post-transaction details, as well as real time, and generate responses to events to create value for the organization. There are two activities that can extract value from digital data according to Pigni et al. (2016):

- **Process-to-actuate:** in this activity the organization initiates action based on real-time processing of the digital data. For example, there is an event occurring that is being informed through digital data, and through the use of existing databases and other contextual data the organization can provide suggestions on which to act.
- **Assimilate-to-analyze:** the organization merges multiple sets of data (real-time and static) to compose datasets that are used for insights later on. For

example, a retailer uses existing correlations between external factors, customer profiles and demand of certain products to determine sales forecasts and inventory replenishment decisions.

There are different factors affecting the extraction of value. First, the delay in processing data from the event until the decision can reduce value. A delay is generated by processes performed on the data such as data collection and preparation for analysis, analysis of the data to transform into information and transformation of the information into decision. Secondly, the set of skills are critical to exploit data streams. Skills depend on the knowledge base of the organization to convert data into improved decision making. The conversion of data to knowledge starts with a decision maker with enough understanding of the issues to request relevant information, followed by processing appropriate data to generate this information when it is available (Pigni et al., 2016). Thirdly, the capacity to effectively identify and access real-time data streams that match organizational needs is necessary to create datasets to generate value (Pigni et al., 2016). Fourthly, an appropriate toolset (software and hardware) is required to access real-time data streams and harvest its content (Pigni et al., 2016). Finally, the organization needs to reach a level of readiness or maturity to exploit digital data and extract value. The level of readiness is associated with strategic, managerial and cultural aspects of the organization as well as data skills. Both level of readiness, or "mindset" in Pigni et al.'s (2016) words, and toolset are key in order to create value from the flow of digital data.

Traditional data management involves a technical or business-oriented perspective in operating and maintaining the organization's information systems structure (Laursen and Thorlund, 2010). Data warehouses may be developed from a technical perspective rather than from the need for information which affects its usability in the business analytics process. If the data warehouse is owned by the technical area associated with information systems, then front-ends may not be user-friendly, not oriented towards the needs of the decision makers or only dependent on internal data warehouses mostly originated from transactional systems (Laursen and Thorlund, 2010). Data acquisition is not thought of in terms of events thus data may not be recorded or recorded inadequately. However, data warehouses offer a common information platform ensuring consistent, integrated and valid data since data is structured and cleansed from the different source systems (Laursen and Thorlund, 2010). Laursen and Thorlund (2010) suggest an architecture and processes for data warehouses:

1) **Source Systems.** They consist of the systems that provide data for the warehouse and they can be internal sources such as ERP, CRM. External sources, among other sources, can be originated from "web scraping" which is the automated extraction of large amounts of data from websites (George et al.,

2016). Web scraping programs are relatively widespread and may come free of charge, such as plugins for Google Chrome (George et al., 2016). Some websites, such as Twitter, offer "application program interfaces" (APIs) to facilitate easy access to its content. Web scraping is used to extract numeric data, such as product prices, and extract textual, audio, and video data generated by firms and individuals, news articles, and product reviews (George et al., 2016). A final consideration of the data sources is their prioritization in terms of usability and availability. Interestingly, the relationship between both concepts is inverse: higher usability may imply lower availability, e.g. questionnaires; and higher availability may lead to lower usability, e.g. call center information.

2) **Extract, Transform and Load (ETL).** These processes transform the data from the source into the data warehouse, merge with another sources, and load them to different locations. Some of the data can be negatively affected during the process of transformation while other data can improve it. In other circumstances, the combination of two lower quality data can lead to a set of data more available but perhaps less usable.

3) **Staging area.** This is an intermediate, temporal, area between the source systems and the final location in the data warehouse. It is usually considered for processes related to the transformation of the data, e.g. to make compatible the different types of formats on databases existing from the source systems.

4) **Data quality process.** This process is performed by firewalls with profiling and cleansing tools. For example, incomplete data, duplicates and inconsistent data can affect the performance of the warehouse so the firewall analyzes the data and rejects improper data. Profiling tools use statistical tools to search for anomalous data, e.g. missing gender or addresses.

5) **Data warehouse.** After the data is treated to have an adequate quality, the data is integrated and categorized in terms of dimensions and metadata for future analysis by the analytics teams. The data is organized using diverse methods such as dimensional modeling. Dimensional modeling adds to transactional data different dimensions to make the data more comprehensive such as adding to items information such as organization, time, place, etc. Metadata is the information related to documenting the data in terms of its origins, sources, size, composition, etc.

6) **Data mart area.** They are the foundation for relational data and cubes for users, as well as access for analytics. They are created based on reporting requirements from the analysts, so they involve organizing and selecting the data to answer users' specific questions.

7) **Analytics Portal.** This area contains the reports for business users such as dashboards, scorecards, and retrospective reports. This is only the tip of the iceberg in terms of analytics processes.

1.4   What is Strategic Management?

There is not a unique definition of strategic management but a series of propositions on the range of the process involved in developing strategies. For example, McGee et al. (2010) suggest strategy can be decomposed into four components: external logic (how a company positions relate to its environment); internal logic (the resources and competences to employ to implement the strategy); the performance over time (the achievement of long-term objectives and survival); and the managerial requirements (the role of general managers and the process of strategic management which involves planning, managing, monitoring and maintenance of strategies). McGee et al. (2010) also explain the nature of strategy: strategy deals with the future which is uncertain, so strategy involves risks that need to be considered in the plans and actions. However, the plans and actions for implementing the strategy are not simple since there are multiple interacting components (external, internal and managerial), which require coordination. Another factor compounding the risk is that plans and actions are irreversible because once a strategy is implemented it changes many external and internal aspects that make it difficult to go back.

Designing and implementing strategy, the realm of strategic management, requires frameworks and tools to address the uncertainty, complexity and risk underpinning it (Pfeffer and Sutton, 2006). Essentially, a strategy framework is a conceptual representation, or a model, that managers can use to design strategies with a clear description of the logic and sources used (Pfeffer and Sutton, 2006). In other words, there are strong indications (e.g. complexity, uncertainty, risk, future-orientation, limited ability to process the problem, evidence requirements, and existence of models) that strategies can be designed and shaped using management science tools. Management science tools work best as part of strategic management frameworks.

In the framework proposed in this book, four components comprise the strategic management process (Figure 1.4). The process starts with a definition/understanding of the business in terms of mission and vision of the business followed by an understanding of the external forces affecting the firm today and in the future (macro factors: political, economic, social, technological, environmental; industry factors: industry structure dynamics and its evolution) as well as a review of the resources and capabilities of the firm in terms of its competitive positioning (products, services, value creation, business model). The results of the previous stage are the basis for designing the strategy in terms of positioning and the conceptualization of the resources and capabilities to sustain it. The design of the strategies involves a creative conceptualization of the resources and capabilities needed for the new strategies (Kunc and Morecroft, 2010). Strategies will be affected by not only the resources and capabilities available to managers but also the life cycle of the organization. For example, some strategies cannot be performed at the

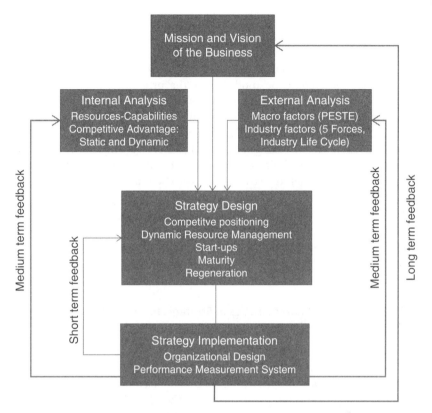

Figure 1.4 Strategic management process.

beginning of the company, e.g. merger and acquisition, and other strategies, e.g. diversification, result from the need for growth occurring when the company reaches maturity. After reaching an agreement in the top management team about the future strategies, their implementation involves managing (reinforcing, building, acquiring, and reorganizing) resources and capabilities to adapt them to the new or updated competitive positioning. Resource management is an inherently complex task because resources and capabilities interact forming a complex dynamic system where feedback processes, delays and external factors affect their dynamic (Kunc and Morecroft, 2009). Consequently, any implementation plans need to consider the future implications in terms of business as usual (base case), potential different external environments (scenarios) and expected contingencies (situations that may eventually happen). Finally, the implementation over time is monitored using performance measurement systems (IT systems, big data and dashboards) which foster organizational learning and adaptation of the organization to emergent situations (e.g. applying descriptive and predictive analytics). The feedback from strategy can be monitored in the short term leading to modifying the management of resources or correcting minor erroneous strategy designs, e.g. data from a customer satisfaction survey indicates that certain product features need to be modified or the product has to be delivered through new distribution channels. However, if the lessons learned involve discovering new external factors, they will need to be tracked over time to observe the relevant trends before making adjustments to the strategy design. Similarly, if lessons from strategy monitoring reflect a change in the qualitative aspects of resources/capabilities, e.g. loss of their uniqueness due to competitors' imitating them, then the strategy needs to be redesigned. Both processes take a longer time to develop than operational issues due to changes in the commitments from the organization. Finally, feedback from strategy monitoring can imply a more substantial change in the organization such as changing the mission, updating its vision and refocusing the business model. Table 1.7 presents a detailed account of the components of the strategic management framework.

1.4.1 What are the Characteristics of Strategic Problems?

Strategic problems, which are at the core of the process of strategic management, have certain characteristics that make them more difficult to solve than *operational problems*. Operational problems are issues generated from daily routine decisions. For example, the development of a new brand will be considered a strategic problem but the definition of the advertising campaign to support the brand is usually an operational problem. The characteristics of problems are (Dyson et al., 2007):

- *Breadth of scope* suggests the existence of implications in and outside of the organization involving multiple stakeholders: owners (individual and institutional shareholders), external (customers, suppliers, local communities, governmental agencies, general society), and internal (employees and managers) with multiple, imprecise and conflicting objectives.
- *Complexity and inter-relatedness* of decision-making context where the interactions between many factors require important coordination in the present and future.
- *Enduring effects*, possibly of an irreversible nature with a *high level of risk* since it involves committing potentially inflexible resources against expected futures that might never materialize affecting the organization's prosperity and survival.
- *Significant time lag* before impact, with widening uncertainty over the timescale involved, which may generate agency problems such as making no decision or leaving the outcome to chance.

Table 1.7 Description of the strategic management process components.

Step	Brief description	Chapter
Mission and vision	The first task in the strategic management process is setting and visualizing the direction of the organization. Even small organizations, which are run by the owners, require a sense of direction that will reflect the intent of the owners. Where is the intent of the owners or top managers coming from? Paradigms, experience and facts define owners' mental models, which are personal explanations about how the real world works. Mental models are responsible for the interpretation of the key external factors affecting current and future performance of the organization and the key internal factors that are at the core of the performance of organization. On the one hand, the mission defines the core purpose of the organization defined by the perception of the key internal factors and the values shared in the organization. On the other hand, the future of the organization using its core purpose in the future is expressed in the vision	Chapter 6 for competitive advantage: static analysis
External analysis	The external environment can affect the organization's actions as well as its performance. Consequently, it is fundamental to consider the external environment in the strategic management process	Chapter 3 for exogenous factors (PESTE)
	The external environment can be divided into three parts according to the closeness to the organization: rivalry with existing organizations (closest); industry dynamics defined by the suppliers, potential entrants, substitutes and customers (mid-range); and the remote environment comprised by the political, economic, social, technological and environmental factors that determine the two closest layers to the organization	Chapter 4 for industry dynamics (5 forces)
	Another important component of the external analysis is the industry life cycle. Industry life cycle can affect any organization, not only for-profit. The life cycle is driven by the usefulness of the industry, or group of similar organizations, for the consumers or users of their services. Industries proceed through four stages (introduction/ birth, growth, maturity and decline), which reflect the rate of growth of sales. The introduction stage is driven by the process of changing buyers' behaviors in order to adopt the new product/service. Sometimes, this stage takes decades. Growth occurs when a large number of buyers change their behavior and adopt the product/service massively surpassing the capacity of the existing organizations to serve them. This situation leads to the entrance of more organizations trying to capture part of this demand. Maturity corresponds to the saturation of the market and growth rate declines towards zero, i.e. when all potential buyers have adopted the product sales are driven by replacements or natural growth rate (ageing). Finally, a new product/service attracts the current buyers and sales will decline determining the disappearance of the industry in its current form. Organizations either regenerate or liquidate	Chapter 5 for industry evolution (industry life cycle)

(Continued)

Step	Brief description	Chapter
Internal analysis	Competitive advantage is at the heart of any organization's performance, from micro business to large corporations through non-governmental organizations. Competitive advantage involves creating value for its buyers differently than competing organizations. Creating value depends on the strengths and weaknesses of the organization without following strategic recipes. Managers can use tools to analyze an organization's capacity to generate value for buyers before designing the strategy	Chapter 6 for competitive advantage: static analysis
	Traditional concepts are complemented with management science tools, e.g. dynamic simulation, to support the process of competitive positioning over time. For example, business-level strategies like Porter's generic strategies are evaluated over time as part of a competitive environment	Chapter 7 for dynamic resource management (dynamic resource-based view of the firm)
Strategy design	Starting a new business is performed by many people but managing a successful start-up is a formidable challenge, especially for those who lack prior business ownership, management skills and experience. Thus, this chapter offers an introduction to the concepts of business model, business plan and financial needs that play an important role in the beginning of a business	Chapter 10 for start-ups
	The set of strategies that companies tend to adopt when they are reaching maturity are driven by, on the one hand, long-term objectives such as economic sustainability; productivity, sustaining competitive position, stance in the value system, product/service positioning, and social responsibility. On the other hand, markets are becoming saturated by competitors and running out of new customers. Thus, strategies to address competition, find new markets and improve efficiency are fundamental for surviving	Chapter 11 for maturity
	Two responses can develop when organizations face a decline in their markets. These responses are important because they can determine the fate of an organization – survival or death. First, innovate and change to offer different products/services. Secondly, they can respond rigidly and fall into organizational decline through a downward spiral. What conditions are needed for each situation to emerge? What signals develop to understand the decline process? Developing a strategic framework for regeneration depends on distinguishing between flexible and inflexible organizations	Chapter 12 for regeneration

| Strategy implementation | Strategy can be affected by the behavior of multiple stakeholders. Thus, strategy implementation is not only a top-down process originated from the top management team but it is also occurs bottom-up when stakeholders and employees make decisions every day. The effectiveness of the implementation of strategies resides in the way that the organization is designed and organized. Organization design implies building the foundations of purpose and core values, policies and structures that determine business decisions and effective learning processes. Therefore, strategy implementation is how to design and improve business processes and organizational structure to achieve the goals and objectives | Chapter 8 for organizational design |
| | The process of defining organizational performance together with the goals and control systems is fundamental to achieve the desired organizational performance. Defining organizational performance is key because managers measure what they value and what they measure affects their behavior significantly. Moreover, this is a key process that defines the data available for the organization that can be exploited through analytics to feed back to the top management | Chapter 9 for performance measurement system |

- *Disagreement* about the motivation for, and the direction and nature of the strategic problem since strategic problems have *no obvious right answers* because of the many uncertainties surrounding their future impacts.
- *Challenging the status quo* and creating a politicized setting where change is contested and the *coordination of a large number of people is complex* and difficult due to the significant scale and importance of the strategic decision to solve the problem.

1.5 Strategy Analytics: Integrating Management Science with Strategic Management

Considering the relationship business analytics can have with respect to strategic management, there are four possible situations suggested by Laursen and Thorlund (2010); these are illustrated in Table 1.8.

The strategic problems can be exacerbated when there is not only dynamic complexity due to existence of feedback processes between the components of the system (organizational and external factors) but also complex behavior in the decision makers, such as personal aspirations, mental models and values (Roth and Senge, 1996). Large multi-business organizations are examples of high dynamic complexity. Under high dynamic complexity, causes of problems cannot readily be determined by direct experience, and actors in the system don't have a deep understanding of the causes of problems. Dynamic complexity requires high level conceptual and systems thinking skills (Roth and Senge, 1996), which is the management science style described at the top level of the hexagon in Figure 1.2. High behavioral complexity exists under conditions of profound conflict in assumptions, beliefs, and perspectives. Consequently, it is difficult to get people to agree on what should be done because they see the world differently and because they have different preferences and goals (Roth and Senge, 1996). Behavioral complexity requires high levels of interpersonal and facilitative skills (Roth and Senge, 1996), which is the management science style described at the bottom level of the hexagon in Figure 1.2. Table 1.9 shows the results of the combination of both dimensions.

Table 1.10 shows a brief explanation of the impact of the issues in terms of formulation and solutions developed using management science tools. Williams (2008) suggests puzzles are fairly easy to tackle since there is no ambiguity in the formulation of the model (either qualitative or quantitative) and there is an expected answer in terms of the outputs. Problems can be defined but there are multiple models that can be employed and none of them are exclusive. Finally, messes involve the most difficult situations since there is no agreement about the issue (so there is no clear formulation) or the solution, as there can be many potential valid outputs.

Table 1.8 Four situations between strategy and business analytics.

Relationship	Consequence	Explanation
Strategic management is dissociated from the use of analytics	Analytics (management science) is used on an ad hoc basis	Companies do not have a clear strategy related to data management and information systems so data is not used for strategic decision making. Analysis is driven by erratic users' requests of information and quantitative models and business analytics is assessed by the speed on answering the request
Strategic management defines the use of analytics	Analytics (management science) supports monitoring strategy performance	Analytics is mostly employed for monitoring the achievement of strategic objectives but there is no feedback from analytics to strategic management. Analysis has a reactive purpose providing reports, or quantitative models, for functional areas or individual departments to support the achievement of strategic objectives
Strategic management maintains a dialogue with analytics	Analytics (management science) supports strategy innovation by offering insights from data as well as testing the robustness of strategic ideas	Strategic management employ analytics to improve the learning process about the performance of the business. Analysis not only reports the achievement of the objectives but also uncovers the reasons for the current performance. Analytics practice is based on strong management science competencies and technological resources to support the dialogue. Information is used to adapt and optimize strategy

(Continued)

Table 1.8 (Continued)

Relationship	Consequence	Explanation
Strategic management has a holistic perspective	Analytics (management science) is used as a strategic resource	Information and analysis is considered as a strategic resource. Analytics is responsible for analyzing and identifying opportunities and threats in the market and issues in the firm. Strategic management uses systematically information to develop strategies. The strength of Analytics resides in people's competencies related to strategic development processes. People have both skills and knowledge of strategy and analytics in all organizational levels

Table 1.9 Complexity facing Strategy Analytics Practitioners.

		Dynamic Complexity	
		Low	High
Behavioral complexity	**Low**	Puzzles	Messes
	High	Wicked problems	Wicked messes

Source: Roth and Senge (1996: figure 1, page 93). Reproduced with permission of Emerald Group Publishing Ltd.

There will always be important questions related to the effectiveness of management science practices, the role of IT functions and how big data analytics is different from traditional analytical frameworks and methods employed in strategic management. Management science practices provide substantive rationality (Simon, 1976) because they force strategists to be methodical and precise in their strategies. Big data analytics offers a platform for organizational learning, which depends on ongoing sensemaking activities. A key question about the use of big data in strategic management is how to relate backward-looking sensemaking from big data that has been accumulated over time to the development of future sensemaking associated with strategic management. Calvard (2016: page 70) suggests "big data is often used in the

Table 1.10 Relationship between the problems faced in the strategic management process and the management science modeling process.

		Puzzles	Problems	Messes
Management science modeling process	**Formulation**	No ambiguity on the formulation about what needs to be solved, issues and options are clear	The definition of the problem is rather clear and agreed	There is a lot of ambiguity, no agreement about the issues, concept relationships or what is the situation
	Solutions	There is a correct answer which requires logical thought even though the answer may not be easy	There is a variety of approaches to solve it so the problem has no single answer that is known to be correct	Unclear formulation implies lack of clarity in the approaches or even if there is a solution at all
Strategic management process		External Factor Analysis	Strategy Implementation	Strategy Design

traditional retrospective sensemaking mode to consolidate and enact a partially existing reality identified by the data". Consequently, there is a need to complement backward-looking analysis with forward-looking foresight. This need can only be satisfied with the use of management science tools such as qualitative methods to structure problems, simulation or optimization, together with strategic management tools.

References

Andrienko, N. and Andrienko, G. (2005). Exploratory Analysis of Spatial and Temporal Data. Springer.

Aggarwal, C.C. (ed.) (2011). Social Network Data Analytics. Springer.

Aggarwal, C.C. and Zhai, C. (eds) (2012). Mining Text Data. Springer Science & Business Media.

Bell, P.C. (1998). Strategic operational research. *Journal of the Operational Research Society*, 49, 381–391.

Belton, V. and Stewart, T. (2001). Multiple Criteria Decision Analysis: An Integrated Approach, Kluwer Academic Publishers.

Berry, M.J. and Linoff, G. (1997). Data Mining Techniques: for Marketing, Sales, and Customer Support. John Wiley & Sons, Inc.

Bryant, J. (2003). The Six Dilemmas of Collaboration: Interorganizational Relationships as Drama. John Wiley & Sons, Ltd.

Calvard, T.S. (2016). Big data, organizational learning, and sensemaking: Theorizing interpretive challenges under conditions of dynamic complexity. *Management Learning*, 47(1), 65–82.

Checkland, P. and Scholes, J. (1990). Soft Systems Methodology in Action. John Wiley & Sons, Ltd.

Chen, H., Chiang, R.H. and Storey, V.C. (2012). Business intelligence and analytics: From big data to big impact. *MIS Quarterly*, 36(4), 1165–1188.

Cohen, M.D. (2004). Exploiting response models – optimizing cross-sell and up-sell opportunities in banking. *Information Systems*, 29(4), 327–341.

Cooper, W., Seiford, L. and Tone, K. (2006). Data Envelopment Analysis: A Comprehensive Text with Models, Applications, References and DEA-solver Software. Springer-Verlag.

Cortinhas, C. and Black, K. (2012). Statistics for Business Economics. John Wiley & Sons, Ltd.

Davenport, T.H. (2006). Competing on analytics. *Harvard Business Review*, 84(1), 98–105.

Davenport, T.H. (2013). Analytics 3.0. *Harvard Business Review*, 91(12), 64–68.

Dhar, V. (2013). Data science and prediction. *Communications of the ACM*, 56, 64–73.

Dykes, J., MacEachren, A., and Kraak, M.-J. (2005). Exploring Geovisualization. Elsevier Science.

Dyson, R. G., Bryant, J., Morecroft, J., and O'Brien, F. (2007). The strategic development process. In: Supporting Strategy: Frameworks, Methods and Models (eds F. O'Brien and R. Dyson), 3–24. John Wiley & Sons, Ltd.

Eden, C. and Ackermann, F. (2013). Making Strategy: The Journey of Strategic Management. Sage.

Gandomi, A. and Haider, M. (2015). Beyond the hype: Big data concepts, methods, and analytics. *International Journal of Information Management*, 35(2), 137–144.

George, G., Osinga, E.C., Lavie, D. and Scott, B.A. (2016). Big data and data science methods for management research. *Academy of Management Journal*, 59(5), 1493–1507.

Hand, D., Mannila, H., and Smyth, P. (eds) (2001). Principles of Data Mining. MIT Press.

Heyman, D.P. and Sobel, M.J. (2003). Stochastic Models in Operations Research: Stochastic Optimization, Vol. 2. Courier Corporation.

Holsapple, C., Lee-Post, A., and Pakath, R. (2014). A unified foundation for business analytics. *Decision Support Systems*, 64, 130–141.

Kaufman, L. and Rousseeuw, P.J. (2009). Finding Groups in Data: an Introduction to Cluster Analysis, Vol. 344. John Wiley & Sons, Ltd.

Keim, D., Andrieko, G., Fekete, J.-D., et al. (2008) Visual analytics: Definition, process and challenges. In: Information Visualization – Human-centered

Issues (eds A. Kerren, J.T. Stasko, J.-D. Fekete, and C. North), 154–175. Springer.

Kunc, M. and Morecroft, J. (2007). System dynamics modeling for strategic development. In: Supporting Strategy: Frameworks, Methods and Models (eds F.A. O'Brien and R.G. Dyson), 157–189. John Wiley & Sons, Ltd.

Kunc, M. and Morecroft, J. (2009). Resource-based strategies and Problem Structuring: Using resource maps to manage resource systems. *Journal of the Operational Research Society*, 58, 191–199.

Kunc, M. and Morecroft, J. (2010). Managerial decision-making and firm performance under a resource-based paradigm. *Strategic Management Journal*, 31(11), 1164–1182.

Lane, D.C. (1995). The folding star: a comparative reframing and extension of validity concepts in system dynamics. Proceedings of the 1995 International System Dynamics Conference. Tokyo, Japan, 111–130.

Laursen, G. and Thorlund, J. (2010). Business Analytics for Managers: Taking Business Intelligence Beyond Reporting. John Wiley & Sons, Ltd.

Liberatore, M.J. and Luo, W. (2010). The analytics movement: Implications for operations research. *Interfaces*, 40(4), 313–324.

Lismont, J., Vanthienen, J., Baesens, B., and Lemahieu, W. (2017). Defining analytics maturity indicators: A survey approach. *International Journal of Information Management*, 37(3), 114–124.

Macal, C.M. and North, M.J. (2005). Tutorial on agent-based modeling and simulation. Proceedings of the 2005 Winter Simulation Conference. Orlando, FL, USA.

Mayer, I.S., van Daalen, C.E., and Bots, P.W.G. (2004). Perspectives on policy analyses: a framework for understanding and design. *International Journal of Technology, Policy and Management*; 4(2), 169–191.

McAfee, A. and Brynjolfsson, E. (2012). Big data: The management revolution. *Harvard Business Review*, 90(10), 60–68.

McGee, J., Wilson, D., and Thomas, H. (2010). Strategy: Analysis and Practice. McGraw-Hill.

Morecroft, J. (2015). Strategic Modelling and Business Dynamics: A Feedback Systems Approach, 2nd edition. John Wiley & Sons, Ltd.

Mortenson, M.J., Doherty, N.F., and Robinson, S. (2015). Operational research from Taylorism to Terabytes: A research agenda for the analytics age. *European Journal of Operational Research*, 241(3), 583–595.

Pfeffer, J. and Sutton, R.I. (2006). Evidence-based management. *Harvard Business Review*, 84(1), 62–75.

Pidd, M. (2009). Tools for Thinking: Modelling in Management Science, 3rd edn. John Wiley & Sons, Ltd.

Pigni, F., Piccoli, G., and Watson, R. (2016). Digital Data Streams. *California Management Review*, 58(3), 5–25.

Robinson, S. (2004). Simulation: the Practice of Model Development and Use. Palgrave Macmillan.

Rosenhead J. and Mingers J. (eds) (2001). Rational Analysis in a Problematic World Revisited. John Wiley & Sons, Ltd.

Roth, G.L. and Senge, P.M. (1996). From theory to practice: research territory, processes and structure at an organizational learning centre. *Journal of Organizational Change Management*, 9(1), 92–106.

Saaty, T. (1980). The Analytic Hierarchy Process: Planning, Priority Setting, Resource Allocation. McGraw-Hill.

Simoff, S., Böhlen, M.H., and Mazeika, A. (eds) (2008). Visual Data Mining: Theory, Techniques and Tools for Visual Analytics. Springer Science & Business Media.

Simon, H.A. (1976). From substantive to procedural rationality. In:25 Years of Economic Theory: Retrospect and Prospect (eds T.J. Kastelein, S.K. Kuipers, W.A. Nijenhuis, and R.G. Wagenaar), 65–86. Springer.

Sterman, J.D. (2000). Business Dynamics: Systems Thinking and Modeling for a Complex World. Irwin/McGraw-Hill.

Van der Heijden, K. (2005). Scenarios: The Art of Strategic Conversations. John Wiley & Sons, Ltd.

Walker, W.E. (2009). Does the best practice of rational-style model-based policy analysis already include ethical considerations? *Omega*, 37(6), 1051–1062.

Williams, T. (2008). Management Science in Practice. John Wiley & Sons, Ltd.

Winston, W.L. and Goldberg, J.B. (2004). Operations Research: Applications and Algorithms. Duxbury Press.

2

Dynamic Managerial Capabilities for a Complex World Under Big Data

Objectives

1) To explain dynamic managerial capabilities
2) To explain the impact of big data and analytics on dynamic managerial capabilities
3) To present the impact of analytics on strategizing

Learning outcomes and managerial capabilities developed

1) Learn the three dimensions comprising dynamic managerial capabilities
2) Learn the concept of models and modeling

Dynamic managerial capabilities are changing in an era of big data, analytics and complexity. Managers need to learn how to apply a combination of strategy concepts and analytical methods (quantitative and qualitative) to address unstructured complex strategic problems using data coming in multiple forms (large, unstructured, fast). The key ability for managers is to integrate strategic concepts with analytical tools in a unique set of capabilities to tackle strategic problems. The main benefit is that quantitative methods, which are essential in an era of big data, are clearly connected with strategy development processes. Moreover, the integration of analytical tools within the abilities of managers aims to reduce behavioral issues in the process of making strategic decisions. To summarize, dynamic managerial capabilities for a complex world under the influence of big data have to tackle complex strategic problems through the integration of analytical (quantitative and qualitative) methods that exploit the availability of a large amount of data (quantitative and qualitative).

Strategic Analytics: Integrating Management Science and Strategy, First Edition. Martin Kunc.
© 2019 John Wiley & Sons Ltd. Published 2019 by John Wiley & Sons Ltd.
Companion website: www.wiley.com/go/kunc/strategic-analytics

2.1 Dynamic Managerial Capabilities

Teece et al. (1997) proposed the concept of "dynamic capabilities" to describe the abilities of managers to configure their organizations to achieve competitive advantage. First, the term "dynamic" denotes the importance of change as a process to renew competences to maintain relevance with the changing business environment. By competences, Teece et al. (1997) define the resources integrated in systems to perform distinctive activities/processes/organizational routines. Secondly, the concept of "capabilities" highlights the important role of the abilities of the top management team and strategic decision-making processes to adapt, integrate, and reconfigure the organizational skills, resources, and functional competences to fit the requirements of the environment. There are multiple definitions of the term by Eisenhardt and Martin (2000), Zollo and Winter (2002), Helftat et al (2007) and even a later refinement by Teece (2007). Further refinements focused on specific characteristics of dynamic capabilities such as differences according to market dynamics and level of complexity, e.g. detailed, analytical which rely on existing knowledge to simple, experiential depending on the situation and new knowledge (Eisenhardt and Martin, 2000).

In a further enrichment of the concept of dynamic capabilities, Adner and Helfat (2003) introduce the concept of "dynamic managerial capabilities" as the capabilities used by managers to build, integrate, and reconfigure organizational resources and competences. This extension focuses the attention towards the role of managers, individually and in teams, on strategic change. It is important to consider that the capability involves performing the activity with a specific purpose and expected outcome and they tend to be repeated in a satisfactory manner. Kunc and Morecroft (2010), and previously Kunc (2005), also assert the importance of managers on the strategic change through the conceptualization and management of the system of resources responsible for the performance of the firm. The management of the system of resources is purposefully achieved through goal adjustment policies (Kunc and Morecroft, 2010) where goals result from the strategic development process.

Barreto (2010: page 271) proposes a more specific definition: "A dynamic capability is the firm's potential to systematically solve problems, formed by its propensity to sense opportunities and threats, to make timely and market-oriented decisions, and to change its resource base." There are a number of interesting features in this definition that better describe the positioning of this book. First, the concept of "systematically solving problems" is aligned to the use of management science tools and methods as discussed in Chapter 1. Secondly, the "propensity to sense opportunities and threats" offers the opportunity for the use of analytical tools performing sensemaking in the external environment, e.g. scenarios and forecasting as well as sentiment analysis. Thirdly, "timely and market-oriented decisions" is at the core of management science practice, i.e. decision making. Fourthly, the implication of "changing its resource base" is strongly aligned with the conceptualization employed for managerial decision-making processes, as stated in Kunc and Morecroft (2010), which underpins the whole book.

In recent times, Harris and Helfat (2013) have expanded the concept of "dynamic managerial capabilities" to suggest impact not only internally but also on the external environment. In that sense, Kunc (2005) proposes that decision-making processes responsible for managing internal resources will inevitably affect other organizations in the industry due to the intrinsic connectedness between firms through their system of resources. Kunc and O'Brien (2007) propose an integrated method using resource management and scenarios to evaluate and configure resources to the requirements of the external environment.

Eisenhardt and Martin (2000) suggest the main mechanisms to create dynamic capabilities are repeated practice leading to experience and trial and error leading to useful rules of thumb. Zollo and Winter (2002) suggested the importance of purposeful cognitive processes such as knowledge articulation by collective discussions and evaluation processes and knowledge codification through tools and manuals. Eggers and Kaplan (2009) suggest that managerial cognition can be seen as a dynamic managerial capability because there are purposeful actions to interpret the environment in order to reconfigure organizational resources and capabilities to match the opportunities and threats arising (Gavetti and Levinthal, 2000). This assertion is based on an important stream of research about the relationship between cognition and strategic change, e.g. how managers perceive and become aware of threats brought about by technological change (Kaplan, 2008), and how entrepreneurs identify potential opportunities (Gaglio and Katz, 2001). This is in line with the cognitive underpinnings of resource conceptualization suggested in Kunc and Morecroft (2010). In this area, management science tools and methods can become useful mechanisms to create and codify dynamic capabilities.

The next three subsections discuss the task (activities), cognitive (interpretation) and behavior (decisions) dimensions of dynamic managerial capabilities.

2.1.1 Task Dimension

The functions of dynamic managerial capabilities include "asset orchestration" (Helfat et al., 2007: page 24). Asset orchestration involves the search for resources and capabilities, selection, investment, deployment and, if necessary, their reconfiguration. Sirmon et al. (2007) propose a similar definition to asset orchestration called "resource management" which is the comprehensive process of arranging the firm's resource portfolio to build capabilities and leveraging the capabilities with the objective of creating and maintaining value for customers.

Another two tasks in asset orchestration are resource investment (Maritan, 2001) and resource deployment (Sirmon et al., 2007). Resource investment decisions determine how to acquire and develop resources and resource deployment defines the specific market segments to use those resources. Kunc and Morecroft (2010) define resource development as the process that "encompasses investment decisions (unplanned or problem-solving decisions) and operating polices (routines) that guide asset stock accumulation. Operating policies, as well as managerial choices and investment decisions, facilitate the accumulation of some resources and capabilities and the decay of others. The result of diverse managerial actions is different rates of accumulation among the resources comprising the firm, which will lead to distinctive firm performance" (Kunc and Morecroft, 2010: page 1167). Teece (2007) proposes a set of "microfoundations" of dynamic capabilities comprised by: (1) sensing opportunities and threats; (2) seizing opportunities by choosing among possible actions, making investments, and deploying resources; and (3) reconfiguring and transforming organizations and their resources and capabilities. From these definitions, the main tasks in managerial dynamic capabilities related to resource management (Sirmon et al., 2007) are:

1) Structuring involves the management of the resource portfolio and it is divided into:
   - Acquiring resources from markets.
   - Accumulating resources by developing internally.
   - Divesting resources through eliminating/selling.
2) Bundling is the process of combining resources to develop capabilities:
   - Stabilizing capabilities by minor incremental improvements.
   - Enriching capabilities to extend their use or withstand changes.
   - Pioneering new capabilities to face competitive issues.
3) Leveraging is the creation of value with capabilities:
   - Mobilizing capabilities in configurations which are suitable for exploiting market opportunities.
   - Coordinating capabilities to achieve efficient configurations.
   - Deploying the capability configuration in a specific strategy.

Sirmon et al. (2007) incorporate additional factors to the resource management process. First, timing in the tasks is important due to their sequential nature. Secondly, there is uncertainty generated by the changes in the external environment such as changes in industry structure, the stability of market demand, and the probability of environmental shocks. Uncertainty affects the suitability of the configurations as well as the understanding of the cause and effect relationships. Finally, Dierickx and Cool (1989) also suggest the role of complexity in the environment. These factors are definitively addressed by management science tools and methods as the following chapters demonstrate.

2.1.2 Cognitive Dimension

Increasingly, researchers are paying attention to the cognition of managers and the interpretive processes in which they engage as key aspects of their capabilities (Tripsas and Gavetti, 2000; Gavetti, 2005; Eggers and Kaplan, 2009; Kunc and Morecroft, 2010; Helfat and Peteraf, 2015). Moreover, managerial cognition scholars suggest that the environment is not purely exogenous but managerial interpretations of the environment define how organizations respond to it (Porac et al., 1989; Barr et al., 1992; Reger and Palmer, 1996). Resources and capabilities exist in a purposeful configuration only when managers conceptualize them (Kunc and Morecroft, 2010). Purposes typically arise because managers perceive an organizational shortcoming or a strategic opportunity external to the organization. However, it is not only recognizing the existence of a configuration but also acting on it by allocating investments to it.

The process used to recognize what an organization can do is non-linear – as it is iterative, building on feedback about efficacy and usefulness from attempts to use the configurations identified (Kunc and Morecroft, 2010). Helfat and Peteraf (2003) argue that the development of dynamic managerial capabilities comes through an iterative process of trials and reflection by management. On the other hand, the learning literature on "problem sensing" (also called problem finding, problem identification, problem recognition, etc.) indicates that managers must be aware of a failure or gap in performance relative to aspirations in order to generate learning about the nature of a problem (Haunschild and Sullivan, 2002). Analogical reasoning (the process of noting similarities between current problems and prior problems) is used by managers to perceive and understand the problems they face (Gavetti et al., 2005; Gary et al., 2012). To summarize, managers may either perceive problems existing objectively, which have to be discovered, or generate them through their actions.

Barr et al. (1992: page 16) suggest, "managers' mental models both facilitate and limit attention to and encoding of salient information about changes in organizational environments" and "lead managers to overlook important environmental changes so that appropriate action at the organizational level is not taken." Attention-based theories suggest that decisions about resource allocation are shaped by how organizations channel managers' attention.

2.1.3 Behavior Dimension

From a behavioral perspective, managers' actions are driven by achieving satisfactory rather than optimal solutions (satisficing behavior); the solutions considered are limited (bounded rationality); and they only look for information if there is a problem (problemistic search) (Cyert and March, 1992).

Managerial decision making under a resource-based paradigm is a processes driving the accumulation of resources through corrective actions aimed to close observed gaps between the desired level of the strategically relevant resources and the actual level of these resources (Kunc and Morecroft, 2010). Thus, resource development is a purposive adjustment of resources (asset stocks) through goal-seeking information feedback influenced by bounded rationality and time constraints derived from resource conditions (Kunc and Morecroft, 2010). The adjustment process is shaped by the goal-setting process. Behaviorally, managers generally search for solutions that are "good enough" to achieve their goals that are determined by the best judgment about the desired amount of a resource given the strategy's requirements.

Managers must draw conclusions and make commitments based on insufficient, unclear, or conflicting information about the results obtained from their investments, causal ambiguity (King, 2007). Causal ambiguity is a concept that describes the degree to which decision makers understand the relationships between resource-building actions and firm performance (King, 2007) and it is related to dynamic complexity in systems of resources. Dynamic complexity exists due to delays between actions and performance responses. Decision makers' learning processes are very important to find the interconnections between firm performance and resource conceptualization but the learning processes are affected by dynamic complexity and causal ambiguity. Therefore, managers employ biases to solve the limitations on understanding.

On account of limited time and resources, managers focus only on the information which they perceive useful (Ocasio, 1997; Cho and Hambrick, 2006). Moreover, managers selectively pay attention to the information that falls within their specialty or interest (Bromiley, 2005) giving them confidence in their decisions and acting quickly. Cognitive biases result from judgmental factors, like overconfidence, or situational factors (Gonçalves and Villa, 2016). Hence, selective perception may result in managers making a sub-optimal decision as the decision process is not an analytical process but rather a biased process. Selective perception can lead to poor performance due to an inappropriate comprehension of the resource system.

Managers also use heuristics to define their resource management decisions. Heuristics are rules of thumb to reduce decision-making time and bring about decisions quickly without necessarily evaluating all alternatives (Kahneman and Tversky, 1972). One example of a heuristic is anchoring and adjustment where decision makers estimate facts that they do not know (Tversky and Kahneman, 1974). Basically, decision makers anchor their decisions on information available and then adjust the anchor using any additional information (different and usually insufficient) to make their decisions.

A final consideration on behavioral decision making is how managers make sense of their reality using different clues (Kunc, 2016). Managers learn about their ambiguous and uncertain environment through clues obtained from their perceptual system. Subsequently, the clues are organized in a deterministic model where they are weighted to form a picture of the environment. However, the weighting process is imperfect and it takes time to learn the correct weights. Thus, behavioral decision making is highly contextual (e.g. tenure, background, experience) so managerial dynamic capabilities are strongly subject to contextual factors. Thus, a contextual aspect of dynamic managerial capabilities is important to highlight. First, O'Reilly and Tushman (2008) propose that diverse dynamic managerial capabilities are critical for implementing ambidexterity (see Chapter 12). Agarwal and Helfat (2009) mention the importance of dynamic managerial capabilities developed in a turnaround situation during strategic renewal (see Chapter 12). Trahms et al. (2013) indicate that the divest function of asset orchestration has a role in turnaround situations (see Chapter 12). Teece (2012) stresses the importance of entrepreneurial managers, which have dynamic managerial capabilities focused on building markets (see Chapter 10).

To summarize, dynamic managerial capabilities are based on a set of underlying managerial resources: managerial cognition, managerial social capital, and managerial human capital (Adner and Helfat, 2003). The three resources provide the basis for managerial intentionality, deliberation, decision making, and action responsible for resource management (Martin, 2011). Managerial cognition consists of mental models and beliefs and mental processes. Managerial social capital consists of goodwill derived from relationships, both formal and informal, that managers have with others and can use to obtain resources and information (Adler and Kwon, 2002). Managerial human capital refers to learned skills and knowledge that individuals develop through their prior experience, training, and education (Helfat and Martin, 2015).

Food for thought 2.1   Find two organizations publicly owned that you are interested in. Then, identify the top management team of the company through the financial information. It is mandatory for public companies to publish the names of the top management team.

Address the following issues:

- What are the demographic characteristics of the top management team: age, background, tenure?
- What are the similarities and differences in the characteristics of the top management team?
- Is there any contextual information that you can infer to explain the similarities and differences?
- If you are working in a company and you participate in meetings related to the strategic planning process, try to pay attention to the arguments exposed by different managers. What are the main characteristics of the arguments? Is there any relation with professional background, functional area, tenure in the company?

2.2 Integrating Management Science and Strategic Management: Managers as Modelers

There is usually a focus on events in strategy, e.g. a diversification, a threat, a growth opportunity, and a focus on patterns (e.g. continuous price discounting, decline in market volume over a period of time) exists in very few instances. However, there is not a focus on models. A focus on models can provide the structures that are behind patterns and ultimately the events observed so the attributions for problems and potential improvements are clearly identified. Models clear thoughts, reduce ambiguity and help to test assumptions. Models in any form, e.g. quantitative or qualitative, are powerful tools for developing strategies.

On the opposite side, the main focus, and outcome, of management science processes is a model and the results obtained from it (Williams, 2008). A model represents or describes a problem simplifying it and abstracting the key elements to provide the information required to solve the problem. The model defines elements, as well as the relationships among them, in a consistent, unambiguous and precise way for its users (Williams, 2008). When a manager becomes a modeler, the manager transforms a real problem into an analytical dimension by finding meaning and structure within the strategic problem that it is dealing with. A model exists in the analytical dimension to help managers visualize the data needed and potential solutions (Williams, 2008). Model structure implies precise definitions of terms reducing ambiguity and imprecisions. However, there may be a set of multiple models supporting each other to triangulate the solutions. The structure of the model can be tested for contradictions. Then the analytical world connects with the real world through data. The construction of models must somehow reflect reality through facts and quantities. More importantly management science is interested in the relationship between structures comprising the real world so measuring the relationships between variables representing the structures is key in defining relationships (Williams, 2008). Data collection is a key part of management science. The results of the model show the behavior of the solutions and compare it with the knowledge schema and beliefs. At this point, the model provides advice, predictions or implications regarding different solutions to the real problem.

One important consideration of management science as tools for thinking is its social nature (Pidd, 2009). When "a model becomes an external and explicit representation of part of reality as seen as people who wish to use it to understand, to change, to manage and to control that part of reality" (Pidd, 2009: page 12), there is an implicit assertion of the need to do models not alone but as part of a social process of discussion and agreement on the design and use of the model. Another implication is that there is no perfect model because there is no fully rational human able to understand reality completely. A further aspect is that models can be qualitative conceptual models, e.g. Porter's Five Forces, qualitative situational, e.g. causal loop diagram, and quantitative models, e.g. linear programming, system dynamics or financial models (Pidd, 2009).

Given these limitations, why do we create models in management science? First, there are some decisions that are discussed over time and with many participants. Secondly, some decisions cannot be experimented with so there is a high level of uncertainty. Thus, it is important to explore the consequences of the strategic decisions and plans before implementing them given the complexity and uncertainties. Therefore, the role of external and explicit models is to provide the platform needed to capture the essential aspects of the decisions and plans to address the problem (Pidd, 2009). In other words, models are supporting procedural rationality (Pidd, 2009), which is concerned with the nature of the deliberation process (search and evaluation) rather than the outcome of the process, and models and modeling are systematic procedures to support decision making of bounded rational decision makers (Pidd, 2009).

Models can reflect different degrees of realism, i.e. model fidelity with respect to real world (Morecroft, 2015). A realistic model with enough detail and scaling can be considered an analogue model. A model that is plausible but has a relative scale is only an illustrative model. A model whose purpose is to transfer insights and is small can be considered a metaphorical model. A list of examples of modeling methods is presented in Chapter 1 (see Section 1.2). Thus, managers, as modelers in an era of Big Data, need to develop capabilities for modeling, understanding systems and evaluate Big Data.

2.2.1 Modeling

Pidd (2009) suggests some principles of modeling, as the process to develop a model not the outcome in itself:

1) **Model simple, think complicated.** A simple model should be supplemented by highly critical thinking and rigorous argument and analysis for a number of reasons. First, a simple model is easier to understand because models are built to help people become more effective in what they do. The results need to be understood and used so trust is a key component in a model, which can be achieved once the user appreciates the overall structure and behavior of the model. Secondly, a simple model is easier to manipulate so it is simpler to produce results that seem relevant. Thus, models are "tools for thinking" not "tools to replace thinking" (Pidd, 2009: page 65) so they extend the power of thinking and support complicated analysis. The previous comment does not mean that there are models which replace humans or are key in decision making, for example in decision automation and routine decision support, since they work on accurate and up-to-date data and are intended to be accurate representations of the business problems faced.

2) **Be parsimonious, start small and add.** The idea is that models should be developed gradually, starting with simple assumptions and only adding complications as they become necessary. The intention is to learn from the simple model and then refine it gradually by adding more realism until it is valid for the purpose of the model.

3) **Divide and conquer, avoid mega models.** In this case, the issue relates to the need to build a model from the components of the problem, where each of them needs to be developed parsimoniously, rather than attempting to develop an all-inclusive model from the beginning.

4) **Use metaphors, analogies and similarities.** The modeler may not develop a model completely anew but may seek an analogy with another system or earlier models so the modeler searches for previous well-developed logical structures similar to the problem. In some cases, we treat the particular problem as an instance of a general case which shares a similar set of properties. The risk is choosing the wrong metaphor or analogy.

5) **Do not fall in love with data.** While the availability of data is increasing rapidly, and its analysis is important, the modeler should not consider that examining the data will reveal all the insights to construct a model. Exploration of data can never replace careful thought and analysis. Modeling drives data collection not the other way around although the modeler should consider the practicality of this process. Thus, the best approach would be to develop a simple model, collect the data to parametrize, and then test its behavior. Further refinements may require additional or different data.

6) **Model building may feel like muddling through.** The model building process is not linear or purely rational but it implies muddling through by using insights, taking time away from modeling, looking at things from different perspectives, and over an extended period through close contact with the client. The process is affected by different steps such as gaining an understanding of the problem and the way of modeling the problem, analyzing the data, developing the model and calibrating it, assessing the validity and usability of the model and its implementation.

2.2.2 Behavior with and Beyond Models

Strategic development processes start often with a strategy workshop that leads to a set of strategy projects. Projects are usually directed by hypothesis testing objectives where the output can be either a business case supporting a decision or a strategic plan (Johnson et al., 2008). Management science modelers have to be aware of this process and how the models will fit within it. This subsection discusses two aspects related to how to use models in the process and the impact of the models on the subsequent behavior of strategists.

Using models is a form of social practice that can be generative and emergent. Modeling can be analyzed using two analytical dimensions: modeling can be used for representing or intervening and the focus of modeling is on individual or group level (White, 2016). When models are used to facilitate information sharing among a group (dimensions: representing and group), they improve collective efficiency. For example, system dynamics models are usually prepared and discussed at group level with the idea to facilitate information sharing. When models help to influence individuals (dimensions: intervening and individual), they are considered as approaches that stress thinking with objects where individuals are able to access common meanings and group processes will emerge through coordination. When models are employed to intervene at group level (dimensions: intervening and group), models have a representational role and help people to think with models as objects. Models shape the way people frame problems.

2.2.3 Modeling Systems

Organizations are systems comprised by multiple interdependent elements. Therefore, it is important to recognize the meaning of system and how it affects the models that can be developed using five characteristics.

First, systems are measured in terms of efficiency and effectiveness (Daellenbach et al., 2012). Efficiency looks at how well resources are used in a given activity. The higher the level of output achieved for a given set of inputs or resources or, alternatively, the lower the inputs or resources needed for producing a given level of output, the higher the efficiency. Effectiveness means the level of achievement of goals or objectives. Operating various parts of a system in the most efficient manner does not necessarily mean the system as a whole is effective in terms of achieving its objectives.

Secondly, it is important to recognize the differences between reductionist and cause-and-effect thinking (Daellenbach et al., 2012). Reductionism is the certainty that systems and every experience of them can be reduced, partitioned, or disassembled into simple indivisible parts. Then the explanation of the behavior of the individual parts can be aggregated to understand and explain the behavior of the system as a whole. Cause-and-effect thinking involves explaining everything by decomposing it into parts while looking for cause-and-effect relationships between the parts. Causal relationships may not be simply one-way as there may be mutual causality or feedback between two things or interdependencies. New relationships or properties may emerge through the interaction between the various parts or aspects of a situation which can be unexpected and counterintuitive.

Thirdly, what to include or exclude in a definition of a system largely depends on what the person viewing the system intends to do with this definition

(Daellenbach et al., 2012). The system become a mental construct, personal to the observer. Systems can be seen as human conceptualizations. Although they may exist out there, it is only the human observer that views something as a system. Any two people viewing the same situation with the same purpose in mind may well form surprisingly different conceptualizations of that organized assembly of things. The view of a system is affected by different factors: formation, cultural and social background, education, practical experience, and personal values or beliefs.

Fourthly, the selection of the boundary is the most critical aspect of systems modeling (Daellenbach et al., 2012). Boundary choice determines not only the nature of the system but also who will benefit from the desirable outputs and who will suffer undesirable consequences. As such, how does one decide what is irrelevant? Which undesirable consequences can be ignored as insignificant or irrelevant to the study?

Fifthly, a system is part of a larger system, its environment, and this larger system is part of an even larger system, the environment of the larger system (Daellenbach et al., 2012). The nesting of systems within systems is referred to as the hierarchy of systems. In most cases, the larger containing system exerts some control over the contained system. The controlling system may set the objectives of the contained system, monitor how well it achieves these objectives, and have control over crucial resources needed by the contained system. One of the advantages of viewing two systems in a hierarchy is understanding their relationships and how the performance of the narrower system is hampered or constrained by aspects of the wider system. Therefore, changes in the wider system may become prerequisites to performance improvement in the narrower system.

There are four different types of systems (Daellenbach et al., 2012). First, *discrete systems:* if the state of the system jumps through a sequence of discrete states which occur at discrete points in time then the system is called a discrete system. The state variables, which describe the situation of the system, also change in discrete jumps. Secondly, *continuous systems:* the state variable changes continuously and it is monitored continuously even though its state is observed and recorded only at regular discrete points in time but the closer consecutive recordings are taken in time, the more accurately the system actual behavior is approximated. Thirdly, *deterministic vs. stochastic systems:* if the behavior of a system is predictable in every detail, the system is deterministic. Given the same starting conditions, a deterministic system will always exhibit exactly the same behavior. Stochastic systems are affected by uncertain, random or stochastic inputs. Sometimes uncontrollable inputs are represented as random in order to keep the narrow system of interest to a manageable size rather than the inputs which are inherently unpredictable. In other cases, the cost to ascertain all the influences is too high so there is a use of a stochastic variable. Fourthly, *closed vs. open systems.* A closed system has no interactions with any environment: no inputs and no output so it is mainly theoretical.

Open systems interact with the environment by receiving inputs from it and providing outputs to it.

Thus, Daellenbach et al. (2012) suggest the art of modeling a system involves:

- **The Ockham's razor principle.** The modeler has to be highly selective about which aspects to include in the model since not all the aspects are essential or contribute little to accuracy.
- **Iterative process of enrichment and reformulation.** Begin with a simple model, abstract from reality, and move in evolutionary fashion towards a more elaborate model that reflects the complexity without overfitting the model. Enrich the model without changing its basic form and structure and incorporate additional aspects that may be important.
- **Use an incremental approach.** Only concentrate on some key subsystems initially and then aggregate more. Do not start from the whole system.
- **Working out a numerical example.** Presenting different set of numbers can help to illustrate the behavior of the system under different representations and interventions.
- **Diagrams and graphs.** Visual representations, e.g. diagrams, can illustrate the boundaries of the system represented and help decision makers make sense of the model. Graphs offer useful information about the trends exhibited in the system behavior in order to infer the dominant behavior.

Food for thought 2.2   Consider two models: one qualitative, e.g. Five Forces or Value Chain;, and one quantitative, e.g. system dynamics. Then, apply both of them to the same strategic issue, e.g. the entry in a new market, and record the process carefully.

Address the following issues:

- What model was simpler to apply?
- What are the reasons for your conclusion?
- What are the sources of data that you employed?
- What model provided more insights?

2.2.4   Big Data Analytics Capabilities

Big data involves a set of challenges related to data (characteristics in terms of volume, variety, velocity, veracity, volatility, and quality), process (how techniques capture, integrate and transform data to feed the right model), and management (governance and ethical). Conceptualizing big data analytics as a capability implies simultaneously (Holsapple et al., 2014):

- Steering specific activities such as data acquisition.
- Using quantitative, qualitative and combinations of techniques.
- Managing statistical tools.

- Employing systematic reasoning.
- Working effectively with models that are descriptive/explanatory, predictive, or prescriptive.
- Ability to deal effectively with evidence in the form of multiple data such as, databases, click-streams, documents, sensors, maps.
- Understanding business models.
- Coordinating the use of different capabilities.

Gupta and George (2016) suggest big data analytics capabilities involve tangible resources, e.g. data, technology and investment, human resources, e.g. managerial skills familiarized with analytics and technical skills related to big data, and intangible resources such as data-driven culture (decisions are based on data instead of intuition) and organizational learning (as the ability to explore, store, share and apply knowledge). Since the data employed in big data analysis is unstructured and beyond the internal transactional systems, the skills are mostly related to software development and quantitative analysis (e.g. statistical analysis, machine learning, modeling, simulation) to develop custom-made solutions.

One of the most important impacts of big data analytics in the organization and dynamic managerial capabilities is sensemaking. However, sensemaking requires being able to appreciate the complex features of big data by reducing its ambiguity through a corresponding set of disciplines and subject areas (Calvard, 2016). The main issue is to learn how to analyze big data by combining disciplines such as management, economics, statistics, applied mathematics and computer science (Calvard, 2016). One of the risks of interdisciplinary approaches is that some groups can bring their biases about the form and content of big data, how to convert data into knowledge to shape future actions and decisions. Therefore, Big Data Analytics capabilities are based on modeling and systems principles capabilities.

In terms of the impact of big data analytics in the dynamic managerial capabilities, managers need to be aware of how to use descriptive analytics seamlessly in order to generate and understand reports. Then, managers should be able to implement inquisitive analytics (drill downs, statistical and factor analysis) to probe data so as to verify or reject business propositions (Bihani and Patil, 2014). At this level of sophistication, managers can trust analysts to perform predictive analytics (forecasting and statistical modeling) in order to to perform search of options. Finally, the process of asset orchestration can be enhanced by prescriptive analytics (optimization and testing).

2.3 End of Chapter

In a complex world awash with big data, dynamic managerial capabilities need to evolve from the traditional reliance on past experience and intuition.

Organizations need to evolve into a data-driven culture where decisions are made based on insights obtained from data. Decisions have to be made at all levels where the data is available and not influenced by the hierarchical position. While it will very difficult not to have specialists in big data analytics, they need to work as functional managers and, even, embed themselves into functional areas. A key aspect of dynamic managerial capabilities in a complex world with plenty of big data is for managers to be willing to override their own intuition if data contradicts it. Moreover, data will not make sense if there is no model to make sense of the data. Therefore, a key dynamic managerial capability is modeling, especially modeling the organization as systems of interconnected elements, e.g. resources. Only with a systems perspective, the integration of data will enhance sensemaking. Modeling is beyond the simple mathematical model or the systematic ordering of qualitative data. Modeling involves performing a social practice by participating actively with the model during strategizing processes.

2.3.1 Revision Questions

1) What is the impact of data velocity on managerial cognition? What new abilities should managers have to manage high data velocity? Think of an example of a company and industry to answer these questions.
2) Find a list of big data analytics tools to perform descriptive analytics. How can you apply descriptive analytics to support asset orchestration processes?
3) How can you ensure a representation of a system is considered during asset orchestration?

2.3.2 Case Study: The Future of Strategizing

Strategizing is a field within strategic management literature which is related to the strategy work. Strategizing involves "the practices and processes through which strategy is conceived, maintained, renewed and executed" (Paroutis et al., 2013: page 7). More specifically, strategizing can be described using the 3P framework (Paroutis et al., 2013: page 11):

- Practitioners: people performing the practices in the organization such as CEO, top management team, managing directors, chief strategy officer, consultants, etc.
- Practices: methods, tools, and procedures employed during strategizing.
- Praxis: strategy activity and its relationship with organizational, institutional and societal contexts.

An example of three potential situations where strategy is being made is presented in Table 2.1 using the 3P framework (Paroutis et al., 2013).

Table 2.1 Praxis and practices for three practitioners in strategizing.

	Chief Strategy Officer	Consultant	Strategy team
Practices	• Outputs are reports for the top management team • Simple strategy tools, e.g. SWOT • Connected with other people responsible for developing strategy	• Outputs are reports and presentation to advice clients • Implementation of recommendations • Use of specific tools developed in-house and adapted to specific problems • Development of a social network	• Participation in the strategy cycle (development of strategies over a certain period) • Ad-hoc organization for dealing with non-routine requirements • Flexibility to deal with variety of initiatives • Multiple stakeholders
Praxis	• Supporting the CEO • Embedded in the business • Facilitating the balance between short- and long-term objectives • Interacting with stakeholders involved in strategy	• Analysis of client's problems • Provision of solutions • Working with client's strategy team • Using high analytical skills • Extraction of information • Collaboration with internal actors in the client	• Preparing documentation • Developing knowledge base • Process development • Initiating new ideas • Starting new initiatives • Applying models and methods to achieve coordination • Supporting the process through knowledge and tools • Performing analyses • Sharing resources and information to develop strategies cross functionally • Defining strategy outputs

Here are a few questions about strategizing:

1) What management science tools and methods are more convenient for each actor? Why?
2) What activities will benefit the most from big data analytics?
3) What will be a key profession to take each role in 10 years?

References

Adler, P.S. and Kwon, S.W. (2002). Social capital: Prospects for a new concept. *Academy of Management Review*, 27(1), 17–40.

Adner, R. and Helfat, C.E. (2003). Corporate effects and dynamic managerial capabilities. *Strategic Management Journal*, 24, 1011–1025.

Agarwal, R. and Helfat, C.E. (2009). Strategic renewal of organizations. *Organization Science*, 20(2), 281–293.

Barr, P. S., Stimpert, J. L., and Huff, A. S. (1992). Cognitive change, strategic action, and organizational renewal. *Strategic Management Journal*, 13(S1), 15–36.

Barreto, I. (2010). Dynamic capabilities: A review of past research and an agenda for the future. *Journal of Management*, 36, 256–280.

Bihani, P. and Patil, S.T. (2014). A comparative study of data analysis techniques. *International Journal of Emergin Trends & Technology in Computer Science*, 3(2), 95–101.

Bromiley, P. (2005). The Behavioral Foundations of Strategic Management. Blackwell.

Calvard, T.S. (2016). Big data, organizational learning, and sensemaking: Theorizing interpretive challenges under conditions of dynamic complexity. *Management Learning, 2016*, 47(1), 65–82.

Cho, T. and Hambrick, D. (2006). Attention as the mediator between top management team characteristics and strategic change: The case of airline deregulation. *Organization Science*, 17(4), 453–469.

Cyert, R.M. and March, J.G. (1992). A Behavioral Theory of the Firm, 2nd edn. Blackwell.

Daellenbach, H.G., McNickle, D.C., and Dye, S. (2012). Management Science. Decision Making Through Systems Thinking, 2nd edn. Palgrave Macmillan.

Dierickx, I. and Cool, K. (1989). Asset stock accumulation and sustainability of competitive advantage. *Management Science*, 35(12), 1504–1511.

Eggers, J.P. and Kaplan, S. (2009). Cognition and renewal: Comparing CEO and organizational effects on incumbent adaptation to technical change. *Organization Science*, 20, 461–477.

Eisenhardt, K.M. and Martin, J.A. (2000). Dynamic capabilities: What are they? *Strategic Management Journal*, 21, 1105–1121.

Gaglio, C.M. and Katz, J.A. (2001). The psychological basis of opportunity identification: Entrepreneurial alertness. *Small Business Economics*, 16(2), 95–111.

Gary, M.S., Wood, R.E., and Pillinger, T. (2012). Enhancing mental models, analogical transfer, and performance in strategic decision making. *Strategic Management Journal*, 33, 1229–1246.

Gavetti, G. (2005). Cognition and hierarchy: Rethinking the microfoundations of capabilities' development. *Organization Science*, 16(6), 599–617.

Gavetti, G. and Levinthal, D. (2000). Looking forward and looking backward: Cognitive and experiential search. *Administrative Science Quarterly*, 45(1), 113–137.

Gavetti, G., Levinthal, D. A., and Rivkin, J. W. (2005). Strategy making in novel and complex worlds: The power of analogy. *Strategic Management Journal*, 26(8), 691–712.

Gonçalves, P. and Villa, S. (2016). Misperception of behavioral operations and bodies of knowledge. In: Behavioral Operational Research: Theory, Methodology and Practice (eds M. Kunc, J. Malpass, and L. White), 105–135. Palgrave Macmillan.

Gupta, M. and George, J.F. (2016). Toward the development of a big data analytics capability. *Information and Management*, 53, 1049–1064.

Harris, D. and Helfat, C. (2013). Dynamic managerial capabilities. In: Palgrave Encyclopedia of Strategic Management (eds M. Augier and D.J. Teece). Palgrave Macmillan.

Haunschild, P.R. and Sullivan, B.N. (2002). Learning from complexity: Effects of prior accidents and incidents on airlines' learning. *Administrative Science Quarterly*, 47(4), 609–643.

Helfat, C.E., Finkelstein, S., Mitchell, W., et al. (2007). Dynamic capabilities: Understanding strategic change in organizations. Malden, MA: Blackwell.

Helfat, C.E. and Martin, J.A. (2015). Dynamic managerial capabilities: Review and assessment of managerial impact on strategic change. *Journal of Management*, 41(5), 1281–1312.

Helfat, C.E. and Peteraf, M.A. (2003). The dynamic resource-based view: Capability lifecycles. *Strategic Management Journal*, 24(10), 997–1010.

Helfat, C.E. and Peteraf, M.A. (2015). Managerial cognitive capabilities and the microfoundations of dynamic capabilities. *Strategic Management Journal*, 36(6), 831–850.

Holsapple, C., Lee-Post, A., and Pakath, R. (2014). A unified foundation for business analytics. *Decision Support Systems*, 64, 130–141.

Johnson, G., Scholes, K., and Whittington, R. (2008). Exploring Corporate Strategy: Text & Cases. Pearson Education.

Kahneman, D. and Tversky, A. (1972). Subjective probability: A judgment of representativeness. *Cognitive Psychology*, 3, 430–454.

Kaplan, S. (2008). Cognition, capabilities, and incentives: Assessing firm response to the fiber-optic revolution. *Academy of Management Journal*, 51, 672–695.

King, A.W. (2007). Disentangling interfirm and intrafirm causal ambiguity: a conceptual model of causal ambiguity and sustainable competitive advantage. *Academy of Management Review*, 32, 156–178.

Kunc, M. (2005). Dynamics of competitive industries: a micro behavioural framework. PhD thesis. London Business School.

Kunc, M. (2016). Modeling behavioral decision making: creation and representation of judgment. In: Behavioral Operational Research (eds M. Kunc, J. Malpasse, and L. White), 161–175. Palgrave Macmillan.

Kunc, M. and Morecroft, J. (2010). Managerial decision-making and firm performance under a resource-based paradigm. *Strategic Management Journal*, 31, 1164–1182.

Lane, D.C. (1995). Modeling for learning organizations. *Journal of the Operational Research Society*, 46(6), 793–795.

Maritan, C.A. (2001). Capital investment as investing in organizational capabilities: An empirically grounded process model. *Academy of Management Journal*, 44, 513–531.

Martin, J.A. (2011). A practice theory of executive leadership groups: Dynamic managerial capabilities and the multi-business team. In: Handbook of Top Management Team Research (ed. M.A. Carpenter), 237–260. Edward Elgar.

Morecroft, J. D. (2015). Strategic Modelling and Business Dynamics: a Feedback Systems Approach. John Wiley & Sons, Ltd.

O'Reilly, C.A., III and Tushman, M.L. (2008). Ambidexterity as a dynamic capability: Resolving the innovator's dilemma. *Research in Organizational Behavior*, 28, 185–206.

Paroutis, S., Heracleous, L. and Angwin, D. (2013). Practicing Strategy – Text and Cases. Sage Publications Ltd.

Pidd, M. (2009). Tools for Thinking: Modelling in Management Science, 3rd edn. John Wiley and Sons, Ltd.

Porac, J. F., Thomas, H., and Baden-Fuller, C. (1989). Competitive groups as cognitive communities: The case of Scottish knitwear manufacturers. *Journal of Management Studies*, 26(4), 397–416.

Ocasio, W. (1997). Towards an attention-based view of the firm. *Strategic Management Journal*, 18(S1), 187–-206.

Sirmon, D.G., Hitt, M.A., and Ireland, R.D. (2007). Managing firm resources in dynamic environments to create value: Looking inside the black box. *Academy of Management Review*, 32(1), 273–292.

Teece, D.J. (2007). Explicating dynamic capabilities: The nature and microfoundations of (sustainable) enterprise performance. *Strategic Management Journal*, 28, 1319–1350.

Teece, D.J. (2012). Dynamic capabilities: Routines versus entrepreneurial action. *Journal of Management Studies*, 49, 1395–1401.

Teece, D.J., Pisano, G., and Shuen, A. (1997). Dynamic capabilities and strategic management. *Strategic Management Journal*, 18, 509–533.

Trahms, C.A., Ndofor, H.A., and Sirmon, D.G. (2013). Organizational decline and turnaround: A review and agenda for future research. *Journal of Management*, 39(5), 1277–1307.

Tripsas, M. and Gavetti, G. (2000). Capabilities, cognition and inertia: Evidence from digital imaging. *Strategic Management Journal*, 21, 1147–1162.

Tversky, A. and Kahneman, D. (1974). Judgment under uncertainty: Heuristics and biases. *Science*, 185, 1124–1131.

White, L. (2016). Behavior beyond the model. In: Behavioral Operational Research: Theory, Methodology and Practice (eds M. Kunc, J. Malpass, and L. White), 65–84. Palgrave Macmillan.

Williams, T. (2008). Management Science in Practice, John Wiley & Sons, Ltd.

Zollo, M. and Winter, S.G. (2002). Deliberate learning and the evolution of dynamic capabilities. *Organization Science*, 13(3), 339–351.

Further Reading

Augier, M. and Teece, D.J. (2009). Dynamic capabilities and the role of managers in business strategy and economic performance. *Organization Science*, 20, 410–421.

Beck, J.B. and Wiersema, M.F. (2013). Executive decision making: Linking dynamic managerial capabilities to the resource portfolio and strategic outcomes. *Journal of Leadership & Organizational Studies*, 20, 408–419.

Bettis, R.A. and Prahalad, C.K. (1995). The dominant logic – Retrospective and extension. *Strategic Management Journal*, 16, 5–14.

Eggers, J.P. and Kaplan, S. (2013). Cognition and capabilities: A multilevel perspective. *The Academy of Management Annals*, 7, 295–340.

Helfat, C.E. and Peteraf, M.A. (2009). Understanding dynamic capabilities: Progress along a developmental path. *Strategic Organization*, 7, 91–102.

Huff, A.S. (1990). Mapping Strategic Thought. John Wiley & Sons, Ltd.

Laamanen, T. and Wallin, J. (2009). Cognitive dynamics of capability development paths. *Journal of Management Studies*, 46, 950–981.

Sirmon, D.G. and Hitt, M.A. (2009). Contingencies within dynamic managerial capabilities: Interdependent effects of resource investment and deployment on firm performance. *Strategic Management Journal*, 30: 1375–1394.

Thomas, J.B., Clark, S.M., and Gioia, D.A. (1993). Strategic sensemaking and organizational performance – Linkages among scanning, interpretation, action, and outcomes. *Academy of Management Journal*, 36, 239–270.

3

External Environment: Political, Economic, Societal, Technological and Environmental Factors

---

Objectives

1) To define exogenous factors
2) To learn tools for foreseeing changes in exogenous factors
3) To organize external environment information for decision making

Learning outcomes and managerial capabilities developed

1) To develop sensemaking managerial capabilities
2) To classify the impact of external factors into threats and opportunities

---

Strategic choices are a function of conditions of the internal and external factors and the possibility of influencing them. The external environment, or external factors, can affect the organization's choices as well as its performance so it is fundamental to consider them within the strategic management process even though it will be impossible to affect them. The closeness of the external factors to the organization implies the possibility for the organization to influence, within a certain time horizon, conditions of these factors. The external environment can be divided into three parts according to the closeness to the organization: rivalry with existing organizations; industry dynamics defined by the suppliers, potential entrants, substitutes and customers; and the general or remote environment defined by the political, economic, social, technological and environmental factors (Figure 3.1).

External factors can not only be threats to the survival of the organization but also opportunities to achieve the vision defined for the organization or even redefine it. Therefore, organizations may need to design strategies to defend themselves against a threat or follow opportunities arising from favorable changes in the external factors. This chapter addresses the factors residing in the general or remote environment.

Strategic Analytics: Integrating Management Science and Strategy, First Edition. Martin Kunc.
© 2019 John Wiley & Sons Ltd. Published 2019 by John Wiley & Sons Ltd.
Companion website: www.wiley.com/go/kunc/strategic-analytics

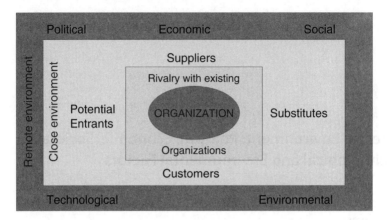

Figure 3.1 External factors affecting the organization.

Political These factors examine the political situation since government regulations and legal issues play a role in its economy and can ultimately affect the organization. Examples of such factors are tax policies, environmental policy, labor laws, international trade barriers and tariffs. It is essential for organizations to asses and align themselves with these policies in order to devise strategies which will enable them to operate successfully in the market and, thus, avoid government pressures as an interested stakeholder. Government policies can become a huge impediment to the growth of an organization if they affect strategic choices in terms of business models. Government policies may also become highly beneficial if they are supporting the growth of the industry or creating barriers to avoid competition.

Economic The macro-economic factors are likely to impact the costs incurred by an organization as well as the revenues. Elements such as exchange rates, interest rates and inflation rates affect an organization's raw material and capital cost, indirectly determining the performance of the business. Additionally, these factors also have an impact on the purchasing power of the consumers which affects the demand for products/services and revenues. Organizations need to actively study the macro-economic trends and factors to understand the dynamics of the financial resources and maintain their profitability during an economic or financial crisis.

Economic factors can be divided into global- and macro-economic factors. The global-economic factors are the external factors which are not determined by national governments. Examples of such factors can include globalization and the state of other economies. These are not controlled forces but have an influence on the whole economy including consumers, suppliers and competitors. On the other hand, macro-economic factors are structured and determined by a country's government in order to control its economy. These include taxes and monetary policies, which directly affect businesses, together with government budget. Macro-economic factors are used to predict the direction and cycle of the economy and the resulting information can aid organizations to plan their strategies accordingly.

Social These factors comprise attitudes and characteristics of the population such as lifestyle trends, age distribution and demographics, health consciousness, and racial and ethnic diversity. All of these factors help in gaining an understanding of the consumers' buying patterns.

An organization can foresee if its products/services can compete in the current and future market by looking at its demographics and cultural elements, as these factors help examine consumer needs. Furthermore, these factors can have a massive impact on the organization's operations since an activity or product that threatens the society's norms will receive negative publicity.

Technological Technological factors refer to the exogenous factors that can affect the technical dimensions of an organization. The impact of changes in technological factors can affect the level of productivity, cost and quality of a product or service. Technological factors can limit or enhance innovation, determine barriers to entry, and eventually impact the decision-making process. Government investment on technical research and/or policies fostering R&D can determine new technologies whose impact may be perceived many years later.

Environmental Environmental factors include ecological factors such as climate, weather changes and geographical events, e.g. earthquakes, that interrupt supply chain processes and/or demand for products. These factors have become increasingly indispensable to monitor due to increasing weather-related incidents. Organizations are also required to do business sustainably due to government and society pressures.

3.1 The PESTE Analysis

The external factors are usually grouped during the strategic management process using a framework called PESTE, an acronym formed by the first letters of the factors mentioned previously. The framework helps managers to identify, organize and qualitatively analyze the external macro-environmental factors that are **likely to affect** an organization's present or future performance. Variations in the framework, mostly concerning the order of the factors, have emerged over the years and the method has also been referred to as STEP, PEST, PESTLE (L stands for Legal factors) or SEPT by different authors (see

Further reading). In any case, the order of the factors does not reflect a preferential method or differences among the variations.

The fundamental purpose of the PESTE analysis is to focus the attention of the organization to the external environment (Figure 3.1) through an "environmental scan" and identify, organize and analyze the factors affecting the present and future performance of the firm. PESTE can also be employed for evaluating strategic decisions that are likely to be affected by issues beyond the control of the organization. PESTE can be helpful for businesses entering new countries or new markets, since the external analysis helps the organization to adapt to the external forces determining the dynamics in the new environment (Nayha and Pesonen, 2012).

Organizations are more likely to survive by adopting a proactive approach rather than a reactive approach in order to align themselves with changing environmental trends (Miller, 1988). However, research in strategic management suggests long-tenured managers tend to ignore their environments (Kunc, 2005). Long-tenured managers are able to detect and interpret events that are in line with historical trends and expectations, but are poor at perceiving, understanding and reacting to significant changes (Miller, 1991). Ferrier (2001) suggested that managerial experience influences sensemaking. Highly analytical strategy processes, which involve exhaustive and comprehensive analyses of the environment and the organization, depend primarily on the availability of enough information. Only stable environments can provide the information needed to implement a comprehensive mode of decision making (Fredrickson and Mitchell, 1984). Given the importance of being proactive and the issues related to the behavior of managers over time, PESTE analysis should be employed regularly in order to be effective since certain external factors may be highly dynamic. Table 3.1 shows the process to perform the PESTE analysis.

3.1.1   Limitations of PESTE Analysis

According to Schoemaker and Day (2009), only 20% of organizations are able to extrapolate valid information from external factors such as macro level indicators. Unfortunately, the PESTE framework does not establish a comprehensive evaluation system for these factors. On the one hand, gathering too much information but losing sight of the main objective may delay the process significantly (Langley, 1995). It is important for decision makers to focus on the identification of only the most fundamental issues and their potential implication. On the other hand, organizations that carry out the process systematically by observing similar factors over time may overlook changes in other external factors, which can become critical. Another issue related to the process is when PESTE analysis is carried out by a limited number of individuals, who always form the same group; it may finish with tunnel vision (Sabherwal and

Table 3.1 PESTE analysis.

Steps	Key activities	Detail
1) **Select the external factors that are critical to the firm**	Selection of the sensemaking team Identification of factors by the team	The team should involve internal (managers) and external (industry experts) actors
		Prepare a workshop with the team and other relevant actors, e.g. board of directors. Using techniques, such as brainstorming, identify the most important perceived external factors
2) **Select sources of significant information for each of the external factors**	The team searches for statistical information, and/ or government and/or research reports that provide information about trends on the external factors	After the trend analysis, try to aggregate variables if they have similar trends and are highly related. Evaluate causality: if one variable depends on the value of another, you will need to separate them
3) **Evaluate the impact of the external factors on the performance of the organization**	The team needs to identify the technique that best adapts to the selected factors, available data, cost, time and skills available	There are many techniques to evaluate the impact of external factors from quantitative and qualitative methods (see Section 3.2 for details)
		You may wish to consider significant impact but low probability events disregarding major disasters
4) **Categorize the external factors into opportunities or threats**	The team categorizes the impact of the factors in the future development of industry, markets and the organization	If a variable has a positive impact, e.g. social changes can expand the size of the market, then you will consider it as an opportunity for the firm. If a variable implies a negative impact, e.g. interest rates may decrease the availability of funding, then you should consider it a threat (to the organization)
5) **Include the insights into the strategic management process**	The team prepares the results of the analysis for consideration in current and future strategies	The result of the process may help the organization to reformulate its mission, identify requirements in terms of internal factors, and to design strategies for achieving its goals and objectives aligned with the external environment

Becerra-Fernandez, 2011). An additional drawback of the PESTE tool is its reliance on assumptions and the oversimplification of data to realistically perform the analysis within time constraints, leading to less accuracy and errors. Consequently, PESTE analysis, which is based on subjective analysis, depends on the capabilities and expertise of the persons participating in the planning process (Kajanus et al., 2012).

Moreover, the qualitative character of the PESTE framework is a limitation (Yuksel, 2012). Decision makers are faced with the complex task of assessing numerous factors without a systematic measurement system to assist in the procedure. For example, it is not correct to assume that every element of the PESTE analysis has equal implications for the organization. Furthermore, the framework noticeably overlooks the existing complex relationship between the external factors, effectively ignoring their inter-dependency. For instance, an economic crisis can produce social changes which may lead to political instability. Thus, a correlation analysis between external factors may address some of these issues. While the PESTE framework is useful to provide a first insight into the set of external factors affecting present and future performance, the framework is insufficient unless it is used in conjunction with management science tools.

To summarize, there are seven limitations to PESTE analysis. First, it relies strongly on the expertise of participants in the analysis. Secondly, participants can transfer their biases into the process making it a highly subjective analysis. Thirdly, factors may be assessed isolated so their interactions may be ignored. Fourthly, factors may not be adequately assessed in terms of relevance and importance to the organization. Fifthly, time and cost constraints can lead to a tunneled vision leaving key factors out. Sixthly, there is no information or too much irrelevant information for many factors. Seventhly, the analysis is static as it focuses on existing knowledge without considering future development.

Food for thought 3.1   The Drax Group is a power generation business which provides 7–8% of the electricity demand in the UK. It also operates a biomass business in the USA, which produces wood pellets for electricity generation.

The company started in 1974 with three generation units and then in 1986 finished three additional coal-fired power generation units. The total capacity is closer to 4000 MW which makes Drax the largest power station in the UK. In 1988, it adopted a desulfurization process so the power station became the cleanest generation unit. After the privatization of the electricity industry in the UK, the company became part of a US-based company.

The privatization of the energy industry led to increased competition, overcapacity and other factors that reduced the electricity price in the early 2000s. Drax came under the ownership of financial institutions due to its financial problems and in 2005 was listed in the London Stock Exchange. In the late 2000s, Drax integrated downstream with a supply company.

Following external changes (environmental, technological and political) in electricity generation, Drax announced its conversion to biomass-based power generation plants, e.g. using wood pellets instead of coal, and transformed three of its units by 2014. To support the conversion, Drax invested in wood pellets plants and port facilities in the USA.

The example of Drax raises some interesting questions in regard to the evolution of external factors affecting an organization that changes over time:

- Identify two factors within each PESTE category for the company between 1974 and 1988. You may look for information in websites describing the situation in the UK energy industry between those years.
- Identify two factors within each PESTE category for the company between 1989 and 2013. You may look for information in websites describing the situation in the UK energy industry between those years.
- Identify two factors within each PESTE category for the company that may be relevant from 2013 until 2030. You may look for information in websites describing future scenarios for the UK energy industry.
- Compare the factors and potential opportunities and threats arising from them in each time period and the strategic changes in the business. What is your opinion about the strategies followed by the company? Are the changes in the business driven internally or externally?

3.2 Integrating Management Science in the Strategic Management Process

When using management science tools to make sense of exogenous factors, managers needs to be aware of more than one technique available so as to make an informed judgment on whether to apply a particular technique. Techniques are usually grouped in three categories. First, qualitative techniques are based on judgment rather than on records of past data. Secondly, causal modeling techniques mean variables are statistically linked in cause-and-effect relationships, e.g. correlations. The relationship is assumed to hold in the future and is used to make the forecasts. Thirdly, time series techniques predict future values of a variable using only historical values. They involve determining patterns in the historical data, e.g. patterns, that are expected to remain into the future.

The objective of the use of systematic methods is to overcome PESTE limitations related to the subjective assessment of factors and to evaluate the PESTE elements according to their relative impact. Table 3.2 presents a list of diverse methods employed to forecast the development of the external factors. The table contains a brief description of each method; an evaluation of the costs to use it in terms of process, data and tools; the perceived level of acceptance; and skills required to implement them together with the type of uncertainty that is addressed. All quantitative methods are associated with predictable futures where there are trends that can be recognized and some methods can uncover alternative futures by identifying probabilities of certain events. Most of the qualitative methods deal with a range of futures and ambiguity in the future.

Table 3.2 Methods to evaluate the impact of external factors.

Methods	Brief description	Cost and effort	Recognition	Level of skills required	Type of uncertainty
Quantitative methods					
Econometric models	(TB)An econometric model specifies the statistical relationship between the variables associated with economic factors. They are essentially multiple regression equations	High since it requires large economic databases and specific software	High due to the importance of economic theory in the management of public policies	This tool is basically employed by economists to forecast future developments in the economy based on past relationships among economic variables such as consumer spending, household income, tax rates, interest rates, and employment. Consequently, it requires knowledge of economic theory	Predictable future
Simple and multiple regression models	They explain the variations in dependent variables due to the impact of one or more independent variables. There are multiple forms such as linear and non-linear	High/medium as it depends on the set of data and the software to be employed. Basic regressions can be performed using widely available spreadsheet software	High due to the availability of software and the widespread existing knowledge about them	A basic regression analysis can be performed by any university graduate with training in quantitative methods, e.g. statistics. More sophisticated regression analyses require specific training, sometimes at master or PhD level	Predictable and alternative futures

Time series models	They evaluate the patterns of variables over time based on historical data with the aim of identifying seasonal and cyclical factors	High/medium as it depends on the set of data and software to be employed	High due to the relatively "safe", and extensively accepted, assumption that the future depends on the past	The level of skills depends on the type of technique to be performed since there are numerous techniques, e.g. linear, exponential, S-curve, univariate, multivariate, with diverse levels of complexity	Predictable future
Trend analysis	These models assume the future will result from the existence of a long-term trend	High/medium as it depends on the set of data and software to be employed. This analysis can also be performed using a widely available spreadsheet software	High due to relatively "safe", and extensively accepted, assumption that the future depends on the past. Additionally, this analysis can also be performed using a widely available spreadsheet software	The level of skills depends on the type of technique to be performed since there are numerous techniques, e.g. simple average, exponential smoothing, logarithmic, with diverse levels of complexity. Additionally, complexity is generated by the identification of changes that may affect the trends	Predictable future

Qualitative or judgmental methods

Operational and executive estimates	These estimates involve aggregating the opinions of diverse people related to the external factors, e.g. social factors may be identified by the sales and marketing areas	Low since it is basically generated by collecting the opinion of people working in the company	High due to extensively accepted assumption that the experience of the people will be able to identify situations where historical data is not available	The skills required will be simple if the number of estimates are low, e.g. a simple average. However, the complexity may increase if the process involves a large number of estimates	Predictable, alternative and a range of futures

(Continued)

Table 3.2 (Continued)

Methods	Brief description	Cost and effort	Recognition	Level of skills required	Type of uncertainty
Customer surveys / Market research	They are primary data collection methods involving the design of questionnaires, definition of the sample and further statistical analysis with the objective to learn the intentions of either current or future customers	High since the design, testing of the accuracy of the process, and data collection is a long and costly process if it is done internally. The cost may decline if it is performed by an external agency	High as every business needs to be informed about changes in social and technological factors affecting its market	The skills required are medium since it requires knowledge about questionnaire design, statistical sampling and analysis even if the research is performed externally	Predictable, alternative and a range of futures
Scenario	It is a systematic method for thinking about the future in a consistent and plausible manner	Low/medium as it depends on the number of people involved in the process from only either the top management team or large groups of stakeholders.	Medium as it is based in qualitative perceptions without quantitative data and, in many cases, surprising results for managers responsible for short- to medium-term decisions	There are simple methods to develop scenarios (see Further reading). However, the difficulty is in the acceptance of issues that may go beyond the tenure of most managers as well as developing a process that is objective and replicable	A range of futures
Delphi method	This method consists in the development of a consensus across a set of experts about the future	Low/medium since it depends on the number of people involved and how accessible they are	Medium given the complexity of the method in terms of access to experts, questionnaire design and process	The only related skill is learning the method and applying systematically as well as identifying and accessing the experts. It is mostly employed in social, political and technological factors	A range of futures and true ambiguity

Source: Adapted from Pearce and Robinson (2000).

3.2.1 Achieving Consistency in PESTE Analysis Using the Analytic Hierarchy Process

AHP, or Analytic Hierarchy Process, was originally developed by Thomas L. Saaty in the 1970s. The AHP is a basic approach to decision making designed to handle both rational and intuitive approaches in order to select the best alternative from a number of options evaluated with respect to several criteria (Saaty and Vargas, 2012). The AHP is able to accommodate subjective opinion, objective data and expert knowledge within the same decision analysis (Kurttila et al., 2000) In AHP, decision makers perform simple pairwise comparison judgments which are then used to develop overall priorities for ranking alternatives (Saaty, 1990). AHP identifies inconsistency in the judgments in order to improve consistency (Saaty, 2008).

AHP, as a decision analysis tool, is of particular importance for group decision-making and while it can be used in a variety of fields and applications, it is extensively used in strategic planning (Vaidya and Kumar, 2006; Kajanus et al., 2012). AHP is also favorable for complex problem solving, especially concerning issues that rely on human perceptions (Bhushan and Rai, 2004). The analytic aspect implies both objective and subjective data are translated into numbers and mathematical formulation is used to evaluate the data so the decision maker can explain choices systematically. The choices can be generated by either one decision maker or a group. As discussed previously, organizations that are undertaking PESTE analysis rely heavily on the expertise of the individuals involved in the task and often, variations in judgment can affect the evaluation process. The hierarchy component of the process implies that the decision problem is structured, in its simplest form, in three levels of hierarchies: the goal at the top level, followed by a second level consisting of the criteria, and the alternatives located in the third level (Saaty and Vargas, 2012). Figure 3.2 shows a hierarchical structure of the attractiveness of a country based on external factors (political and economic factors) with their respective criteria and a rating of their intensities (high to low). Finally, the process aspect of the method involves thinking over the concepts identified, gathering new information, negotiating data and formulating group consensus through the proper running of decision-making sessions (Wu and Wu, 1991).

In more detail, the application of AHP to a PESTE analysis will involve the steps given in the following.

The first step is PESTE analysis. The key activity in this step is to define the external factors pertaining to each concept of the PESTE framework. The maximum number of factors within each concept should not be large due to the impact of the rapid increasing number of pairwise comparisons. It is important to organize the structure of the PESTE factors in hierarchy if there is more than one level of analysis.

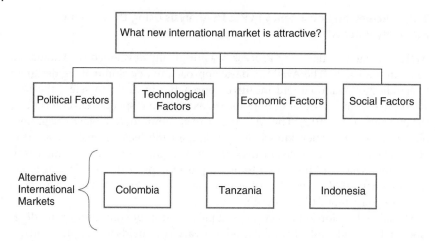

Figure 3.2 A PESTE analysis to evaluate international market attractiveness.

The case to be addressed to illustrate the AHP analysis corresponds to a medium size company which is interested in expanding internationally. An initial evaluation suggested three potential markets: Colombia, Tanzania and Indonesia. The management team has a brief discussion about the PESTE factors to evaluate each potential market and they decided to focus on: political, economic, social and technological factors. Figure 3.2 shows the structure of the problem that is going to be addressed using AHP.

In the second step, a group discussion was organized, a questionnaire is prepared if it is not possible to arrange a meeting, to compare the factors pairwise and add a numerically evaluation according to their relative importance based on Saaty's "scale of relative importance" (Wu and Wu, 1991). Each numerical value reflects the decision makers' preference for a factor with respect to another factor and the strength of the preference (Table 3.3).

Thirdly, a pairwise comparison normalized matrix with the PESTE factors is developed to calculate the weights of each factor. Basically, each row contains the evaluation of the factor with respect to another PESTE factor obtained in the previous step. For each value in the first row, a reciprocal value is defined in the corresponding column. For example, economic factor has moderate importance with respect to political factor and political factor has a very strong importance with respect to social factor. See the example in Table 3.4.

Then, each element of the pairwise matrix is divided by the aggregate sum of its respective column to calculate its corresponding normalized element. This generates a new matrix with the normalized values where the sum of the elements in each column is 1. See the example in Table 3.5.

The priority vector is calculated for each PESTE factor where the priority vector (Table 3.6) is calculated by dividing the aggregate sum of each row by

Table 3.3 Scale of relative importance to evaluate PESTE factors.

Verbal preference	Numerical scale
Factor A has equal importance with respect to factor B	1
Factor A has a moderate strong importance with respect to factor B	3
Factor A has a strong importance with respect to factor B	5
Factor A has a very strong importance with respect to factor B	7
Factor A is extremely important with respect to factor B	9
Values 2, 4, 6 and 8 are intermediate values of preferences	

Table 3.4 Pairwise comparison matrix for the PESTE factors.

	Political	Technological	Economic	Social
Political	1	5	2	4
Technological	1/5	1	1/2	1/2
Economic	1/2	2	1	2
Social	1/4	2	1/2	1

Table 3.5 Normalized pairwise comparison matrix for the PESTE factors.

	Political	Technological	Economic	Social
Political	0.5128	0.5000	0.5000	0.5333
Technological	0.1026	0.1000	0.1250	0.0667
Economic	0.2564	0.2000	0.2500	0.2667
Social	0.1282	0.2000	0.1250	0.1333

Table 3.6 Priority vector for PESTE factors.

	Priority vector
Political	0.5115
Technological	0.0986
Economic	0.2433
Social	0.1466

the number of pairwise comparisons. Each element of the priority vector reflects the weighted importance of the factor. Therefore, the sum of all priorities must be equal to 1. The initial analysis indicates the economic factor is the most important factor followed by the political factor. The result will be used as a scaling factor to obtain the global priorities for each alternative international market.

Fourthly, it is necessary to verify any inconsistencies in the matrix regarding the relative importance given by the decision makers. The technique involves Consistency Ratios (CRs) which have to below 0.10 to be consistent (Saaty, 1980). To calculate CR, there is a procedure:

1) Compute **Aw** where **A** is the matrix calculated in Table 3.4 and **w** is the priority vector in Table 3.6. You can multiply the two matrices because matrix **A** has the same number of column as **w**'s number of rows. The row for the new matrix is obtained by summing the products of the elements in row 1 of Table 3.4 with the corresponding elements in the column of Table 3.6.

$$
\mathbf{Aw} = \begin{matrix} \text{Results} \\ 2.0774 \\ 0.3958 \\ 0.9894 \\ 0.5933 \end{matrix}
$$

2) Calculate the ratio of each element of **Aw** with its corresponding element in the priority vector (Table 3.6) and average these ratios:

$$
\left(\begin{array}{l} 2.0774 / 0.5115 + 0.3958 / 0.0986 + \\ 0.9894 / 0.2433 + 0.5933 / 0.1466 \end{array} \right) / 4 = 4.0477
$$

3) Calculate the Consistency Index (CI) using the following equation:

$$
CI = \left[\left(\text{result from the equation in step 2} \right) - \text{number of factors} \right] / \left(\text{number of factors} - 1 \right)
$$

$$
CI = \left(4.0477 - 4 \right) / \left(4 - 1 \right) = 0.0159
$$

4) Calculate CR by dividing CI with RI (Random Index). The values of RI shown in Table 3.7 provide the average value of CI if the entries in the

Table 3.7 Priority vector for PESTE factors.

2	3	4	5	6	7	8	9	10
0.00	0.58	0.9	1.12	1.24	1.32	1.41	1.45	1.51

Table 3.4 were selected randomly. If the ratio of CI to RI is small, the decision makers' pairwise comparisons will be consistent. Thus, the suggestion that CR < 0.10. If CR > 0.10, there are important inconsistencies and AHP analysis will not be useful. In this case, CI/RI= 0.0159/0.90=0.0177.

The next step is to assign a score for each alternative international market with respect to each PESTE factor. To perform these evaluations, the scale from Table 3.3 is used and a pairwise comparison matrix, such as Table 3.4, is generated and the scales are discussed collectively. Table 3.8 shows the pairwise comparison matrices (top) and the four PESTE factors and the normalized comparison matrices (bottom) for the three alternative international markets. The procedures to calculate the matrices are similar to steps 2–4 mentioned previously

Table 3.9 shows the priority vectors for each international market. It is interesting to observe that Indonesia is the best alternative when technological and social factors are considered while Tanzania is only interesting from an economic perspective and Colombia from a political perspective.

The final step is to determine the best market by combining all four separate scores for each country in Table 3.9 with the priority vector for each PESTE factor in Table 3.6.

Colombia = 0.57 * 0.5115 + 0.16 * 0.0986 + 0.09 * 0.2433 + 0.08 * 0.1466 = 0.3409

Tanzania = 0.29 * 0.5115 + 0.25 * 0.0986 + 0.67 * 0.2433 + 0.32 * 0.1466 = 0.3829

Indonesia = 0.14 * 0.5115 + 0.59 * 0.0986 + 0.24 * 0.2433 + 0.60 * 0.1466 = 0.2761

The final results show Tanzania is the preferred market followed by Colombia. While Indonesia has strong scores in two PESTE factors, both of them are not significantly important for the decision maker.

An extension for the previous analysis can involve a second level of factors, e.g. the economic factor can be decomposed into a set of additional factors such as GDP per capita, GDP growth, etc. In this case, the AHP process has to be performed for the lowest level hierarchy and then the priority vector for the highest level PESTE factor acts as a global priority, or scaling, factor (Wu and Wu, 1991).

Table 3.8 Pairwise comparison matrices for alternative international markets.

	Political			Technological			Economic			Social		
	Col.	Tanz.	Ind.	Col.	Tanz.	Ind.	Col.	Tanz.	Ind.	Col.	Tanz.	Ind.
Colombia	1	2	4	1	1/2	1/3	1	1/7	1/3	1	1/4	1/7
Tanzania	1/2	1	2	2	1	1/3	7	1	3	4	1	1/2
Indonesia	1/4	1/2	1	3	3	1	3	1/3	1	7	2	1
Colombia	0.57	0.57	0.57	0.17	0.11	0.20	0.09	0.10	0.08	0.09	0.08	0.09
Tanzania	0.29	0.29	0.29	0.33	0.22	0.20	0.64	0.68	0.69	0.33	0.31	0.30
Indonesia	0.14	0.14	0.14	0.50	0.67	0.60	0.27	0.22	0.23	0.58	0.61	0.61

Table 3.9 Priority vectors for alternative international markets.

	Political	Technological	Economic	Social
Colombia	0.57	0.16	0.09	0.08
Tanzania	0.29	0.25	0.67	0.32
Indonesia	0.14	0.59	0.24	0.60

Some implications of the AHP analysis for decision making are:

- Visualization of the highest global priorities for the organization as those factors that are the most important for the decision makers within a PESTE analysis.
- Improvement of decision-making process since AHP eliminates the assumption that all factors have equal implications.
- The initial evaluation of the PESTE concepts can be replaced by sensitivity analysis to identify scenarios determined by diverse preferences among decision makers.

A summary of the process to perform AHP comprises three steps (Wu and Wu, 1991):

1) Development of the hierarchy structure using a graphical presentation of the objective, the criteria, sub-criteria and various alternatives (Figure 3.2 and Table 3.3).
2) Establishing normalized weights for the main criteria; establishing normalized weights for all sub-criteria; and defining normalized weights for each alternative with respect to each sub-criterion. All these normalized weights are generated by pairwise comparison matrices developed with the decision makers.
3) Combine the normalized weights or priority values of step 2 to establish the overall normalized weights and priorities of the alternatives.

Food for thought 3.2 You have been hired by Drax to evaluate the development of a new generation plant based on four types of technologies: coal, natural gas combined cycle, nuclear and biomass. After an initial evaluation using PESTE analysis, the management selected a set of criteria (Table 3.10). Your task is:

1) To evaluate the generation plant technologies with respect to the criteria selected in order to rank them in terms of desirability. Follow the procedure explained previously to calculate the priorities for each criterion and then evaluate it. Which is the most desirable technology? Which is the least desirable?
2) To replace the priorities obtained through AHP by performing different sensitivity analysis, e.g. varying the weights for the PESTE factors. What are the main changes in the ranking with diverse weights emphasizing certain PESTE factors? For example, what will happen if there is more concern for environmental and social factors than economic and technological and vice versa?

Table 3.10 Criteria selected.

Political	Economic	Technological	Social	Environmental
Land requirement	Job creation	Radioactivity	Social acceptance	Non-radioactive emissions

Land requirement   The land required by a plant is important for their evaluation because the quality of life is affected directly and indirectly by the technology of the plant. First, land is valuable, especially when power plants are located near metropolitan areas. Secondly, visual disruption can be caused by the buildings and noise pollution from equipment, such as wind generators, that are difficult to be financially assessed but definitely affect the area near the plant. Thirdly, the process of building the plant: excavations, tunnels and other work necessary for plant operation disrupt the flora, the fauna and the ecosystem generally generating reactions from diverse stakeholders. Biomass power plants seem to occupy more land than coal, natural gas combined cycle and nuclear power plants (Chatzimouratidis and Pilavachi, 2008) but this measure may be controversial since biomass can also come from secondary sources, e.g. chips from forest or corn discarded. The land required in square kilometers per 1000 megawatts produced is: 2.5 for plants using coal, natural gas combined cycle and nuclear, and 5000 for biomass power plants (Chatzimouratidis and Pilavachi, 2008).

Job creation   Depending on the technology, power plants can employ many people during their life cycle (from construction and operation until decommissioning). The average number of jobs created by a 500 MW power plantis: 2500 for coal and nuclear, 2460 for natural gas combined cycle, and 36 055 for biomass (Chatzimouratidis and Pilavachi, 2008).

Radioactivity   Interestingly, even small amounts of radioactivity are released to the atmosphere from both coal-fired and nuclear power stations (Chatzimouratidis and Pilavachi, 2008). In the case of coal combustion, small quantities of uranium, radium and thorium present in the coal produce various levels of radioactive fly ash such as 490 (person-rem/year) for a 1000 MW power plant (Chatzimouratidis and Pilavachi, 2008). Nuclear power stations and reprocessing plants release small quantities of radioactive gases such as krypton-85, which can be detectable in the environment with sophisticated monitoring and analytical equipment (4.8 [person-rem/year] for a 1000 MW power plant) (Chatzimouratidis and Pilavachi, 2008). No radioactivity is released from natural gas combined cycle and biomass power plants.

Social acceptance   Social acceptance can be defined by pairwise comparison of the types of power plant with respect to their acceptance by the local community (where 1 is of equal importance up to 9 meaning extreme importance). Each type of power plant in a row of Table 3.11 is compared with a type of power plant in a column but the figures represent how much better or worse a power plant in a row of the table is in comparison with a power plant in a column (Chatzimouratidis and Pilavachi, 2008).

Non-radioactive emissions Non-radioactive emissions can be either gaseous or small particles and they tend to affect people's respiratory system, cause cancer, cardiovascular and vision problems as well as ecosystem instability and the global warming effect (Chatzimouratidis and Pilavachi, 2008). Each type of power plant releases different amounts of substances during their life cycle such as 986 000 (mg/KWh in CO_2-equivalent) for coal, 450 000 (mg/KWh in CO_2-equivalent) for natural gas combined cycle, 21 435 (mg/KWh in CO_2-equivalent) for nuclear, and 58 000 (mg/KWh in CO_2-equivalent) for biomass (Chatzimouratidis and Pilavachi, 2008). It is clear coal is the more contaminating technology.

Table 3.11 Subjective pairwise evaluation of social acceptance for types of power plants.

Type of power plant	Coal	Natural gas combined cycle	Nuclear	Biomass
Coal	1	1/5	3	1/3
Natural gas combined cycle	5	1	5	1/3
Nuclear	1/3	1/5	1	1/5
Biomass	3	3	5	1

Source: Adapted from Chatzimouratidis and Pilavachi (2008: table 8, page 1080). Reproduced with permission of Elsevier.

3.2.2 Understanding the Evolution of PESTE Factors Using Visualization Analytics

PESTE factors evolve over time through slow and regular progressions, abrupt changes, and turnarounds. For example, a discussion on a regulation can take many years since the regulation is shaped over time. Therefore, temporal patterns can be useful to understand how certain PESTE factors evolved and predict future developments. Bach et al. (2016) introduce the concept of time curves. The time curve technique is an approach to visualize temporal data based on their similarity, which can be quantified using a metric, in discrete time points (Bach et al., 2016). Basically, all data is arranged on an initial timeline where each position encodes time but then the timeline can be stretched and folded depending on their similarity. Therefore, space reflects similarity. Time curves are useful to identify patterns in the development of a factor such as degree of stagnation (progression – lines vs. stagnation – multiple crossing curve lines), point density (sparse – few instances vs. dense – multiple instances), oscillations (no oscillation – stable vs. high oscillations – unstable).

3.3   End of Chapter

Evaluating the external environment of the firm is important for firms because changes in PESTE factors can: alter the demand for products both for a company and the whole industry; change how products and services reach consumers; and change prices and ways in which organizations relate to stakeholders. There are many methods to evaluate the external environment, either qualitative or quantitative, but all of them start with identifying the critical factors that might be opportunities or might become threats to the future of the organization. The methods can have diverse planning horizons, some may be more suitable for short to medium term, e.g. time series or regressions, while others may be more amenable to long-term horizons with more uncertainties, e.g. scenarios.

In terms of developing a system to support foreseeing the dynamics of external factors, there are some guidelines that can be followed. First, it is important to evaluate the decisions that are being supported by the system. Secondly, define what type of analysis is needed in terms of variables, frequency of the analysis, time horizon and accuracy levels. Thirdly, a conceptual model is prepared by indicating the ideal methods and causal linkages with the variables being forecasted. For example, it may indicate the historical patterns which might influence the future, causal variables, and whether volatile conditions might point to the use of a qualitative method. Fourthly, what data is, and is not, available. Fifthly, test the method's accuracy comparing the past data and the forecasted results. Sixthly, decide how to incorporate judgments into forecasts. Finally, monitor the performance of the system by measuring accuracy by using MAD (mean absolute deviation) and MSE (mean square error).

The managerial capabilities developed in this chapter are: the ability to identify environmental factors that can affect an organization's performance (in the past, present and future); the ability to identify management science tools suitable to evaluate the importance of the factors and additional tools to evaluate trends and how factors change over time given their strengths and weaknesses; and the ability to avoid biases or errors with individual methods by learning how to combine more than one technique.

This chapter explored one management science tool: AHP to facilitate the evaluation of the diverse factors identified in a PESTE analysis. In this situation, the mathematical-based tool can help to clarify arguments and values while democratize the evaluation of external factors rather than using only subjective judgements on the factors. In this chapter, the management science styles are clearly participative and interactive as indicated in Figure 3.3.

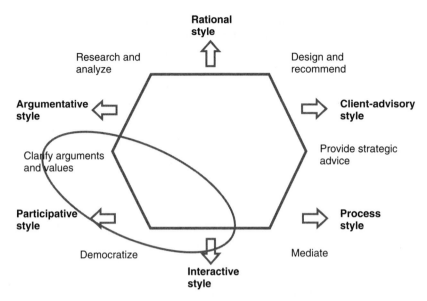

Figure 3.3 Management science styles. *Source:* Walker (2009). Reproduced with permission of Elsevier.

3.4.1   Revision Questions

1) What are the main differences between PESTE factors affecting a capital intensive industry, such as energy generation, and a service industry, e.g. fast food?
2) What are the key organizational processes related to evaluate the external environment?
3) What are the weaknesses of PESTE analysis? You may want to use Burt et al. (2006).
4) What can be an appropriate management science tool to support PESTE analysis in the clothing industry? Why?
5) Visit the websites of www.imf.org, www.worldbank.org and www.oecd.org . What are their main forecasts? How are they prepared? Prepare a critique of their methods.
6) Find out information about the Big Mac Index published by *The Economist.* Explain how it can be employed for a PESTE analysis.

3.4.2   Case Study: Westmill Co-op and the Rise of Renewable Energy

The energy industry is changing very rapidly with the rise in renewable energy such as wind and solar. This case study discusses one company specializing in wind energy with very special characteristics.

Westmill Co-op was established in 2004 to build and operate a community-owned wind farm in Oxfordshire, UK. Westmill Co-op is the first wind farm co-operative which gave local people the priority to invest in the production of renewable energy. The opportunity was launched at the end of 2005 and remained available until February 2006. Westmill Windfarm Co-op has 2374 members.

The Co-op financed the purchase and construction of five wind turbines using £4.6 million obtained from the shares sold, supplemented by a bank loan and a capital grant from the South East England Development Agency (SEEDA). The wind farm also involved 25-year operation of the five wind turbines. The turbines are connected to an electricity sub-station on the site, from where the electricity generated is metered and sold. The wind farm started commercial generation in February 2008.

One interesting aspect of the Co-op is the operation and design of the wind farm was managed by a specialized consulting firm and the Co-op is established in an existing farm owned by an organic farmer with an interest in community and environmental issues.

In 2012 a second co-operative was launched. The Westmill Solar Cooperative raised £16 million to develop the largest community-owned solar project.

Recent developments The *Daily Mail* (2015), a British newspaper, reported negatively about wind energy saying that wind turbines take energy from the National Grid (the UK national electric system) when they are not generating any electricity. Wind turbines use electricity to keep spinning in cold weather to stop icing so turbines only operate when the wind is between 10 mph and 50 mph. While wind energy can produce enough electricity to power 8.8 million homes, low wind speeds reduce the output from wind turbines.

Here are two questions:

1) Identify key PESTE factors that will determine the future of the renewable energy in the UK. Categorize them into threats and opportunities.
2) Find a method to develop scenarios, e.g. O'Brien and Dyson (2007), and develop a set of scenarios for wind energy generation in the UK.

References

Bach, B., Shi, C., and Heulot, N., et al. (2016). Time curves: Folding time to visualize patterns of temporal evolution in data. *IEEE Transactions on Visualization and Computer Graphics*, 22(1), 559–568.

Burt, G., Wright, G., Bradfield, R., et al. (2006). The role of scenario planning in exploring the environment in view of the limitations of PEST and its derivatives. *International Studies of Management and Organization*, 3, 55–58.

Bhushan, N. and Rai, K. (2004). Strategic Decision Making, 1st edn. Springer.

Chatzimouratidis, A.I. and Pilavachi, P.A. (2008). Multicriteria evaluation of power plants impact on the living standard using the analytic hierarchy process. *Energy Policy*, 36(3), 1074–1089.

Daily Mail. (2015). New wind turbine farce: How they take power from the National Grid even when they are NOT generating any electricity. http://www.dailymail.co.uk/news/article-2893708/New-wind-turbine-farce-power-National-Grid-NOT-generating-electricity.html#ixzz3NroIqDVT (accessed January 2015).

Ferrier, W. (2001). Navigating the competitive landscape: the drivers and consequences of competitive aggressiveness. *Academy of Management Journal*, 44, 858–877.

Fredrickson, J.W. and Mitchell, T.R. (1984). Strategic decision processes: comprehensiveness and performance in an industry with an unstable environment. *Academy of Management Journal*, 27, 399–423.

Kajanus, M., Leskinen, P., Kurttila, M., and Kangas, J. (2012). Making use of MCDS methods in SWOT analysis – Lessons learnt in strategic natural resources management. *Forest Policy and Economics*, 20, 1–9.

Kunc, M.H. (2005). Dynamics of competitive industries: a micro-behavioural framework. PhD thesis. London Business School.

Kurttila, M., Pesonen, M., Kangas, J., and Kajanus, M. (2000). Utilizing the analytic hierarchy process (AHP) in SWOT analysis – a hybrid method and its application to a forest-certification case. *Forest Policy and Economics*, 1(1), 41–52.

Langley, A. (1995). Between "paralysis by analysis" and "extinction by instinct". *Sloan Management Review*, 36, 63–63.

Miller, D. (1988). Relating Porter's business strategies to environment and structure: Analysis and performance implications. *Academy of Management Journal*, 31(2), 280–308.

Miller, D. (1991). Stale in the Saddle: CEO tenure and the match between Organization and Environment. *Management Science*, 37, 34–52.

Nayha, A. and Pesonen, H. (2012). Diffusion of forest biorefineries in Scandinavia and North America. *Technological Forecasting and Social Change*, 79(6), 1111–1120.

O'Brien, F. and Dyson, R. (2007). Supporting Strategy: Frameworks, Methods and Models. John Wiley & Sons, Ltd.

Pearce, J.A. and Robinson, R.B. (2000). Strategic Management: Formulation, Implementation, and Control, 7th edn. Irwin/McGraw-Hill.

Saaty, T. (1980). The Analytic Hierarchy Process, 1st edn. McGraw-Hill International Book Co.

Saaty, T. (1990). How to make a decision: the analytic hierarchy process. *European Journal of Operational Research*, 48(1), 9–26.

Saaty, T. (2008). Decision making with the analytic hierarchy process. *International Journal of Services Sciences*, 1(1), 83–98.

Saaty, T.L. and Vargas, L.G. (2012). Models, Methods, Concepts & Applications of the Analytic Hierarchy Process, Vol. 175. Springer Science & Business Media.

Sabherwal, R. and Becerra-Fernandez, I. (2011). Business Intelligence, 1st edn. John Wiley & Sons, Inc.

Schoemaker, P.J.H. and Day, G.S. (2009). Why we miss the signs. *MIT Sloan Management Review*, 50(2), 43–44.

Vaidya,O. and Kumar, S. (2006). Analytic hierarchy process: An overview of applications. *European Journal of Operational Research*, 169(1), 1–29.

Walker, W.E. (2009). Does the best practice of rational-style model based policy analysis already include ethical considerations? *Omega*, 37(6), 1051–1062.

Wu, J.A. and Wu, N.L. (1991). A strategic planning model: structuring and analysing via the Analytic Hierarchy Process. *Industrial Management & Data Systems*, 91(6), 5–9.

Yuksel, I. (2012). Developing a multi-criteria decision making model for PESTEL analysis. *International Journal of Business and Management*, 7(24), 52–65.

Further Reading

Haberberg, A. and Rieple, A. (2008). Strategic Management: Theory and Application. Oxford University Press.

Rowe, G. and Wright, G. (1999). The Delphi technique as a forecasting tool: issues and analysis. *International Journal of Forecasting*, 15, 353–375.

Saaty, T. and Vargas, G. (2012). Models, Methods, Concepts & Applications of the Analytic Hierarchy Process, 2nd edn. International Series in Operations Research & Management Science, Vol. 175. Springer.

Van der Heijden, K., Bradfield, R., Burt, G., et al. (2009). The Sixth Sense: Accelerating Organizational Learning with Scenarios. John Wiley & Sons, Inc.

4

Industry Dynamics

Objectives

1) To define the structure of the industry
2) To learn the impact of the Five Forces on the dynamic behavior of the industry
3) To identify analytic tools to manage the behavior of the actors in the industry

Learning outcomes and managerial capabilities developed

1) To apply the Five Forces to analyze the industry
2) To manage the dynamic behavior of industry actors

As the environment is important to an organization's existence, strategic issues identified within this context will enable an organization to gain advantage over its competitors. It is suggested that through the analysis of the five competitive forces: bargaining power of suppliers; bargaining power of buyers; threat of new entrants; degree of rivalry; and threat of substitutes, a strategist can evaluate the current industry structure, profitability and attractiveness. Within this framework the organization is viewed as a bundle of strategic activities aiming to adapt to industry environment by seeking an attractive position in the market arena.

This chapter is based on Porter's Five Forces framework but focuses on employing a dynamic perspective to consider all potential strategic interactions within each force. The dynamic analysis brings into consideration strategic actions such as competitive action/response sequences. Strategic interaction analysis is supported by a set of management science tools like revenue management and system dynamics simulation. Dynamic managerial capabilities are necessary to anticipate and influence other actors in the industry (competitors, buyers, suppliers, new entrants, and substitutes) in order to generate opportunities and reduce threats.

Strategic Analytics: Integrating Management Science and Strategy, First Edition. Martin Kunc.
© 2019 John Wiley & Sons Ltd. Published 2019 by John Wiley & Sons Ltd.
Companion website: www.wiley.com/go/kunc/strategic-analytics

4.1 Defining the Industry

Before analyzing the industry, it is necessary to define the structure of the industry. While there are different authors offering suggestions on how to define it, the common ground is reflected in the following questions:

1) **What are the boundaries?** The boundaries define the set of companies offering products/services that customers perceive to be substitutable for one another. The definition of the boundary is important because it focuses attention on the arena where the company is competing: substitutes, competitors, customers, goals, and key success factors. The main issue affecting the definition of industry boundaries is the evolution of the industry since it affects the main components of the industry.

2) **What is the structure?** Structure is defined by a set of attributes that provide a distinctive character and generate the requirements for success: concentration, economies of scale, product differentiation and barriers to entry. Concentration indicates the level of domination of the industry by only a few companies which affects the level of competition and barriers to entry. Economies of scale refers to the costs savings obtained due to volume of production which determines the intensity of competition. Higher economies of scale imply lower costs and lower prices which also deter entry to the industry. Product differentiation denotes the extent to which customers perceive products or services similar to or different from in reality or in perception. Differentiation affects the level of competition for customers among companies. Barriers to entry define the level of obstacles, e.g. capital requirements, brand image, etc., that a company must overcome to start competing in an industry. Barriers to entry reduce the numbers of potential companies in the industry reducing competition.

3) **Which companies are competitors?** Competitors are those companies that share a similar definition of the benefits customers derive from the products and services offered by a company. Another dimension affecting competitors is their level of commitment in the industry as it sheds light on the long-term intentions and goals. Some issues affecting the identification of competitors are: focusing on current and known competitors; only considering large and not small competitors, not evaluating international competitors; similar behavior over time; and misreading signals and focusing on only a few and tangible signals.

4.2 Porter's Five Forces and Industry Dynamics

The first fundamental determinant of a company's profitability is industry structure (Porter, 1985). Competitive strategy starts understanding the rules of competition that determine an industry's dynamics (Porter, 1985). Five forces determine the structure, and the attractiveness, of an industry: bargaining power of suppliers; bargaining power of buyers; threat of new entrants; degree of rivalry; and threat of substitutes embody the rules of competition. The collective strength of these five competitive forces determines the ability of companies in an industry to earn, on average, rates of return on investment exceeding the cost of capital (Porter, 1985). By understanding the strength of each of these forces, an organization can develop strategic initiatives which would maximize gain or minimize losses. The five forces determine industry profits because they influence the prices, costs and required investment in an industry (Porter, 1985).

The industry in which the organization operates determines the strategic issues from a structural perspective of strategy. Strategic issues are defined as developments, events and trends that have the potential to impact on an organization's strategy which can present problems or opportunities to decision makers (Duncan and Dutton, 1987). Strategic issues identified can then pose either an opportunity or a threat for organizations within the industry. For example, a company operating within an industry that is experiencing an increase in substitute products can develop strategic initiatives such as modifying their products to reduce profit losses. Beyond opportunity and threats, strategic issues are also signs for decision makers to drive the collection and interpretation of information from the industry.

The strategic issues are derived from the relative strength of the determinants of the five forces: higher strength implies a higher level of importance of the issue. A key consideration in the strategic formulation process is how to prioritize and segment strategic issues. Environmental analyses usually classify issues as threats and opportunities dependent on the strength of the determinant within each force. Thus, these issues as opportunities or threats in turn influence the strategic formulation process.

4.2.1 Bargaining Power of Suppliers

One of the elements of industry structure is the bargaining power of suppliers. Suppliers capture most of the value generated by charging high prices for their products, limiting quality or services, or shifting costs to industry participants (Porter, 2008). Companies and their suppliers are tied to one another through economic relationships, and these relationships are characterized by uncertainty, due both to demand variability and relative power positions (Harrigan, 1985). Sometimes the relationships between suppliers and companies are regulated by governments (Sanderson, 2001).

Table 4.1 shows the dimensions that define the bargaining power of suppliers and help to define suppliers as weak, which offer either opportunities or not depending on their strategic importance, or strong, which generate threats if they are strategically relevant. When suppliers are concentrated in only a few companies compared with the companies in the industry, they have higher

Table 4.1 Dimensions to evaluate suppliers.

Weak suppliers	Dimension	Strong suppliers
Low	Supplier concentration	High
High	Importance of volume to supplier	Low
Weak	Differentiation of inputs	Strong
Low	Impact of inputs on cost or differentiation	High
Low	Switching costs	High
High	Presence of substitute inputs	Low
Unlikely	Threat of forward integration	Credible

bargaining power to influence price and other aspects of the economic relationships. If suppliers do not depend on the industry in term of sales, suppliers have more negotiation power than suppliers which have strong relationships with the industry. If the products/services from the suppliers have an important impact on companies' strategies and are difficult to switch, suppliers have high bargaining power. Suppliers are also strong when there are no substitutes to their products or when they have the capacity to acquire companies in the industry by forward integration.

4.2.2   Bargaining Power of Buyers

Customers capture most value when they are able to define prices, demand better quality or more services (so driving up costs) and generally make industry participants compete against each other (Porter, 2008). Buyers have also power if they have negotiating influence in comparison with industry participants, particularly when they are price sensitive and can use their influence primarily to reduce prices.

Table 4.2 reports the dimensions to classify buyers/customers according to their bargaining strength and price sensitivity. Buyers have low bargaining power when the products/services represent a significant fraction of their costs (although they may be more interested in negotiating prices), there are no substitutes available or they have high switching costs. Buyers have higher bargaining power when they are more concentrated, i.e. they are larger companies, than their suppliers, and there is no threat of backward integration. Buyers can be highly sensitive to price if the product/service does not have a strong brand identity, is undifferentiated, the price is not significant with respect to the total purchases, and the products/services have low impact on quality/performance. Finally, buyers will be more sensitive to price when their profits are low.

Table 4.2 Dimensions to evaluate buyers.

Weak buyers	Dimension	Strong buyers
Low	*Bargaining leverage*	*High*
Low	Buyer volume	High
Sparse	Buyer information	Abundant
Low	Buyer concentration vs. industry	High
Low	Substitutes available	High
Unlikely	Threat of backward integration	Credible
High	Switching costs	Low
Low	*Price sensitivity*	*High*
Strong	Brand identity	Weak
High	Product differentiation	Low
Low	Price/total purchases	High
High	Impact on quality/performance	Low
High	Buyer profits	Low

4.2.3 Substitutes

A substitute product/service performs the same or similar function as the industry's product/service, defining the limit for industry prices and profits (Porter, 2008). The degree of the threat of substitutes within any industry determines the strategic issues that companies within the industry face.

Table 4.3 shows the dimensions employed to define the level of threat. For example, buyer inclination to look for substitutes can result in companies within the industry facing customer retention issues which force product differentiation, improvements in performance and quality, etc. Some factors that limit this threat are the existence of switching costs for the buyers and a lack of inclination to substitute products. Sometimes substitutes take time to develop until their price performance trade-off is high enough to move

Table 4.3 Dimensions to substitutes.

Limited threats	Dimension	Substantial threats
High	Switching costs	Low
Low	Buyer inclination to substitute	High
Low	Price performance trade-off of substitute	High

buyers to acquire them. Table 4.3 shows the determinants of the threats from substitutes.

4.2.4 Threat of New Entrants

New entrants to an industry bring new capacity and a desire to gain market share that puts pressure on prices, costs and the rate of investment necessary to compete (Porter, 2008). The threat of entry in an industry depends on the difficulty of entry barriers that are present and on the reaction from incumbents to the entrant (Porter, 2008). It is the threat of entry, not whether entry actually occurs, that affects profitability because of the need to keep prices low and high investments (Porter, 2008).

Table 4.4 displays the key determinants of the strengths of the barriers to entry and define the existence of a threat for existing companies. Exclusive product differentiation implies the existence of value creation factors (e.g. advertising, brand, customer service, product characteristics) that sustain customer loyalty. When access to distribution, which determines the access to customers, is covered by existing companies, it generates important issues for entrants in terms of costs and actions to reach customers. Government policy can limit or restrict the entry of new companies through regulations and access to inputs. Economies of scale (which refers to the decreasing function of costs as a result of increasing volume of production/activity) forces new entrants to make large investments in order to reach similar costs to existing companies or accepting cost disadvantages. Capital requirements reflect the requirements of financial resources that need to be invested in overcoming the barriers to entry. Three aspects are significant for this dimension: amount; risk; and recoverability. Switching costs are the monetary, knowledge or time costs facing customers if they want to change from one supplier to another supplier.

Table 4.4 Dimensions to evaluate the threat of entrants.

Weak threat	Dimension	Strong threat
Sustainable	Proprietary product differences	Low or easily copies
Difficult	Access to distribution	Easy
Protection	Government policy	Deregulation
Substantial	Economies of scale	Limited
High	Capital requirements	Low
High	Switching costs	Low
High	Absolute cost advantages	Low
High	Expected retaliation	Low

Absolute cost advantages are other costs not related to economies of scale and they may be proprietary product technology, access to inputs at low costs, locations, subsidies, learning curve, etc. Expected retaliation describes the reactions of the existing companies to the threat of an entrant (e.g. price reductions) which are fostered by their level of resources (e.g. financial, commitment to the industry, asset specificity, and the situation of the industry, low growth).

4.2.5 Intensity of Rivalry

Rivalry among existing competitors can take many forms: price discounting; new product innovations; and advertising campaigns (Porter, 2008). Rivalry drives down industry profits depending on the intensity of the competition and the type of competition employed (Porter, 2008). For example, highly specialized assets result in companies being unable to leave the market so they are likely to compete more intensively (Porter, 2008). As competition intensifies, company performance will no longer be determined by its own actions but it may become uncertain since the company's behavior is heavily influenced by the actions and contingences undertaken by competitors (Menguc and Auh, 2005).

Table 4.5 shows the key dimensions defining rivalry. Exit barriers are factors that preclude companies leaving the industry if their profitability is negative. Some factors are specialized assets, fixed costs, strategic interrelationships, emotional barriers and regulatory restrictions. Industry concentration refers to the number and size distribution of companies competing within a market (Grant, 2013). When the industry is dominated by a few companies, oligopoly, price competition may not be intense due to either collusion or imitation, so the competition occurs in other dimensions such as advertising or product development. When the industry has many balanced competitors in terms of resources, then instability is expected as they try to overcome each other.

Table 4.5 Dimensions to evaluate competitive intensity.

Low rivalry	Dimension	Intense rivalry
Low	Exit barriers	High (difficult to exit)
Low	Industry concentration	High
Low	Fixed costs	High
High	Industry growth	Low
High	Differentiation	Low
Infrequent	Intermittent overcapacity	Frequent
Low	Diversity of rivals	High

Finally, an industry dominated by one company will be fairly stable given the ability of the leader to discipline other companies. High fixed costs relative to the value added generate strong incentives for companies to fill capacity through price cutting. Industries with low growth rate imply companies which need to steal market share from competitors when they try to expand, generating competitive reaction. If the growth is high, then companies can keep their market share and growth together with the industry. Industry with similar products or services, low differentiation, tend to compete based on price and become volatile compared with industry with differentiated products or high switching costs. Industries which need to expand capacity on large increments may suffer from overcapacity leading to price cutting in order to generate demand to fill the new capacity. Diverse rivals in terms of strategies, goals or intentions with respect to the industry can accidentally generate periods of strong competition as they cannot understand each other and misunderstand the industry recipes.

4.2.6 Strategic Issues Derived from Five Forces Analysis

Dimensions within each force are usually classified as either opportunities or threats to the organization during the strategic formulation process. How issues are interpreted depends on their perceived characteristics, and the presence of particular issue characteristics affects whether managers interpret issues as threats or opportunities (Jackson and Dutton, 1988). The "opportunity" category relates to a situation where there is, or will be, a positive impact on the situation of the company and is under control of the company. In contrast, a "threat" is defined as a negative situation that is, or will be, generating a loss and the company has relatively little control (Dutton and Jackson, 1987).

In order to address a strategic issue, it has to be clearly described since issue interpretation affects the actions to be taken. Jackson and Dutton (1989) suggest that interpretation will be certain when available information is distinctive of a threat or opportunity rather than neutral. Subsequent research also highlights the importance of labels on the strategic actions undertaken to address strategic issues (Chatoopadhyay et al., 2001). Walton et al. (1989) suggest focusing on a few dimensions when deciding how to categorize strategic issues to take into account the similarities between strategic issues. Strategic issue categorization is important because it influences the allocation of attention and resources used to address them. For example, organizations facing a loss of profitability are more likely to be risk-seeking (Kahneman and Tversky, 1979). Thus, after the industry environment has been assessed, interpreted and categorized, the company prepares a strategic response that will depend on how environmental conditions have been labeled (Mukherji and Hurtado, 2001).

Food for thought 4.1   One of the most interesting industries to apply the Five Forces framework is the airline industry for a number of reasons: transparent and diverse business models, high availability of information, and personal experience. Here is a brief explanation of industry performance after the economic crisis based on IATA Economics (2015b):

Airline shares (Figure 4.1) have remained subdued between 2008 and 2015 due to the low profitability of the airline industry. However, there are some special cases where performance has been excellent, e.g. the European low-cost carriers such as Ryanair or easyJet, because low price tickets were more suitable for travelers during the recent economic crisis. Recently, the decline in oil prices has impacted positively on profits which was reflected in the market valuation of most airlines, especially the US airlines.

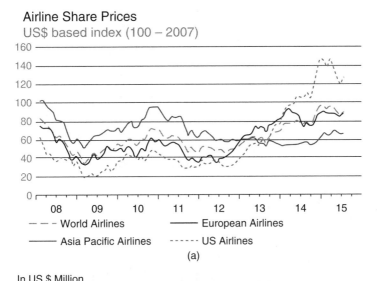

Airline Share Prices
US$ based index (100 – 2007)

- – – – World Airlines
- ——— European Airlines
- ——— Asia Pacific Airlines
- · · · · · US Airlines

(a)

In US $ Million

# Airlines*	Regions	Q2 2014		Q2 2015	
		Operating profit	Net post-tax profit	Operating profit	Net post-tax profit
9	North America	5210	3083	6737	5236
7	Asia-Pacific	131	82	462	432
7	Europe	1734	893	1881	1213
2	Latin America	8	−13	42	29
0	Others	0	0	0	0
25	**Sample total**	**7083**	**4045**	**9122**	**6910**

(b)

Figure 4.1 Financial performance of the airline industry. (a) Airline share prices by region. (b) Airline operating profits by region. *Source:* IATA Economics, 2015b. Reproduced with permission from IATA Economics.

Ticket price (without fuel surcharges and ancillary revenues) at industry level had not shown similar performance to the stock market (Figure 4.2a). Some reasons for this performance were the decline in fuel costs, exchange rate and stronger growth in capacity relative to demand (Figure 4.2b). Another factor for keeping ticket prices restrained was the impact of low-cost airlines which had increased the geographic breadth of their service and enjoy low operating costs. A final important factor (which has developed over the past decade and makes airline prices more transparent) was internet-based search and booking solutions such as

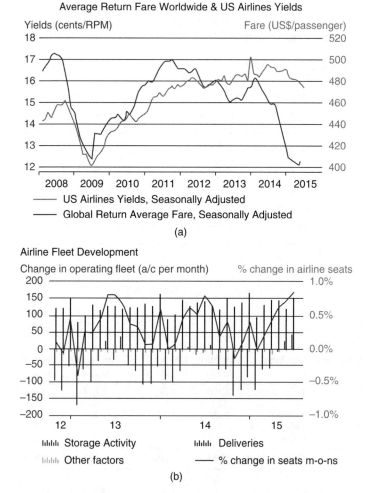

Figure 4.2 Price and capacity performance of the airline industry. (a) Average return fare worldwide and USA airline yields. (b) Airline fleet development. *Source:* IATA Economics, 2015b. Reproduced with permission from IATA Economics.

Opodo, Expedia and Travelocity, which account for a large percentage of airline tickets.

Finally, a key metric in the airline industry is the load factor, which measures the percentage of the airplane capacity occupied by either passengers or cargo, presented in Figure 4.3. Given the high fixed costs, load factors were important in evaluating the profitability of the industry and specific airlines. Interestingly, airlines did not have stable demand, as shown by the graph in Figure 4.3b. Peak

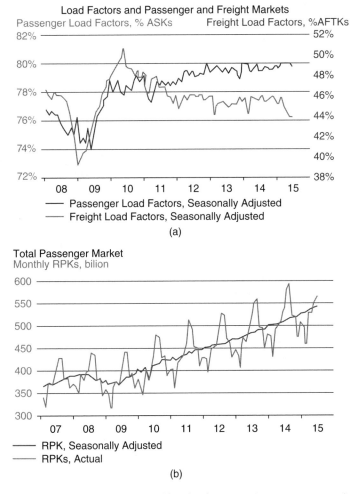

Figure 4.3 Load factors for passenger and freight: the two main revenue streams in the airline industry. (a) Load factors for passengers and freight markets. (b) Total passenger market with seasonality. *Source:* IATA Economics, 2015b. Reproduced with permission from IATA Economics.

season corresponds to the summer months in the Northern Hemisphere and the differences in capacity utilization between peak and off-peak seasons can be 30% or more. However, the trend shows strong growth since 2009.

Table 4.6 provides a suggested description of the determinants of the Five Forces for the airline industry.

After a review of the diverse material offered by the internet (tips: a search using Google will give more than 800 000 results; a key source for information about the

Table 4.6 Five forces analysis of the airline industry.

Five Forces	Conditions
Buyer power	High buyer independence without threat of backward integration (mainly consumers)
	High price sensitivity due to high price/total purchase (traveling)
	Highly discretionary product (traveling is a discretionary activity)
	Low switching costs but fairly differentiated product (similar product – travel – but differences among providers)
Supplier power	Depending on the input for airline operations, airlines can have high independence (e.g. fuel), large fairly differentiated suppliers with high switching costs (e.g. aircraft engines), high importance on quality/cost (e.g. food), no substitutes and concentrate (Airbus and Boeing)
	Other suppliers, e.g. airports, also have high switching costs and high importance on quality/cost and no substitutes (central airports)
	Low dispensability and threat of forward integration
Substitutes	Low switching cost
	Low price performance trade-offs (compared with car or train over long distances)
New entrants	Strong market growth
	Economies of scale that are important but achievable and high fixed costs
	Suppliers accessible
	Low proprietary product differences and low switching cost
	Strong brands but accessible distribution
	Incumbents that can retaliate strongly
	Highly regulated operations but open entry
Rivalry	Highly diverse industry with differentiated products (similar product – travel – but differences among providers) and competitors of diverse size
	Low switching costs
	High fixed costs with intermittent overcapacity
	Potential zero sum game in certain markets
	Exit barriers relatively high

airline industry is www.iata.org, which is the International Air Transport Association), you will be able to answer the following questions:

- Do you agree with Table 4.6? Explain the reasons in favor and against for each force.
- Will the analysis change if we segment the industry across the main type of business models (also known as strategic groups which are the group of companies employing similar strategy to compete in similar segments (Porter, 2008)): low-cost airlines (e.g. Ryanair, Southwest, Air Asia, Gol), flag airlines (e.g. Qantas, British Airways, Lufthansa, Aerolineas Argentinas), or full-service airlines (e.g. United Airlines, TAM, Air Europe)? Try to develop a Five Forces analysis for at least two of the strategic groups. What are the differences and similarities?

4.3 Integrating Management Science into Strategic Management

A key problem with Five Forces is that Porter gives no indication of how to operationalize an analysis based on the Five Forces or how to determine what counteractions can be taken (O'Shaunessy, 1984). The introduction of management science tools can help to mitigate this problem. Management science tools provide the opportunity for companies to gain a competitive advantage or neutralize a threat. The evaluation of these tools can identify which ones are more useful in relation to the industry in question. One of the important issues with using management science tools is all elements related to a problem have to be quantified but all variables do not lend to quantification and models may not take into account qualitative factors or emotional factors which can be important. Continuing with the analysis of the airline industry, IATA analysis suggested industry's bargaining power is low with respect to customers (IATA, 2015a) due to the following aspect: Customers have high bargaining power because air travel is a standardized product, which is part of discretionary spending, with low switching costs and they have increasing price transparency. Simultaneously, airlines sell a perishable product with limited product differentiation and high fixed costs.

The next subsection provides a management science tool to address some of the concerns raised with buyers. This tool has been successfully implemented in other industries with similar strategic issues: find out those industries and check if its use is justified.

4.3.1 Revenue Management

Airlines are able to collect a great quantity of information about buyers' behavior. For instance, bookings and cancellations are used to forecast demand, as

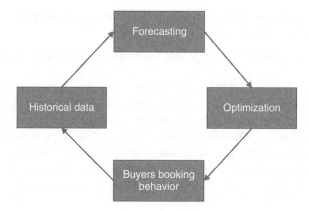

Figure 4.4 Simple description of RMS.

well as to determine, based on this forecasted demand, scheduled inventory (fleet allocation) and prices, which determine the value of each unit in the inventory (seats available in the fleet/network) at a certain point in time, optimizing their revenues (Oancea, 2014). This system is called the Revenue Management System (RMS) (Talluri and Van Ryzin, 2006). One important aspect is related to its influence in the market since the prices and capacity offered may affect positively, buyers behave in the way it is expected, or negatively, buyers dislike prices and offerings. Figure 4.4 shows a simple description of the system. Basically, the system is a combination of databases with historical sales and buyers' behavior (e.g. percentage of no-shows by flight) that are used to forecast future demand. Then using the forecasted demand, linear programming (see Chapter 11) combines the demand with the availability of airplanes (e.g. location and size of the fleet) to generate a profile of revenues and profits. The profile is optimized through repeating the linear programming model multiple times until the best profile is obtained and key decisions regarding pricing are made. The system is continuously learning from the results of the pricing strategy as the resulting buyers' behavior is captured in the databases.

RMS has evolved making the models more accurate. For example, the third generation of RMS generated an increase of 4–6% in revenues (Belobaba, 2011). The entry of low-cost airlines implies a structural change in pricing as they promoted a simplified fare structure which implied the elimination of previous methods such as restrictions on low fares related to round-trip purchases and minimum stay requirements, which were employed to segment leisure from business passengers (Belobaba, 2011).

The use of RMS helps airlines to implement strategies that can dynamically change the availability of inventory in real time depending on buyers' requests coming toward the airline's reservation system (Oancea, 2014). The main objective of RMS is to support the airline in order to: "offer the right price at the right time to the right customer" (Oancea, 2014). Since its first implementation, RMS has contributed to reducing the disadvantage that airlines have with respect to buyers' bargaining powers. The use of RMS has some issues:

- Changes to the inventory, such as adding/removing destinations/frequencies/ airplane size, can affect the performance of RMS in terms of standard metrics employed by airlines. For example, adding one long-haul destination may increase the Average Ticket Value (AVT), potentially Load Factor but it may reduce the Revenue per Available Seat-Kilometers (RASK) (Oancea, 2014). Consequently, using simulation can minimize the risks of doubtful operational decisions with potential impact on the performance of the company at a strategic level (Oancea, 2014).
- Technical limitations, poor design or lack of qualified staff to optimize the parameters employed by the RMS can easily affect the quality of the decisions generated if the buyers' behavior changes (Oancea, 2014). Most popular models supporting RMS use recent transactions to estimate demand and generate subsequent decisions about pricing in terms of optimal use of the capacity. However, RMS cannot evaluate the true willingness to pay from buyers (real price sensitivity) or eliminate the randomness of buyers' behavior.

Table 4.7 shows a process used to manage a RMS (Parker, 2003) with the intention to serve not only as an operational tool but also as a strategic feedback system.

Table 4.7 Process to manage RMS.

RMS area	Procedure	Strategic implication
Seat allocation	• Compile historical data about buyers' behavior (seat demand, class distribution and market fares) • Compare with planned capacity utilization (flights scheduled, seats available and expected) • Classify the differences in terms of importance (market, regions, and specific flights schedules) in key metrics: load factor, composition of the revenue profile (type of passengers)	This exercise detects changes in buyers' behavior which need to be investigated given their level of importance as they may have strategic impact: new entrants, rivals' competitive actions, changes in price sensitivity, or simply erroneous assumptions about pricing or capacity allocation

(Continued)

Table 4.7 (Continued)

RMS area	Procedure	Strategic implication
System calibration	• New offerings need to be included in the system and calibrated into the system by using historical data from another route with similar competitive environment (buyers' and rivals' behavior) to be able to optimize revenues • Verify that the historical data fits with the future patterns of activity in the new offering (departure times, completely new route, special events, seasonality patterns)	This activity can inform the expected conditions of the new market and serve as a platform to learn about the market once the offering is launched
Commercial exception policies	• The system will provide the optimal configuration of the seat inventory to maximize the revenues after using the expected information • Management may decide to override some of the results in order to adjust to specific policies to achieve strategic goals	While the system can only provide the best solution to a defined competitive market, managers may want to explore policies to achieve goals that exceed optimizing the current set of resources.
Performance monitoring	• Recurrent reviews to compare advance with historical data or post-flight are performed	This activity allows the company to react to erroneous expectations or changes in the market

Food for thought 4.2   The Qantas Group employs more than 30 000 people and offers services across a network of more than 180 destinations in more than 40 countries in Australia, Asia, the Americas, Europe, Middle East and Africa (Qantas, 2010). The Qantas Group has two airline brands: Qantas; and Jetstar, which is a low-cost airline (Qantas, 2010). In the domestic market (Australia), Qantas, QantasLink and Jetstar operate more than 5000 flights a week serving 59 cities and regional destinations. Jetstar operates 160 domestic flights a week in New Zealand (Qantas, 2010). Internationally, Qantas and Jetstar operate more than 900 flights each week (Qantas, 2010).

The Qantas Group operates a fleet (approximate number of airplanes in brackets) comprising: Boeing 787s (10), Boeing 747s (11), Boeing 737s (79) and Boeing 717s (79); Airbus A380s (12), Airbus A330s (27) and A320s (108); Bombardier Dash 8s (46); and Fokker F100 (13) (Qantas, 2010).

The Qantas Group suggests the following strategies for managing its revenue (Qantas, 2010):

1) **Yield management.** Yield managers employ widely accepted statistical tools to forecast seat demand, taking into account historical data and seasonal variables. For example, there is heavy demand on domestic routes during weekday peak periods and to leisure destinations during holiday periods, but there is low demand at other times. Therefore, each flight has its own individual forecast. Yield managers look at external and internal factors as diverse as economic indicators which affect longer term demand, seasonal schedule changes and changes in aircraft capacity to achieve an optimal mix of fares.

2) **Overbooking.** A component of yield management is the overbooking of flights. Overbook occurs because there is a percentage of passengers and travel agents that make reservations without ever trying to use them and others make multiple bookings. Overbooking profiles are monitored and managed so flights are not closed for bookings ahead of departure. Therefore, fewer seats are wasted and more customers have the opportunity to travel.

3) **Pricing initiatives.** A range of fares is offered to meet overall revenue targets since not everyone is prepared to pay the same price at the same time. Some customers are driven by price and choose to purchase discounted fares, such as sale or promotional airfares. Other customers want to book early or travel on a particular day or time in order to secure a seat. Customers who are time sensitive or want greater flexibility are often willing to pay a higher price. The full range of fare types is available for sale for some time during the booking lifecycle. In its aim to maximize seat sales, pricing initiatives play a role in identifying areas of weaker demand and releasing special fares to stimulate demand.

4) **Capacity to meet demand.** When it is viable, peak travel periods are matched with additional capacity to meet customer demand. In periods of lower demand, a combination of pricing initiatives and/or capacity changes is applied in order to best match seat demand and supply.

Using the insights of the RMS and the information about Qantas, answer the following questions:

- Which market (national or international) will you consider most difficult to predict in terms of demand? Explain your reasons based on the Five Forces operating in the market and the PESTE factors.
- What variables, in addition to current buyers' behavior, will you consider in order to forecast the demand for the most difficult market? Think about the impact of the Five Forces operating in the market.
- What planes will you suggest to consider for the international market: large size (e.g. Airbus 380) or medium size (e.g. Boeing 777)? Explain your reasons based on the Five Forces operating in the market.
- How frequent will you review the performance of the RMS? Why? What signals indicating changes in the Five Forces will generate your review?

4.3.2 Evaluating Competitors' Performance in the Market Using Text Mining

Companies have a strong presence on social media nowadays using various services such as Facebook and Twitter to offer products/services and obtain feedback from customers. Customers and companies generate an important amount of content on social media that is amenable for analysis. More importantly, the content can be employed to monitor and analyze the performance of the company and competitors with respect to satisfying customers (He et al., 2013). More specifically, the content can be used to understand the strength of buyers' power and rivalry intensity.

Activities employing social media are brand management, advertising, sales, customer support, and product development and trial (Di Gangi et al., 2010). One of the characteristic aspects of social media data is the lack of structure: customers' opinions, professional reviews, competitors' prices and promotions, competitors' product information and distribution channels' own contents. Consequently, the use of traditional quantitative methods is not possible with this type of data but there is technology called text mining that can be used (Romero and Ventura, 2010). Text mining aims to produce models describing relationships between variables and trends/patterns in the text. Text mining differs from content analysis because it is data driven rather than word coding driven (He et al., 2013). Some applications of text mining are clustering, which can reveal hidden trends or correlations among data, and text summarization, which extracts information (He et al., 2013).

He et al. (2013) performed a case study in the pizza industry comparing the three main companies in the USA: Pizza Hut; Domino's; and Papa John's. The pizza industry uses multiple channels to reach its customers: direct mail, TV advertising and social media, and it is a very popular industry so it generates a large amount of interest among customers and the visibility of competitors is high. The process for the text mining analysis of competitors' activities involved:

1) Identification of social media targets: Facebook and Twitter, and period of time.
2) Extraction of posts in social media targets into a file for analysis, e.g. Excel.
3) Data cleaning, e.g. elimination of posts not useful, and formatting, e.g. integrating into one format for use by the mining techniques.
4) Use of text mining software to explore and extract key concepts, generate categories and gain insights. Then query search on the data to identify patterns, linkages and information based on hypothesis.
5) The social media data can be presented as tweets, comments to posts, shares and likes. See Figure 4.5 for an example of the information found by He et al. (2013).

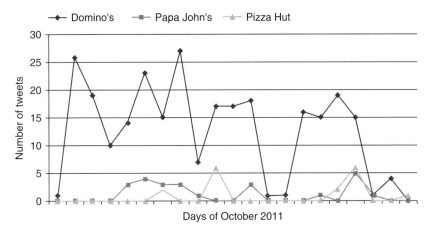

Figure 4.5 Trend of tweets for the companies during October 2011. *Source:* He al. (2013: figure 2, page 467. Reproduced with permission from International Journal of Information Management.

6) Some of the data can be quantitative such as number of followers, postings, comments, likes, frequency of posting, posting and response time. The information collected by He et al. (2013) indicates that Pizza Hut had the largest number of Facebook fans (almost 5 million), followed by Domino's (4.3 million) and Papa John's (almost 2 million) but Domino's had the largest number of Twitter followers. This information confirms the trend in tweets observed in Figure 4.5 where Twitter is the preferred means to communicate with buyers for Domino's. Facebook information also shows that Domino's was highly active with two wall posts in Facebook compared with Pizza Hut with only one wall post.

7) In terms of means of engagement, the analysis found that questions generated the highest response from social media where Pizza Hut received almost 100 000 likes and more than 15 000 comments but Domino's obtained more than 200 000 likes and 30 000 comments during a month.

8) Text mining was employed initially to identify emerging themes so combining all data from the three companies offered a broad overview of the main discussions among buyers. Five themes appeared in Twitter: ordering and delivering (positive and negative); quality (taste and ingredients); purchasing decision; community building (connecting with customers in other aspects than pizza); and marketing. Facebook's analysis is more challenging since there are not only texts but also videos and photos. The six themes observed were: posting photos related to events not specific for the business; questions to obtain input from customers regarding the products; highlighting events that could be associated with consumption occasions; community building; signs of appreciation to customers; and promotions/rewards.

The observation of the patterns of behavior among the three companies suggest different levels of engagement with their customers and potential buyers. While there should be a correlation between their presence on social media and their market share, the data does not support it. Domino's had a market share of 7% compared with Pizza Hut's 11%. Potentially, the comparison should be made between the growth rate in market share and the level of activity on social media. Another piece of important information from social media is the level of service and product quality: positive and negative communications can affect customers' perceptions about the companies offering temporal competitive advantages if companies' responses are fast (Browne and Kunc, 2010).

Finally, He et al. (2013) propose a set of recommendations for companies. First, monitor your own and competitors' social media presence using free and commercial internet tools such as Google Alerts, Quora, etc. Secondly, use the information gather to perform competitive benchmarking regarding key metrics such as followers, posting, comments, tweets, etc. Thirdly, perform text mining to understand the conversations on social media and detect changes in customers and social trends (see Chapter 3 for PESTE analysis). Fourthly, evaluate the impact of findings on the business's competitive advantage such as the links between business actions (price, promotions) and social media responses (consumer sentiments).

4.4 End of Chapter

The industry dynamics is determined by the actions of different companies, each trying to achieve their own strategic and financial objectives. The Five Forces framework provides a suitable grouping of actors across their main behaviors in the industry and their impact on the profitability of the industry and the company. A key issue is to draw the boundaries of the industry: what is a valid substitute product? How far in the supply chain should suppliers be considered? Understanding the behaviors of key actors is necessary in order to predict and foresee the future dynamics of the industry leading to its evolution over time (see Chapter 5 for a more detailed explanation of industry evolution). Knowing about the potential changes is fundamental to the design of robust strategies. While the Five Forces framework is simple, and somewhat imprecise, the task of implementing the strategic recipes is complex. For example, managing customers implies considering not only customers' needs and bargaining power but also the role of substitute products as well as competitors providing similar products. The implementation of actions to manage the dynamics of the industry is the area of analytics tools such as Revenue Management to manage customers' demand or text mining to learn customers' and competitors' actions. Management science can support the

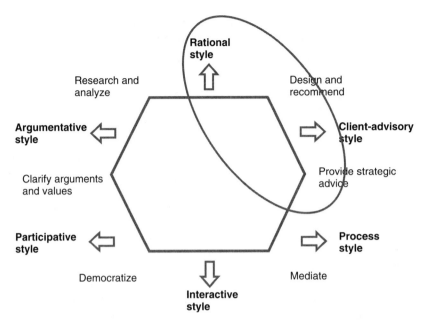

Figure 4.6 Management science styles. *Source:* Adapted from Walker (2009). Reproduced with permission from Elsevier.

design of actions to overcome issues raised by a Five Forces analysis. In this chapter, management science provides rational advice for designing and recommending strategies to overcome the forces driving the industry behavior, as Figure 4.6 indicates.

4.4.1 Revision Questions

1) Find other frameworks to evaluate the dynamics of the industry and compare with the Five Forces. For example, read Holmberg and Cummings (2009) on selecting strategic partners for alliances.
2) What factors will you consider to expand Five Forces analysis? For example, companies that are neither suppliers nor buyers but complement the companies in the industry can be an addition to the analysis.
3) What other management science tools will you employ to identify, evaluate or address strategic issues raised by the Five Forces?
4) Develop a 2×2 matrix using two dimensions: duration of the service (predictable vs. unpredictable) and price variability (fixed vs. variable). Then allocate industries that you know in each quadrant. In which quadrant do buyers have high bargaining power? Why? Which industries will use revenue management intensively?

4.4.2 Case Study: Strategic Evaluation of Entering in a New Market as a Low-cost Airline Using System Dynamics Modeling

The following case study is adapted from Kunc and Morecroft (2007).

4.4.2.1 Describing the Key Strategic Aspects of a Business Using a System Dynamics Model

The concept of stock accumulation appears as the cornerstone of system dynamics models (Sterman, 2000; Morecroft, 2015). Simultaneously, any balance sheet item (such as inventory, manufacturing and operational equipment, buildings and financial resources) and key tangible or intangible resource (e.g. people, knowledge, reputation) in an organization can be represented as a stock accumulation. Since it takes time to develop such assets or to reduce them, it makes it important to understand their dynamics. Balance sheet items and resources, which we define as asset stock, accumulate their inflows and outflows in just the same way as the concept of stock in system dynamics models (Sterman, 2000: Morecroft, 2015). Graphically, an asset stock is represented as a rectangle and on each side is an inflow/outflow drawn as a valve (or tap) superimposed on an arrow. The arrow enters the stock and originates from a source, shown as a cloud. The complete picture is called a "stock and flow" network. The equations for a stock and flow network contain the arithmetic of accumulation. Thus, the value of an asset stock at the present time is equal to its value at a previous point in time added to the difference between the inflow and the outflow over the time interval between the previous and present times. Each asset stock has an initial value at the start of the simulation. Since asset stocks cannot be adjusted instantaneously and change only occurs through adjustments captured by flow rates, stocks are useful to represent the dynamic performance of companies within industries.

4.4.2.2 The easyJet Case

While the case study reflects the situation described in "easyJet's $500 million gamble" (Sull, 1999), this situation is similar to any low-cost airline attempting to enter a new market. Sull (1999) explained the rapid growth of easyJet, which started operations in November 1995, and its consideration of the model low-cost European airline becoming a strong competitor to traditional airlines. Using Table 4.8, we can describe the Five Forces affecting EasyJet:

Therefore, a system dynamics model can generate scenarios to verify if it will be difficult or impossible to fill the planes considered for investment. There are two key issues related to the Five Forces: how to attract enough passengers to fill 12 planes (initial investment); and how to deal with retaliation by rivals.

There are multiple system dynamics models of low-cost airlines which offer realistic opportunities to develop the intuition to run an airline. One of the most popular system dynamics models is People Express (Sterman, 1988).

Table 4.8 Five Forces analysis for the easyJet case.

Five Forces	Conditions
Buyer power	Since they have low switching costs, passengers may be attracted to easyJet easily. However, the service is fairly differentiated: no frills vs. full service so there is a need to educate potential passengers to use easyJet
Supplier power	Airlines can have high independence for fuel so it is not relevant for a model
	There are only two suppliers of aircraft(Airbus and Boeing), so the choice is simple and it depends on the economies achieved by buying a large quantity of aircraft. Thus, the importance of attracting enough passengers
Substitutes	Given the low price and key performance trade-offs (compared with car or train over long distances), there is no threat from substitutes
New entrants	There is strong market growth with accessible suppliers (aircraft companies and secondary airports) together with accessible distribution (internet-based ticket sales)
	The key issue is incumbents that can retaliate strongly by reducing prices
Rivalry	It is a highly diverse industry with differentiated products (similar product – travel – but differences among providers – service) and competitors of diverse size. Simultaneously, there is low switching costs and a potential zero-sum game in certain markets
	Rivalry is key for the model

However, the starting point of this systems dynamics model is a map of the business to think about the task of attracting and retaining passengers and the factors that might drive competitor retaliation.

The dynamics of attracting potential passengers   The building blocks of system dynamics models are stock accumulations, causal links and feedback loops. Causal links show simple cause and effect relationships. Feedback loops represent closed paths of cause and effect generating the dynamics of the business. Feedback loops can be either reinforcing or balancing. Reinforcing loops are responsible for growth dynamics and balancing loops are responsible for goal-seeking dynamics. Figure 4.7 presents the dynamics of potential passengers using one stock accumulation (potential passengers), one reinforcing feedback loop (increase of potential passengers), one balancing feedback loop (loss of potential passengers) and several causal links related to the process of attracting new passengers.

Potential passengers are shown as an asset stock representing the cumulative number of passengers who have formed a favorable impression of the start-up airline. This is a convenient simplifying assumption that enables the model to focus on growth of interest in low-cost flights without the need to model the detailed operations of the company (e.g. airplanes, people, airports, etc.).

The driver of growth of passengers is a reinforcing feedback loop shown at the center of Figure 4.7 (labeled R, Growth Engine). In this loop potential

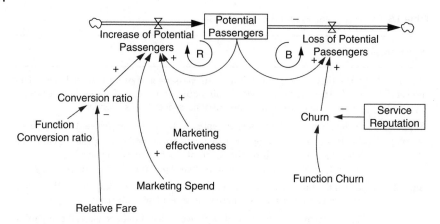

Figure 4.7 The dynamics of potential passengers.

passengers attract new converts through positive word-of-mouth. The more potential passengers, the greater the rate of increase of potential passengers. This causal link is drawn as a curved arrow with a "+" sign on the arrow head to indicate a link with positive polarity (more passengers, greater inflow). The increase of potential passengers then accumulates in the stock of potential passengers, leading to even more potential passengers and a greater rate of increase in potential passengers, thereby completing the reinforcing loop. Since potential passengers have low switching costs, their response to word-of-mouth depends on relative fare, which subsequently determines the conversion ratio. As relative fare increases the conversion rate decreases, a causal link drawn as a curved arrow with a "–" sign on the arrow head to indicate a link with negative polarity. This part of the model captures the price sensitivity of the potential passengers, a bargaining power of customers in the Five Forces.

The increase of potential passengers is also influenced by marketing spend, another causal link. This link is formulated as the product of marketing spend and marketing effectiveness. Marketing effectiveness represents the number of new potential passengers per marketing pound (£) spent. The loss of potential passengers depends on service reputation. The lower service reputation, the greater the churn (hence the "–" sign on the arrow head of the causal link). The greater the churn, the more the loss of passengers. Industry specialists say that service reputation depends on ease-of-booking, punctuality, safety, on-board service and quality of meals. For short-haul flights punctuality is often the dominant factor. The model does not represent all these factors explicitly but simply represents service reputation as a stock accumulation that can be initialized anywhere on a scale between very poor and very good. If reputation is very good then fliers retain a favorable impression of the airline, so the annual loss of potential passengers is small. If reputation is poor then the loss of potential passengers per year is damagingly high, up to 100% per year. Notice there is no inflow or outflow to reputation even though it is a stock variable. The reason is that the factors driving change in reputation are outside the boundary of the model.

Retaliation by existing companies   The stock and flow diagram presented in Figure 4.8 shows the response of existing airlines to the low-cost airlines.

Figure 4.8 shows how the competitors could affect easyJet's growth ambitions. Remember that word-of-mouth feedback relies on easyJet's fare (Fare Set by Start-up in Figure 4.8) being lower than existing competitors for its contagion. But what if competing airlines try to match the start-up's low price? Figure 4.8 shows how such price adjustment might take place. At the heart of the formulation is a balancing loop (labeled B, Restructuring). Rivals' fare is shown as a stock that accumulates the change in rivals' fare, which in turn depends on three factors: the fare set by the start-up; rivals' fare; and the time to change costs, all depicted as causal links. The use of a stock accumulation implies that it takes time and effort for the established airlines to lower their fares. They cannot reduce fares until they cut costs and large airlines can take years to achieve cost parity with a low-cost start-up. The process of achieving cost parity is essentially a goal-seeking process represented by the balancing loop.

While large airlines will match low seat prices regardless of cost by providing some seats at a discount (price cuts can be implemented very quickly through on-line RMSs – see Section 4.3.1), narrow discounts are an ineffective weapon in the competitive fight with low-cost airlines. Thus, only cost parity can deliver competitive prices and profitability in the long term for large airlines catering to a growing population of price-conscious fliers. Such an enormous change can only be achieved through major restructuring of

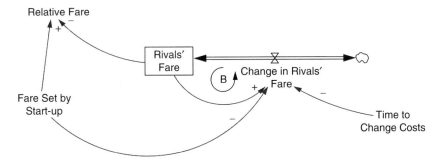

Figure 4.8 Balancing loop and other causal links describing rivals' retaliation through fare reduction.

the business. The change in rivals' fare is controlled by the "restructuring" balancing loop that gradually reduces the fare to equal the fare set by the start-up. The pace of restructuring depends on the time to change costs. Normally one would expect this adjustment time to be several years.

Route saturation   The stock and flow diagram presented in Figure 4.9 is a way to visualize the limits imposed by the strategy in terms of capacity, the number of planes and the seats available to offer in different routes. The loop is peripheral to the immediate question of whether or not easyJet can fill 12 planes but is important in the long run to ensure realistic limits to the growth of potential passengers in the region. The balancing loop reflecting route saturation eventually restricts the increase of potential passengers. Basically, planes can make a certain number of flights per day to a certain distance and transporting a certain number of passengers. Planes serve a certain number of days per year and the maximum passenger miles that can be served is also limited by the expected market share attained. On the other hand, passengers will fly a certain number of flights per year and a number of miles per flight. The comparison between the capacity, maximum passenger miles, and the demand, potential passenger miles, determines the level of saturation in the route.

We can have a 2×2 matrix describing all potential scenarios based on the strength of the two feedback loops for the new company. Rival's retaliation is determined by the variable "Time to change costs" where low retaliation is 4 years and fast retaliation is 2 years. Marketing spending to attract customers is determined by the variable "Marketing Spend" and low is £1 million and high is £2.5 million.

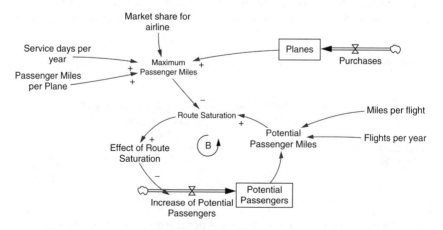

Figure 4.9 The dynamics of route saturation.

Here are a few questions that you can answer using the simulation model:

1) Which strategic option will help easyJet to be successful considering that it needs 1 million passengers?
2) What will happen if easyJet starts with a price similar to large airlines? Adjust variable "Fare Set by Startup" to 0.25.
3) What other adjustment will you make to the model? Try to implement and discuss the new insights generated.

References

Belobaba, P. (2011). Did LCCs save airline revenue management? *Journal of Revenue and Pricing Management*, 10, 19–22.

Browne, M. and Kunc, M. (2010). Corporate Reputation in Chile. In: Corporate Reputation and the News Media (ed. C. Carroll), 279–292. Routledge.

Chatoopadhyay, P., Gick,W.H., and Huber,G.P. (2001). Organisational actions in response to threats and opportunities. *Academy of Management*, 44(5), 937–955.

Di Gangi, P.M., Wasko, M., and Hooker, R.E. (2010). Getting customers' ideas to work for you: Learning from Dell how to succeed with online user innovation communities. *MIS Quarterly Executive*, 9(4), 163–178.

Duncan, R.B. and Dutton, J.E. (1987). The influence of the strategic planning process on strategic change. *Strategic Management Journal*, 8(2), 103–116.

Dutton, J.E. and Jackson, S.E. (1987). Categorizing strategic issues: links to organisation action. *Academy of Management*, 12(1), 76–90.

Grant, R.M. (2013). Contemporary Strategy and Analysis: Text and Cases, 8th edn. John Wiley & Sons, Ltd.

Harrigan, K.R. (1985). Vertical integration and corporate strategy. *Academy of Management Journal*, 28(2), 397–425.

He, W., Zha, S., and Li, L. (2013). Social media competitive analysis and text mining: A case study in the pizza industry. *International Journal of Information Management*, 33(3), 464–472.

Holmberg, S.R. and Cummings, J. L. (2009). Building successful strategic alliances: strategic process and analytical tool for selecting partner industries and firms. *Long Range Planning*, 42, 164–193.

IATA Economics (2015a). Air Passenger Market Analysis, June 2015. www.iata. org (accessed 17 August 2015).

IATA Economics (2015b). Airlines Financial Monitor, June–July 2015. www.iata. org (accessed 17 August 2015).

Jackson, S. and Dutton, J. (1989). Discerning threats and opportunities. *Administrative Science Quarterly*, 33,370–387.

Kahneman, D. and Tversky, A. (1979). Prospect theory: An analysis of decision under risk. *Econometica*, 47, 263–292.

Kunc, M. and Morecroft, J. (2007). System dynamics modelling for strategic development. In: Supporting Strategy: Frameworks, Methods and Models (eds R. Dyson and F. O'Brien), 157–189. John Wiley & Sons, Ltd.

Menguc, B. and Auh, S. (2005). Balancing exploration and exploitation: The moderating role of competitive intensity. *Journal of Business Research*, 58(1), 1652–1661.

Morecroft, J.D.W. (2015), Strategic Modelling and Business Dynamics: A Feedback Systems View, 2nd edn. John Wiley & Sons, Ltd.

Mukherji, A. and Hurtado, P. (2001). Interpreting, categorising and responding to the environment: the role of culture in strategic problem definition. *Management Decision*, 39(2), 105–112.

Oancea, O. (2014). Pitfalls of airline revenue management observations. *Journal of Revenue & Pricing Management*, 13(4), 334–338.

O'Shaunessy, J. (1984). Competitive Marketing. Allen & Unwin.

Parker, G. (2003). Optimising airline revenue management. *Journal of Revenue and Pricing Management*, 2(2), 138–149.

Porter, M.E. (1985). Competitive Advantage: Creating and Sustaining Superior Performance, 1st edn. The Free Press.

Porter, M.E. (2008). The Five Competitive Forces That Shape Strategy. *Harvard Business Review*, 86(1), 25–40.

Qantas, (2010). Fact File - September 2010. Obtained from Qantas.com on 28/06/2011

Romero, C. & Ventura, S. (2010). Educational data mining: A review of the state of the art. *IEEE Transaction on Systems, Man, and Cybernetics, Part C: Applications and Reviews*, 40(6), 601–618.

Sanderson, J. (2001). The impact of regulation on buyer and supplier power. *The Journal of Supply Chain Management*, 37(1), 16–21.

Sterman, J.D. (1988). People Express Management Flight Simulator: Software and Briefing Materials. Sloan School of Management-MIT.

Sterman, J.D. (2000). Business Dynamics: Systems Thinking and Modelling for a Complex World. Irwin McGraw-Hill.

Sull, D. (1999). easyJet's $500 million gamble with commentary by Costas Markides, Walter Kuemmerle and Luis Cabral. *European Management Journal*, 17(1), 20–38.

Talluri, K.T. and Van Ryzin, G.J. (2006). The Theory and Practice of Revenue Management, Vol. 68. Springer Science & Business Media.

Walker, W.E. (2009). Does the best practice of rational-style model based policy analysis already include ethical considerations? *Omega*, 37(6), 1051–1062.

Walton, E.J., Dutton, J., and Abrahamson, E. (1989). Important dimensions of strategic issues: separating the wheat from the chaff. *Journal of Management Studies*, 26(4), 379–396.

Further Reading

Belobaba, P., Odoni, A., and Barnhart, C. (eds) (2015). The Global Airline Industry, 2nd edn. John Wiley & Sons, Ltd.

Garrow, L.A., Jones, S.P., and Parket, R.A. (2007). How much airline customers are willing to pay: An analysis of price sensitivity in online distribution channels. *Journal of Revenue and Pricing Management*, 5(4), 271–290.

Gary, S., Kunc, M., Morecroft, J. and Rockart, S. (2008). System dynamics and strategy. *System Dynamics Review*, 24, 407–430.

Morecroft, J.D.W. (2015). Strategic Modelling and Business Dynamics: A Feedback Systems View, 2nd edn. John Wiley & Sons, Ltd.

Smith, B.C., Leimkuhler, J.F., and Darrow, R.M. (1992). Yield management at American airlines. *Interfaces*, 22(1), 8–31.

Warren, K. (2002). Competitive Strategy Dynamics. John Wiley & Sons, Ltd.

5

Industry Evolution

Objectives

1) To define industry evolution
2) To identify the drivers responsible for industry evolution
3) To understand the behavior of the companies and its effects on industry evolution

Learning outcomes and managerial capabilities developed

1) To apply system dynamics to evaluate the evolution of the industry
2) To understand the concept of interdependency between companies and competitive landscape

---

Industry structure analysis, which is discussed in Chapter 4, helps to define the competitive forces existing in an industry. However, the competitive forces are not static since they change as their dimensions become stronger or erode over time. For example, buyer behavior shifts from price sensitivity to quality focus depending on the economic cycle. Technology can erode barriers to entry and create new substitutes. Understanding the drivers of industry evolution and transforming this insight into predictions is fundamental for achieving a sustainable competitive advantage for a number of reasons. Firstly, the cost of reacting increases as the need to change increases. Secondly, the first company defining the industry structure can have important benefits, e.g. first mover advantages. The basic tool for identifying the industry evolution is the "Product Life Cycle", which portrays the phases that products follow in the market (Porter, 2004). Figure 5.1 shows the basic pattern of the industry life cycle driven by the aggregated sales of its products. Industries evolve in four stages: introduction, growth, maturity and decline, which reflect the rate of growth of industry sales. The introduction stage is mostly determined by the launch of a new product in the market and the process of changing buyers' behaviors to

Strategic Analytics: Integrating Management Science and Strategy, First Edition. Martin Kunc.
© 2019 John Wiley & Sons Ltd. Published 2019 by John Wiley & Sons Ltd.
Companion website: www.wiley.com/go/kunc/strategic-analytics

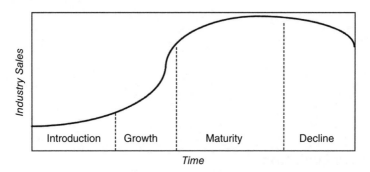

Figure 5.1 Industry life cycle in four stages.

adopt the new product. Growth occurs when a large number of buyers change their behavior and adopt the product massively. Maturity corresponds to the saturation of the market, when all potential buyers have adopted the product, so growth rate declines. Finally, a new substitute will attract the current buyers and sales will decline determining the decline of industry sales.

The second dynamic process in the industry life cycle is the evolution of the population of companies (Keppler, 1996) as shown by Figure 5.2. Gort and Klepper (1982) provides a concise description of the dynamics of the population of companies, which is briefly presented here. Stage I (Introduction) begins with an introduction of a new product in the market by one company, and ends when the rate of entry of new competitors into the industry has a substantial increment. During Stage II (Growth), the number of companies grows strongly as a large number of new competitors enter the industry but, by the end of the stage, the net entry rate fails. During Stage III (Maturity), the number of new companies is almost equal to the number of companies abandoning the industry. Thus, the industry's population arrives at a plateau, but not a steady state. In Stage IV (Decline), net entry is negative as exits intensify.

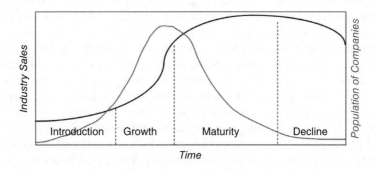

Figure 5.2 Industry life cycle and the number of companies in an industry.

The period of negative net entry concludes when the industry reaches a steady state. The absence of entries or exits can be considered the final state of the industry if there is not an external shock, such as a product that substitutes the actual industry's main product.

Table 5.1 shows the changes in the dimensions of the industry forces as the industry transits from introduction to decline. Industries can have multiples variations of the life cycle: a shorter or longer time horizon or they can even miss one of the stages, and the depth of the changes on the industry forces. For example, technology-intensive industries resemble industries in a continuous emerging process. Other industries will not decline because their products satisfy basic needs for multiple buyers, e.g. food industry. Some industries may emerge again after a decline due to technology innovations. Consequently, the life cycle model is a useful analytical tool to foresee the evolution of industries but it may not be accurate in predicting exactly a determined pattern or the specific stage where the industry is located.

Table 5.1 Factors driving the evolution of industries through the life cycle model.

	Stages			
Dimension	**Introduction**	**Growth**	**Maturity**	**Decline**
Buyer behavior	High income buyers so low price sensitivity Buyer inertia so they need to be convinced about trying the product	Buyer acceptance and additional buyers buying the product. Buyers accept uneven quality	Mass market is reaching saturation Repeat buying behavior Brands become more important	Buyers form niches where specialist buyers are knowledgeable.
Product development	Poor quality and basic design Product design and development is important given the rapid changes in design Multiple variations, no standards	Products have technical and performance differentiation but there is increasing standardization Continuous improvement in products with good quality	Superior quality with less differentiation (commoditization) Minor and limited product changes	Little product differentiation Differentiation in specific dimensions creates niches

(Continued)

Table 5.1 (Continued)

	Stages			
Dimension	Introduction	Growth	Maturity	Decline
Manufacturing	Short production runs High production costs Skill intensive in labor Excessive capacity	Move towards mass production with more process improvements Competition for distribution channels Capacity is insufficient	Stable production process Lower labor skills Large production runs to achieve lower costs Distribution channels more selective Mass channels Increasing overcapacity	Considerable overcapacity Specialty channels Mass production
Technology	Rapid product innovation	Product and process innovation	Incremental innovation	Technology is widely available
Competition	Few companies	Entry of many competitors Mergers and exits	Shakeout Consolidation Price competition Private brands	Exits Fewer competitors
Profits	High prices and margins but low profits	High prices but slightly lower than introduction leading to higher profits	Declining prices Lower profits and margins Stable market share and prices	Low prices and margins Prices may decline but at the end of the cycle they may increase given the exclusiveness of the product

One important aspect to consider is that the industry evolution is not independent from the investment decisions by existing and new companies in the industry. Companies drive demand through investments in marketing, reduce costs by innovating in manufacturing processes, and displace suppliers by researching for new materials. Simultaneously, businesses need to consider the implications of their objectives and strategies for the different stages of the life cycle and evaluating their positioning to keep with the changing conditions. The analysis needs to evaluate projections of market conditions and

Table 5.2 Measures to track the evolution of the industry.

Industry level concepts	Product competition and marketing concepts
Number of product changes	Level of customization
Technology changes	Product breadth comparative
Development time for new products	Product quality comparative
Relative payment/compensation	Price and market share
	Sales force costs/revenue comparative
	Marketing budget/revenue comparative
R&D concepts	**Production and efficiency concepts**
Percentage of sales from new products	Inventory/sales
Percentage of R&D investment in new products from sales	Capacity investment/sales
	Capacity utilization
Percentage of R&D investment in process improvement from sales	Employee productivity
	Value generated/sales
Vertical integration concepts	**Performance concepts**
Relative integration upstream (suppliers' acquisition/ development)	Return over investment
	Relative market share
Relative integration downstream (retail acquisition/ development)	

competitors' strategies. For example, decisions concerning short-term profitability and market share during the growth stage can have a critical impact on the success of the company as the market matures.

Table 5.2 presents a set of variables to track the changes in the industry over time as suggested in Anderson and Zeithaml (1984). However, the attention to the measures can change over time due to exogenous factors (PESTE) such as during an economic crisis (Kunc and Bhandari, 2011).

5.1 Dynamic Behavioral Model of Industry Evolution

In this perspective, the industry is seen as an information feedback system whose dynamic behavior is captured by the industry life cycle concept. The dynamic behavior is controlled by two feedback loops: a reinforcing loop that controls the growth and decline of companies; and a balancing loop that determines the evolution of the market. In this model, the market evolution is endogenous and determined by the actions of managers. The industry structure is important for understanding behavior; however, how managers perceive this structure is more important. The following subsections describe the model in more detail.

5.1.1 Industries as Feedback Systems

Basically, the industry life cycle is driven by two main dynamic processes: the development of the market; and the dynamics of the population of companies. On the one hand, companies provide services or products to satisfy customers' needs. On the other hand, potential customers have needs that must be satisfied. The rate at which potential customers adopt the products feeds back to companies indicating their success in satisfying these needs. This process is the main driver of the market development. Some companies grow as an increasing number of potential customers adopt their products and become customers; but other companies are forced to abandon the industry because their products do not satisfy customers' needs.

Market development can be measured by the total cumulative sales of a product, which usually follows an S-shaped growth curve (Mahajan et al., 2000). Markets follow three stages: introduction; growth; and maturity. In the introduction stage, sales are small because product awareness is low. Since it is difficult to overcome buyer inertia, the initial customers for the product tend to be innovation-oriented. The growth stage is characterized by accelerating market penetration as product technology becomes more standardized and accepted. Ownership spreads by word of mouth. The maturity stage is driven by an increasing market saturation that reduces the growth rate as few potential customers remain. In some products, the demand for the new product gives way to replacement demand (Mahajan et al., 2000). This dynamic process has been extensively studied under the concept of Diffusion of Innovations; for a comprehensive review of product diffusion models see Mahajan et al. (2000). From a feedback system point of view, the market development is represented as a balancing feedback loop. Potential customers represent people that have requirements to be satisfied. These people will become users of the products offered by the companies in the industry if the products satisfy these requirements. Actual customers represent the users of these products. As companies gain customers, they reduce the pool of potential customers: more actual customers mean less potential customers. The number of actual customers increases if there are potential customers: more potential customers means more actual customers once they adopt the product. However, the number of actual customers stops increasing when there are no more potential customers to attract, which is called market saturation. Market saturation is the natural limit for the industry unless companies engage in diversification (selling their products to other customers who may be using different products, also known as product substitution) or product innovation (changing characteristics of the product to make it attractive to new potential customers whose needs have not been satisfied with the initial product).

The second dynamic process in industries is the dynamics in the population of companies. Companies enter the industry trying to capture the market as it develops; some of them are successful and capture most of the potential customers

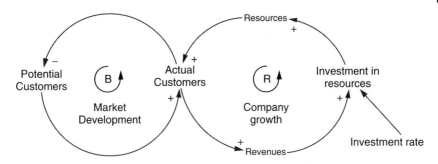

Figure 5.3 Industry as a feedback system.

while others have to leave being pushed out by the lack of customers. The company growth process is a reinforcing process that drives successful companies. Successful companies attract customers that generate revenues, which are invested in resources (e.g. manufacturing plants, brands, new products) to attract more customers. Unsuccessful companies go bankrupt because they cannot capture enough customers to drive the reinforcing process (so growth does not occur).

Figure 5.3 is a summary of the previous discussion using a causal loops diagram. Causal loop diagrams are employed in system dynamics to represent feedback systems together with stocks and flows (see the case study in Section 4.4.2). On the left, the causal loop diagram represents markets as feedback systems. The development of markets is driven by a balancing feedback process due to the constraints imposed by the number of potential customers. The causal link between "actual customers" and "potential customers" is drawn as a curved arrow with a "−" sign on the arrow head to indicate a link with negative polarity (more actual customers, less potential customers). As the number of customers increases, there are less potential customers. The causal link between "potential customers" and "actual customers" is presented as another curved arrow with a "+" sign on the arrow head to specify a link with a positive polarity (more potential customers, more actual customers). On the right, the causal loop diagram describes the growth of companies as a reinforcing feedback process. More customers lead to higher revenues, a positive causal link, which are invested in additional resources, another positive causal link. Additional resources are used to attract more customers, a final positive causal link. One of the critical variables in the dynamic process described is the investment rate because it can accelerate or reduce the industry evolution. The investment rate depends on the managers' decision-making process.

5.1.2 A Behavioral Model of Organizations

The behavioral approach to organizational behavior defines organizations as systems of coordinated actions among members whose interests, information and knowledge differ (March and Simon, 1958). The concept of organization is based on a network of decision-making processes that comprehend all its members. Among the members of an organization, the management team makes most of the critical decisions to guide the organization. Management determines objectives, or goals, that the organization must achieve and is responsible for their achievement. The behavioral theory implies that decision makers are bounded rationality and there is imperfect environmental matching (Cyert and March, 1992). The main outcome of the behavior of companies is reflected in their investment rate (Figure 5.3). For example, if decision makers consider the industry has reached market saturation due to imperfect information, they will reduce investment in new resources and will focus on cost efficiency leading to price decline instead of investing in attracting more potential customers. In this approach, decision processes are viewed as a continuous stream of decisions rather than a discrete choice selection process.

From a behavioral feedback point of view, the decision-making process consists in setting goals responsible for regulating prices, developing products, expanding sales force, determining production capacity, and managing financial resources (Morecroft, 1985; Simon, 2001). For example, the management modifies goals for the sales force based on information about internal and external requirements (see Chapters 3 and 4) and expectations such as current customer growth rate, salesman productivity and expected number of customers. The difference between the desired goal and the actual size of the sales force determines the investment rate on the sales force. The key element in the behavioral feedback view of management is the process of goal setting, which is affected by uncertainties, limited cognitive capabilities, dynamic complexity and competitors' actions.

There are three main uncertainties during the evolution of an industry, which are ordered as they emerge: competitors' actions; market size; and evolution of customers' needs over time. The first uncertainty is closely related to the management of an organization's growth and its impact on other organizations. The second uncertainty affects not only the investment in capacity expansion of existing organizations but also the attractiveness of the market for potential entrants. Finally, the initial customers' needs and their evolution over time influence the product development and technological innovation as well as the market attractiveness for potential competitors. The uncertainties can be tracked over time using some of the measures indicated in Table 5.2. While uncertainties are important for decision making, Simon (2001) affirms the formation of expectations has higher destabilizing effects in a system because expectations can lead to overreactions or to unstable oscillations. Feedforward in markets can become especially destabilizing when each actor tries to anticipate the actions of the others and hence their expectations. Table 5.3 presents a summary of each uncertainty.

Table 5.3 Key uncertainties affecting managerial decision making during industry evolution.

Uncertainty	Description
Competitors' actions	The lack of information about competitors' actions generates a potential dilemma with the investment rate. On the one hand, the company wants to attract most of the potential customers in order to generate the highest revenue not only during the development of the market but also from a large customer base when they need to replace their product. While a competitor may bring a better product and attracts the customer base, a company with a larger customer base has more resources than a small company, which may deter potential competitors. On the other hand, an aggressive growth strategy may generate bold reactions from other companies, which results in a hypercompetitive industry as companies escalate their reactions
Market size	In new markets, the management team does not know the exact size of the pool of potential customers, so forecasts are the base for its decisions. The management team may forecast the market size based on similar products. However, the exact size of the market is only revealed over time as the market develops, so forecasting is difficult because data is scarce at the beginning of the market when it is especially required. The forecast of the market size becomes the base for decisions on initial and future investments. Optimistic forecasts can generate excessive capacity in the industry. Periods of excess capacity mean low prices resulting in low or negative profits, which force some companies to abandon the industry. Pessimistic forecasts imply smaller investments in capacity depressing the future market development since potential consumers cannot find the product in the retail channel
Evolution of customers' needs over time	Initial customers' needs and their evolution over time influence managerial decisions about the technology trajectory that companies will pursue. Customers' needs change over time because they learn from other technologies and products as well as different uses of the actual product. While the number of customers is a function of the current product characteristics, changing the product may attract additional customers as they find that the new product satisfies their requirements. Consequently, the pool of potential customers as well as the number of current customers change over time as the product changes. Investment in product development through R&D is a key factor to maintain the current customers as well as attract additional customers

5.1.3   Dynamic Behavioral Model of Industry Evolution

In order to capture the behavioral influences on the industry evolution and complete the model of industry evolution, the causal loop diagram presented in Figure 5.3 has to be expanded to include dynamic behavioral processes. Figure 5.4 presents the complete dynamic behavioral model of industry evolution. The variables "customer needs", "population attracted" and "competitors' actual customers" reflect the uncertainties described in the previous subsection: What is the population attracted to the industry? How fast are competitors gaining potential customers? What are the customer needs and how attractive is the technology for the potential customers? The variable "investment rate" represents the outcomes – or actions – of the decision-making process that controls the growth of the operational resources and the investment on the company's technology. The flows of information (broken lines in Figure 5.4) for the decision-making process are: one direct from the evolution of the number of actual customers; and the other flow comes from the perception of the level of saturation in the market.

The dynamic behavioral model of industry evolution that determines the industry dynamic contains the key investment decisions made using two information sources: the evolution of the number of actual customers; and the perceived market saturation. These two sources of information are extensively captured nowadays, generating big data and opportunities for the application of analytics. In a competitive industry, other companies are also capturing customers from the same pool of potential customers (causal loop diagram on the left in Figure 5.4). Companies can engage in a race in order to capture the largest amount of potential customers, increasing the gain of the reinforcing feedback loop through aggressive investment in resources. The number of potential customers is a function of how attractive (represented by features such as

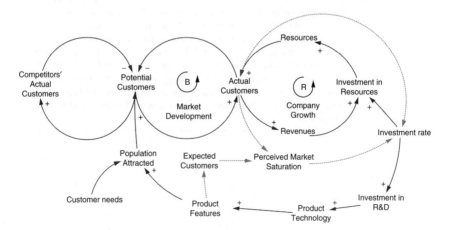

Figure 5.4 Dynamic behavioral model of industry evolution.

design, usability, quality, etc.) the product is with respect to population needs, see causal links connecting product technology to product features at the bottom of Figure 5.4. Hence, companies are able to increase the pool of potential customers if they change their technology leading to more or different product features to satisfy more or new needs from the population.

Companies in this model compete in two dimensions: resources and technology, which are the basis of the Schumpeterian competition. As Schumpeter (1950: pages 82–83) suggests:

> Capitalism, then, is by nature a form or method of economic change and not only never is but never can be stationary. The fundamental impulse that sets and keeps the capitalist engine in motion comes from the new consumers' goods, the new methods of production or transportation, the new markets, the new forms of industrial organization that capitalist enterprise creates. This process of Creative Destruction is the essential fact about capitalism.

Regarding Schumpeterian competition, Barney (1986: page 795) suggests:

> For Schumpeter, these revolutionary innovations in product, market, or technology can only be imperfectly anticipated by companies. Sometimes companies in an industry may survive a revolutionary innovation to become important actors in a succeeding industry. It may even be the case that investments made by a currently successful company will themselves generate a Schumpeterian revolution. Other times, a revolutionary innovation will have the effect of displacing all currently competing companies. Moreover, in the competitive setting envisioned by Schumpeter, when major innovations do appear, their ultimate impact may not be known for some time, at which point it may be too late for older companies with older technologies and skills to compete in new markets requiring new skills. On the other hand, guessing too early that a given innovation will become dominant may jeopardize a company's long term survival by betting on a technology or market that turns out not to be dominant.

Therefore, the behavior of companies as well as the evolution of industries, are determined by the behavioral approach employed to perceive the structure of the industry and its dynamics. Consequently, industry evolution patterns have to be inferred from the interaction of behavioral types existing in an industry.

5.1.4 Types of Dynamic Behavior and Strategic Implications on the Evolution of Industries

The dynamic behavior of organizations can be characterized in two types that reflect management preferences as well as biases with respect to what information is used and its influence on the decisions: reactive; and proactive. "Reactive" behavioral types tend to mainly use information provided by the market, and "reacting" to the events as the market evolves. In some way, reactive companies tend to focus on descriptive analytics. This behavioral type of management team seems to be more conservative as the information arrives with delays, and it only reacts after some time has passed from the events. The goal setting process is based on past events or backward-looking (Gavetti and Levinthal, 2000). This behavioral type heavily discounts present and future information, so its desired state of the organization is only an update of the actual conditions to past events.

The "proactive" behavioral type "creates" its own information based on expectations that "forecast" the evolution of the market. This behavioral type of management tries to proactively manage the evolution of the market through their decisions. This type of companies use predictive and prescriptive analytics continuously. The goal is based on forecasts and expectations, a concept similar to forward-looking (Gavetti and Levinthal, 2000). Management adopts a "proactive" approach when it aims to manage the balancing feedback loop related to market development. This approach is close to the concept that organizations do not respond to defined environmental conditions but instead create their own environments through a series of choices regarding markets, and desired scale of operations (Weick, 1979). This behavioral type uses the actual situation of the organization to verify the discrepancy with respect to its desired state, so the greater the discrepancy the greater the resulting action even though the actual state clearly represents the optimal situation given the existing constraints.

The behavioral types are influenced by managers' mental models. Mental models are filters that interpret the information and associate it with an adequate action; for example, these filters may determine the adequacy of discrepancies, response time under different situations or even preferred information type. Mental models change over time so the behavioral type of a company may change reflecting learning and adaptation to environmental feedback or simply changes in the top management team, such as the replacement of a CEO.

In conclusion, "reactive" organizations grow as the market develops, or metaphorically, they "chase" the market; and "proactive" organizations grow by controlling the development of the market, or metaphorically, they "make" the market. If one type of organization or the other has better performance, it will depend on the interaction effect between all organizations and the market given the uncertainties that organizations face during the evolution of the industry (Kunc and Morecroft, 2010). Table 5.4 shows the strategic implications for the behavioral types.

Industry evolution patterns can be inferred based on the strategy types that most of the companies follow in the industry (Kunc and Morecroft,

Table 5.4 Evaluating behavioral types, strategic actions and industry implications.

Industry measurements	Strategic behavior	Industry implications
Market saturation in terms of product breadth and market share	Proactive companies do not respond to defined market conditions but they create their own conditions based on their assumptions, so their investment rate may decline when they are achieving the real potential (forward-looking) Reactive companies respond to the signals from the market, so they react to rapid growth reinforcing their investments thus pushing growth even more (backward-looking)	Reactive industries reach, and overshoot, the saturation level sooner than proactive industries
Distribution in terms of production capacity and market-related resources	Reactive companies may start small in the first stages of the industry due to low demand but they grow fast once market develops leading to complex organizations (high vertical integration levels) Proactive companies start with a size that reflects their assumptions about the market size leading them to manage their investments to capture markets and rely on alliances or networks to remain flexible (low vertical integration levels)	Proactive (reactive) industries tend to have their company size distribution skewed to the right (left) or smaller size (larger). Reactive industries have higher vertical integration levels
Technology and product changes	Management has two issues in respect of customer requirements: initial technological level to attract the first customers; and the pace of technology development to keep revenues stable If the initial technology and products provides a satisfactory level of revenues, reactive companies will lock in to the initial technology level Proactive companies will continuously engage in the development of new technologies because these companies reach their perceived saturation level sooner than reactive companies. So, proactive companies may be successful in conditions where consumers evaluate technology continuously	Proactive industries engage in search for new technologies sooner than reactive industries and invest more in R&D
Competition focus	Reactive companies assign low importance to competitors' actions considering market pace as the key focus Proactive companies consider the impact of competitors' actions on their expectations, so they focus on continuous change	Proactive industries tend to focus more on technology development and new products Reactive industries tend to focus more on resource development and efficiencies

2007, 2010). Firstly, industries whose companies follow reactive strategies reach the saturation level sooner than industries with participants that follow a proactive strategy. Secondly, industries where most of the participants adopt a proactive (reactive) strategy will tend to have company size distribution skewed to the right (left) or a lot of relatively small (large) companies. Reactive industries will have large companies during the initial stages of the industry leading to abrupt shakeouts in the maturity stage due to their overoptimistic and delayed investment decisions. Thirdly, industries with proactive companies will engage in the search for new technologies sooner than industries with reactive companies. Finally, companies may obtain good (bad) performance in industries where most of the companies follow different (similar). In summary, industries tend to be competitive in different dimensions with different predominant behavioral type of companies.

Food for thought 5.1 One of the most dynamic industries in recent years has been the camera industry. Figure 5.5 shows almost 40 years of sales of cameras from film based to digital. The information displayed in Figure 5.5 corresponds to the shipments from the Camera and Imaging Producers Association, which includes the largest producers of cameras in the world such as Canon, Konica Minolta, Nikon, Olympus and Panasonic. The association was established in 1954 as the Japan Camera Industry Association but in 2002 the association transformed into Camera & Imaging Products Association (CIPA) as the industry changed from conventional film photography to digital photography. The association aims to discuss specification standards and product compatibility not only on cameras and lenses but also related products, components, software and systems.

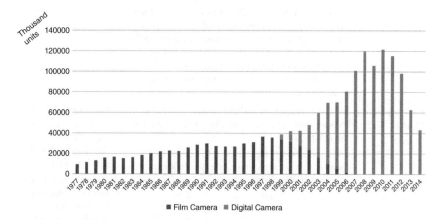

Figure 5.5 Worldwide shipments from Japanese camera makers. *Source:* CIPA, 2015. Reproduced by permission of John Wiley & Sons.

While the history of the camera as a product can be traced back to over one thousand years ago, e.g. the camera obscura, the modern history of the camera, e.g. obtaining a photograph from a camera image, dates from 200 years ago but the mass market adoption of the cameras and film-based photography started at the beginning of the twentieth century with Brownie, an inexpensive box camera pre-loaded with film, provided by Eastman. The initial evolution of the industry started when plate cameras had been replaced by cameras using photographic film pioneered by Eastman and its company, Kodak, was the main driver of this stage. Then, camera manufacturers started using 35 mm film for photography which became the standard and dominant design for the first part of the twentieth century. Innovations in 35 mm film made it more accessible and simpler to use for mass consumers. In the 1930s, Japanese manufacturers began to produce their first cameras. Innovations in camera equipment also began improving functionality and quality, e.g. single and twin-lens reflex cameras, given the development of low-cost electronic components, e.g. automatic exposure. Japanese manufacturers were rapidly adopting the single reflex cameras and providing interchangeable components, e.g. lenses, transforming the camera into a system comprised by multiple accessories. Innovations avoiding some processes, e.g. film development, were introduced later such as the Polaroid instant-picture camera. The volume of sales for film-based cameras from 1977 until 2007, when CIPA stopped recording them, can be observed in Figure 5.5. The industry could have disappeared by 2007 given the disappearance of film-based cameras without reinventing themselves successfully into digital cameras producers. This was not the fate of Kodak as it went bankrupt and it had to demolish many film manufacturing plants before restructuring into a specialist imaging company in areas such as healthcare.

The recent stage in the evolution of the camera industry was determined by the appearance of the digital camera. Digital cameras differ from film-based cameras in terms of the means to store the images captured: digital memory cards or internal storage. As can be observed in Figure 5.5, they have replaced the sales of film-based cameras in the last 15 years due to a key factor: low operating costs, e.g. no need to buy and process films and easiness to capture, transfer, manipulate and store images. Interestingly, the first attempt formally recorded for a digital camera was in 1975 by an engineer from Eastman Kodak, Steven Sasson (see his interview in Kodak's channel, Kodak Moments, on YouTube: https://youtu.be/wfnpVRiiwnM). The prototype weighed 3.6 kg and the black and white image was recorded in a cassette tape. More surprising was the reaction from the management once he showed the prototype: "But it was filmless photography, so management's reaction was, 'that's cute – but don't tell anyone about it.'" (Deutsch, 2008). Kodak, the leading company in film photography, filed for bankruptcy in January 2012. The components for digital camera were available to every company in the industry: sensors, digital memory, etc. so innovation was not restricted but the improvement in quality and functionality depended on the development of other technologies. In the late 1980s, the first producers were Sony, Casio, Nikon, Fuji and Canon and the initial adopters were the news media driven by costs and the ability to transmit images quickly. Kodak brought to market a digital camera system in 1991. Most of the initial cameras still use the same bodies of the lens reflex cameras. Changes in digital formats, JPEG and MPEG, helped to capture more images due to their ability to be compressed for storage. Additional innovations were liquid crystal display on the back of the camera to see the picture taken. The market segmented in diverse categories: compact digital still cameras, which are small and do not have removable lens; bridge cameras, which occupy the gap between simple point-and-shoot and professional single-lens reflex cameras; digital

Table 5.5 Prior industry affiliations of the companies that entered the consumer digital camera market.

Photography	Customer electronics	Computing
Achiever	Arches	Aiptek
Agfa	Casio	Apple
Argus	Creative DXG	BTC
Canon	Hitachi	BenQ
Chinon	JVC	D-Link
Concord	LG Electronics	Dolphin
Fuji Photo Film	Mitsubishi	Epson
Jazz Photo	Oregon Scientific	Gallant Computer
Kodak	Panasonic	Gateway
Konica	Philips	Hawking Technology
Kyocera	RCA	Hewlett-Packard
Leica	Relisys	IO Magic
Minolta	Samsung	Intel
Minox	Sanyo	Jeninage
Nikon	Sharp	KB Gear
Olympus	SiPix	Logitech
Pentaz	Sony	Micro Innovation
Polaroid	Syntax Brillian	Microtex Labs
Praktica		Mastec
Premier		NEC
Ricoh		SoundVision
Ritz Camera		Spot Technology
Rollei		Toshiba
Sigma		UMAX Technologies
Vivitar		Visioneer

Source: Benner and Tripas (2012: table 1, page 283). Reproduced with permission of John Wiley & Sons.

single-reflex cameras, and mirrorless compact cameras, which are smaller and lighter than single-reflex cameras but they have interchangeable lens. This set of cameras can be observed as having taken over the market since the beginning of 2000 in Figure 5.5.

From the evolution of industry framework discussed, the digital camera industry is characterized by high uncertainty and the entry of companies from three diverse industries – photography (25 companies), computing (25 companies), and consumer electronics (19 companies) – observed in a sample from the entrants to the US from 1991 to 2006 (Benner and Tripsas, 2012). See Table 5.5.

The digital camera market is unique since technical capabilities were not a primary driver of choices for which features to introduce but instead a well-developed supply chain gave all companies access to the same core features, even if they had no capabilities (Benner and Tripas, 2012). After studying the digital camera industry, Benner and Tripas (2012: page 279) suggest "firms from the same prior industry shared similar beliefs about what consumers would value as reflected in their concurrent introduction of features—firms were significantly more likely to introduce a feature, such as optical zoom, to the extent that other firms from the same prior industry entered with the feature in the same year." The case discussed raises some interesting questions:

- Explain the reasons that influenced existing companies to consider innovation in similar fashions, e.g. optical zoom, rather than disruptive or radical.
- Why would a company producing MP3 players, e.g. Sony in consumer electronics, be interested in entering the digital camera industry? What would have been their strengths and weaknesses compared with existing companies, e.g. Nikon or Kodak?
- What complementing technologies supported the emergence of the digital camera? Identify the most important technology which could have derailed the development of the digital camera and explain your reasons.
- Why was the market development process faster and stronger for digital cameras than for film-based cameras, as seen in Figure 5.5?
- Which companies use their reinforcing feedback process more efficiently in the digital camera age?

5.2 Integrating Management Science into Strategic Management

One of the important issues raised in the behavioral model of firms is the management of expectations regarding the dynamics of the industry. Reactive companies may be accustomed to the use of descriptive tools, to infer the development of the market in the future based on the past performance.

Some proactive companies may be users of predictive tools while other proactive companies may use prescriptive tools. The next subsection provides two examples of the use of management science tools, prescriptive tools, to understand and manage the evolution of industries:

5.2.1 Exploring Industry Evolution Using System Dynamics

This subsection explains an illustrative system dynamics model based on the dynamic behavioral model of industry evolution discussed previously. The model represents the two main feedback processes described in Figure 5.3: market development; and a company's growth. Kunc (2004, 2010) and Kunc and Morecroft (2007) present more detailed system dynamics models and modeling processes to evaluate industry evolution.

Market development The balancing feedback process described in Figure 5.3 indicates that the number of actual customers (or adopters of a product) directly relates to the number of potential customers (potential adopters) but as the number of adopters increases, the number of potential adopters decreases over time. A basic model to reflect this process was developed by Bass (1969) in 1969 and is known as a product diffusion model. Bass's diffusion model is widely used in system dynamics Sterman, 2000; Morecroft, 2015) due to its simplicity and close relationship with customer and company behaviors. The Bass model provides a clear structure and dynamics for market development leading to the S-shaped growth pattern characteristic of products and services in diverse markets.

Figure 5.6 shows the stock and flow representation (see section 4.4.2 for an explanation of stock and flow) of the market development where the behavior of two key actors is represented in a stylized way. The two stocks and a flow captures the movement of people from being potential buyers of a product to having actually purchased the product. Where does the information for each stock come from? It is safe to assume that the number of potential adopters originated from either market research (e.g. focus groups across the entire population to detect purchase intention after showing a new product) or previous experience in the company (e.g. similar product launched previously). Adopters are initially zero since the product is not in the market. When we zoom into the balancing feedback loop in Figure 5.6, we can observe two other feedback loops reflecting the behavior of companies and adopters.

First, we analyzed the behavior of customers. Diffusions are essentially a social contagion process (Rogers, 1983). Adopters show and tell their new product to other people, e.g. friends, colleagues, etc., spreading the product. Mathematically, this process is reflected by the contact rate (the number of people an adopter knows or talks with about the product) multiplied by the

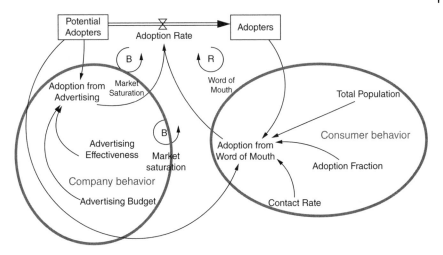

Figure 5.6 Market development model.

success of the contact measured by the adoption fraction (how many people from those who hear about the product really buy the product). However, the possibility that the social contagion will occur is determined by how large the number of potential adopters compared with the total population is (a very popular product will be adopted by almost all the population so it will have higher chances but a very specific product will not attract many potential adopters so the chances are smaller). Then, what is driving the reinforcing feedback process? Essentially the number of adopters generates a self-reinforcing process. More adopters mean more contacts and more future adopters (if there are enough potential adopters). The process is usually known as word of mouth.

The second actor in the market development is the company. Let us try a simple experiment. What is the result of "Adoption from word of mouth" if the number of adopters is zero? The result is zero. There is no possibility to successfully develop a market unless there are some people out there showing and talking about the product. So how do we get people to start talking about the product? One possibility is to give free samples so that the initial value of the stock of Adopters is more than zero. Another possibility is to start promoting the product through advertising campaigns. Company behavior is captured by its actions to develop the market through investment in advertising (Figure 5.6). Large advertising budgets mean more potential adopters being aware of the product but the real impact of advertising may not be too high. Rogers (1983) suggests receiving advice from a trusted user, word of mouth, generates more impact than seeing a product on TV or on the Internet. Thus, the impact of the

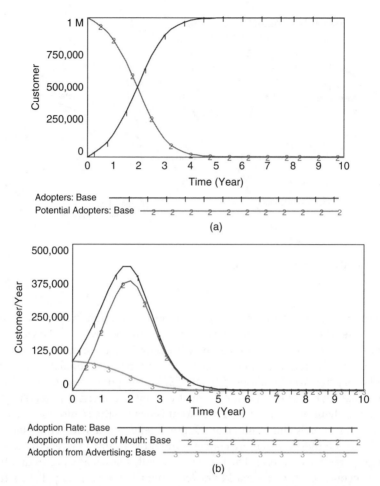

Figure 5.7 Market development simulations. (a) Growth in the number of adopters and the decline in potential adopters over time; and (b) rates at which the transition occurs.

advertising budget is not high and it varies a lot depending on the product or the media employed so the model captures this situation by the concept of advertising effectiveness. The information for advertising effectiveness can come from diverse sources: market research, advertising agencies and previous experiences. Figure 5.7 shows the results from the simulation: Figure 5.7a shows the growth in the number of adopters and the decline in potential adopters over time; and Figure 5.7b describes the rates at which the transition occurs (line 1 shows total number of adopters, line 2 presents the adopters from word of mouth and line 3 indicates the adopters from advertising). Now, you can experiment with the speed of the development of a market by running the model whilst considering different situations: higher advertising effectiveness or more advertising budget, less or more popular product (different number of initial potential adopters with the same total population), and more or less successful word of mouth due to the complexity of the product or price (change the adoption fraction).

Figure 5.8 presents the stock and flow diagram that synthetically represents the behavior of the company while it tries to chase the growth in the market (Morecroft, 2015). There are two main areas where the companies invest to develop the market. First, managers invest in advertising in order to develop the market by attracting potential adopters (this structure is captured in Figure 5.6). Secondly, managers invest in production capacity (e.g. physical resources and human resources to deliver the products bought by adopters). This investment is described in the sector named "capacity expansion" in Figure 5.8.

The production capacity accumulates gradually, which is reflected by the time taken to adjust capacity, to expand a factory or train human resources so capacity adjustment is not instantaneous. How does the company decide on the amount of capacity to adjust? There are two components: the future capacity required, which can be defined by forecasting the development of

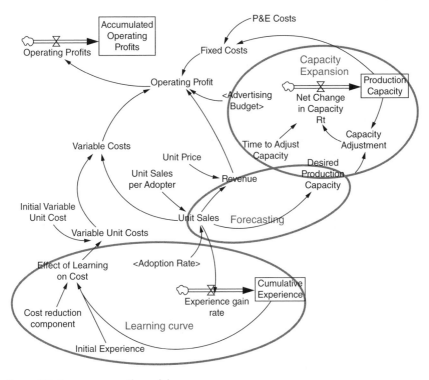

Figure 5.8 Company growth model.

the market ("forecasting" in Figure 5.8), and a calculation of the adjustment needed based on the market forecast, variable "desired production capacity" in Figure 5.8, and the current capacity. This process reflects a goal adjustment process. Forecasting is based on matching the current sales, which is a usual process followed by most companies, but there are a wide set of forecasting methods that can support managers in this process (Mahajan et al., 2000).

There are two outcomes from the growth of the company: learning; and financial results. Learning is a process well documented in the strategic management literature and known as the learning curve, see "Learning curve" in Figure 5.8. Companies can reduce costs as they learn to be more efficient in

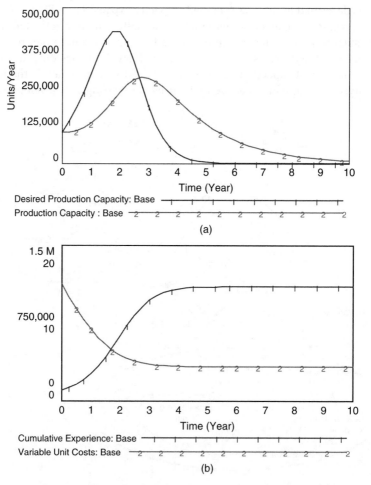

Figure 5.9 Company growth simulation. (a) Production capacity adjustment. (b) Learning curve and unit costs. (c) Financial performance. (d) Operating profits.

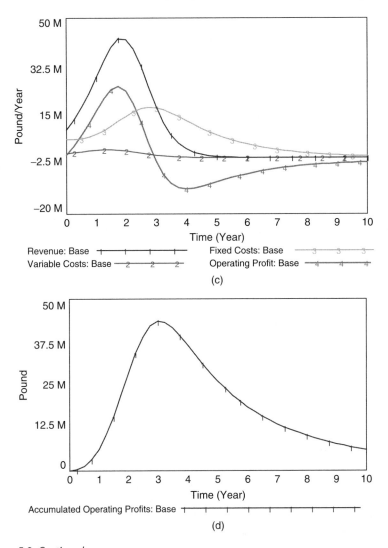

Figure 5.9 *Continued*

manufacturing their products or delivering their services. Learning reduces variable unit costs over time and generates entry barriers because new companies start without the accumulated experience. Financial results come from the revenues obtained and the subtraction of the variable and fixed costs to produce the product. Variable costs are related directly to the sales but the production capacity is responsible for the fixed costs, so fixed costs vary at a slower rate than sales. The final operating profit is determined by the revenues minus all costs and the investment in advertising. A stock is included to accumulate the profits over the life cycle of the industry. Figure 5.9 shows a set of results from the base simulation. Figure 5.9a and b represent the results from the expansion of the production capacity: Figure 5.9a depicts the lag that exists between the desired production capacity, which is based on the sales, and the implemented capacity whereas Figure 5.9b shows how production experience accumulates (line 1) and variable costs decline over time due to the learning curve (line 2). It is interesting to observe the important disadvantage a new entrant may face as variable costs declined more than 70%. Figure 5.9c and d reflect the financial performance of the company. Figure 5.9c shows the operating profit (line 4) and its components: revenue (line 1), variable costs (line 2) and fixed costs (line 3). While revenues achieved a peak relatively fast driven by the growth in the market, the fixed costs reached their peak when the sales are declining. The impact on operating profits is clear: the delay in building up resources has an impact on the profits as fixed costs remain high. This is usually the situation when shakeouts occur in industry, many companies enter the market when the sales are declining so they incur losses. While the accumulated operating profits remain positive at the end of the simulation, the final level is well below the peak in operating profits since losses absorb a large part of the initial surplus. The results shown in the simulation reflect in a synthetic way the "Get Big Fast" behavior observed in many dot.com companies in the 2000s (see Oliva et al., 2003 and Sterman et al., 2007 for detailed models of this behavior). Now, you may explore diverse industry scenarios: diverse learning curve due to different levels of complexity in the production process (change cost reduction component), different prices and costs, and more or less complex production capacity (change time to adjust capacity).

Food for thought 5.2   The model discussed previously can be expanded. For example, once all the potential adopters have adopted the product, there are no sales related to continuous purchases for either replacement or additional units. Figure 5.10 incorporates replacement sales. Replacement sales are driven by the average life for each product. Once the product reaches its end of life, adopters will buy the product again following the same behavior discussed in market development. What will the shape of revenues be? What will happen if the advertising budget is reduced after 5 years?

Additional questions to consider in developing the model further are:

- How can competing companies be represented in the model? Imagine a race to attract potential adopters so more outflows will depart from the stock of potential adopters.
- How can services be represented in the model? Will sales originate from the rate of adoption or from the stock of adopters? What differences can you observe in revenues?

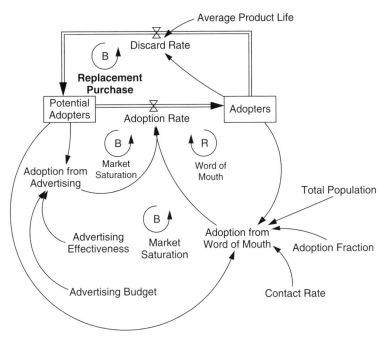

Figure 5.10 Replacement sales.

5.2.2 Understanding How the Levels of Integration/Interaction Between Companies Affect the Evolution of Companies Using NKC Models

This subsection discusses the principles of NKC models before presenting the results of a study using them.

NKC models are derived from Kauffman (1993) models. In this type of models, companies are represented using N dimensional vectors of binary variables (0 or 1). The value of each dimension represents organizational arrangements related to the activities constituting the company, e.g. purchasing, manufacturing, marketing, R&D, in a similar fashion as defining the parts of the value chain managed internally by the company. Since each strategy requires a certain set of activities to deliver the competitive dimensions, not all companies have similar activities. Consequently, companies can be modeled as 2^N possible different configurations (2 reflects the binary variable and N is the number of dimensions representing the company) resulting in different performances. This information can be obtained from a study of companies in the industry or simply use a random variable to connect configuration with performance.

The set of all potential configurations, and their corresponding performance in terms of profits, constitute the potential performance landscape of each company. For example, a company may have a certain configuration in its value chain where it performs 6 activities out of 10 available while another company can perform 8 activities with a different profitability. Both companies can change their configuration, e.g. the first company can execute 8 activities instead of 6, with a certain profitability. Thus, companies' behavior in the industry is represented by considering their need to modify their configurations through either small changes, which can be visualized as a local search without much risk, or large changes, without knowing the consequences, exploring the performance landscape. Small changes reflect incremental innovations and large changes show radical innovations in their businesses.

The second parameter of the model, K, reflects the number of trade-offs between the different activities of the model. When $K = 0$, there are no trade-offs because the activities do not interact. Without trade-offs, managers can improve their performance by simply optimizing each single activity so that the total improvement of the performance is the sum of all local improvements. Then, the changes made in each activity will lead to better performance. Making organizational changes will lead to a clear maximum performance related to the best possible strategy. When $K>0$, there are trade-offs between activities when the manager wants to implement a new strategy. The development and implementation of strategies become complex and finding the best strategy is more difficult. Companies may be trapped in configurations that give a good performance (local peaks) but not the best. In this situation, the performance landscape is rugged since there are many organizational configurations providing good performance but changing an organization may imply a decline in the performance due to the trade-offs, e.g. reducing costs in manufacturing (which increases profitability) may imply lower quality reducing sales so the net effect is a decrease in profitability.

The third parameter of the model, C, measures the number of companies which are interdependent. It can be considered a measure of the closeness between competitors in an industry. The interdependencies constitute the competitive dimensions that characterize competition in the industry (Caldart and Oliveira, 2010). For example, a reduction in manufacturing costs can help a company to reduce prices in order to attract customers but its competitor will also reduce price once it sees the company is reducing price. Now all performance landscapes (e.g. the possible organizational configurations and their potential performance) from each individual company are interconnected. Therefore, all performance landscapes change simultaneously and one strategic change by a single company can impact the rest of the industry, a process call co-evolution (Caldart and Oliveira, 2010). However, there are different levels of interdependency. If $C = 1$, the competitive complexity is low because competitive rivalry is based on a single organizational dimension, e.g. advertising.

A final aspect to consider is the behavior of the companies. In this model, the company follows a simple improvement behavior: it compares the current performance with a potential performance by changing some of its activities in an incremental process and if the potential performance is better, then it will change its activity. For example, the management team is not satisfied with the current profitability and asks a consulting company to evaluate potential changes. Then, the consulting company suggests some changes in the organizational activities, e.g. outsourcing. The management team implements those changes and it improves the performance of the company but the changes simultaneously affect competitors' performance. Competitors' react by making changes as well. The consequence is the performance landscape as visualized by both management teams is not static or fixed but coevolves in unexpected ways due to the complexity. The complexity is defined by the number of N (activities), K (the interdependencies between activities), and C (the interconnections in the competitive dimensions). For example, in an industry where only 5 companies are strongly interconnected: the number of possibilities for $N=10$, $K=8$, and $C=2$ is closer to 1.5 million and for $N=10$, $K=3$, and $C=5$ is more than 160 million. This perspective is discussed extensively in Robertson and Caldart (2009).

5.2.2.1 Insights from the Model

The number of companies competing in an industry increases over time so the ability of each company to notice its competitors' moves decreases making competitive interaction complex (Caldart and Oliveira, 2010). Another factor which increases complexity is the number of dimensions that determine the value created by companies, for example advertising, manufacturing costs, product quality, customer relations, channel coverage, and customer service can define the strategic positioning of a company in a market. As the number of competitors following similar strategies increases, the intensity of competition increases and the profitability declines since customers can choose across more options with similar value. Since companies can formulate their strategies over a broad range of competitive dimensions with the aim to differentiate their value proposition, the complexity of competing within the industry increases as the variety of possible changes in companies' value propositions grows exponentially increasing the potential of competitive clashes (Caldart and Oliveira, 2010). Such complexity makes it difficult for managers to plan ahead in the long run, as their competitive landscapes are likely to suffer frequent alterations, damaging the performance associated with their current strategies. This situation reduces the managers' ability to improve performance by varying their value proposition incrementally as they learn based on the feedback received from the market. This situation forces them to explore alternative strategic directions.

Caldart and Oliveira (2010) run a NKC model with $N = 12$ organizational activities; $K = 5$ interconnected organizational dimensions; and different

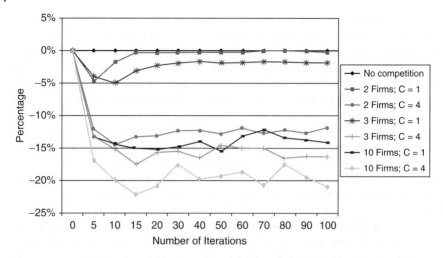

Figure 5.11 Simulated industry performance over time and differences in profitability. *Source:* Caldart and Oliveira (2010: figure 6, page 101). Reproduced with permission of Elsevier.

number of companies in the industry = 2 (duopoly), 3 (oligopoly), 10 (fragmented); and diverse levels of interdependence $C = 0$ (no interdependence), 1 (low), 2 (moderate) and 4 (high). As the model was dynamic and probabilistic, the simulation experiments had to be repeated in order to ensure the robustness of the results, so they run each simulation experiment 100 times.

Figure 5.11 shows the differences in profitability between different types of industries after 100 periods (iterations). The simulations show an initial decline in the performance which indicates the fall into a wrong configuration and then the companies remain without possibility of improvement except for small industries, e.g. 2 and 3 companies with low interdependencies ($C = 1$). Another insight from the simulation experiments, as observed in Figure 5.11, is that an increase in the number of competitive dimensions ($C = 4$) means a decline in industry performance. Industries with high number of companies also impact negatively on the performance of the whole industry.

5.2.3 Uncovering the Evolution of the Technology in an Industry Using Latent Topic Modeling

Technological advancements can be tracked through technical and scientific publication repositories together with patent applications. One of the methodologies for extracting specific trends (topics) from textual data is topic modeling, more specifically latent Dirichlet allocation (Blei et al., 2003). Latent

Dirichlet allocation is a natural language processing method that uses machine learning to do semantic analysis of documents to uncover structures that approximate concepts without a priori knowledge about them. Topics are determined by their distribution over the words in the documents but this distribution is learned from the data since the distribution is unknown. In this case, the technological advancements, our topics, are identified through their presence in patent applications (Saraswat et al., 2016). The data for this analysis can be obtained from patent search analysis tools such as Google Patent (https://patents.google.com/) and FreePatentsOnline (http://www.freepatentsonline.com). Then, topic extraction is presented as a set of phrases that are associated with certain technologies and documents (Saraswat et al., 2016). Topics extracted are organized by timeline and linked to identify topic significance and evolution (Saraswat et al., 2016). Topics are associated if they overlap in terms of documents and phrases containing them. Topics can have different trajectories: exponential growth, emergence and then merge, slow growth, steady or short-life. This modeling can identify topic evolution. Additional use of latent topic modeling is to evaluate the potential bankruptcy of companies (Shirata et al., 2011).

5.3   End of Chapter

Understanding the evolution of industries is important for managers to make the right decisions in terms of investments and commitments of organizational energy and resources. Life in new and exciting industries is not simple because there are numerous uncertainties. Market research cannot overcome limitations in understanding buyers' needs and the technology to satisfy them but this uncertainty supports the existence of varied products with different features and approaches in the first stages of the industry. It is a natural process to have many companies attempting to satisfy needs by experimenting and exploring diverse products. However, there is simultaneously a process of product selection as users experiment with diverse products and learn about them. Users become more knowledgeable about the product and demand more specific features leading to the emergence of a victorious product design; the dominant design. Some companies reduce their search for alternative products and concentrate on improving processes to satisfy the demand for the product. Other companies continue experimenting. Competition is driven by other dimensions, such as price and availability, rather than technology. Over time only a few companies remain. One important lesson to acknowledge by strategy scholars is the difficulty to predict how industries will change. Industries are interrelated systems so a change in one element of the structure triggers changes in other areas, not only in the same industry but upstream (suppliers) and downstream (buyers) (Porter, 2004). Consequently, there is no specific way in which industries evolve but there are few key relationships that tend to occur:

- long term changes in demand growth
- changes in market segments
- buyers' learning
- diffusion of knowledge related to manufacturing and processes
- accumulation of experience
- changes in minimum efficient scale
- changes in costs
- product and process innovation
- marketing innovation
- government influence on the industry.

Typical questions in this area can be answered using management science tools. For example, what multiple combinations of features and technologies can be experimented with? This type of question is answered by optimization tools, e.g. Nelson et al. (2001). While this tool will not develop the strategy around a new product, it can provide a set of options that can be explored with

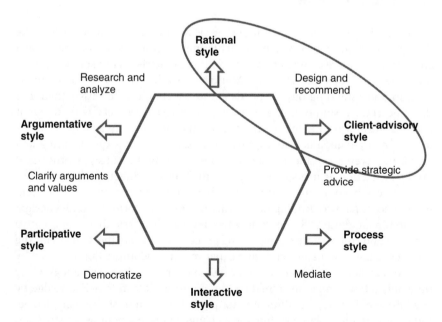

Figure 5.12 Management science styles. *Source:* Walker (2009). Reproduced with permission of Elsevier.

potential users and addresses questions regarding costs and production facilities. Another example is: how many users will adopt the product? Forecasting techniques have developed extensively in recent years to provide more accurate answers to this question (Goodwin et al., 2015). Consequently, the role of management science in this area of strategic management is to provide different design options for the strategies based on "what if" situations addressing uncertainties and potential changes in the forces driving the evolution of the industry. The role of management science tools is to provide design solutions to complex problems while offering strategic advice on the potential paths the industry may take, as Figure 5.12 indicates.

5.3.1   Revision Questions

1) There are numerous literature streams explaining the evolution of industries. See Further reading for some examples. Explore one stream in particular and infer the implicit behavior of companies: how realistic is the description of the companies? Is it useful in practice?
2) What is the role of timing to market in the success of a company? What stage will be simpler in terms of strategies?
3) What other management science tools will you employ to identify, evaluate or address strategic issues existing in each stage of the industry evolution?
4) What types of forecasting methods are employed to predict the development of a market?

5.3.2   Case Study: The Rise of Smartphones and its Impact on the Camera Industry

Reports indicated that the smartphone has decimated digital camera sales (CIPA, 2015). Figure 5.13 shows the sales of cameras, both film-based and digital, and smartphones. While the growth rate of smartphones has been relentless in recent years (+38% in 2013) reaching and passing a billion units, digital camera sales have declined by 36% in 2013 falling from 120 million to 40 million units in 4 years. Some reports suggest consumers believe that recent smartphones are taking better pictures than their digital cameras but it is not correct in real terms. Megapixels in smartphones, a measure for digital photography quality, has grown steadily in recent years with cameras from 5 to 13 megapixels in current phones. In the simplest point-and-shoot cameras, the number of megapixels grew from 4 in the 2000s to 16.5 in 2014. However, the average phone's camera has enough pixels for most of the photography needs for amateur photography. This seems to be a case where a product with inferior specifications has displaced an existing product.

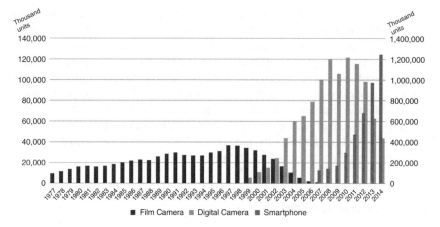

Figure 5.13 Sales of cameras from 1977 to 2014. *Source:* CIPA (2015).

The integration of the camera into the smartphone facilitates the activity of taking pictures since there is no need to carry an additional device. While the quality cannot impress camera owners, it has improved over time with better technologies in image sensors and other parts. However, one of the most important aspects of the cameras in the smartphone is the ability to share an image in in the digital world (WhatsApp, Facebook, Twitter, etc). The changes in the market generated a completely different ecosystem supporting the industry as Figure 5.14 shows.

Nowadays, there are many more participants than camera manufacturers. For example, phone manufacturers; wearable devices; software for editing photographs; photo management services; and social media, among others.

The current situation in the camera industry is becoming difficult. Digital cameras displaced film-based cameras, which were operating for almost 70 years in mass markets, in 3 years. Smartphones seem to be displacing digital cameras, which were the leading product for 12 years, in just 4 years. It seems the speed of innovation is accelerating in the camera industry. Using the theoretical frameworks learned and the simulation models, you may be able to answer the following questions:

1) What drivers have pushed the displacement of the film-based and digital cameras over the last 20 years? Did you see any similarities between the two?
2) Based on Figure 5.14, what group of companies will create the next innovation in the industry? Explain your answer.
3) What are the most important feedback processes in the development of the camera industry over time? Did the feedback processes change from one type of product to another?

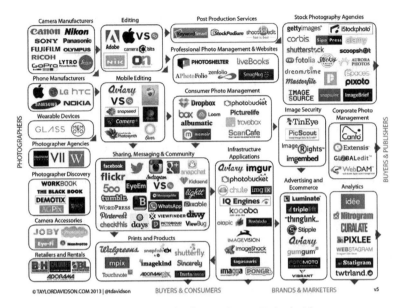

Figure 5.14 The photography industry landscape. *Source:* Taylordavidson.com.

4) Produce a map of the competitive dimensions that exist in the industry and the level of interconnectedness between companies. What will be the size of a NKC model?

References

Anderson, C. and Zeithaml, C. (1984). Stage of the product life cycle, business strategy, and business performance. *Academy of Management Journal*, 27(1),5–24.

Bass, F. (1969). A new product growth for model consumer durables. *Management Science*, 15(5), 215–227.

Barney, J.B. (1986). Types of competition and the theory of strategy: Toward an integrative framework. *Academy of Management Review*, 11(4), 791–800.

Benner, M.J. and Tripsas, M. (2012). The influence of prior industry affiliation on framing in nascent industries: The evolution of digital cameras. *Strategic Management Journal*, 33(3), 277–302.

Blei, D.M., Ng, A.Y. and Jordan, M.I. (2003). Latent Dirichlet allocation. *Journal of Machine Learning Research*, 3(Jan), 993–1022.

Caldart, A.A. and Oliveira, F. (2010). Analysing industry profitability: A "complexity as cause" perspective. *European Management Journal*, 28(2), 95–107.

CIPA. (2015). Total Shipments of Film Cameras. CIPA Report. Camera & Imaging Products Association.

Cyert, R.M. and March, J.G. (1992). A Behavioral Theory of the Firm, 2nd edn. Blackwell Publishers.

Deutsch, C.H. (2008). At Kodak, some old things are new again. *The New York Times* (2 May). http://www.nytimes.com/2008/05/02/technology/02kodak.html?_r=0 (accessed 2 September 2015).

Gavetti, G. and Levinthal, D.A. (2000). Looking forward and looking backward: cognitive and experiential search. *Administrative Science Quarterly*, 45, 113–137.

Goodwin, P., Meeran, S., and Dyussekeneva, K. (2014). The challenges of pre-launch forecasting of adoption time series for new durable products. *International Journal of Forecasting*, 30(4), 1082–1097.

Gort, M. and Klepper, S. (1982). Time paths in the diffusion of product innovation. *The Economic Journal*, 92(367), 630–653.

Gort, M. and Konakayama, A. (1982). A model of diffusion in the production of an innovation. *The American Economic Review*, 72(5), 1111–1120.

Kauffman, S. (1993). The Origins of Order. Oxford University Press.

Keppler, S. (1996). Entry, exit, growth, and innovation over the product life cycle. *The American Economic Review*, 86(3), 562–583.

Kunc, M. (2004). Simulating the evolution of industries using a dynamic behavioural model. 22nd International Conference of the System Dynamics Society, Oxford.

Kunc, M. (2010). Revisiting Porter's generic strategies using system dynamics: when taking book's recipes conduces your organization to dysfunctional behavior in a competitive environment. In: Computational Analysis of Firms' Organization and Strategic Behavior (ed. E. Mollona), 152–169. Routledge.

Kunc, M. and Bhandari, R. (2011). Strategic Development Processes during Economic and Financial crisis. *Management Decision* 8, 1343–1353.

Kunc, M. and Morecroft, J. (2007). Competitive dynamics and gaming simulation. *Lessons from a fishing industry simulator. Journal of the Operational Research Society*, 58, 1146–1155.

Kunc, M.H. and Morecroft, J.D. (2010). Managerial decision making and firm performance under a resource-based paradigm. *Strategic Management Journal*, 31(11):1164-1182.

Mahajan, V., Muller, E., and Wind, Y. (eds) (2000). New-Product Diffusion Models. Kluwer Academic Publishers.

March, J.G. and Simon, H.A. (1958). Organizations. John Wiley & Sons, Inc.

Morecroft, J.D. (1985). The feedback view of business policy and strategy. *System Dynamics Review*, 1(1), 4–19.

Morecroft, J.D.W. (2015). Strategic Modelling and Business Dynamics: A Feedback Systems View, 2nd edn. John Wiley & Sons, Ltd.

Nelson, S.A., Parkinson, M.B., and Papalambros, P.Y. 2001. Multicriteria optimization in product platform design. *Journal of Mechanical Design*, 123(2), 199–204.

Oliva, R., Sterman, J.D., and Giese, M. (2003). Limits to growth in the new economy: exploring the 'get big fast'strategy in e-commerce. *System Dynamics Review*, 19(2), 83–117.

Porter, M.E. (2004). Competitive advantage: creating and sustaining superior performance. The Free Press.

Rogers, E.M. (1983). Diffusion of Innovations, 3rd edn. The Free Press.

Saraswat, N., Dey, L., Verma, I., and Gupta, H. (2016). Integrated analysis of research publications and patents for strategic decision making. 2016 IEEE 16th International Conference on Data Mining Workshops (ICDMW), 210–217. IEEE.

Schumpeter, J.A. (1950). Capitalism, Socialism, and Democracy, 3rd edn. Harper.

Simon, H.A. (2001). The Sciences of the Artificial, 3rd edn. The MIT Press

Shirata, C.Y., Takeuchi, H., Ogino, S., and Watanabe, H. (2011). Extracting key phrases as predictors of corporate bankruptcy: Empirical analysis of annual reports by text mining. *Journal of Emerging Technologies in Accounting*, 8, 31–44.

Sterman, J.D. (2000). Business Dynamics: Systems Thinking and Modeling for a Complex World. Irwin/McGraw-Hill.

Sterman, J.D., Henderson, R., Beinhocker, E.D., and Newman, L.I. (2007). Getting big too fast: Strategic dynamics with increasing returns and bounded rationality. *Management Science*, 53(4), 683–696.

Walker, W.E. (2009). Does the best practice of rational-style model based policy analysis already include ethical considerations? *Omega*, 37(6), 1051–1062.

Weick, K.E. (1979). The Social Psychology of Organizing, 2nd edn. McGraw-Hill, Inc.

Further Reading

Armstrong, J.S. (2001). Principles of Forecasting A Handbook for Researchers and Practitioners. Kluwer Academic Publishers.

Baum, J.A.C. and Amburgey, T.L. (2002). Organizational ecology. In: Companion to Organizations (ed. J.A.C. Baum), 304–326. Blackwell Publishers.

Geroski, P.A. (1991). Market Dynamics and Entry. Blackwell.

Kauffman, S. (1993). The Origins of Order. Oxford University Press.

Mahajan, V., Muller, E., and Wind, Y. (eds) (2000). New-Product Diffusion Models. Kluwer Academic Publishers.

Robertson, D.A. and Caldart, A.A. (2009). The Dynamics of Strategy: Mastering Strategic Landscapes of the Firm. Oxford University Press.

Sterman, J.D. (2000). Business Dynamics: Systems Thinking and Modelling for a Complex World. Irwin McGraw-Hill.

Sterman, J.D., Henderson, R., Beinhocker, E.D., and Newman, L.I. (2007). Getting big too fast: Strategic dynamics with increasing returns and bounded rationality. *Management Science*, 53(4), 683–696.

Tirole, J. (1990). The Theory of Industrial Organization. The MIT Press.

6

Competitive Advantage: Static Analysis

Objectives

1) To define the concept of value
2) To learn tools to evaluate how the company is creating value
3) To identify basic business strategies to create value and achieve a competitive advantage

Learning outcomes and managerial capabilities developed

1) To apply tools to identify the activities responsible for value creation
2) To have an overview of the analytic tools to support value creation

---

There is no competitive advantage if the company cannot deliver more value to customers than competitors. Companies need to perform a set of discrete processes, e.g. delivering products, which cut across traditional functions, e.g. logistics, in order to deliver value. A competitive advantage is achieved when the strategy develops a coherent configuration of processes that deliver value differently than other companies in the industry. Thus, strategy implies choosing and developing specific sets of processes which require a distinctive bundle of resources and capabilities. Processes determine the connections between the internal aspects of the company, e.g. resources and capabilities, and the product market position, as well as the boundary of the company due to the location of the processes, either in-house or outsourced.

Strategies are intended to help companies focus their efforts on satisfying their customers. Therefore, effective strategies have a clear statement of the value created for their customers. While there can be many different value statements for customers (see any company's website), there are two basic types of value that a company can achieve: low price or differentiation (Porter, 1998). Low price means the intended value is realized through giving buyers the opportunity to buy products at the lowest price in the market for average

Strategic Analytics: Integrating Management Science and Strategy, First Edition. Martin Kunc.
© 2019 John Wiley & Sons Ltd. Published 2019 by John Wiley & Sons Ltd.
Companion website: www.wiley.com/go/kunc/strategic-analytics

market quality. Differentiation means the creation of value occurs when customers can acquire products with functionalities unique or above the "average" product in the market. Based on the two value creation's positions, companies seem to follow two generic types of strategy: cost leadership; and differentiation (Porter, 1998).

Before this chapter begins to discuss the concept of value, it is important to define the key driver of the type of strategy pursued by companies: their direction. Then, this chapter will address the concept of generic strategies in terms of configuration of activities and risks involved with the strategies.

6.1   The Direction of a Company: Vision and Mission

Managers define the direction of an organization using a simple question: "What does the organization want to be?" The answer to this question is not only a personal choice but also a consideration of the long-term sustainability of the company as well as the culture, reputation and other characteristics of the organization. While there are a number of recipes for the concept of *vision*, a *vision* is conceptually the "image" of the organization in the future and it makes the ideology connecting the organization explicit. The "image" of the organization presents the desired future for the organization within the areas of operation and competencies defined in the *mission. Mission* defines the core purpose of the organization. The mission aims to provide unanimity of purpose, a basis for the use of an organization's resources and capabilities, and the translation of the purpose into goals that can be accessed and controlled.

Without a clear direction, it is difficult to define value and market segmentation. Direction provides an anchor so as to not pursue all opportunities available in the market and have a stable value creation process over time.

6.2   Defining Value and Market Segmentation

Value is a difficult concept to delineate because there are many different definitions of value held by different consumers. Value depends on the subjective appreciation of a product/service realized by a buyer/user and this subjective appreciation is then translated into their willingness to pay for the value received (Lepak et al., 2007). There are two implications from this description:

- The payment must be at least similar to or exceed the company's costs of creating value.
- Payment is a function of the perceived performance of the product/service.

Therefore, the process of value creation involves two perspectives that are intrinsically connected: an internal view based on the processes responsible for generating value and an external value perspective originated from the consumer understanding about the value offered by the product.

Given the differences in terms of value, there is a need to segment consumers who have similar perceptions of value, so the company can target them with the right product/service. This process is called segmentation. Segmentation is particularly important not only for creating value to similar consumers but also for understanding the competing products fighting for the same group of consumers. The segmentation process consists of:

1) **Identify segmentation variables**. The segmentation variables are the dimensions that we can employ to characterize the purchasers in the market. Dimensions can be grouped into three areas: consumers' characteristics; product/service characteristics; and consumers' behaviors.

   - Purchasers' characteristics mostly depend on their type: businesses (size, requirements); people (geographic location, demographics, lifestyle, culture).
   - Product/service characteristics: size, technical complexity, price, features, design, performance, general/personalized.
   - Consumers' behaviors: purchase occasion, cultural, social and ethical influences.

   While marketing is usually the discipline in charge of the segmentation in detail, few dimensions are conceptualized at a strategic level in order to divide the market into clearly different sectors. There are two considerations in the process of identification: substitutes and correlation. Substitution defines the limit by which a product can be replaced by a similar product, e.g. the automobile market is segmented by type of car since a buyer of a luxury car, such as Jaguar, will not find a cheaper car, e.g. Fiat, as a substitute. Correlation implies dimensions that are strongly related so they can be subsumed into a single variable, e.g. type of hotel can be a general dimension comprising price level, services available and location so type of hotel has strong correlation with the rest of the variables.

2) **Visualize the market segments**. Once you have the key dimensions to segment the market, you can organize them in a matrix or map where the market segments can be visualized. For example, the airline industry can be organized in terms of service offered: no-frills and full service and then geographical coverage (short and long haul). Additional information can be included in each of the segment such as size of the market (number of consumers, price levels and sales), competitors and geographical location. One potential outcome of mapping the segment is the identification of unoccupied segments. See Figure 6.1.

3) **Evaluate market segment attractiveness**. Profitability is a key factor to consider at strategic level when we analyze market segments. The same principles employed for the industry can be applied in each market

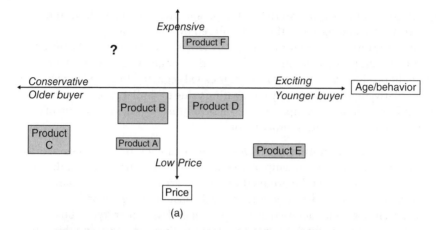

Figure 6.1 Mapping market segmentation: (a) mapping age/behavior vs. price and market size (size of boxes indicates market size); and (b) matrix: age vs. type of drinks in pubs.

segment: Five forces (see Chapter 4); and life cycle (see Chapter 5). However, there are some differences to consider. First, substitutes are products that are employed by consumers in other segments in the same industry and can also be employed in this market segment without modifications, e.g. the automobile industry. Secondly, competitive movements between segments are constrained by the barriers to mobility, which follow similar principles as the barriers to entry and include proprietary product differences, access to distribution channels, economies of scale, capital requirements, switching costs, and level of retaliation (see Chapter 5).

4) **Select the segment or segments to compete.** The final decision is to compete focused on only one segment (specialist or narrow strategy) or on multiple segments (broader or generalist strategy). The decision is made as a function of the analysis performed previously (characteristics of the segments) and the relative easiness of competing across multiple segments which can be related to: similarity of processes; shared resources/capabilities; and economies of scope.

Porter (1998) synthesizes the sources of value to two mechanisms: lowering the costs of the consumer/buyer; or providing consumer/buyer with higher performance than the performance obtained from similar products/services. This broad simplification provides the two extremes in a continuum of strategic positioning that companies can adopt: low cost; or differentiation, as shown in Figure 6.2. Later on, Section 6.4 discusses tools that can be used to identify the activities that lead to cost or differentiation advantage.

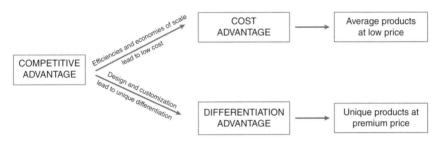

Figure 6.2 Competitive advantage paths and generic strategies.

6.3 Mapping the Activities to Deliver Value

From an operational perspective, strategies are a set of coherent activities that contribute in delivering value to customers (Porter, 1998). While companies have multiple activities, a number of frameworks are available to identify what activities/processes are responsible for delivering value and how they interact to deliver value. This section presents three frameworks: Value Chain; Activity System Map; and Business Model Canvas. The frameworks translate the highly aggregated contents of strategies into more specific models of the company's business operational processes.

6.3.1 Value Chain

The competitive advantage originates from the set of activities/processes performed to deliver products/services to consumers/buyers in a way that generates value to them. Porter (1998) introduces the concept of value chain in order to systematically analyze the set of activities/processes responsible for value creation. While the level of analysis is the business unit, there can be variations by product categories, location and other dimensions that make activities specific for different market segments.

A value chain reflects nine generic categories of activities/processes comprising the business and how they are linked together. The activities/processes existing in a value chain reflect the history, strategy and their intrinsic characteristics, e.g. technological, economic, etc. A process/activity employs inputs and resources to perform its function while it generates information, intermediate assets/outputs (e.g. inventory) and financial results (cash, account receivables, liabilities). There are two large groupings for the nine categories: primary and support activities. Primary activities are responsible for the delivery of the product/service and the support to consumers after purchasing the product. Support activities provide assistance to primary activities through the procurement of inputs and human resources for production processes, as well as technology and information for other processes. Each process can be analyzed with respect to its contribution to generating value to customers and its impact on costs. The traditional visual representation of the value chain is displayed in Figure 6.3 where the support activities are located on top of primary activities because they service all activities responsible for delivering products and the primary categories are arranged in a form to reflect their linkages to fulfilling customers' needs.

The primary activities involve inbound logistics (reception, storage and delivery of inputs for operations), operations (transformation of inputs into product/services), outbound logistics (storage and delivery of products to customers), marketing & sales (advertising, promotion, price, sales force and channel management), and service (installation, repairs and training). Support activities comprise procurement (purchasing, asset investment), human resource management (recruiting, hiring, training, and payroll), company infrastructure (general management, planning, finance, accounting, legal,

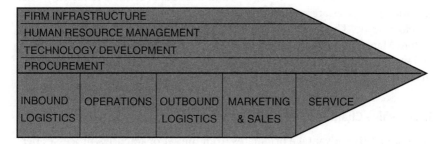

Figure 6.3 Value chain.

information systems) and technology development (process and product improvement, R&D). The configuration of the value chain, as well as the importance of each process, depends on the industry and the strategy adopted by the company, e.g. some companies outsource part of the value chain. Some of the activities directly influence the creation of value while others have an indirect impact.

It is important to consider that activities/processes interconnect to form a complex system. Therefore, each activity can influence and be influenced by another activity in terms of cost or performance, e.g. inbound logistics that do not deliver inputs on time impact production (operations), outbound logistics and sales. Consequently, coordination is a more important managerial action in the creation of value than the optimization of discrete activities. The importance of coordination needs to be considered not only internally but also externally through linkages with suppliers and distributors. Linkages have a significant influence on the definition of the boundaries of a company within an industry together with the relative bargaining power of the suppliers providing the linked activities.

6.3.2 Activity System Map

Porter (1996) suggests strategy consists of choosing to perform either activities in a different manner than competitors or different activities in order to achieve a competitive advantage. He also suggests combining activities in a unique systematic way is also a source of competitive advantage. Considering the activities as part of a system implies the need to consider how they fit among them. There are three ways in which activities can fit: fit with respect to the strategy; reinforcing fit among activities when they support each other; and optimization of effort when activities are coordinated to minimize effort (Porter, 1996). The sustainability of strategies resides in the difficulty of imitating the whole system rather than copying individual activities. However, the existence of a system of activities makes it more difficult to achieve sustainable growth as it implies compromises that can reduce the fit between activities.

Porter (1996) presents a diagram called an "activity system map" to support this perspective. According to Porter (1996: page 71): "Activity system maps, show how a company's strategic position is contained in a set of tailored activities designed to deliver it. In companies with a clear strategic position, a number of higher-order strategic themes…can be identified and implemented through clusters of tightly linked activities …." See Figure 6.4 for an example about a full-service Asian airline. The key strategic themes (in dark circles) are the long-haul direct flights to key markets in USA, Europe and Asia using full inflight service (supporting activities are in light circles) complemented by services for business customers in airports such as lounges and parking services. Another important strategic theme complementing direct flights is the

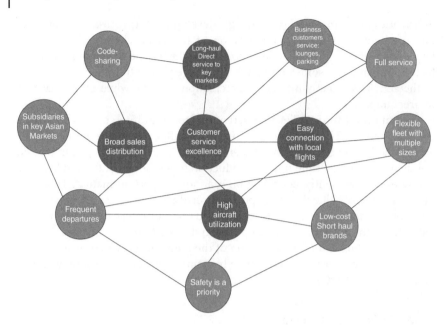

Figure 6.4 Activity system map for a full service airline in Asia.

existence of broad sales distribution through code-sharing and subsidiaries that allow seamless services from the Asian destination to any part in the world. Simultaneously, the airline offers easy connections with local flights for travelers from USA, Europe and Asia through the use of its own subsidiaries and frequent departures. Operational efficiency measured by high aircraft utilization is achieved through a flexible fleet and high security standards. Operational efficiency allows the company to offer short-haul services in the low-cost categories for local and foreign travelers.

While the activity system map looks visually attractive and may facilitate a discussion about the key components of the business, the method to design it and the criteria to separate between strategy themes and supporting activities is unclear. The only explanation for the method suggested by Porter (1996) is to consider strategic themes as concepts closely related to the value proposition for the customer segments identified in the process for defining the strategic positioning.

6.3.3 Business Model Canvas

Another widely employed tool to identify the building blocks of a business is called the Business Model Canvas (Osterwalder and Pigneur, 2010). Figure 6.5 displays an example for easyJet, which is one of the largest European low-cost airlines. The first building block comprises the partners that provide services

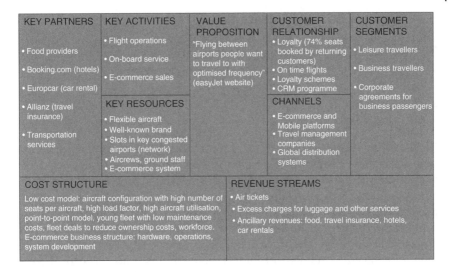

KEY PARTNERS	KEY ACTIVITIES	VALUE PROPOSITION	CUSTOMER RELATIONSHIP	CUSTOMER SEGMENTS
• Food providers • Booking.com (hotels) • Europcar (car rental) • Allianz (travel insurance) • Transportation services	• Flight operations • On-board service • E-commerce sales **KEY RESOURCES** • Flexible aircraft • Well-known brand • Slots in key congested airports (network) • Aircrews, ground staff • E-commerce system	"Flying between airports people want to travel to with optimised frequency" (easyJet website)	• Loyalty (74% seats booked by returning customers) • On time flights • Loyalty schemes • CRM programme **CHANNELS** • E-commerce and Mobile platforms • Travel management companies • Global distribution systems	• Leisure travellers • Business travellers • Corporate agreements for business passengers

COST STRUCTURE	REVENUE STREAMS
Low cost model: aircraft configuration with high number of seats per aircraft, high load factor, high aircraft utilisation, point-to-point model, young fleet with low maintenance costs, fleet deals to reduce ownership costs, workforce. E-commerce business structure: hardware, operations, system development	• Air tickets • Excess charges for luggage and other services • Ancillary revenues: food, travel insurance, hotels, car rentals

Figure 6.5 easyJet Business Model Canvas.

and perform activities for the company. Partners are included in order to optimize the configuration of the business and generate particular revenue streams. The second building block is the key activities related to the value proposition, support distribution channels and customer relationships together with the generation of revenues. The third building block involves the description of the resources supporting the value proposition, distribution channels, customer relationships and revenue streams. The fourth building block corresponds to the value proposition: description, type of problems solved to customers, products/services offered and needs from the customer. The fifth building block is how the company establishes relationships with customers explained in terms of segments, level of development of the relationships, integration with the rest of the business (activities and resources), and the costs involved. The sixth building block describes the channels where the product/service is delivered to the customer segments and how the channels are servicing customers. The seventh building block portrays the customer segments targeted by the company. In the case of easyJet, it presents an interesting contrast with respect to other low-cost airlines since it also targets business customers. The management believes it has a competitive advantage with respect to full service airlines in this segment due to its frequency and price. The two building blocks at the bottom of Figure 6.5 present the financial aspects of the business: cost structure by resources and activities and its drivers (economies of scale and scope); and revenue streams (price method, perceived value of the product/service, methods of payment).

6.4 Type of Business Strategies

This section discusses the generic strategies that can be employed to create value for customers and their impact on activities/processes in more detail.

6.4.1 Cost Advantage

Achieving a cost advantage implies selling products/services that provide functionalities required by customers at a lower price than competitors. This type of business strategy involves performing activities, which do not differ substantially from existing products in the market, in an efficient way while controlling the costs associated with the activities. The drivers of costs have a strong influence on the "cost advantage" strategy. However, they are usually not clearly understood in their systemic nature, e.g. the interrelationships and feedback processes between activities. The lack of understanding is partially influenced by the lack of information systems tracking costs' drivers from a strategic perspective. When companies need to consider their cost position with respect to competitors, it is usually very difficult to assess the competitors' cost positions which complicates the design of cost advantage strategies.

The basic process to design a cost advantage strategy starts with an understanding of the activities to generate value (see Section 6.3 for examples of the process). Then, each activity needs to have the costs and assets involved in the activities together with their cost drivers assigned. More importantly, it is the identification of the drivers, or structural factors, affecting the dynamics of the costs. Porter (1998) defined a number of cost drivers responsible for the behavior of an activity (Table 6.1). More than one driver can be operating simultaneously in each activity so quantification of the relationship between level of activity and cost driver can be difficult to obtain.

A strategy aiming to take a company into a cost advantage position will consider two main options: controlling the cost drivers better than competitors or reconfiguring the set of activities in a more efficient way than competitors. A dynamic perspective on cost drivers is important to consider when designing strategies looking for a cost advantage.

6.4.2 Differentiation Advantage

Strategies based on differentiation advantage create unique value for the buyers/consumers in dimensions that result as critical for them. The only way to provide unique value is through a set of processes directly related to critical dimensions responsible for consumers' satisfaction: product/service use and value perception (information provided: signaling). Porter (1998: page 119) asserts: "Firms view the potential sources of differentiation too

Table 6.1 Cost drivers.

Cost drivers	Description
Economies of scale	Economies of scale operate when: activities are executed more efficiently at larger volume, the cost of certain activities can be divided over large sales volume, or activities have less proportional cost increases compared with the output growth
	Diseconomies of scale occur when the increase in the volume of an activity creates complexity in its management and coordination costs
	Technology, specialization and minimum size are important factors influencing the dynamics of economies of scale
Learning	The costs of activities may decline over time as the activity is performed more efficiently due to the learning process. Learning improves how processes are performed. Learning can occur due to the volume of activity, level of investment, or simply time
Capacity utilization	If an activity has fixed costs, the utilization of the activity will have an important impact on the production costs per unit. The configuration of the activity (internal factor), as well as demand fluctuations (external factors), determine the utilization of the capacity
Linkages	If the competitive advantage arises from strongly linked activities (internally and externally), then their costs depend on the performance of other activities. Therefore, it is necessary to undergo a systemic evaluation of the drivers by considering all other activities connected
	When linkages are external, external actors may be integrated into the company (vertical integration) as a way of controlling costs for the activity
Interrelationships between businesses	Multi-business companies have activities shared between business units. These type of activities provide the possibility of increasing output (or utilization) by sharing it among multiple businesses. Sharing an activity implies obtaining economies of scale and learning
Timing	Timing implies enjoying low costs when the assets for the activity are acquired in favorable conditions, e.g. business cycles, or generate more demand for an activity, e.g. being the first mover in a market
Strategic choices	Certain strategic choices can impact on the costs of the activities such as product configurations and variety, service, customer segments, technology, location, human resources policies, and process efficiencies

narrowly. They see differentiation in terms of physical products or marketing practices, rather than potentially arising anywhere in the value chain". Being unique in the market allows companies to have premium price in order to compensate for activities that are tailored to consumers' needs. Uniqueness can originate from any or multiple sets of drivers. See Table 6.2 for a list of them.

Differentiation advantage originates from offering consumers a performance for product/service that is unique in the market. A strategy aiming to generate differentiation advantage needs to consider the key activities responsible for meeting consumers' requirements. The first step will clearly involve understanding who the consumer is (see Section 6.2), what is driving the consumer's behavior, and what the product/service being offered is together with its limitations. One important aspect to evaluate is the cost of implementing a differentiation advantage which can lead to trade-offs between activities based on their contribution to value creation. Consequently, some activities are performed considering low cost options while other activities will be executed offering unique value to consumers. To summarize, a strategy aiming at a differentiation advantage will enhance uniqueness in existing activities, define the criteria for uniqueness in the industry or create a completely new system of activities.

Table 6.2 Differentiation drivers.

Differentiation drivers	Description
Strategic choices	Strategic choices such as product configurations and variety, service, level of customer's information, quality, technology, and location
Linkages	Complex products/services comprise more than one activity performed in a coordinate way including external linkages
Location	Being the only option in a specific location offers uniqueness to consumers
Learning	Learning from consumers' experience helps to develop activities continuously in order to satisfy customers differently to competitors
Integration	Integrating external activities can help the company offer key activities in a unique way rather than depending on an external supplier
Scale	Certain activities, e.g. sales, require a minimum volume to support other activities, e.g. R&D, design, that deliver uniqueness
Perception of value	Understanding how the product/service is perceived by, and affects, the consumer is a key driver in achieving differentiation

6.4.3 Blue Ocean Strategy

Blue Ocean strategy is based on the premise that companies should focus their strategies on finding or creating new, uncontested market space (a "blue ocean") rather than to compete against companies in existing markets ("red oceans") (Kim and Mauborgne, 2005). The main instrument for finding blue oceans is a "strategy canvas," a visual representation of value curves. Value curves reflect the value proposition in terms of the elements constituting it (e.g. dimensions of uniquess). Kim and Mauborgne (2005) introduced the concept of the value curve, which they later used in developing the strategy canvas. The strategy canvas allows the comparison of competitors. The strategic factors and value proposition elements that the industry considers critical are displayed on the horizontal axis. The vertical axis shows the level buyers receive for each element. Most of the considerations are usually judgmental based on the information obtained during workshops or discussions among managers. Figure 6.6 shows an example in the mobile telephone industry considering the introduction of unbranded mobile handsets (bandit cellphone). The handsets are low cost with customized value-added features and compete with the traditional cellphone makers, e.g. Samsung, Apple, etc. Their market is consumers with a low budget and diverse needs in emerging economies.

Blue Ocean strategy is about focusing on alternative customers, who place less weight on the current elements of the value proposition and value other (new) propositions (Kim and Mauborgne, 2005). Essentially, Blue Ocean

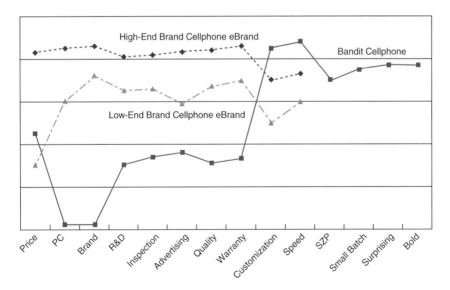

Figure 6.6 Mobile telephone handset strategy canvas. Source: Chang (2010: page 222). Reproduced with permission of Technology in Society.

strategy defines new market boundaries by reaching consumers beyond the existing demand for a certain product. The implementation of the strategy implies reducing the elements of the propositions that are below the standards in the industry, creating new elements that are not in the market, improving elements above the standard and eliminating those elements in the current value proposition that are not important (Kim and Mauborgne, 2005). Blue Ocean strategy, and its tools, can be integrated with the Business Model Canvas method (see Section 6.3.3) in order to have a comprehensive set of tools to develop strategies that compete with traditional Porterian methods.

Food for thought 6.1 (extracted from Kunc and Morecroft, 2007) For many years, bar soap has been the leading product in the personal care products market, but washing habits have changed over the years. With consumers taking showers more regularly they have been changing their preferences for liquid washing products over bar soaps. PZ Cussons (hereafter "Cussons"), with its brand Imperial Leather, had been the leader in the bar soap market for 50 years, as it exploited a brand that was familiar to the majority of adults in the UK since childhood. But Imperial Leather started losing some of its mainstream relevance when Lever Fabergé launched the Dove bar soap in 1992. Dove bar, which is a "syndet" (synthetic non-soap), reached the number one position in the bar soap sector by 1997 with a new proposition: skin moisturizing. IT was not only the effect of Dove that affected the Imperial Leather bar; consumers had been building very different expectations and requirements in personal care because, as consumers experienced novel products offering value added benefits, most consumers started considering bar soap as being outmoded.

Thus, in addition to Dove, the bar soap market grew into a personal washing category with the arrival of shower gels and bath foams offering value added benefits. The shower gels and bath foams segments had been the domain of Radox, a well-known foaming bath brand since the 1950s, owned by Sara Lee Household & Body Care UK. Radox had the leadership in shower gels with its defining hook – specifically designed to hang in the shower – and their value adding strategy through therapeutic elements based on herbal ingredients. In the midst of these strong brands, Cussons was also competing against own-label products, which had been a strong and vibrant category since the major retailers (Marks & Spencer, Boots, Tesco, Sainsbury's) had also become interested in bathroom ranges.

The management response   Cussons' management responded to the strategic dilemma that they faced in the 1990s with two different strategic actions. First, they launched an innovative liquid soap – Carex – aimed at the handwash segment in 1994. Until 1993, the liquid soap handwash market in the

UK had been stagnant. Sales were flat, own-label products were commoditizing the market, and liquid soaps were only differentiated by cosmetic properties. Cussons' managers identified the opportunity for an antibacterial moisturizing liquid for handwashing based on the success of similar brands in the USA. They developed an everyday product based on a rational proposition of tackling dirt and germs as well as leaving fresh, clean and moisturized hands. While Carex had been launched as a product oriented towards the kitchen rather than the bathroom, as most of the traditional liquid soaps were at that time, it had also attacked Dove's moisturizing message. Secondly, in 1998 Cussons launched a foam-burst gel, as part of its portfolio in shower gels. A premium product, highly differentiated on the shelf through its packaging (in a can, not a plastic bottle as other shower gels) and its performance, changing itself from a tiny drop of gel into a mass of rich lather during the shower.

The market response Dove reacted to Cussons' Carex by strengthening the offer of Dove in the bathroom, rather than expanding into the rational alternative of an antibacterial liquid soap. Thus, Lever Fabergé followed Cussons in the bath and shower category with a whole range of products based on its moisturizing proposal. However, Dove and Carex were not the only competing products in what seemed to be a very crowded personal care market in 2004 with the own-label products joining the battle for the liquid soap. Figure 6.7 shows a time series with the sales in volume for the bar soap market divided among the main companies (lines 1–3) and the total volume for the liquid soap market (line 4).

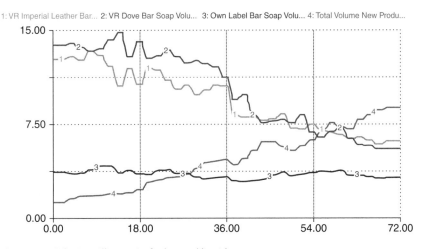

Figure 6.7 Sales in million units for bar and liquid soap.

Questions:

- How can Cussons' management grow and sustain Carex in the face of stiff competition?
- What are the drivers of differentiation in fast moving consumer goods and personal care in particular? Look for some answers by reviewing information from the key players.
- What other innovations could Cussons have implemented to keep differentiation? Justify yourself based on the drivers of innovation and the system of activities.

6.5 Integrating Management Science into Strategic Management

Bell et al. (2003) coined the term "strategic operations research" (SOR) to define when an operations research/management science application creates a sustainable competitive advantage. Essentially, the implementation of SOR impacts on either costs or differentiation drivers in the companies supporting their cost or differentiation advantage, respectively. The evidence considered to categorize the use of management science as SOR is the extended use of the methods, systems and databases over time, changes in the organization to accommodate the prescriptions of the SOR as well as the response from the competitors to the implementation of SOR. In other words, the application of SOR becomes an inherent component of the activities performed by the company in a similar way to a marketing plan, supply chain management or human resources policies. Traditionally, management science has been recognized as supporting efficiency improvement and cost reduction (the cost advantage), see examples in Table 6.3, but more recently management scientists have also been working on the revenue side of the organization (the differentiation advantage) supporting pricing activities, see examples in Table 6.4 (Bell and Chen, 2006).

6.5.1 Uncovering Market Segments Using Analytics Tools: Market Basket Transactions Analysis

Market basket transactions are the most basic piece of information retailers can collect from their business. Transaction ID, product description, transaction date, volume and sales are the key parts of a transaction record and some more informative transactions also include a customer profile (if it runs a loyalty program). Thus, every transaction can tell a story about a customer (Blischok, 1995).

Table 6.3 Cost drivers and the use of Management Science methods to manage costs.

Cost drivers	Management Science methods	Examples of applications
Economies of scale	Evaluation of the improvement on economies of scale of organizational units through the comparison of efficiency ratios. Efficiency ratios are determined by comparing the inputs (resources) vs. outputs (services and products). The method employed is called data envelopment analysis	A study by Ferrier and Valdmanis (2004) compared the situation between merged and non-merged hospitals in the USA. A hospital merger is the union of independent hospitals through either the dissolution of one hospital and its assimilation or the creation of a new hospital from the combination of hospitals. After two hospitals become merged, activities, such as support services, management, patient care and professional services, become joined reducing duplication of services and decreasing costs.
Learning curve	A learning curve model defines an explanatory variable called "experience" using a cumulative measure of production or use. Then the change in "cost", the explained variable, provides a measure of learning improvement. The learning curve was explored with a variety of functional forms to describe the relationship between cumulative capacity and cost but a log-linear function is the most common function employed due to its simplicity and high goodness-of-fit to observed data	The applications of the learning curve are extensive in new technologies. An example of the study on the reduction of costs due to the learning curve in photovoltaics is presented by Nemet (2006) where he highlighted the existence of additional factors to the learning curve influencing the decline in costs
Capacity utilization	Fleet assignment supports the allocation of assets with different sizes according to expected demand. The method supporting this process is mathematical programming algorithms	Delta Airlines employed a fleet assignment application to minimize the costs associated with flights by allocating the right airplane according to demand (Subramanian et al., 1996)

(Continued)

Table 6.3 (Continued)

Cost drivers	Management Science methods	Examples of applications
Linkages	An integrated manufacturing planning system to improve linkages across the production chain employs mathematical programming	Sadia, a Brazilian company and one of the largest meat processing companies in the world, developed a system called PIPA (an integrated poultry planning system) to optimize planning across the supply chain (Taube-Netto, 1996).
Interrelationships between businesses	Sharing resources to reduce costs in diversification strategies can misfire due to erroneous inferences in the linkages between activities. A system dynamics study was employed in order to demonstrate this problem	A simulation was based on a real case study of a service company engaged in diversification and showed the issues faced with stretching a shared resource with additional activities without investment to expand it (Gary, 2005)
Timing	Capacity management in a legacy plant aims to keep production volume while harvesting the asset. Optimization model combined with data analytics can evaluate order history and define decreasing production plans so the asset can be harvested.	A study on a chemical S&P 500 company was performed by Ali et al. (2014). Legacy plants built decades before have had to adapt existing plant asset configurations and manufacturing practices to new demand and customer profiles.

For shops that have a large number of products, it is almost impossible to analyze all possible combinations using only the staff analytical capabilities. Therefore, a data mining solution can take advantage of the existence of transaction information: market basket analysis (Nishi, 2005). Market basket analysis is based on the assumption that purchase decisions are made in multiple product categories during one shopping trip (Russell and Petersen, 2000). Market basket analysis is based on association rules (Agrawal et al., 1993). The approaches to market basket analysis can be broadly categorized into exploratory, or data mining techniques, and explanatory methods (Mild and Reutterer, 2003). Exploratory methods only focus on identifying data patterns and do not consider business related interpretation to the results whereas explanatory methods tend to identify marketing-mix information variables and study their effects by using cross-category relationships (Solnet et al., 2016). Therefore,

Table 6.4 Differentiation drivers and Management Science methods to control differentiation drivers.

Differentiation drivers	Management Science methods	Examples of applications
Strategic choices	Product portfolio management to manage variety in product offering using combinatorial optimization.	HP has developed a revenue coverage optimization tool to define product portfolio based on importance (order history) and portfolio size (Jain, 2008)
Linkages	Optimization models can be employed to evaluate the promotion of bundled products and the use of multi-channel structures The challenge of customer relationship management is to know which product to offer to each customer using certain channels under certain constraints, e.g. budget	In the retail banking industry, companies need to develop profitable long-term relationships with their customers and use customer relationship management in order to maintain and increase the demand of the multiple products in bundles (e.g. mortgages and insurance) through multiple channels (e.g. branches, online and call centers) (Delanote et al., 2013)
Location	Strategic decisions related to segmenting the existing store portfolio into a number of retail offerings based on the location of customers. Combination of factor and cluster analysis is employed to design the portfolio	Convenience grocery stores have become common in UK retailing due to their adoption by retailers associated with supermarkets. Segmentation of the convenience market into a series of clusters by location type is suggested by Hood et al. (2016)
Perception of value	Revenue (or yield) management has been employed to segment the market according to price or other product features and match up the perception of value for the same product or service. The tools involved are optimization and decision making under uncertainty	American Airlines implemented the first yield management system (Bell et al., 2003). See Chapter 4 for another application

both methods generate a "story" from the data either by identifying simple unexpected behaviors which reflect unexpected combinations of products creating value creation or by understanding the impact of marketing mix and product development variables on value creation reflected through specific purchase decisions.

Market basket analysis provides insights on which products tend to be purchased together by identifying product affinities or association rules among shopping baskets. Association rules mining is the data mining technique most closely linked with market basket analysis. Association rules explore patterns in data without a specified target (Berry, 2004). The outputs of market basket analysis can be easy to understand by expressing them in the form of a transaction rule: set of items X influences the purchase of the set of items Y. It expresses the incidence across transactions of one set of items as a condition of another (Chapman and Feit, 2015). The transaction rule indicates that the purchase of items $\{X_i\}$ will likely lead to the purchase of items $\{Y_j\}$. The following three metrics are the measures for association rules in market basket analysis:

- The *support* for a set of items is the proportion of the transactions that contain the set which occurred among all the transaction data. The support of products X_i and Y_j refers to the proportion of times that products X_i and Y_j are purchased together. Support for multiple items can be considered as a joint probability.
- *Confidence* is defined as the conditional probability of the consequence given the antecedent, which is mathematically stated as confidence $(\{X_i\} \Rightarrow \{Y_j\})$ = $p(Y_j \mid X_i)$. A rule with higher confidence denotes that it is more likely for Y_j to be purchased with X_i in one single transaction.
- The *lift* of a rule is defined as lift $(\{X_i\} \Rightarrow \{Y_j\}) = p(Y_j \mid X_i)/p(Y_j)$ where $p(Y_j)$ is the probability that a randomly selected transaction will contain products Y_j. Lift is in place to show the difference between the confidence of a rule and the expected confidence (Allenby, 2010) and is measured as a ratio. For example, if the lift of "if wine then cheese" is 2, it means customers who purchase wine are 2 times more likely to purchase cheese than randomly chosen customers. Therefore, if lift $(\{X_i\} \Rightarrow \{Y_j\})$ is larger than 1, it indicates that X_i results in an upward lift on Y_j. An interesting case is that if the lift of a rule is very low, it implies that the two sets of products are substitutes (e.g., whisky and gin) which tend not to be in the same basket very often.

Market basket analysis is commonly used to compare stores with different geographic location within a single chain, e.g. which store is creating the highest value for customers? The selling patterns of different stores are not the same due to factors like regional trends, the effectiveness of operation and management, and demographic patterns. For example, customer behavior of a fast food chain in a business area will vary a lot from the one with high traffic of tourists or in rural towns. Market basket analysis can help to figure out the differences between these cases for further business understanding and identifying market segments (Berry, 2004). The process to identify customers' segments consists of applying market basket analysis to the different sets of transaction data and generating effective association rules that explain consistent stories about customers' behaviors. With the same method, market basket analysis can be used for some other types of comparisons:

- Sales patterns during business interventions (marketing campaigns, product launch, etc.) compared with sales before business actions.
- Sales patterns due to seasonal differences.
- Sales patterns before and after pricing changes.

Food for thought 6.2   A coffee chain (the name of the chain is not given for reasons of confidentiality) was founded in 1986 and now has 397 shops worldwide in the UK, USA, France, and China. The company has a mission to create handmade, natural food, avoiding additives and preservatives used in "prepared" and "fast" food on the market. The milk and coffee is 100% organic and there are no "sell-by" dates on the packages. The company offers the unsold food to charity at the end of each day rather than keeping it to sell the next day. As a leading fast food retail company in the UK, the company is well-known for providing high quality, natural, fresh sandwiches, salads and drinks, which is a clear differentiation with respect to other fast food retailers on the high street.

It has put most of its efforts in food management and service delivery so that it has very limited marketing, promotions and advertising interventions. The methods to communicate to its customer are basically by using its official social media account and customer responses obtained by the customer service department. To maximize its two key competitive edges, the company wants learn more about their customers. Although it does not have a loyalty program, the huge amount of data collected every day can provide insights on customer purchase patterns to facilitate better business decisions on value creation through product development and the impact of differentiation strategies.

The company has implemented data warehousing and business intelligence in the last couple of years. Around 50 000 transactions happen in every single shop per month. As a result, the company is quite rich in data and can learn different "stories" from customers. Therefore, the use of market basket analysis can provide the company with very insightful information to help understand the drivers of perceived value among the clients in terms of the products offered and understand the drivers of differentiation better.

Questions:

- If you had a limited budget and time, what locations would you choose to perform a market basket analysis? Justify your choice based on the considerations related to drivers of differentiation and market positioning.

- What time horizon would you consider for your data? What special considerations would you make?
- The mission of the company is "to create, handmade, natural food, avoiding chemicals, additives and preservatives common to 'fast' food on the market today." Based on the mission, what type of products would you expect to find associated in your analysis? Would the location of the shop affect the associations? What implications would the findings have for the strategy of the company? What caveats would you have about the results?

6.6 End of Chapter

Competitive advantage is generated by either offering high value to customers allowing the company to charge higher prices or achieving greater operational efficiency resulting in lower costs than the rest of competitors. Generic strategies are a simple recipe that can be followed when deciding where to position a company with respect to market segments. Generic strategies also indicate what type of actions to implement, on the drivers of costs or differentiation, in order to achieve the market position. However, positioning a company is not simple and implies complex work on the whole company and not only on particular parts of the company.

Operational effectiveness is the realm of traditional management science, as Tables 6.3 and 6.4 show. While operational effectiveness is necessary in order to move activities towards the productivity frontier, it is not sufficient. The differences in value or costs originate from hundreds of activities employed to create, produce, sell and deliver the products or services. Therefore, it is important to map the activities responsible for value creation in a systematic way (see Section 6.2) because sustainable strategy involves the whole system of activities where activities fit and reinforce each other. Managers fail to make choices and visualize the trade-offs especially when there is a strong desire to grow. Managers have to define the strategic position, make the trade-offs while achieving a good fit among the activities supporting the strategic position: either differentiation or cost advantage. This is the realm of strategic analytics: to offer a systemic perspective where the use of management science models is to learn and explore the complexity associated with fitting multiple activities and decisions. It is clear that the use of management science tools provides managers with rational approaches to implement generic strategies by supporting their design or providing strategic advice, as indicated in Figure 6.8.

6.6.1 Revision Questions

1) Find other strategy recipes and compare with the two business strategies.
2) What drivers do you consider most difficult to control in a cost advantage strategy? Use examples of current companies to support your consideration.

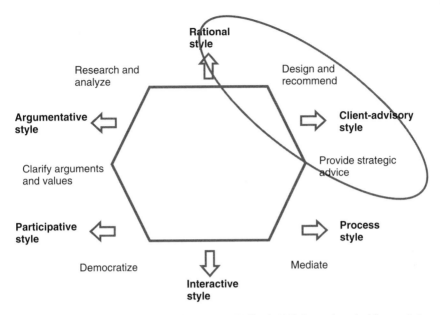

Figure 6.8 Management science styles. Source: Walker (2009). Reproduced with permission of Elsevier.

3) What drivers do you consider most difficult to control in a differentiation advantage strategy? Use examples of current companies to support your consideration.
4) What do you think the proportion of companies following cost advantage vs. differentiation advantage is? What is usually informed in the business press?
5) What other management science tools will you employ to identify, evaluate and address the drivers behind the business strategies?

6.6.2 Case Study: Revisiting Porter's Generic Strategies Using System Dynamics

Following the experience of using system dynamics for understanding the dynamic behavior in chapter 5, this case study is based on previous work developed in Kunc (2010) that extends the model presented in chapter 5. The model presented here portrays managerial decision-making processes using the generic strategies described previously: cost and differentiation advantage. The physical structure of any business is important as it imposes operating constraints (practical rules for how resources work and combine to deliver products and services) on managers. However, the effect of operating policies (managers' decision-making processes related to the level of coordination and development of activities related to the value chain of the company) is more relevant to the dynamic behavior of companies. Porter's generic strategies intend to be proposals for managing operating policies in a coherent way, e.g. if a company follows a cost leadership strategy, operating policies aimed at minimizing costs are key for this company, in order to achieve profitability.

Table 6.5 displays the expected differences in four key areas (market size, customers' requirements, resources that need to be developed to perform activities, and competitors' reactions) faced by companies following the two generic strategies based on an analysis of Porter's generic strategies. These key issues are translated into differences in the managerial decision-making styles employed in the simulation model to explore company performance.

The decision-making processes in the simulation describes decision functions as simple rules of thumb in a similar way to behavioral simulation models (Morecroft, 1985a, 1985b; Sterman, 1987). Figure 6.9 represents a simplified

Table 6.5 Differences in decision-making styles using Porter's generic strategies.

Key areas	Cost advantage	Differentiation advantage
What is the expected market's size?	The expected market size is based on extrapolations of past market growth rate	Market size is based on the number of consumers that the managers expect to attract with the product
What are the requirements of potential customers?	Broad requirements in terms of product characteristics, but highly sensitive to price	The consumers are highly demanding in terms of product characteristics and less sensitive to price
What is the set of resources necessary to perform the activities that satisfy customers' requirements and maintain a competitive advantage?	Management expects to build their competitive advantage by improving the efficiency of the existing operations. Thus, they allocate most of their investment to increasing the effectiveness of their operational resources as a mean to reduce costs. Market share is a key goal for the achievement of economies of scale. However, they try to maintain close product parity with the differentiation leader	Management believes that customers' requirements are mostly related to better products rather than lower prices. Consequently, management allocates most of the investment in the development of new product technology as a means to achieve a competitive advantage.
How will the companies react to competitors' actions?	Management will increase their efforts to reduce costs without increasing the gap with their competitors' product	Management will tend to further differentiate the product from competitors if they face competitive pressures

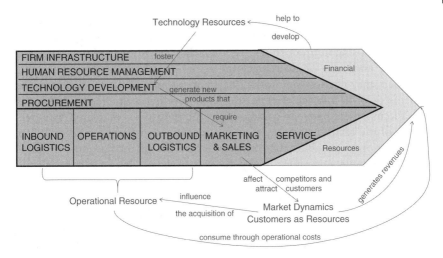

Figure 6.9 Mapping the sectors of the model with the concept of value chain.

view of the structure of the simulated companies using both the value chain and sector map concepts. Management focuses its attention on sources of information related to the performance of the company such as profits or market share in order to coordinate the sectors of the company. There are four sectors that represent the main resources of the simulated company: financial; technology; operational; and market. Financial resources are basically accumulated profits, which are later invested in resources related to the competitive positioning of the company. For example, the level of profits and the existence of financial resources determine the investment in technology. Technology resources are employed to develop new technologies (activity) which increase the attractiveness of the product. Higher product attractiveness and signaling actions (sales and advertising) lead to an increasing number of customers, revenues and profits. This business process is driven by a reinforcing feedback process. An increasing number of customers request more products, which need to be manufactured using operational resources (located in inbound logistics, operations and outbound logistics). Then, operational resources increase operating costs that reduce the level of profits. There is also a balancing feedback process driven by the increasing costs associated with serving customers. These are the trade-offs suggested by Porter when he developed the concept of activity systems.

6.6.2.1 The Model

The model represents a duopoly, which is an industry with only two companies. The model was calibrated so as to have an initial run with the industry in equilibrium given a certain set of initial conditions, e.g. equal number of consumers which are price sensitive and product features sensitive, and no changes in the conditions over time. Consumers use price, product functionality and advertising in order to decide upon the best alternative to adopt, as a first buyer, and, later on, to replace the actual product as a repetitive buyer. Customers may change the product as competitors offer better products for the same price or a lower price for the same product technology. The movement of customers between companies in the industry is regulated by a perception of the relative position of each alternative (cost leader alternative or differentiation leader alternative) in each dimension (price or product technology). For example, customers may perceive situations where the prices of the differentiation leader is 28% higher than the cost leader as good value for money, but only if the differentiation leader's product is at the same time 28% better than the product of the cost leader. Whenever companies in the industry change these perceived relationships, customers will respond by switching to the company that offers the best combination of price and product technology. If the rival does not react promptly, it may find itself out of the market.

The first component of the model is the market dynamics (Figure 6.10) which comprises the total market, potential customers and both companies' customers.

First, the total market changes over time as the product functionality improves attracting people who have not previously been interested in the product. When the industry improves product technology (and then product functionality), the proportion of the total available market interested in the product increases. However, the rate of growth of the industry diminishes over time, as the number of members of the population not using the products of the industry declines leading to the saturation of the market.

Secondly, people who are interested in the product (potential market) decide to adopt one of the products available. There are three effects in the process of adoption. The initial effect is word of mouth generated by the consumers. Then, the additional effect is advertising. The final effect is a basic consumer choice model where a weighted decision is obtained for each product alternative (Cost Leader or Differentiation Leader alternatives). The function includes the relative weights that heterogeneous consumers (Price or Product functionality sensitive adopters) have about each dimension (price, product functionality or advertising) and the relative strength of each product alternative (e.g. Cost Leader product functionality compared with average product functionality). The function provides an overall value for each alternative in terms of market share of the potential customers adopting the product.

Thirdly, customers change their products as companies offer better products (Differentiation Leader) or lower price (Cost Leader). The movement of customers between companies in the industry is driven by a perception of the relative position of each product alternative (Cost Leader or Differentiation Leader alternatives) in each consumer dimension (price or product technology).

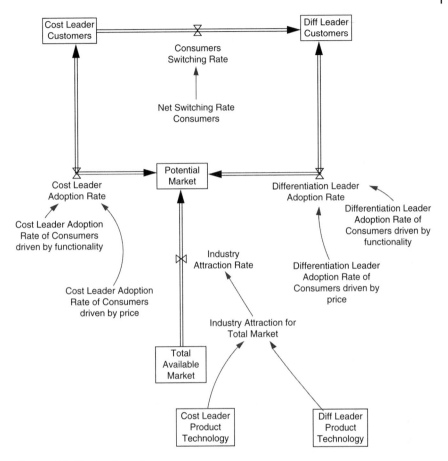

Figure 6.10 Market dynamics.

Operational resources capture the physical and human resources necessary to provide the products requested by customers (e.g. production and transportation). Companies start with an initial endowment of resources that reflect their initial investments. The development of these resources depends on the expectations that managers have about the evolution of the market size, which basically reflects a simple extrapolation of current growth. Operational efficiency determines the productivity per unit of operational resources. Higher productivity reduces the cost per unit of product in addition to the economies of scale obtained by the level of the operational resource. Operational resources are subject to a normal depreciation rate; however, when the company changes its technology the normal depreciation rate increases due to technological obsolescence. The basic cost per unit of product decreases influenced by the effect of economies of scale. Figure 6.11

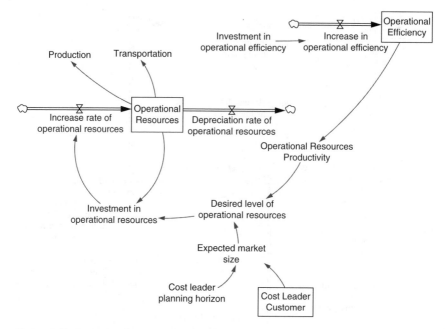

Figure 6.11 Operational resources.

presents a simplified stock and flow diagram of the operational resources sector.

Technology resources comprise two types of resources: Product technology and Operational efficiency (Figure 6.12). Product technology describes the technological level of the product and is a key resource for companies following a differentiation strategy. Product technology represents an index of the level of the product characteristics. The product characteristics can be directly associated to the level of consumers' requirements; for example, a product technology level of 100 is close enough to cover all the possible consumers' requirements, and, consequently, the company can attract a huge number of consumers from the potential market. A higher product technology level relative to competitors' technology level will attract customers from existing competitors. Cost Leaders will invest less to change the technology of its products because it erodes the gains obtained from investing in operational efficiency. However, if there is a widening gap between the Differentiation Leader's product and Cost Leader's product technologies, a Cost Leader company will allocate some resources to promptly reduce the existing gap (Porter 1998: chapter 3). Decisions to change the level of the product technology are implemented through the allocation of financial resources.

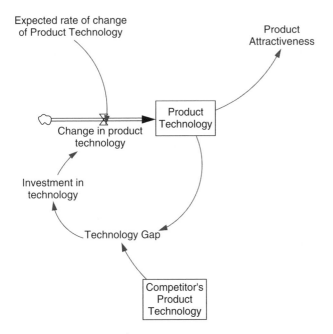

Figure 6.12 Operational resources.

Operational efficiency indicates the level of productivity of the operational resources and is a key resource for companies following a cost leadership strategy. The management of a company can also invest financial resources to increase the efficiency of operational resources. Operational efficiency represents the cumulative efforts of the company to refine the actual operating technology for the existing type of products. Operational efficiency reflects the management's efforts to reduce costs independently of the economies of scale. Operational efficiency is related to the concept of process innovation (Porter (1998: chapter 8). Management following a Cost Leader strategy believes that the main competitive advantage is to have the lowest cost so management will invest more resources to increase the efficiency of its operational resources and less in the technology of the product.

The management decisions in the model describe functions as simple rules of thumb where decisions are driven by goal adjustment processes. Goals are one of the key outputs in strategic planning as they are employed to guide organizations towards the outcomes defined by the strategies. For each resource, a goal is defined to control it according to the generic strategy being implemented. For example, a cost-oriented strategy will require a stable operating income, so the goal is keeping the profit rate similar to previous periods. Table 6.6 presents the list of goals for each type of resource under different generic strategies.

Table 6.6 Main decision-making processes existing in each model of the company.

Management decisions	Cost-oriented company	Differentiation-oriented company
Financial resources	The objective is to maintain a stable operating income. If actual profit rate is lower than past profit rate, more financial resources will be allocated to the development of technology or operational efficiency in order to increase revenues	The objective is to maintain a stable operating income. The evolution of profits determines the intensity of the resources allocated to technology development
Technology resources	The configuration of technology resources is principally oriented to reduce costs by increasing operating operational efficiency. However, if there is an important gap with the competitor's product, resources allocated to technology are mostly used to reduce the gap with the competitor's technology	The source of competitive advantage is believed to be the development of new products. Consequently, the resources are mostly allocated to develop the product technology
Operational resources	The expected size of the market, which is adjusted by an extrapolation of the actual market growth rate, determines the expansion rate of this asset stock	Operational resources are developed over time based on the management's expected size of the market. Managers have defined a priori a certain market size
Market sector/ Competitive actions	Price: It aims to be lowest in the market by reducing costs of goods sold and, later on, gross margin Advertising intensity: lower budget than the Differentiation Leader	Price: higher than average in market but it will tend to cut gross margin aggressively if the expected market size is not achieved. However, it will increase the price very fast when the expectations about market size achieved are fulfilled Advertising intensity: highly intensive

Here are a few questions that you can answer using the simulation model:

1) Which company will achieve the highest market share if the market is split evenly between price sensitive and product feature sensitive consumers?

2) What is the impact on prices for both companies when a differentiation advantage company wants to achieve a high market share? Adjust variable

"Differentiation leader expected market size" from it current value to 25% and 50% higher.

3) What will happen to a cost advantage company if the product technology gap is large? Adjust variable "Differentiation leader Product technology" from its current value to 25% and 50% higher.

4) What will be the best possible combination of goal setting for both companies for the previous two variables?

References

Agrawal, R., Imieliński, T., and Swami, A. (1993). Mining association rules between sets of items in large databases. *ACM Sigmod Record*, 22(2), 207–216.

Ali, A.I., Ghoniem, A., and Franke, A. (2014). Evaluating capacity management tactics for a legacy manufacturing plant. *Journal of the Operational Research Society*, 65(9), 1361–1370.

Allenby, G.M. (ed.) (2010). Perspectives on Promotion and Database Marketing: The Collected Works of Robert C. Blattberg. World Scientific.

Bell, P.C., Anderson, C.K., and Kaiser, S.P. (2003) Strategic Operations Research and the Edelman Prize Finalist Applications 1989–1998. *Operations Research*, 51(1), 17–31.

Bell, P.C. and Chen, J. (2006). Cutting costs or enhancing revenues? An example of a multi-product firm with impatient customers illustrates an important choice facing operational researchers. *Journal of the Operational Research Society*, 57, 443–449.

Berry, M.W. (2004). Survey of text mining. *Computing Reviews*, 45(9), 548–560.

Blischok, T. (1995). Every transaction tells a story. *Chain Store Age Executive with Shopping Center Age*, 71(3), 50–57.

Chapman, C. and Feit, E.M. (2015). R for Marketing Research and Analytics. Springer.

Delanote, S., Leus, R., and Talla Nobibon, F. (2013). Optimization of the annual planning of targeted offers in direct marketing. *Journal of the Operational Research Society*, 64, 1770–1779.

Ferrier, G.D. and Valdmanis, V.G. (2004). Do mergers improve hospital productivity? *Journal of the Operational Research Society*, 55, 1071–1080.

Gary, M.S. (2005). Implementation strategy and performance outcomes in related diversification. *Strategic Management Journal*, 26, 643–664.

Jain, S. (2008). Decision sciences: A story of excellence at Hewlett-Packard. *OR/MS Today*, 35(2).

Hood, N., Clarke, G., and Clarke, M. (2016). Segmenting the growing UK convenience store market for retail location planning. *The International Review of Retail, Distribution and Consumer Research*, 26(2), 113–136.

Kim, W.C. and Mauborgne, R. (2005). Blue Ocean Strategy: How to Create Uncontested Market Space and Make the Competition Irrelevant. Harvard Business School Press.

Kunc, M. (2010). Revisiting Porter's Generic Strategies using System Dynamics: When taking book's recipes conduces your organization to dysfunctional behavior in a competitive environment. In: Computational Analysis of Firms' Organization and Strategic Behavior (ed. E. Mollona), 152–169. Routledge.

Kunc, M. and Morecroft, J. (2007). System dynamics modeling for strategic development. In: Supporting Strategy: Frameworks, Methods and Models, 157–189. Jon Wiley & Sons, Ltd.

Lepak D.P., Smith K.G., and Taylor, M.S. (2007). Value creation and value capture: a multilevel perspective. *Academy of Management Review*, 32(1), 180.

Mild, A. and Reutterer, T. (2003). An improved collaborative filtering approach for predicting cross-category purchases based on binary market basket data. *Journal of Retailing and Consumer Services*, 10(3), 123–133.

Morecroft, J. (1985a). The feedback view of business policy and strategy. *System Dynamics Review*, 1(1), 4–19.

Morecroft, J. (1985b). Rationality in the analysis of behavioral simulation models. *Management Science*, 31(7), 900–916.

Nemet, G.F. (2006). Beyond the learning curve: factors influencing cost reductions in photovoltaics. *Energy Policy*, 34(17), 3218–3232.

Nishi, D. (2005). Market-basket mystery. *Retail Technology Quarterly*, 12A, 12–14.

Osterwalder, A. and Pigneur, Y. (2010). Business Model Generation: a Handbook for Visionaries, Game Changers, and Challengers. John Wiley & Sons, Inc.

Porter, M.E. (1996). What is strategy? Harvard Business Review, November–December, 61–78.

Porter, M.E. (1998). Competitive Advantage: Creating and Sustaining Superior Performance. The Free Press.

Russell, G.J. and Petersen, A. (2000). Analysis of cross category dependence in market basket selection. *Journal of Retailing*, 76(3), 367–392.

Solnet, D., Boztug, Y., and Dolnicar, S. (2016). An untapped gold mine? Exploring the potential of market basket analysis to grow hotel revenue. *International Journal of Hospitality Management*, 56, 119–125.

Sterman, J.D. (1987). Testing behavioral simulation models by direct experimentation. *Management Science*, 33(12), 1572–1592.

Subramanian, R., Scheff, R.P., Quillinan, J.D., et al. (1994). Coldstart: fleet assignment at delta air lines. *Interfaces*, 24(1), 104–120.

Taube-Netto, M. (1996). Integrated planning for poultry production at Sadia. *Interfaces*, 26(1), 38–53.

Walker, W.E. (2009). Does the best practice of rational-style model based policy analysis already include ethical considerations? *Omega*, 37(6), 1051–1062.

Futher Reading

Chen, H., Chiang, R.H., and Storey, V.C. (2012). Business intelligence and analytics: from big data to big impact. *MIS Quarterly*, 36(4), 1165–1188.

7

Dynamic Resource Management

Objectives

1) To define a resource-based view of organizations
2) To learn the origin of dynamic performance in companies
3) To identify analytic tools to manage a company dynamically

Learning outcomes and managerial capabilities developed

1) To be able to use a framework for decision making under a resource-based paradigm
2) To manage resources and capabilities using a dynamic perspective

---

Chapter 6 discussed a set of strategies used to deliver value to consumers in markets: differentiation or cost advantages. The implementation of strategies implies identifying and nurturing activities that deliver the value proposition embedded in the strategic intent. One aspect that has not been discussed in Chapter 6 is how to develop and deliver those activities over time. The answer from the strategic management field is to deliver activities through the use of resources and capabilities. However, the use of resources and capabilities to implement strategy has other considerations. Resources and capabilities offer better anchors for the design of long-term sustainable strategies than adapting continuously to market changes and the product/industry life cycle (see Chapter 5) (Grant, 2013). Additionally, it is more difficult to build new resources and capabilities to serve current customers who are looking for something different than to employ existing resources and capabilities to serve new customers who may be looking for products developed with them, e.g. Apple employed the same resources and capabilities, such as technology, design and brand image, to deliver new products (from computers to smartphones to watches) to new customers rather than focusing only on its computer users.

Strategic Analytics: Integrating Management Science and Strategy, First Edition. Martin Kunc.
© 2019 John Wiley & Sons Ltd. Published 2019 by John Wiley & Sons Ltd.
Companion website: www.wiley.com/go/kunc/strategic-analytics

There are also linkages between resources and the structure of the industry, e.g. Porter's Five Forces (Grant, 2013). First, competitive positions are sustained by the existence of barriers to entry, which result from the ownership of difficult to replicate resources such as patents and knowledge. Secondly, the bargaining power of actors is enhanced by owning strategic resources. Thirdly, strategy making as industry selection and positioning (see Chapter 6) leads to the adoption of similar strategies which need similar resources. Similar resources generate competition to acquire resources leading to a reduction of profits in the long term due to increasing costs. As a recipe to overcome the issues mentioned, a resource view of strategy suggests focusing on the unique strengths of the company to design and implement a strategy as opposed to imitating other companies (Barney, 1986, 1991). This chapter discusses the process of strategic planning from this perspective and the use of management science tools to support it.

7.1 Resources and Capabilities

Resources are assets owned, or under sufficient control,[1] by the company, and capabilities are the ability of the company to perform activities. Resources by themselves are not able to deliver activities but they are the basis of the capabilities, e.g. a skilled worker is a resource but the impact of a skilled worker on the organization is only through its ability to perform a certain activity not by simply having the worker under a contract. Without resources and capabilities, the company cannot perform activities. Activities result from the combination of multiple resources and capabilities. Then activities are responsible for creating and delivering value to customers.

It is easier to identify activities (processes) than resources and capabilities because neither resources nor capabilities are usually accounted for in any system of the company. However, there are some useful guidelines to identify them:

- From the strategy perspective, resources are strategic when they are Valuable (they generate value to the company through either capabilities or activities),

---

[1] From this point of view, some resources are not directly owned by the company but the company has sufficient control. Sufficient control implies the possibility of manipulating their level (number or size) over time due to decisions originated by the management in the organization. For example, customers may be a resource if the company can maintain their loyalty over time. However, customers may not fit within the concept of strategic resources (see definition of strategic resources) since customers may be able to change but they are important to generate sustained revenues that can pay for developing or maintaining other strategic resources, e.g. brands. While customers may not be strategic resources per se, they are intrinsically interconnected and mutually dependent with brands, which are strategic resources from a traditional resource-based perspective.

Rare (only the company or a few companies have the resource), Inimitable (they cannot be imitated by another company), and provide Organization (they help other resources as well). This perspective is called the VRIO framework as suggested by Barney and Hesterley (2015). VRIO reduces the number of resources that can be employed in strategic planning substantially. However, additional categories can be considered for resources that have some characteristics but not all of them. For example, a resource, e.g. cash, can be valuable because it supports other resources (Organization) but it is not rare or inimitable. This type may be called a generic resource (Huh, 2013). Another resource can be valuable, rare and inimitable, e.g. a famous actor, but it does not support other resources. This type of resource is called a discrete resource (Miller and Shamsie, 1996).

- Resources can be tangible such as a plant, stores, inventory or cash (Grant, 2013). Tangible resources are easier to identify than intangible resources due to their physical appearance. Tangible resources are constrained in the exploitation of their physical or technological characteristics. For example, a plant by itself may not be a strategic resource because the manufacturing services provided can be replaced (by a third-party manufacturer) – Rare – or easily replicated by competitors (due to its low technological sophistication) – Inimitable. However, a plant may be strategic from the Organization dimension because it helps to control costs which may not be possible if the production is outsourced. Thus, tangible resources may fall into non-VRIO categories such as generic or discrete resources.

- Resources can be intangible such as reputation, technology, intellectual property and brand (Grant, 2013). Intangible resources can be more valuable than tangible resources but some hint of their impact can be observed in the differences between the accounting value of a company and its stock market valuation. Intangible resources can be exploited in more ways than tangible resources, e.g. reputation can be used to sell different products in a range of markets. Intangible resources fulfill the VRIO requisites easier than tangible resources.

- Human resources is a different category than tangible due to the intrinsic relationship between the abilities of the resource, e.g. skills, and the lack of ownership, a company only purchases services from employees (Grant, 2013). Employees tend to stay with a company for a long period of time, a key consideration for resources, even though they can move freely. Employees can be developed over time through training and they can develop through learning processes increasing their value for the company. Similar considerations can be employed for customers: they tend to stay with the company for long periods if the product delivers value and they can increase their value to the company by cooperating with the company through sharing experiences, e.g. social media, or purchasing additional products, e.g. Apple customers buy computers, phones and MP3 players.

- Capabilities can be considered in two levels: organizational and dynamic/ strategic. Organizational capabilities are the abilities to perform a certain activity reliably over time using resources. Organizational capabilities are based on routines. Therefore, they can be identified together with their activities. For example, functional areas can be useful to identify activities and their subsequent capabilities as well as other activity-based methods explained in Chapter 6: an activity system map or a value chain. Similar consideration to VRIO can be employed to distinguish the contribution of the organizational capabilities. Different to organizational capabilities, dynamic capabilities are located at the strategic level. Dynamic capabilities are the abilities by which managers "integrate, build, and reconfigure internal and external [resources and organizational capabilities] to address rapidly changing environments" (Teece et al., 1997: page 516). See also chapter 2. These capabilities are usually related to new value creation processes, e.g. product development, strategic planning, acquisition of resources, and they tend to vary with industry dynamism (Eisenhardt and Martin, 2000). Dynamic capabilities in stable industries (see Chapter 11) tend to be routines based on detailed and analytic processes employing existing knowledge due to predictable outcomes (Eisenhardt and Martin, 2000). Dynamic capabilities in dynamic industries are simple and based on experiential learning and iterative execution due to the unpredictability of the outcomes (Eisenhardt and Martin, 2000).

7.2   Resource Management

Traditionally, the literature on strategic management considers resources as productive factors that can be acquired in strategic factor markets (Barney, 1986) or they can also be asset stocks that can be accumulated over time (Dierickx and Cool, 1989). The strategic factor market logic, which considers resources tradeable like commodities, implies that a company can earn profits above other companies only if the cost of obtaining those strategic resources is less than the value created by that resource in the implementation of a strategy. Barney (1986) indicated only two ways to achieve this situation: a company has specific information about the value of the resource before it acquires it; or the company is lucky because it acquires it without knowing its impact on value creation. Dierickx and Cool (1989) proposed that non-tradeable resources, which cannot be acquired in strategic factor markets, tend to be company specific and therefore must be developed internally. The mechanism of internal resource accumulation is a process with certain characteristics such as time compression diseconomies (a resource cannot be created instantaneously), causal ambiguity (the linkages between resources and the resulting value created is not clear), asset interconnectedness (resources are interconnected), and asset mass efficiencies (certain resources in large quantities produce better outcomes than in small quantities). These characteristics help to sustain a competitive advantage by the internally accumulated resources. However, there are no prescribed methods to manage resources from an operational point of view of strategic implementation, except for Kunc and Morecroft (2010) who propose "resource management" as a description of an operational approach to implement strategy using resources.

The key component of resource management is managerial decision-making (Kunc, 2005; Kunc and Morecroft, 2010). Managerial decision-making is fundamental in this approach because it extends throughout the company and determines which particular resources managers identify as strategically important and, as such, are built over time. This capability for innovative resource building, a dynamic capability, comprises two distinct components: resource conceptualization, a creative managerial cognitive process; and resource management, the operating polices that guide resource accumulation. The result of accumulating strategically relevant resources is heterogeneous company performance. Then company performance feeds back to reinforce or undermine the initial conceptualization of the set of relevant resources as shown in Figure 7.1.

7.2.1 Resource Conceptualization

Strategic resource conceptualization is a creative and sometimes visionary process of defining which resources the business really needs. This is essentially a cognitive process. Interestingly, managers can define different combinations of resources in order to deliver similar value to customers and different combinations can coexist in an industry for two reasons. First, management has a limited capacity to understand complex systems such as the whole interrelationships between the activities comprising the value chain. Thus, management simplifies complexity using metaphors and mental representations in order to handle strategic problems (Huff, 1990). Managerial mental

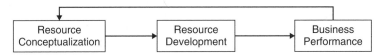

Figure 7.1 Managerial decision-making process responsible for resource management. *Source:* Kunc and Morecroft (2010). Reproduced with permission of John Wiley & Sons.

representations or knowledge structures concerning the system of resources are a result of complex selection, sorting, manipulation and conversion processes shaped by experience and existing knowledge (Walsh, 1995). In other words, mental models affect what managers see, and two managers with different mental models can observe the same industry or even the same company and conceptualize not only the resource system differently but also suggest different relevant resources to achieve competitive advantage. This is one of the key principles behind the replacement of managers when companies are not performing in the way they expected to by shareholders.

Secondly, managers can gain a competitive advantage simply by exploiting limited and diverse representations of the resource system that exists in the industry. Varied managerial conceptualizations of the set of strategic resources, which can be called cognitive asymmetries, facilitate the existence of different and, sometimes, successful strategies. Clearly, the existence of variation of conceptualization of the system of strategic resources is aligned to differentiation strategies where the concept of uniqueness is fundamental to achieve a different positioning in the industry. See Table 7.1 for an example of resources and capabilities for differentiation strategies.

In the case of cost advantage, the resources and capabilities may tend to be similar since the focus is on standard products (with few or no uniqueness) and cost drivers. Thus, managers may try to close their cost positions by imitating

Table 7.1 Differentiation drivers and their resources and capabilities.

Differentiation drivers	Key resources and capabilities	Description of the driver
Strategic choices	R&D (resource) Patents (resource) Service personnel (resource) New product development (capabilities) Customer service (capabilities)	Strategic choices can generate uniqueness for consumers. For example: product configurations and variety, service, commitments to customers, information, level of quality, technology, and human resources policies
Linkages	Logistics systems (resource) Customer relationship management systems (resource) Supply chain coordination (capabilities)	Complex products/services involved more than one activity performed in a coordinate way, especially if it involves external linkages such as channels
Location	Store locations (resource) Real estate management (capabilities)	Being the only option in a specific location offers uniqueness to consumers in the area

Table 7.1 (Continued)

Differentiation drivers	Key resources and capabilities	Description of the driver
Learning	Customer relationship management systems (resource) Knowledge management systems (resource) Customer experience delivery (capabilities)	Learning from consumers' experience to perform key activities better is an important source to being continuously different than competitors imitating products/services
Integration	Logistics (resource) High quality materials production (resource) Distribution systems (resource) Quality assurance (capabilities) Delivery as requested by customers (capabilities)	Delivering certain external activities internally can help the company to offer activities in a way they are envisaged by the company rather than depending on an external supplier
Scale	Brand (resource) Customer relationship management system (resource) Reputation (resource) Development of perceived value (capabilities) Global services (capabilities)	Certain activities, e.g. global sales, require a minimum volume to support other activities, e.g. design, delivering uniqueness
Perception of value	Market research department (resource) Customer relationship management system (resource) Customer experience delivery (capabilities)	Understanding how the product/service is perceived by, and affects, the consumer is a key driver in achieving differentiation. Mostly, helping the buyer to perceive the value correctly is another driver of differentiation

other managers' recipes for success; however, the existence of feedback processes (resources are interconnected) and characteristics of the bundle of resources make it difficult for decision-makers to learn all dimensions of competitors' strategies. Experiential learning, e.g. observing the activities of competitors, may not be useful when behavior is not repeated. For example, if companies are continuously experimenting with different strategies, they will create instability in the behavior of the system of resources. Consequently, managers may observe unexpected changes in activities in competitors, which will reduce their experiential learning and the possibility of reducing asymmetries with competitors. An additional important aspect that prevents the imitation of cost advantage strategies is the concept of time diseconomies (Dierickx and Coo, 1989). Economies of scale are not easily replicated in a short time given the time that is needed to build the necessary scale. Table 7.2 shows a list of cost drivers and the resources and capabilities involved.

To summarize, resource conceptualization is viewed as a managerial cognitive process performed during the design and implementation of strategies. Cognition determines the subset of resources perceived to be strategically

Table 7.2 Cost drivers and related key resources and capabilities.

Cost drivers	Key resources and capabilities	Description
Economies of scale	Manufacturing (resources)	Economies of scale operate when activities perform more efficiently at larger volume, the cost of certain activities can be amortized over greater sales volume or they have less proportional cost increases compared with the output growth
	Shared services (resources)	
	Distribution system (resources)	
	Production at decreasing costs (capabilities)	Diseconomies of scale occur when the increase in an activity leads to complexity in its management and coordination costs.
	Expansion of product/services at similar costs (capabilities)	Technology, specialization and minimum size are important factors affecting economies of scale
Learning	Knowledge management system (resource)	Costs of activities may decline over time as the activity is performed more efficiently due to learning processes. Learning affects the manner in which processes are performed through improvements. Learning can occur due to the volume of activity, slack, level of investment, or simply time
	Skilled personnel (resource)	
	Production process improvement (capabilities)	
Capacity utilization	Yield management systems (resource)	If an activity has its associated costs mainly fixed, the utilization of the activity will have an important impact on the costs associated with it. The configuration of the activity (internal factor), as well as demand fluctuations (external factors), can affect its utilization
	Sales force (resource)	
	Sales fulfillment process (capabilities)	
	Sales forecasting (capabilities)	

Table 7.2 (Continued)

Cost drivers	Key resources and capabilities	Description
Linkages	Planning department (resource) Coordination and supply chain management personnel (resource) Distribution systems (resource) Production planning and coordination (capabilities) Distribution at low cost (capabilities)	If the competitive advantage arises from strongly linked activities (internally and externally), then the costs of any activity depend on the performance of other activities. Therefore, it is necessary for a systemic evaluation of the drivers to consider not only the activity but also all other activities connected with it
Interrelationships between business	Group-based operational and strategy controlling department (resource) Business unit synergy creation process (capabilities)	In multi-business companies, when an activity is shared between business units it provides the possibility of increasing its output (utilization), achieving economies of scale and learning
Timing	Planning department (resource) Forecasting and market research (capabilities)	Timing implies the possibility of enjoying low costs when acquiring the assets for the activity, e.g. business cycles, or obtaining more demand for an activity, e.g. first mover in a market

valuable through attributions about their future effect on company performance, which is a forward-looking choice selection (Gavetti and Levinthal, 2000), in the areas to be considered strategically relevant (see Tables 7.1 and 7.2 for examples for generic strategies). Managerial cognition comprehends managerial beliefs and mental models that serve as a basis for decision making. Managers' vision and value system shape selective perceptions forming the basis for managerial decisions (Adner and Helfat, 2003). The development of these perceived to be strategically relevant resources, which is discussed in the next section, will usually be controlled over time because they will receive managerial attention and managers will attribute the performance of the company to them. However, there may be some resources which are important but are not within the managers' belief and may be a surprise to the managers later (e.g. the concept of "luck" from Barney's point of view). There is no assurance a priori that managers' selection of resources is correct. If the selection proves to be effective, then managers' investment in building them up will transform them into resources that are costly to imitate due to time compression diseconomies (in the cost advantage) or complex interdependencies (in the differentiation advantage).

Another possibility is to implement strategies with little foresight, then based on market feedback recognize the sources of their performance retrospectively, and further develop and exploit the sources of strength. This view is emergent in contrast to the design approach to strategy (Mintzberg et al., 1998; Gavetti and Levinthal, 2000) suggested. In this case, managerial cognition is not imprinted by beliefs but it develops over time based on learning from success and failures, as a hypothesis-testing behavior.

7.2.2 Resource Development

This step consists of controlling the acquisition and composition of resources over time. The process can be represented as purposeful adjustment of resources through goal-seeking information feedback decisions (Sterman, 2000: Morecroft, 2002). Decisions lead to corrective actions intended to close observed gaps between desired and actual resource levels (Figure 7.2). Resource development is an information processing activity which is imperfect,

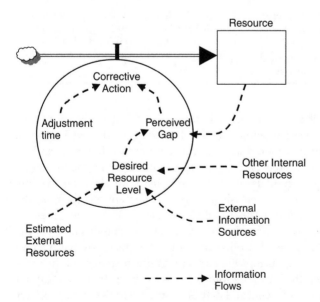

Figure 7.2 Resource development concept. *Source:* Adapted from Morecroft (2002).

judgmental and behavioral – subject to the practical constraints of bounded rationality (Morecroft, 1985).

Practically, every manager has a large number of information sources available to control the development of a company's resources. However, each manager selects and uses only a small fraction of all available information due to background education, experience and time to define the desired level of their resources. Desired resource levels are operating goals linked to the overall strategy. Hopefully, the achievement of local goals leads to a successful implementation of strategy, thereby achieving a competitive advantage.

A different perspective regarding resource development is presented in the field of dynamic capabilities. Eisenhardt and Martin (2000: page 1107) propose a definition of dynamic capabilities as "the company's processes that use resources – specifically the processes to integrate, reconfigure, gain, and release resources – to match and even create market change." Sirmon et al., (2007) suggest resource management processes consist of three main processes:

- Structuring involves purchasing resources, developing resource internally and divesting resources.
- Bundling relates to combining resources to develop capabilities: incremental improvements to existing capabilities, extending current capabilities to new markets, and creating new capabilities.
- Leveraging implies the use of capabilities to create value through mobilizing capabilities to exploit opportunities, coordinating the capabilities by integrating multiple capabilities, and deploying the configurations to implement the strategy.

7.2.3 Business Performance

The decision-making process proposed is complete when information about business performance feeds back to modify or reinforces the initial conceptualization of the relevant resources for implementing the strategy, as shown in Figure 7.1. The management of resources is evolving and dynamic as managers adapt to environmental contingencies and market results, where changes in the resource are stimulated by the lack of achievement of goals (see Section 7.2.2) and are directed toward finding a solution to performance problems.

Resources and the competitive environment are both essential in the strategy-making process. A business can be viewed as a set of interdependencies among resources forming a unified system that comprises a network of interconnected internal and external resources. While not all resources of the system may be strategically relevant under certain circumstances, all of them are responsible for the performance of the business over time. Companies as open systems of resources are closely interrelated with their environments, and the managerial capability to acquire and maintain a well-balanced set of resources determines the performance and competitive advantage of the company.

However, management actions aimed at meeting the company's goals affect, unintentionally, the resources of other rival organizations, leading to competitive reactions that will sooner or later influence or even redefine the configuration of resources needed to compete effectively. Hence, the achievement of an appropriate balance of resources is not static but dynamic and often uncertain due to the reactions of rivals who try to change the competitive landscape, and consequently undermine or invalidate the established resource position.

On strategic issues, managers must draw conclusions and make commitments based on insufficient, unclear, or conflicting information about the results obtained from their investments (King, 2007). There are two types of uncertainties that affect the understanding of the business performance:

1) **Internal causal ambiguity.** This concept refers to the degree of understanding of the relationship between resource management actions and the resulting business performance. A higher degree of causal ambiguity means lower levels of understanding. One of the key drivers of causal ambiguity is dynamic complexity. Dynamic complexity exists due to three factors. First, delays between actions and the performance response. For example, investment in a brand may not be observed until months or years later. Secondly, misperceptions of the feedback processes existing in dynamic environments given the existence of multiple interacting feedback processes. For example, the growth of customers may be affected positively by building a brand but negatively by not investing in resources related to customers' services. Thus, the resulting effect on business performance is difficult to quantify. Thirdly, non-linear cause-effect relationships existing between resources which make it difficult to calculate relative results of investments. For example, investing in a manufacturing plant which is subject to economies of scale will not provide a linear decline in costs and its transference to price will be influenced by the costs of other resources related to manufacturing, e.g. logistics, raw materials, etc.

2) **External causal ambiguity.** The degree of understanding of the relationship between resource management actions and the resulting business performance can also be affected by the complexity existing in the dynamics of industries driven by processes such as rivalry, industry life cycle, etc. Motivations of other managers, which determine industry rivalry, can be very difficult to read and incorporate their effects on the business performance. Moreover, the rival managers are also subject to similar internal causal ambiguity. Industry life cycle can be an important factor in

confounding the information coming from the maker. For example, a growth of low price products or services can indicate either decline or growth of an industry. A decline is driven by decreasing demand of the product and a fight for market share and volume, e.g. consumer goods is a typical case. Growth of an industry can occur when low price uncovers new market segments such as the case of low-cost airlines.

Learning processes arising from connecting the business performance to resource management and resource conceptualization are critical in improving decision making over time. However, it will not be easy to learn about the best set of resources for two reasons. First, if too many resources change simultaneously, the ability to understand the impact of resource management decisions is reduced due to the interconnectedness between resources. Secondly, delays, or temporal distance, can lead managers to attribute business performance to resources that are being managed now but are not related to the current performance.

7.3 Integrating Management Science into Strategic Management

We are going to discuss the tools from the management science field that can be employed to support dynamic resource management. The first tool is based on a qualitative method, resource mapping, to support managerial cognition in order to select the set of resources and understand their linkages. The second tool is an integration of resource mapping with a simulation method to develop resources under future scenarios. The third tool, decision trees, provides a simplified way of evaluating the development of resources under conditions of uncertainty using probabilities. Finally, there is a discussion of the use of decision trees within analytics.

7.3.1 Resource Conceptualization Using Resource Mapping (as a Problem Structuring Method)

Basically, there are two procedures to conceptualize resources. First, Barney (1995) introduced the VRIO framework to identify what resources are important for sustainable competitive advantage by considering the following questions:

- How valuable is the resource? Resources have to provide little sustainable advantage for the company. For example, resources (particularly mobile resources) such as equipment, staff, and suppliers may not be valuable to sustain an advantage.

- How replicable is the resource? Resources that can be easily copied by rivals offer little scope for competitive advantage.
- Can the resource be substituted? If the business can fulfill its demands using two indistinct resources then the resources cannot sustain competitive advantage. Resources cannot be copied or traded.
- Are the resources complementary? Resources work together with other resources but there are different levels of interdependency. For example, brand is of little value without the distribution channels to generate sales.

Warren (2002) suggests problems with the VRIO framework such as:

- It is difficult to find a resource which is valuable for all strategies, completely non-tradeable, or totally impossible to copy or substitute.
- VRIO fails to portray the inherent dynamic nature of the resources. There is always the problem of how fast a resource can be built or may decay (resource management).
- VRIO does not consider the resource interdependencies so it is necessary to capture how resources actually work together through time.

Problem structuring methods, which are a stream of management science developed mostly in the UK, helps managers to represent the complex problems, analyze the problem and bring solutions for them based on the facilitated workshops. Mingers and Rosenhead (2004), who are two of the key authors in the problem structuring methods area, identify the following as characteristic of problem structuring methods: enable several alternative perspectives to be brought into conjunction with each other and operate iteratively so that the representation adjusts to reflect the state and stage of discussion among the actors. One of the problem structuring methods specifically designed for supporting the conceptualization of resources is called resource mapping (Kunc and Morecroft, 2009).

Resource mapping consists of a series of steps which lead to obtaining a resource map, which is a picture or visual aid to understand the set of strategic resources, their sources of dynamic change and the interdependencies among them. Resource mapping can be performed with individuals or groups for solving strategic problems or negotiation about strategy. Through resource mapping, the managers or management team discuss their different perspectives about the resources deemed strategically important and how to manage them. Resource maps, which are the outcome of a resource mapping process, are stock and flow diagrams similar to strategic architecture maps (Warren, 2002). An example of a stock and flow diagram is shown in Figure 7.2 where a resource is represented as a box, the adjustment process of a resource is a flow, and the decisions to control the adjustment process are valves. Stocks represent the resources as asset accumulation processes described by Dierickx and Cool (1989). Flows are the increases and decreases in the resources controlled by the resource management processes as presented in Figure 7.2. Then, the set of connectors or linkages between resources and flows reflect the causal attributions perceived by the managers or management team. While the resource map can be transformed into a system dynamics model adding parameters and equations to formalize the dynamics of the stocks and flows, resource maps can be considered as pictures to focalize the resource conceptualization process. The typical resource mapping process is presented in Table 7.3.

Table 7.3 Resource mapping process.

Stage	Activities
1) Identifying resources and capabilities	Previous explanation of the concept of resources and capabilities, managers identify resources/capabilities perceived to be fundamental for the performance of the business without any limitation
2) Assessing the strength and importance of the resources and capabilities	Managers discuss a numerical evaluation (1–10) for each of the resources/capabilities identified in terms of their strategic importance and relative strength with respect to competitors. The evaluation is plotted on a 2×2 matrix where one dimension is importance divided into low (5 or less) and high (6–10) and the other is strength also divided into low (5 or less) and high (6–10). Each quadrant shows the combination of low/high values for the resources/capabilities in each dimension
3) Mapping resources and capabilities	Using specific notation, participants prepare a resource map in four steps. First, they draw (boxes) only the resources that are strategically important. Secondly, they identify the processes (flows) responsible for increasing or decreasing the resources. Thirdly, the relationships between resources and flows are presented using connectors and type of relationship (if both move in the same direction the sign is positive or if they move in opposite directions the sign is negative). Fourthly, feedback processes are recognized and labeled as either reinforcing (growth) or balancing (stagnation)
4) Quantifying resources and capabilities	Each resource has a certain level related to the actual accumulation of the resource in the business. The level needs to be indicated in the resource map. Potentially, a desired level for the resource given the future strategic plans can be considered in the map to understand the adjustment for the resource

Food for thought 7.1 Traditional bookstores were different from modern bookstores. Traditional bookstores had only one mission: to sell books. Therefore, they were simple in terms of shop design and layout. Now, consumers shop at large stores which conveniently carry books and other entertainment merchandise while small-scale bookstores have closed because of low customer traffic. Independent bookstores continue to exist in spite of big chain book retailers and online services while some independent bookstores, which are mainly specialists, are also using the Internet to increase bookstore sales. Some bookstores serving niche markets moved completely to e-commerce to increase their reach. However, some people still enjoy the browsing experience gained solely from visiting stores. Some business models, such as Waterstones in the UK, try to have their stores in strategic locations in the high streets followed by a unique design following new trends.

The sales of printed books decreased in the main markets while sales of digital books increased substantially. The e-book market is exploited by both pure internet players such as Amazon and other chains with presence in the high street such as WHSmith in the UK. Amazon has become the largest seller of books on the internet with its differentiated offerings, customer service, and low prices.

Address the following issues:

- What are the key strategic resources and capabilities of a bookstore chain? And of an independent bookstore?
- Find information about the number of bookstores over a period of 15 years and map it with the sales of books (print and e-book). Is the number of the bookstores following sales of books in print? What other resources and capabilities can be linked to sales of books in print? What drivers may be affecting the trend? If you were a bookstore (either independent or a chain), how would you manage your resources (think in terms of the three processes mentioned by Sirmon et al., 2007) and capabilities?
- What are the key strategic resources and capabilities for a pure internet bookstore? How can a pure internet bookstore gain market share? What will be the main ambiguity between the development of the resources/capabilities and the resulting performance in terms of market share and profits? Think about the issues faced by dot.com companies.
- Figure 7.3 shows a resource map of a bookstore chain. Identify the resources and capabilities in the map and write down the feedback processes that you can observe in the resource map as if telling a story. What are the critical resources? Why? What external factors are missing in the map? What resource does it need to develop (be included in the resource map) to compete with Amazon?

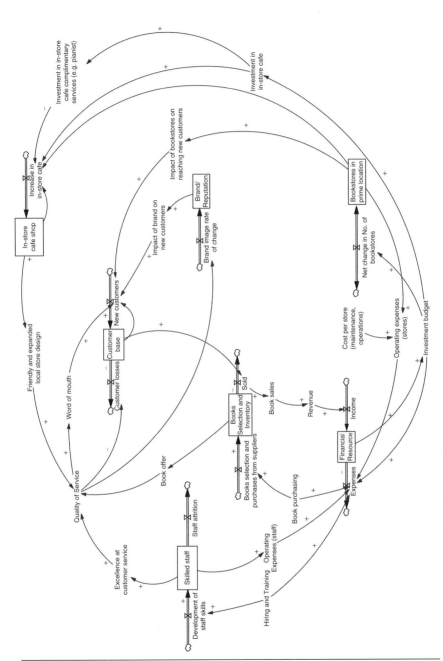

Figure 7.3 Resource map of a bookstore chain.

7.3.2 Resource Development Using Resource Mapping, System Dynamics and Scenarios

The resource development process can be represented as purposeful adjustment of resources towards goals, as presented in Figure 7.2, using system dynamics modeling (Sterman, 2000; Morecroft, 2015). Since goals are defined as part of the strategic planning process, investment decisions (which follow the strategic plan) are corrective actions used to close observed gaps between desired and actual resources. The implementation of system dynamics modeling in this context implies the following aspects:

1) Resources can increase due to actions performed by exogenous actors or factors. For example, cash inflows from revenues, which increase cash balance (resource), are generated by customers' purchases. A factor affecting human resources departures is salaries in the market.
2) Resources can decrease by factors that are not related to managerial actions specific for the resource. For example, departures from human resources can be influenced simply by tiredness from having large workloads.
3) Increase in a resource can result in a decline in another resource due to their interconnectedness and is performed without a specific managerial action, i.e. it is performed by an organizational process. For example, customers' purchases, which increase cash balance (resource), decrease inventory (resource).
4) Increase in a resource is indirectly and non-linearly affected by the current level or increase in another resource and is generated without a specific managerial action, even by an external actor. For example, cash inflow from revenues can be associated non-linearly with the current level or increase in brand or reputation since customers usually buy a product after considering the brand or the reputation.
5) Resources are purposefully managed when there is an information processing task comprising inputs, process, and outputs. The inputs are originated from multiple sources: resources, external information (markets), and internal information (financial). The information processing task involves goal formation (desired level of the resource), evaluating the gap between desired and actual level, and a remedial action (the change of the resource to reach the desired level) (Morecroft, 2015). The output is the remedial action. The impact of the remedial action is not immediate but it takes time, so the adjustment time needs to be considered in the flows affecting a resource (Figure 7.2). The basic equation for the calculation of the change in a resource is:

$$Change\,in\,resource = (Desired\,level\,of\,the\,resource - Actual\,level\,of\,the\,resource)\,/\,Adjustment\,time$$

6) Financial performance results from associating costs and revenues to the level of the strategic resources responsible for the business operations. For example, sales force, as a resource, generates costs from their salaries and operational

expenses but it can also generate revenues from the capability to sell products.

7) Investment in resources comprises the rate of change of the resource (inflow) and the amount of money associated with the rate of change. For example, an expansion in manufacturing capacity (a change in the level of a resource) can be associated with a certain amount of money necessary to generate an additional unit of capacity.

8) Disinvestment in resources involves costs associated with the reduction of the resource. For example, the reduction of human resources through lay-offs involves legal costs and salaries.

Secondly, resource development processes need to include the impact of external factors, as mentioned previously in point 1. Kunc and O'Brien (2017) propose to combine resource mapping with scenarios to develop a comprehensive method covering both external and internal analysis for dynamic resource management. Table 7.4 shows the steps of the method that continue from step 3 in Table 7.3.

Table 7.4 Integrating external and internal analyses: scenarios and resource mapping.

Stage	Activities
4) Mapping the impact of external events on resources and capabilities/ Integrating the insights from scenarios	Once the resource map is completed, managers connect the internal aspects of the business (resources and capabilities) with the external environment (variables identified during the scenario process). Managers connect the scenario variables to the resources/capabilities that can be directly affected by them, e.g. new technological advances (scenario variable) affect the portfolio of patents (resource). Scenario variables can take qualitative or quantitative values depending on the scenarios, e.g. new technological advances can be high or low so the impact on the portfolio de patents will vary depending on the scenario, and the purpose of the resource mapping process, e.g. present quantitative results
5) Rehearsing future performance paths	Having completed the resource map with the impact of scenarios on the resources/capabilities, managers can rehearse and test the future performance paths for the business by considering three aspects: new strategies in a stable environment; changes in the environment affecting current strategies; or new strategies responding to the impact of the changes in the environment. Essentially, rehearsing strategies using the resource maps consists of following the linkages between resources and understanding the accumulation processes for the different resources/capabilities. This process is defined as conceptual simulation. There are two outcomes related to rehearsing future performance paths. The first outcome is understanding if the strategies are internally and logically consistent. The second outcome is evaluating the robustness of strategies in the face of external changes

(Continued)

Table 7.4 (Continued)

Stage	Activities
6) Presenting the results from rehearsing strategies	Results may be presented in two ways: using either a qualitative approach or by following a quantitative approach
	If the managers are satisfied with qualitative insights, the conceptual simulation exercise can be explained using a story-telling approach to narrate the organization's different performance paths in the face of uncertain future
	However, if the managers need numerical results, the resource map can be converted into a System Dynamics model. In this case, the process may extend to gather data and develop the equations behind the resource map in order to develop a quantitative model

7.3.3 Resource Development Under Uncertainty Using Decision Trees

When managers develop strategy, they foresee how their organizations will be in the future and the path they need to follow to reach the destination. Financial tools are usually employed to estimate the value of the business after implementing strategy, e.g. discounted cash flow, but they assume implementation plans tend to be predetermined independently of the occurrence of events. A technique that conveys the uncertainty surrounding the options for developing resources to implement strategy is *decision analysis*. Under this view, implementing strategy is a sequence of major decisions regarding acquisition and development of resources over time surrounded by uncertainty. Decision analysis aims to helping find the best decision (on average) when the decision involves a series of sub-decisions, which imply choices, distributed over time and being affected by certain events. The decisions are not quantitatively complex and the criterion to identify good decisions from bad decisions is clear. Decision analysis involves four elements (Targett, 1996):

1) **Decision tree** represents the sequence of decisions/events. The decision tree includes *decision nodes* that reflect when a decision is made (usually boxes), *event nodes* (usually circles) where an event that will occur is presented and the logical sequence of the decisions and events.
2) **Payoffs** are the outcomes of a decision path followed through the tree. It represents the outcome in monetary or non-monetary terms. They are presented at the final part of the tree (extreme right hand).
3) **Probabilities** are allocated to each event nodes to indicate the likelihood of the event. Events can be market research reports, results from the launch of a product, the outcome of a research project, etc. Probabilities can be logical or theoretical (the possibility of an outcome over a number of outcomes), experimental (based on data), or subjective (judgmental).

4) **Expected monetary value** (EMV) is the average outcome of the decision or event determined by the probability of occurrence of each option and their respective payoffs. Basically, it is the multiplication of the payoff by the probability to obtain it.

Here are some considerations about the method:

1) **Payoffs.** There may be a lack of transparency on the calculation of payoffs unless assumptions/data are thoroughly documented and discussed during the process. Payoffs can be evaluated through sensitivity analysis by varying the different assumptions and developing more than one decision tree with all the potential payoffs. The aim of the sensitivity analysis on the payoffs is to check the robustness of the decision. Robustness is obtained when the optimal path does not change under variations in assumptions and data.

2) **Probabilities.** The sources of information for probabilities tend to be either subjective or logical. However, big data can be a unique source to obtain probabilities from large samples of events if they are captured in the relevant systems. A class of big data can be viewed as samples from a probability distribution over a very large domain and it occurs in almost any setting: financial transactions, sensor nets, etc. (Rubinfeld, 2012). One of the issues is the lack of explicit description of the distribution of probabilities since there are only samples. Therefore, there is a need to estimate parameters and understand basic properties of the underlying probability distribution in order to use the data to calculate the probabilities (Rubinfeld, 2012). Other issues are: elements that have non-zero probability in the distribution; the type of distribution; and the type of probability (joint distribution independent) (Rubinfeld, 2012).

3) **Events.** Probabilities are continuous functions that describe the state of the world but they are transformed into a discrete set of values in order to have a limited, and manageable, number of branches in a decision tree. Discretization of outcomes can generate extreme results in the analysis whilst the future results may not be extreme due to the actions of actors to maintain the status quo. Discretization also shows the impossibility of capturing all aspects of the future, so the continuous function may not even be revealed for decision makers.

4) **EMV.** The EMV is the average outcome of the decision or event determined by the probability of occurrence of each option and their respective payoffs. Basically, it is the multiplication of the payoff by the probability to obtain it. Uncertainty about EMV can be reduced at a certain cost also known as the value of information (see point 2). Decision analysis has one concept to measure the cost of information: expected value of sample information (EVSI), which involves a specific set of information (Taggert, 1996). EVSI gives the value of the information to be compared with the cost of the information to have a maximum amount to pay for the extra information. The

calculation of EVSI is equal to the EMV with the extra information minus the EMV without the extra information.

5) **Interpretation of results.** The EMV will select the option that will be on average the most favorable but this situation does not preclude the possibility of having extremely good and bad outcomes included in the EMV. Therefore, there may be situations where the results are not acceptable such as the absolute magnitude of the payoffs (e.g. billions vs. thousands) compared with the wealth of the company, huge losses for the financial situation of the company with low probabilities can be hidden or large gains with low probabilities to be achieved with low costs can encourage gambling. Consequently, other non-optimal factors independently of EMV can be used to select the desired path, e.g. reputational issues, financial risk.

Targett (1996) suggests five steps to perform decision analysis that mimic the components of decision analysis techniques. Table 7.5 presents the five steps.

Table 7.5 Decision tree process.

Steps	Activities
1) Drawing the decision tree	It involves discussing the sequence of decisions and events together with the relationships between them. It usually starts with a single decision node which leads to different branches determined by the events that will happen after the decision is taken. After the event, a new decision may follow or additional events may branch out. The process is repeated until the last event
2) Including the payoffs	The payoffs are included at the end of all branches of the tree. They may be monetary or non-monetary. The calculation of the payoffs needs to be consistent across all branches and include a final profit to be obtained. Costs related to events or other activities are included in the corresponding nodes
3) Inserting probabilities	Event nodes have probabilities associated to them in order to account for the uncertainty affecting their occurrence. The probabilities are based on three sources: logical; experimental; or subjective
4) Calculating the EMV	Targett (1996) calls this step "roll-back" as it starts from the payoffs and moves backwards to the initial decision commencing the tree. You also begin from the top right of the tree and move to the initial decision. After finishing with the initial decision in one tree, you move to the next branch a level below. In each event node, the EMV is calculated. Then, you compare all the EMVs coming to a decision node and eliminate all of them except the most favorable

Table 7.5 (Continued)

Steps	Activities
5) Presenting the optimal path and defining the risk profile	In this step, the optimal path of the decisions is identified which is the branch with the largest EMV coming to the initial decision A risk profile is also defined as the summary of all the possible outcomes that can occur when the optimal path is followed together with their probabilities. The risk profile shows the probabilities attached to each payoff. One of the key uses is to show the range of outcomes that can be obtained with their probabilities since the EMV can hide a large range of results, including negative results with low probabilities Other considerations can be employed to choose the optimal path depending on the criteria set up by the decision maker

EMV, Expected monetary value.

Food for thought 7.2 Huawei technologies Co. Ltd is a Chinese company providing information communication technology solutions to consumers, enterprises and telecommunication carriers. It is a private company founded by Ren Zhengfei in 1987 in Shenzhen, Guangdong Province. The main business, which accounts for 60% of total revenues, is comprised of networking and telecommunication equipment and services to telecommunication companies. Consumer business and Enterprise business only generate 40% of total revenues (Huawei, 2015).

Nowadays, Huawei is recognized for its innovation and the internationalization strategy implemented in recent years, which led to having sales in more than 170 countries and a third of the world's population. Huawei's sales grew from US$20 billion in 2007 to more than US$40 billion in 2015 when sales of Alcatel dropped from US$25 billion to US$ 10 billion and Ericsson only reached US$28 billion from US$24 billion in the same period. Its key factor is cost performance where the price of Huawei's product decreased by 50% over the same period of time (Bloomberg, 2016). Huawei followed an internationalization strategy as a result of the strong competition faced in China by ZTE, a state-controlled company.

Huawei was a late comer into the telecommunications industry and had to catch up with the leaders in a very short period of time through strong investment in R&D amid the relentless pace of technology innovation in the industry, e.g. from 2G to 5G technology in only 20 years. Huawei now faces some dilemmas in building the next phase of its development: competing on the Internet of Things. Below is a list of the strategic initiatives aimed at acquiring resources in order to maintain the current growth rate. Our task is to find the most robust path for Huawei for the next 5 years.

1) The strategic resource is an R&D facility leading to patents and products for the European market. It will imply building up an R&D facility in Italy with a cost of US$ 5 billion. The expectation is to develop new products for the European

market with a certain probability of achieving certain revenue targets. Products will generate operating profits of US$ 8 billion (50%), US$ 10 billion (30%) or US$ 3 billion (20%) under normal market conditions. If the EU collapses, the expected revenues will decline by 50% with similar probabilities. The expected chance that the EU will collapse is 20%.

2) Another strategic resource necessary to enter into the European market is to establish a joint venture with Siemens to develop products. The development of the joint venture will help to develop additional strategic resources such as knowledge about the German and European markets and products shared with Siemens through co-branding, which will increase reputation. The joint venture will have a cost of US$ 1.5 billion but the property of the innovations will be shared with Siemens. Consequently, the expected net profits will be US$ 2 billion (35%), US$ 1.5 billion (50%) and US$ 1 billion (15%). The same effect of the EU collapse can be applied to this option.

3) Another initiative is to invest aggressively in the manufacturing and sales channel in Latin America by opening a manufacturing facility in Brazil and developing retail stores in the capitals of 10 Latin American countries in order to sell phones and equipment as well as establishing the brand image. An investment of US$ 3 billion in those resources can generate four potential payoffs: US$ 8 billion (30%), US$ 4 billion (20%), US$ 2 billion (25%) or US$ 1 billion (25%).

4) There is an option investing in a short term joint venture with a Latin American mobile company in order to understand the markets better at a cost of US$ 500 million but it will imply lower payoffs with greater certainty. The new payoffs are US$ 2.5 billion (30%), US$ 1 billion (50%) and US$ 800 million (20%).

The top management team at Huawei must to make a robust decision about the next steps in the internationalization strategy and the evolution of the company from an orientation on cost performance and market share to leadership in technology. Figure 7.4 shows the decision tree for the European options. The right-hand side contains all payoffs and each branch leading to a certain payoff is the probability expressed in units, e.g. 30% is presented as 0.30, for obtaining the payoffs. There is one key event which is the collapse of the EU. In each event node, the EMV is calculated as the addition of all payoffs and their respective probability. Table 7.6 contains the calculations of the EMV. The R&D lab can produce an EMV equal to US$ 6.84 billion which is US$ 1.84 billion above the investment required but the joint venture generates a loss of US$ 0.04 billion.

The risk profile for the optimal decision (Table 7.7) in the European option reflects the conditional probabilities originated from the impact of an EU collapse on the resulting outcomes from investing in the R&D lab and the payoffs. The conditional probabilities come from the multiplication law of probabilities where:

$$P(\text{"No EU collapse" and "Best outcome"}) = P(\text{"No EU collapse"})$$
$$\times P(\text{"Best outcome" / "No EU collapse"})$$
$$P(\text{"No EU collapse" and "Best outcome"}) = 0.8 \times 0.3 = 0.24$$

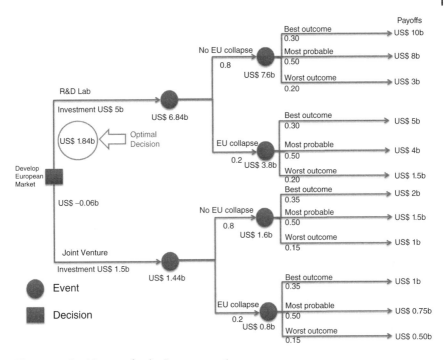

Figure 7.4 Decision tree for the European option.

Table 7.6 EMV calculation.

Branch	Calculation
R&D lab and no EU collapse	US$ 7.6b = 0.30 × US$ 10b + 0.50 × US$ 8b + 0.20 × US$ 3b
R&D lab and EU collapse	US$ 3.8b = 0.30 × US$ 5b + 0.50 × US$ 4b + 0.20 × US$ 1.5b
R&D lab	US$ 6.84b = 0.80 × US$ 7.6b + 0.2 × US$ 3.8b
Join venture and no EU collapse	US$ 1.6b = 0.35 × US$ 2b + 0.50 × US$ 1.5b + 0.15 × US$ 1b
Joint venture and EU collapse	US$ 0.8b = 0.35 × US$ 1b + 0.50 × US$ 0.75b + 0.15 × US$ 0.5b
Joint venture	US$ 1.44b = 0.80 × US$ 1.6b + 0.2 × US$ 0.8b

The risk profile uncovers very interesting information about the potential outcomes. There is a strong impact by a highly successful net payoff (US$ 5 billion) and the total probabilities of the two positive net payoffs is 64%. There is a 36% probability of making losses on the investment although there is only 6% probability to lose US$ 3.5 billion.

Table 7.7   Risk profile.

Outcome	Net payoffs (operating profits less investment)	Probability
No EU collapse and best outcome	US$ 5.0b	$0.24 = 0.80 \times 0.30$
No EU collapse and most probable outcome	US$ 3.0b	$0.40 = 0.80 \times 0.50$
No EU collapse and worst outcome	US$ –2.0b	$0.16 = 0.80 \times 0.20$
EU collapse and best outcome	US$ 0.0b	$0.06 = 0.20 \times 0.30$
EU collapse and most probable outcome	US$ –1.0b	$0.10 = 0.20 \times 0.50$
EU collapse and worst outcome	US$ –3.5b	$0.04 = 0.20 \times 0.20$
	Total =	1.00 (100%)

Your task is to perform a similar study for the Latin American option and integrate both decision trees. After you integrate both decision trees answer the following questions:

- What is optimal decision for Huawei: Europe or Latin America?
- What other considerations can you include to choose a different path? What additional information will be looking to support the choice of the new path? Is there more than one path?
- What limitations can you find with the decision tree developed? What benefits will the use of the decision trees provide?

7.3.4   Developing Decision Trees from Big Data

Decision trees are employed widely to analyze large datasets as a data mining tool. Decision trees are generated by an algorithm that recognizes various ways of dividing data into branches (de Ville and Neville, 2013). The branches form an inverted decision tree that originates with a root node at the top containing the field of the data and spread/distribution of the values of the target variable. Then, the algorithm creates the branches underneath the root node considering decision rules based on identifying the relationships between the variable object of the study (which is located in the root node) and different fields in the data. The values in the input fields (variables characterizing the target variable) are used to estimate the likely value in the target variable. While decision rules are used to show the tree-like network of relationships that characterize the input (rest of the variables in the data) and target values, they can also predict the values for new or unobserved data that contain the values for the inputs but not values for the targets.

Some applications are related to detecting a subset of customers to understand their profitability or target through marketing campaigns. Detecting the right customers help to manage them as a stable resource over time. For companies with thousands or millions of customers, this is an ideal method to decide which customers should be targeted while reducing costs by not performing activities targeting non-profitable customers.

7.3.5 Inferring Business Performance from Management Science Methods

It is clear that the use of management science tools can reduce the causal ambiguity affecting the understanding between the development of resources and the business performance obtained. While numerical analyses are important and necessary, the key aspect to understanding business performance and reducing causal ambiguity is to map the expected relationships between resources/capabilities and the resulting performance. This is essentially a cognitive task and management science tools, such as problem structuring methods and system dynamics, which help to elicit managerial cognition are essential in order to untangle ambiguity related to business performance.

However, two positions related to business performance can be inferred from the management science tools discussed. First, system dynamics, a deterministic and continuous simulation method, offers the possibility of establishing direct relationships between resources/capabilities and business performance. Basically, operational or financial performance can be obtained from attaching respective costs or revenues generated to each resource/capability. Dynamic complexity is originated by the interaction of multiple feedback processes simultaneously; however, each feedback process can be evaluated individually in terms of their causal relationships, reducing the causal ambiguity between resource levels and business performance.

Secondly, decision trees can be employed to elicit a managerial thinking process related to the implementation of strategy through the acquisition and development of resources. The paths of decisions and events described in decision trees offer an account of the dominant logic behind the investment decisions, expected events and resulting payoffs. After a decision tree, the dominant logic is explicit and subject to discussion between the managers and management team. The information from decision trees can be the source for budgeting and financial control. Informally, a set of causal relationships between decisions, events and results is presented in a clear way and accounts for the uncertainties affecting the implementation of strategy.

7.4 End of Chapter

Implementing strategies based on resources and capabilities has not yet been addressed in the field of strategic management with an analytic perspective. Existing methods are either theoretical, e.g. strategic factor markets, or qualitative, e.g. VRIO (Barney and Clark, 2007). One of the key issues of implementing strategies using resources and capabilities is to unambiguously establish the relationship between the resources/capabilities and the resulting business performance. This chapter offers three paths to address these shortcomings. First, there is a process of identification and mapping of the resources and capabilities called resource conceptualization that can be supported with visual interactive tools in workshop environments such as resource mapping. Resource mapping contains the same functionalities as system dynamics without the need to develop a quantitative model. Secondly, there is a process of resource management through investment decisions, controlling factors affecting their levels and understanding their interrelationships. Managing resources involves numerical simulation, i.e. system dynamics, to understand how the investments increase their levels and their levels affect other resources and capabilities. The dynamics of the resources drive the financial performance of the business. In an unusual approach to traditional strategic management, resource development integrates the impact of the environment, which is obtained from scenario analysis, in order to understand the dynamics of resources/capabilities and the business performance in the medium to long term. Thirdly, decision analysis using decision trees offers the opportunity to elicit the sequence of decisions and events that can affect the implementation of a strategy through the investment of resources. Decision trees can provide a base to evaluate the logic and risk profile of the management team. However, the limitations are important in terms of linking the resources to business performance. For example, payoffs need to be calculated in a transparent way including the assumptions and data, especially when resources are interrelated generating dynamic complexity over time. Another important observation is the calculation of the probabilities attached to each of the resulting payoffs and events occurring. Big data can help to calculate probabilities if there is data covering the events the management team expects to happen. This situation comes back to one of the suggestions: discuss as a team in an open-minded workshop all factors (internal and external) affecting the implementation of strategy.

In terms of style (Figure 7.5), the methods/tools discussed in this chapter can be allocated in the process, interactive and participative styles since the main objectives is to elicit as much information as possible about the causal linkages between resources and capabilities and the business performance.

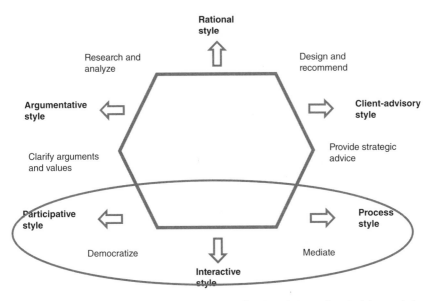

Figure 7.5 Management science styles. *Source:* Walker (2009). Reproduced with permission of Elsevier.

7.4.1 Revision Questions

1) What are the different classifications of resources existing in the literature? What are the types of capabilities discussed in the literature?
2) What are key factors affecting the development of resources? How will you identify the delays in the process of building resources? What will be delays for the resources identified in the previous question?
3) What other management science tools may be suitable for resource management processes?
4) What are the limitations of financial modeling in understanding the business performance?

7.4.2 Case Study: Majestic Wines

Majestic Wine started in 1980 when its wine warehouses opened in order to sell 12-bottle cases directly from the warehouses with the possibility of tasting the wines before buying them. Majestic Wine was listed in the London Stock Exchange in 1996 leading to a period of strong growth. The company currently operates 210 branches in the UK with its headquarters located in Watford. Selling wine directly to the public is not the sole channel of distribution for the company since Majestic acquired other businesses to sell wine (through channels such as business-to-business, online) and have access to the market segment of fine wine for the wealthy. In 1994, Majestic Commercial was established and specialized in serving businesses such as pubs, bars, event companies and hotels. The business still struggles to penetrate the UK's business-to-business market, with a market share of 2.28 % in 2016. In 2009, the group acquired Lay and Wheeler for £6 million – a wine specialist with over 100 years of experience in selling, storing and evaluating fine wine – to gain access to the high-end market. Majestic's most recent acquisition was a £70 million bid for the retailing platform Naked Wines in 2015 in order to improve the digital aspect of the group.

Wines in the UK are sold legally through two types of license: on-trade; and off-trade. On-trade are the sales of alcohol which are consumed directly, such as restaurants, pubs, bars and hotels, in the premises. Off-trade is when consumers purchase alcoholic beverages from retailers such as specialist shops, supermarkets or convenience stores and consume them privately. Supermarkets account for more than 70% of all off-trade sales, especially in the lower end of the price range. Therefore, specialist wine shops focus on selecting good quality wines that can be bundled with others to create attractive offers.

In the case of Majestic, the key resources are numerous and involve diverse levels of strategic importance. Majestic's brand is synonymous with high quality wine and good bargains but supermarket competition can offer the same types of wine at lower prices without promotion. The existing relationship with suppliers (another key resource) is not strong enough to provide competitive advantage by getting better prices from them to fight a price war with supermarkets. Naked Wines' platform is creating value, rarity and something that supports other resources well, e.g. warehouse sales. However, the time required to create a similar platform is not significant enough to stop other businesses joining the e-commerce market, so it only provides a temporary advantage. The two key resources delivering a sustainable competitive advantage are the capability to effectively deliver wine in the UK and the expertise of employees on wine obtained from a training program.

The resource map shown in Figure 7.6 was constructed based on the market development of a wine brand through a wine specialist shop, such as Majestic wine. The model intends to be generalist, so it can be applied to any country with similar sales channels as the UK.

Essentially there are only three resources: wine tasting employees; stores selling the wine; and customers. Two of the resources, stores selling the wine and customers, are embedded into a reinforcing feedback process since customers will buy the product if it is in stores and stores will buy the product only if there are interested customers. There are two drivers of the reinforcing feedback process. First, wine tasting employees persuade stores to sell the wine through wine tasting sessions. Wine tasting employees can convince stores to sell the wine if they find the wine profitable. Stores which stock wine are

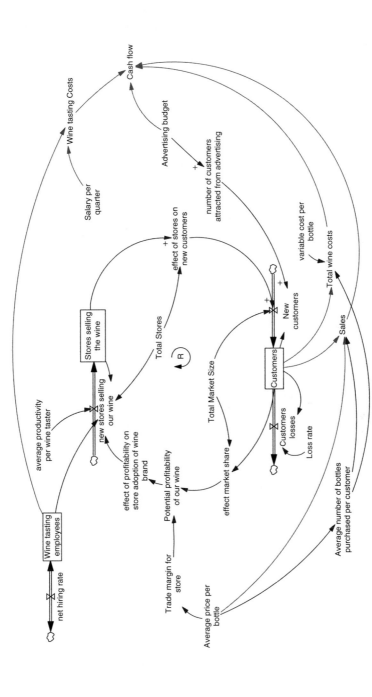

Figure 7.6 Resource map of a wine brand sold through specialist wine stores.

necessary to transform customers who are only aware of the product into customers who will buy the product. Secondly, advertising persuades customers to ask for the wine from the stores. However, customers are not the only factor in making a wine profitable: the trade margin for the store is another driver. The trade margin is directly related to the price of the bottle of wine and the price influences the bottles purchased by customers as well as the profitability of the wine company.

Here are a few questions to consider about the case study:

1) What additional resource will you add to the map for your specific case?
2) What are the external factors in the map? What additional external factors can you include in the resource map?
3) Using the simulation model in the website, answer these two questions:

- What is the best combination of wine tasting employees, average price per bottle and advertising budget in order to achieve positive cash flow in the shortest time? Explain the key aspects affecting the results.
- What is the best combination in order to maximize the cash flow over 3 years? Explain the key aspects affecting the results.

References

Adner, R. and Helfat, C.E. (2003). Corporate effects and dynamic managerial capabilities. *Strategic Management Journal*, October(Special Issue 24), 1011–1025.

Barney, J.B. (1986). Strategic factor markets: expectations, luck and business strategy. *Management Science*, 32, 1231–1241.

Barney, J.B. (1991). Firm resources and sustained competitive advantage. *Journal of Management*, 17, 99–121.

Barney, J.B. (1995). Looking inside for competitive advantage. *The Academy of Management Executive*, 9(4), 49–61.

Barney, J.B. and Clark, D.N. (2007). Resource-based Theory: Creating and Sustaining Competitive Advantage. Oxford University Press.

Barney, J.B. and Hesterly, W. (2015). Strategic Management and Competitive Advantage Concepts and Cases. Pearson.

De Ville, B. and Neville, P. (2013). Decision Trees for Analytics Using SAS Enterprise Miner. SAS Institute.

Dierickx, I. and Cool, K. (1989). Asset stock accumulation and sustainability of competitive advantage. *Management Science*, 35, 1504–1511.

Eisenhardt, K.M. and Martin, J.A. 2000. Dynamic capabilities: What are they? *Strategic Management Journal*, 21, 1105–1121.

Gavetti, G. and Levinthal, D.A. 2000. Looking Forward and looking backward: cognitive and experiential search. *Administrative Science Quarterly*, 45, 113–137.

Grant, R.M. (2013). Contemporary Strategy Analysis: Text and Cases, 8th edn. John Wiley & Sons, Ltd.

Huawei. (2015). Building a Better Connected World. Huawei 2015 Annual Report. http://www.huawei.com/en/press-events/annual-report/2015 (accessed 20 August 2017).

Huff, A.S. (1990). Mapping Strategic Thought. John Wiley & Sons, Ltd.

Huh, K.K. (2013). Strategic resource development process: a behavioral view. PhD thesis. University of Warwick.

King, A.W. (2007). Disentangling interfirm and intrafirm causal ambiguity: A conceptual model of causal ambiguity and sustainable competitive advantage. *Academy of Management Review*, 32(1), 156–178.

Kunc, M.H. (2005). Dynamics of competitive industries: a micro behavioural framework. PhD thesis. London Business School.

Kunc, M. and Morecroft, J.D. (2009). Resource-based strategies and problem structuring: using resource maps to manage resource systems. *Journal of the Operational Research Society*, 60, 191–199.

Kunc, M. and Morecroft, J.D. (2010). Managerial decision making and firm performance under a resource-based paradigm. *Strategic Management Journal*, 31(11), 1164–1182.

Kunc, M. and O'Brien, F.A. (2017). Exploring the development of a methodology for scenario use: Combining scenario and resource mapping approaches. *Technological Forecasting and Social Change*, 124, 150–159.

Miller, D. and Shamsie, J. (1996). The resource-based view of the firm in two environments: the Hollywood film studies from 1936 to 1965. *Academy of Management Journal*, 39, 519–543.

Mingers, J. and Rosenhead, J. (2004). Problem structuring methods in action. *European Journal of Operational Research*, 152(3), 530–554.

Mintzberg, H., Ahlstrand, B. and Lampel, J. (1998). The design school. In: Strategy Safari: A Guided Tour through the Wilds of Strategic Management, 23–45. The Free Press.

Morecroft, J.D. (1985). The feedback view of business policy and strategy. *System Dynamics Review*, 1(1), 4–19.

Morecroft, J.D.W. (2002). Resource management under dynamic complexity. In: Systems Perspectives on Resources, Capabilities and Management Processes, Advanced Series in Management (eds J.D.W. Morecroft, R. Sanchez, and A. Heene), 19–40. Pergamon.

Morecroft, J.D.W. (2015). Strategic Modelling and Business Dynamics: A Feedback Systems View, 2nd edn. John Wiley & Sons, Ltd.

Rubinfeld, R.(2012). Taming big probability distributions. *XRDS: Crossroads, The ACM Magazine for Students*, 19(1), 24–28.

Sirmon, D.G., Hitt, M.A., and Ireland, R.D. (2007). Managing firm resources in dynamic environments to create value: Looking inside the black box. *Academy of Management Review*, 32(1), 273–292.

Sterman, J.D. (2000). Business Dynamics: Systems Thinking and Modeling for a Complex World. Irwin/McGraw-Hill.

Targett, D. (1996). Analytical Decision Making. Pitman Publishing.

Teece, D.J., Pisano, G.P., and Shuen, A. (1997). Dynamic capabilities and strategic management. *Strategic Management Journal*, 18, 509–533.

Walker, W.E. (2009). Does the best practice of rational-style model based policy analysis already include ethical considerations? *Omega*, 37(6), 1051–1062.

Walsh, J.P. (1995). Managerial and organizational cognition: Notes from a trip down memory lane. *Organization Science*, 6(3), 280–321.

Warren, K. (2002). Competitive Strategy Dynamics. John Wiley & Sons, Ltd.

Futher Reading

Albright, C. and Winston, W.L. (2010). Business Analytics: Data Analysis & Decision Making. Cengage Learning.

Ledolter, J. (2013). Data Mining and Business Analytics with R. John Wiley & Sons, Inc.

Talia, D., Trunfio, P., and Marozzo, F. (2016). Data Analysis in the Cloud: Models, Techniques and Applications. Elsevier.

8

Organizational Design

Objectives

1) To identify organizational aspects that facilitate the implementation of strategies
2) To define organizational structures and processes
3) To identify analytic tools to design organizational structures and processes

Learning outcomes and managerial capabilities developed

1) To be able to use analytic tools to support organizational design
2) To learn the critical aspects of organizational structures and processes

---

Chapter 7 discussed the use of resources and capabilities in implementing strategy. However, the strategy must be translated into organizational structure, processes, goals and control systems in order to be implemented on a daily basis. Strategy is operationalized through the coordination of multiple stakeholders (employees, suppliers, government, etc.). While strategy can be affected by the behavior of multiple stakeholders, strategy implementation is not only a top-down process originated from the top management team but it also occurs bottom-up when stakeholders make decisions every day. Therefore, the effectiveness of the implementation of strategies resides in the way that the organization is designed and organized. Peter Senge suggests the most important role of a leader is to be the designer of the organization who is not visible but whose consequences have impact over a long period of time. In his perspective, organization design implies building the foundations of purpose and core values, policies and structures that determine business decisions and effective learning processes (Senge, 1990). In this chapter, we develop how to design and improve business processes and organizational structure while Chapter 9 will review performance and control systems.

Strategic Analytics: Integrating Management Science and Strategy, First Edition. Martin Kunc.
© 2019 John Wiley & Sons Ltd. Published 2019 by John Wiley & Sons Ltd.
Companion website: www.wiley.com/go/kunc/strategic-analytics

One important aspect needs to be considered in terms of the size of the organization. Small businesses may not have the same needs in terms of organizational structure and control systems since the owner is inherently part of the implementation of the strategy. Owners make most of the key decisions. In large organizations, strategy formulation and implementation needs to be clearly communicated. One of the reasons for the development of organizations is the efficiency in producing products and delivering services, which originates from specialization and division of labor to tackle processes. However, specialization and division bring two problems: coordination to integrate the different tasks performed; and cooperation to align the interests of stakeholders performing the different tasks in the processes (Grant, 2013). Cooperation can be achieved through the establishment of hierarchies. Hierarchies employ different mechanisms to achieve coordination such as incentives (both positive and negative), authority and shared values. In terms of coordination, the methods are rules and norms, routines, and mutual adjustment (Grant, 2013).

8.1 Organizational Components

8.1.1 Structure

Organizational structure is the basic outcome of the implementation of hierarchies. Hierarchy is a system in which members of an organization are ranked according to relative authority in vertical segments. Simply put, each segment includes a member of the organization, a supervisor (who supervises other members) and subordinates. In this way, cooperation is achieved through top-down control. This is known as bureaucracy where there is not only top-down control but also division of labor and formalization of routines through standard rules with the intention to obtain a rational and efficient organization (Grant, 2013). Simultaneously, a hierarchy helps to economize coordination when it is compared with self-organizing. Self-organizing teams will need to incur multiple interactions in order to achieve mutual adjustment while a team supervised by one person only needs to interact with the supervisee to coordinate their actions. Hierarchies also create modules (self-contained units) which can operate independently but achieve coordination through a superior layer of control.

The main two types of organizational forms are: mechanistic; and organic (Grant, 2013). Mechanistic forms are rigid and highly specialized where rules are vertically imposed. The communications are only vertical, so the knowledge is centralized in the upper echelons. Mechanistic organizations are suitable for stable environments with low uncertainty (Grant, 2013). Organic organizations are flexible with tasks broadly defined which require mutual adjustment to achieve coordination and a common culture to control them. The communication is fluid and dispersed across the organization since knowledge is decentralized. Organic organizations thrive in dynamic environments with high uncertainty due to continuous changes (Grant, 2013). However, the organizational form will depend definitively on the strategy adopted, the business model, technology and environmental conditions. For example, low cost strategies imply highly standardized products which need simple and efficient organizations with mechanistic characteristics. Additionally, organizations may combine both types of forms depending on the activities performed: standardized activities, e.g. procurement, may use mechanistic arrangements and creative activities, e.g. R&D, may be structured around organic forms; or the location of their activities (Grant, 2013). Figure 8.1 provides examples of some organization structures.

Grant (2013) proposes three questions to design the correct organizational structure:

- What basis should be employed to group organizational members into units? Some of the basis can be common tasks, products, location and processes but the key factor is the needs of coordination due to the level of interactions necessary by members of the organization. The interdependency can be

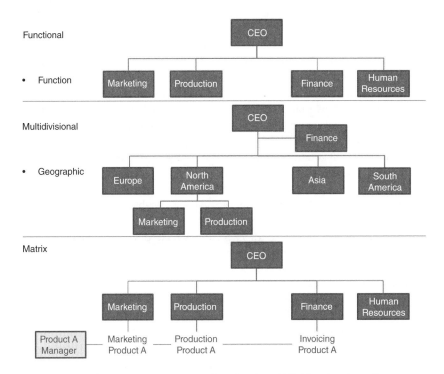

Figure 8.1 Typical organization structures: functional, multidivisional and matrix represented using organizational charts.

identified in three levels: members can operate independent but depend on each other's performance (pooled interdependence); members' outputs are inputs for some other member of the organization (sequential interdependence); and members are mutually dependent (reciprocal interdependence).

- What is the configuration of the units into the organizational structure? Some of the most well-known structures are functional, multidivisional and matrix. Functional structure occurs when the grouping of the members are around similar functions, e.g. logistics, in order to achieve economies of scale, learning and capability and standardized processes and controls. Integration of the structure happens at the top level, so this type of organization tends to be highly centralized. One of the main issues is cooperation and coordination due to the high levels of independency (goals, values, routines) of each unit and the issues when the organization grows to multiple businesses, products and geographic places. A multidivisional structure consists of the arrangement of organizational units in terms of product or geographical locations. This arrangement means the units are loosely coupled so business strategies are decided at unit level and the corporate level makes decisions on business portfolio and support the business units with centralized services. While it fosters autonomy, and leadership, one of the issues is the potential duplication of efforts on production, markets and customers. Matrix structures reflect the attempt to coordinate organizations across different dimensions, for example: functions, markets and products, with one of the dimensions being more important than the others in terms of authority. Some of the key issues are increased reporting and conflicts due to overlapping responsibilities which can be exacerbated if there is formalization and centralized decision-making processes in the corporate level.
- What drivers will generate changes in the configuration of the organizational structure? There are a number of factors that can lead to hybrid structures such as reduction in organizational vertical segments (delayering), more emphasis on controls through shared values, flexible communication and limited hierarchies (adhocracy and team-based) and emphasis on formal and informal networks (networked). Two factors related with the changes due to flexibility requirements are focus on projects (project-based) and virtual structures through outsourcing and partnerships with other organizations (virtual organizations).
- Reduction in organizational vertical segments (delayering).
- More emphasis on controls through shared values, flexible communication and limited hierarchies (adhocracy and team-based).
- Focus on projects (project-based).
- Emphasis on formal and informal networks (networked).
- Development of virtual structures through outsourcing and partnerships with other organizations (virtual organizations).

Greiner (1972) proposes five phases for changes in organization structure when businesses grow and age:

- In phase 1 when the organization is small and young, the organizational structure is informal where the top management team is mostly based on one person and entrepreneurial.
- Phase 2 implies a centralized structure organized by functions due to the increasing emphasis on efficient operations and decision making directed by the top management team.
- When the focus is on expanding the market (phase 3), the structure becomes more decentralized in geographical terms and decision making is delegated in the units.
- Phase 4 coincides with the consolidation of the organization across units based on products and supporting units where the top management team is involved in the development and control of investment centers.
- Finally, organizations become focused on innovation and problem solving in phase 5. Decisions are made participative and the organizational structure tends to become matrix-based with teams involved in new products and projects.

8.1.2 Processes

Organizational processes are directly linked to the strategy of the company since they are the main source for delivering value to customers both internally and externally. Therefore, their effectiveness can substantially affect the success of a strategy. Organizational processes are lateral or horizontal arrangements, that encapsulate the interdependence of tasks (activities), roles, human resources, organizational units and functions required to provide a product or service to either internal or external customers (Earl, 1994). Kettinger et al. (1997) suggest the main components of processes are:

- management
- human resources,
- information technology
- coordination mechanisms

Another way of establishing an overview of a process is to focus on:

- **Mission:** what is the purpose of the process? How does it contribute to the strategy?
- **Inputs:** what are the resources (human, technologies, monetary)? What is the flow of information coming into the process (forms, documents, reports, databases)? What is the flow of physical inputs (raw materials, energy, etc.)?
- **Activities:** what is the transformation activity (information, physical, decisions) occurring inside the process?
- **Outputs:** what are the resources, information and physical outputs generated?

Processes can be intra-functional when they are performed inside organizational units organized by functions (Kettinger et al., 1997). For example, manufacturing processes are performed inside the production unit. Processes can also be across functions when they involve human resources and information technology from multiple organizational units leading to complex coordination mechanisms. For example, a customer service process may involve organizational units such as inventory, logistics, sales and after sales. Processes can also extend between organizations, inter-organizational, when they need to involve multiple businesses. For example, supply chain processes comprise suppliers of raw materials, transportation companies, manufacturing facilities, outbound logistics firms and retail companies. Processes can also be classified into operating and management processes. Table 8.1 provides an overview of this classification:

Table 8.1 Generic set of organizational operational and management processes.

Generic process	Second level classification	Specific process
Operating processes	Understand customers	• Determine customers' needs through quantitative and qualitative assessment and its achievement • Monitor changes in markets through scanning competing products/services
	Design products and services	• Develop new product/services based on customer needs: design, build and test • Define product/services life cycle • Refine existing product/services
	Market and sell products and services	• Price, advertise, sell and process orders for products/services • Forecast sales and control targets
	Produce and deliver products and services	• Plan and acquire assets, human resources, technology • Generate products/services: scheduling, sourcing, production, storage, delivery • Assure quality and efficiency
	Customer service	• Invoice customers • Provide customer support
Management processes	Information systems	• Plan and develop components: hardware, software, human resources • Manage information system • Evaluate and improve performance
	Human resources	• Plan overall human resources strategy • Hire and develop human resources • Manage reward and motivation

Table 8.1 (Continued)

Generic process	Second level classification	Specific process
Management processes	Financial and accounting	• Manage financial resources: budgeting, allocation, and control • Process accounting and financial transactions • Control cash requirements: cash flow, bank accounts, financing needs • Manage tax • Financial reporting: internal and external
	External relationships	• Communication with stakeholders and shareholders • Develop public and community relationships • Interface with board of directors and corporate governance • Manage legal and environmental compliance
	Strategic development	• Scan external environment: competitors, political, economic, social, technological and environmental trends • Define and maintain mission and vision • Define strategy and business model • Define and maintain organization structure • Define organizational goals • Measure and monitor organizational performance • Implement organizational improvements

8.2 Integrating Management Science into Strategic Management

The tools from the management science field that can be employed to support the design and optimization of organizational structure and process are now going to be discussed.

8.2.1 Network Analysis for Organizational Structure Design

Organizational structures can be seen as networks of decision makers inter-acting in either formal (rules and procedures) or informal (problem solving events, projects, teams) ways. One of the key and well-established tools is social network analysis, which has roots in anthropology, sociology, psychology, and applied mathematics. Network analysis is a widely employed tool in Management Science which improves multiple problems in transportation, project management, telecommunications, etc.

Social network analysis studies social relations and represents structures as relations between social actors. Thus, a critical assumption in network analysis is actors are interdependent and the interactions among them (relational ties) are important for each actor as well as for the system that contains them. The interactions can take any form: formal or informal, face-to-face interactions, telecommunication interactions, web-based interactions or email interactions. The actors, which can be individuals, groups or organizations, are usually called nodes or members of the network. Social network data sets are multi-dimensional and/or longitudinal including information about actor attributes and the set of relational ties among them. Social network analysis analyzes data on patterns of relational ties in order to examine how the existence and functioning of ties are affected by the network structure where actors are embedded. Structure is studied at different levels: dyad (pair of actors), subgroup (sample of actors also known as ego-centered network), or even the entire network. The objective of social network analysis is to study network structure using different concepts, e.g. density, centrality, mutuality, and role.

It is important to distinguish the approach taken here with other approaches such as organizational networks, which are also called inter-organizational networks or network organizations. In this case, the level of analysis is not internal between members of an organization but between organizations (e.g. supply chains) or individuals in different organizations (e.g. researchers in universities and scientists in private companies) connected through different links (e.g. social, economic, information, knowledge, etc.). In this level, the key factor generating the networks is trust or contractual arrangements. There is a large amount of literature that evaluates the impact of organizational networks on different areas such as innovation, knowledge creation and sharing, etc., and there are multiple characterizations such as cooperative networks, strategic alliances, clusters, outsourcing networks, and innovation systems such as triple helix (which are networks of industry, university and government). However, similar principles, such as flows, centrality, etc., employed to evaluate social networks may also be employed to evaluate the dynamics in an inter-organizational network.

Figure 8.2 shows a simple diagram of an organizational network in the finance area. The finance managers are at the center of the network having the strongest link with D from the "payments section" due to the payment approval process. The finance manager also works closely with an external consultant who provides advice about financial issues. The "invoices section" is fairly independent and most of the contact is external with either customers or the warehouse manager due to the invoicing process. While G has many links with

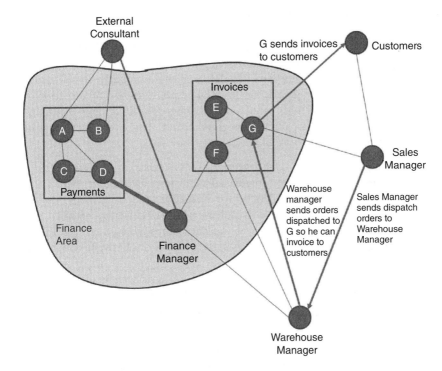

Figure 8.2 Organizational network in the finance area includes direct and non-direct linkages as well as links with diverse intensity.

external actors, G depends on F to resolve issues requiring the approval of the finance manager.

There are a variety of methods used to represent networks with the intention of facilitating the description of the networks compactly and systematically. Two will be discussed here: adjacency matrix; and graph theory.

A basic matrix in social network analysis is formed by as many rows and columns as there are actors in the network or data set containing indications of the ties between actors, e.g. emails. The simplest common matrix is binary where a tie is presented by a "1" in a cell corresponding to two actors and a "0" if there is no link. In a matrix, the sender of a tie is the row and the target of the tie is the column. The matrix is called an "adjacency matrix". Thus, an adjacency matrix is a matrix of size $n * n$ where n is the number of nodes in the network and each cell contains either 1 or 0 to indicate the existence of a link between nodes (Baesens et al., 2015).

Graph theory is also a mathematical treatment of networks (Boccaletti et al., 2006). A graphical representation of a network, or "sociogram," is an intuitive and simple visualization of a network (Baesens et al., 2015). A graph of a network consists of a set of nodes (vertices) and a set of links (edges). A node can represent a person, a computer or an activity. A link represents a relationship between the nodes it connects, such as formal or informal relationships between people, a physical connection between computers or an event between two activities. A graph where the links define a direction between the nodes (line with arrows) in the network is a directed graph. If there is no direction in the network, the graph is undirected. A graph where the links show the intensity of the relationships, is called a "weighted graph". There are three types of weighted graph (Baesens et al., 2015):

- **Binary weight:** when the weight is either 1 (a link exists) or 0 (a link does not exist). If the link wants to be categorized as positive or negative, then 1 will be employed for a positive link or –1 for a negative link.
- **Numeric weight:** it is employed to indicate a level of closeness between two nodes. The level of closeness can be measured through surveys, e.g. Likert scales, or using quantitative measures of the interactions between two nodes, e.g. emails, forms, etc.
- **Normalized weight:** it is a variation of the numeric weight where all the links of a node add up to 1 so the numeric weight for each link is divided by the total numeric weight of all links to obtain a value lower than 1.

There is a set of metrics to understand the characteristics of a network. First, the number of connections of a node is defined as a "degree" (Baesens et al., 2015). Secondly, "density" reflects how connected the nodes are. Density is represented as the division between 2 * number of links and the multiplication between the number of nodes and number of nodes minus one (Baesens et al., 2015). Thirdly, "centrality" measures the nodes that are central, which have most of the links to other nodes. The centrality of a node in a network is a measure of the structural importance of the node. A central node, typically, has a stronger capability of connecting other network members. Fourthly, "closeness" indicates the mean distance from a node to another node in the network (Baesens et al., 2015). Closeness can be regarded as a measure of how long it will take information to spread from a given node to other nodes in the network. Fifthly, "betweenness" measures the degree to which a node lies on the paths linking other nodes (Freeman, 1979). This is a measure of the level of control over information flowing between others by a node. For example, a node with high betweenness can facilitate interactions between the nodes. Some of the issues that network analysis using metrics can uncover are:

- Individuals or a group of people isolated in the organization.
- Key individuals or a group of people that are central to the network.
- Strongly interconnected individuals or group of people due to high density connections.
- Key individuals that have the only link to a resource or another individual/group.

Food for thought 8.1 One of the most dynamics industries is the computer industry in all its variations, e.g. equipment makers such as Hewlett Packard or Dell, software developers such as Microsoft or Oracle, internet-based businesses such as Google or Amazon, smartphone and computer producers such as Apple, and social networks like Facebook. Instead of finding a sophisticated organizational structure drawing, which is called an organizational chart like in Figure 8.2, for this task, I found a satirical cartoon of the organizational structure of firms in the industry. "Manu Comet" developed a satirical cartoon of six organizational charts from very well-known firms in the industry, which was posted on 27 June 2011, as presented in Figure 8.3. This type of cartoon is a non-realistic style of drawing intended for caricature or humor. However, they intend to portray parts of reality.

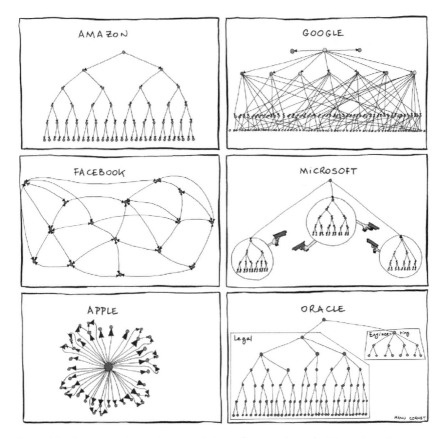

Figure 8.3 Six organizational structures in the software industry by "Manu Cornet".
Source: www.bonkersworld.net (creative common license).

You need to address the following issues:

- What network analysis based on the cartoon can tell us about the organizational structure: density, centrality, nodes?
- Find information describing the organizational structure for each of the firms and evaluate whether the cartoon reflects the situation.
- What are the benefits and issues facing each real organizational structure?
- What are the main factors defining the real organizational structures?

8.2.2 Business Process Modeling

Organizational processes are directly linked to the strategy of the company since they are the main source for delivering value to both internal and external customers. Therefore, their effectiveness can substantially affect the success of a strategy. Effectiveness can be measured in terms of throughput and efficiency in terms of costs related to the throughput. Organization, or business, processes have seen the largest efforts from consulting and software firms in terms of conceptual modeling to analyze, improve and develop software to support them. Business literature has produced very well-known bestsellers relating to ways in which to improve processes, such as Hammer and Champy (1993) or Davenport (1993), and there are a plethora of methods and tools to improve them, e.g. Lean and Six Sigma. This situation creates a problem with selecting the right technique and tool. Aguilar-Savén (2004) reviewed some of most employed process modeling techniques in business, which are briefly described in Table 8.2, and

Table 8.2 Business process modelling techniques and methodologies.

Concept	Activities
Flow chart	It is a formal graphic representation of the logic sequence of a process in terms of its flow. It is a very flexible technique since the only formal part is the building blocks, e.g. boxes are actions, rhomboids are decisions, arrows connect the sequence, etc., which facilitates communication. Some weaknesses are related to the size that can take, no differences between type or importance of the activities, and it is difficult to include responsibilities in the chart
Role activity diagrams	They are a graphic representation of the process taking the perspective of individual roles related to their organizational functions
Workflow	It is a computerized facilitation of a business process where information or tasks are transferred between participants of a process based on rules. The process is controlled by a work management system which executes the workflow based on logic rules. The steps to implement are: information gathering, business process modeling, workflow modeling and implementation/verification/execution. There are number of computer languages employed to develop workflows

Table 8.2 (Continued)

Concept	Activities
Soft systems methodology	It is a methodology employed to structure thinking related to complex organizational problems with a social systems perspective. It consists of seven steps: define the problem situation; express the problem situation; formulate root definition; build conceptual models; compare the problem situation and the conceptual model; define feasible and desirable changes; and take action to improve the situation. Its main advantage resides in the description of the interaction of the different processes comprising the social system and their relationship with organizational problems
Simulation	It is an umbrella concept for many mathematical methods and software to replicate the behavior of real systems. Simulations can be deterministic (data is constant) or stochastic (data is random) depending on the input data employed. Simulations can be continuous (changes are continuous) or discrete (changes occur at separated points in time). Two of the most well-known methods are system dynamics (deterministic and continuous simulation) and discrete event (stochastic and discrete). It is clear that simulation models require conceptual models which can be prepared using the techniques discussed previously. Simulation is not employed when the processes improvement can be estimated analytically, e.g. Little's law.

additional sources are presented in Further reading. However, the focus on business process improvement should not exclude a continuous analysis of their alignment with the strategy and customer value creation dimensions.

Two of the most recent and famous methods to improve business performance are Lean, which focuses on cost reduction, and Six Sigma, which improves quality and reducing costs by reducing the variability in processes (Spector, 2006).

Lean is the systematic elimination of wasteful, or non-value adding, activities in the organization (Womack and Jones, 1994). Its approach is based on mapping and analyzing activities in processes, which is called value stream mapping (Womack and Jones, 1994; Womack, 2006). Value stream reflects the activities necessary to produce products or deliver services and the analysis refers to identifying those that generate "waste": waiting times, transportation, overproduction, excess inventory, etc. Lean can also be considered a pull system since it only tries to meet market demand (Näslund, 2008). Näslund (2008) suggests five steps to apply Lean are:

1) Define what is value for the customers and the processes responsible for it.
2) Identify the chronological flow of activities in the process to add value: mapping the value stream.
3) Redefine activities which do not add value by eliminating or minimizing them so the flow is without interruptions.

4) Implement just-in-time so customers pull the product or service.
5) Keep reviewing the flow so as to ensure the process is improved continuously.

Six Sigma basically employs statistical methods in order to understand variations in process outputs and identify the root causes of the problems (Pojasek, 2003). Additionally, the use of statistical controls helps to control processes and avoid the appearance of defects. Six Sigma also includes designing, improving and monitoring business processes (Revere et al., 2004). Six Sigma means the chance of finding a defect is only 3.4 per million. Näslund (2008) suggests the methodology is based on the DMAIC (Define, Measure, Analyze, Improve and Control) cycle for continuous improvement and it is related to the earlier Total Quality Management methodology developed by Deming, including the use of statistical tools.

Food for thought 8.2   One of the key measures of the performance of process is the time that it takes for inputs to go through the process. When there are not enough resources or the process is wrongly configured, the first indication is usually the existence of queues and time waiting in queues. Queues can occur in production lines, services or administrative processes. Queues are the most pervasive element of any process. Thankfully, the mathematical analysis of queues is appropriate for any type of queue but it includes simplifications in order to reduce the complexity of the real process. The basic queueing models consist of three components (Albright and Winston, 2010):

1) **Arrivals.** Arrivals are categorized in terms of timing and type. Timing is described through '"inter-arrival times"', which is the time between successive arrivals. While arrivals may be known in some situations, most of the time arrivals are random so the probability distribution is the only information available. The most common probability distribution is the exponential distribution where the density decreases from left to right ($f(x)= \lambda e^{-\lambda x}$ with $x>0$) and its mode is closer to the left side. The mean and standard deviation are equal to the reciprocal of parameter λ, so λ is equal to 1/mean of the inter-arrival times.

   Type of arrivals either can be in batches or one at a time and they may be similar or in different classes.

2) **Service discipline.** Service discipline indicates the rules applied to process the arrivals. The most common is the "First-Come-First-Served" where the first arrival is processed first. Other possibilities are "Service-in-Random-Order", which treats the arrivals in random order, "Last-Come-First-Served", or "Shortest-Processing-Time", which ranks arrivals in terms of their processing time before processing the arrival with the shortest processing time.

Another issue is the discipline of the arrivals. If arrivals arrive and see a line of arrivals waiting, they may leave the process; this action is called "balking". This action can occur due to a decision of the arrival or the process can contain a limit on the number of arrivals waiting so it rejects arrivals when the waiting line is full. Another possibility is arrivals, which are already queueing, who do not wait to be treated and leave, this action is called "reneging", or they decide to change waiting line, which is called "jockey".

3) **Service characteristics.** Each arrival is treated by a specific actor, who is called a "server", over a period of time. The "service time" is usually random so it is necessary to define the probability distribution of a typical service time. The probability distribution, which has an exponential distribution, may be equal for all arrivals and servers or it may be different for arrival type or server. Servers can be configured to run in "parallel", e.g. one single queue of arrival is processed by multiple servers, or "series", e.g. each arrival is processed by a different server following certain rules.

   Service also needs to consider the impact of initial conditions on the throughput achieved. If the initial conditions significantly affect the performance of the service over the time period analyzed, then the initial conditions or short-run behavior are predominant. Most of the mathematical analysis is performed with service under "steady-state" so the parameters of the queueing system (inter-arrival times, service time, etc.) remain constant for the entire period and the system is "stable" because the servers can process arrivals fast enough to avoid the queue growing to infinite.

The most famous formula to evaluate time average and entity average for a queuing system in steady state is Little's formula. The formula states that:

$$L = \bar{\lambda}W$$

where L is the expected number of entities in the system and $\bar{\lambda}$ is the average rate of arrivals to the queueing system together with W being the expected time a typical unit spends in the system. The purpose of the formula is to find any of the parameters when there is information about the other two parameters, which is the usual situation. For example, if there is information about the arrival rate and the number of customers in the system (both of them measured in similar units of time), then the formula will be able to quantify how long customers wait in the system. One of the most important features of Little's formula is the reduced amount of information required, for example, there is no requirement about the number of servers, inter-arrival times or service times. Table 8.3 gives some examples about the application of Little's formula in different processes (Little and Graves, 2008). Little (2011) asserts that Lean Six Sigma methodology is intrinsically related to Little's formula where the formula can be used to evaluate ex-ante

Table 8.3 Applications of Little's formula in the analysis of business processes.

Situation	Description
Manufacturing process	Knowing the manufacturing time is critical for scheduling and delivery plans. If there is information about the average number of products started per day and the size of the work-in-progress, then it will be possible to infer the *average manufacturing time* for the factory
Administrative process	Understanding the time to manage customers' complaints can be very important in maintaining reputation. If there is information about the arrival rate of complaints per day and the system keeps the number of complaints pending (so it is possible to calculate an average number of complaints unsolved), then it will be easier to calculate the *time required to solve a customer complaint* without necessarily knowing the number of people involved in the process
	However, if there is a target for the time taken to answer complaints and the average number of complaints remain steady, then it will be possible to infer the *average number of complaints pending in the system* (queue length). The difference between the current situation and the required number divided by an average productivity will provide a basic approximation of the *number of people required in the process*
Sales processes	By observing a sample of customers' activities in a short period of time, you may be able to infer the total sales. For example, you may visit a shop at random times over a certain period of the day and observe the length of the queue and the time taken to get in and out of the shop. If the information is typical, then it will be possible to obtain the *total throughput rate* during the period, which is *equal to the arrival rate* (assuming that all customers are served once they arrive at the shop). If each customer spends a typical amount of money, total sales will be equal to the arrival rate multiplied by customers' expenditure in the shop

the situation of the process and ex-post the results of the use of the methodology.

You need to answer the following questions:

- Which organizations have significant queueing systems in their core processes?
- Identify and describe three to four core processes of one of the organizations mentioned in the previous question.
- Consider the application of Little's formula to one of the core processes: what information do you need to apply the formula? What are the sources of the information?

8.2.3 Improving Manufacturing Productivity Using Predictive Analytics

Data analytics can be very useful for achieving productivity gains in manufacturing. Predictive analytics can lead to production improvement with respect to the cost, quantity, quality and sustainability of manufactured products by anticipating changes to the manufacturing system (Lechevalier et al., 2014).

Data in manufacturing can come from many different sources and have differing formats (Lechevalier et al., 2014). The data can be archived data collected from previous operations, simulated data (if the real data are not available), or real time data collected from machine monitoring. The data module should be able to collect the data from a wide variety of sources and formats. Moreover, the data can be collected from a data stream and the module must support the tools needed to handle data flows of high volume and velocity. Data collected from sensors in manufacturing operations are generally structured data.

The most important functionality provided by an analytics framework is the automatic generation of a predictive analytics model from the system specification (Lechevalier et al., 2014). The diagnostic and predictive model to be defined depends on the variables that the user wants to observe and predict, and the characteristics of the systems being defined. One of the main components of a discrete manufacturing system is the machine tool. In a meta-model, the machine tool needs to be represented in a way that allows users to model the machine, to interconnect several machines, and to model the parameters of the machine.

Predictive techniques have also been used to address challenges in product quality. A Bayesian network approach has been developed to predict and avoid defects in castings called micro-shrinkage or secondary contraction (Lechevalier et al., 2014). With a Bayesian method, the initial step is the construction of a probabilistic network from a database of records. Once constructed, such a network can provide insight into probabilistic dependencies that exist among the variables in the database. One application is the automated discovery of dependency relationships. The computer searches for a probabilistic-network structure that has a high posterior probability given the database, and outputs the structure and its probability. A related task is computer-assisted hypothesis testing: The user enters a hypothetical structure of the dependency relationships among a set of variables, and the program calculates the probability of the structure given a database of cases on the variables.

8.3 End of Chapter

Designing organizational structures and organizational processes is not as appealing as defining the grand strategy. Organizational structure and organizational processes are two areas usually left to be dealt with in operational terms. However, most successful organizations have clear templates to develop these areas beyond the operational level. First, business process design needs to have a broad strategic vision which is translated into specific objectives for the process in terms of costs, time, quality and learning/empowerment of the actors in the system. Secondly, there has to be a list of core processes and a continuous evaluation of the importance of the rest of the processes. Processes must be redesigned as often as possible usually following changes in strategies. Thirdly, all processes have to be understood and measured. There is a plethora of tools and methods to support this aspect. Moreover, the extensive adoption of information systems and the existence of big data as well as the Internet of Things offer a strong platform from which to measure processes thoroughly. Fourthly, the relationship between processes and organizational structure is fundamental in controlling and managing them. Organizational structure may need to be defined along key processes and hybrid structures combining processes with pools of skills, e.g. functional structure, can be considered. Fifthly, processes require resources, behavior and information so redesigned processes must consider the changes in resources, behavior and information together. Managing processes can also require contributions from behavioral science, design science and computer science together with management science.

In terms of style (Figure 8.4), the tool discussed in this chapter can be allocated in the rational style since the main objective is to research and analyze

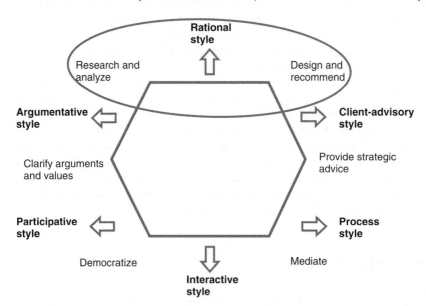

Figure 8.4 Management science styles. *Source:* Walker (2009). Reproduced with permission of Elsevier.

the current situation of the organizational structure and business processes in order to provide recommendations on improvement and design of them.

8.3.1 Revision Questions

1) What are the strengths and weaknesses of the methods (both presented in this book and other methods found through your own research) used to evaluate social networks? What is the impact of Big Data and Analytics on evaluating social networks?
2) What is the concept of structural holes in social networks? What is modularity in social networks?
3) What are the strengths and weaknesses of using simulation and statistical methods to evaluate and redesign organizational processes?
4) What are the implications of integrating organizational processes in information systems in terms of Big Data and Analytics? What are the perils of Big Data and Analytics without a clear model of the organizational processes?

8.3.2 Case Study: Improving Processes in Health Services Using Simulation

One of the key components in health services are hospitals. Simulation studies performed in hospital are widely published and cited in management science literature (Gunal, 2012). Three simulation methods are usually employed: discrete event simulation; system dynamics; and agent-based models. A brief comparison between them is presented in Figure 8.5. Discrete event simulation consists of passive objects, e.g. people, gadgets, documents, called entities which are routed through diverse servers (resources) using different rules or behaviors (events) as a way of representing processes. Queues are explicit and the time intervals are discrete. Processes are stochastic in nature. Additional detail on discrete event simulation is found in Robinson (2008). Agent-based modeling focuses on active individuals (agents) which have individual deterministic rules (e.g. they are internal to each agent). There is not a general process governing the dynamics, so the behavior of the system arises from local interactions between the agents, which may or may not lead to the formation of queues. More information about agent-based modeling is discussed in Macal and North (2010). System dynamics treats entities as groups or aggregates which are consolidated in levels/stocks (see chapters 5, 6 and 7). The entities move along the processes through rates (flows). Rates reflect the rules managing the process and they are defined either externally as constants or endogenously by information feedback processes. Queues are represented as stocks/levels in an explicit

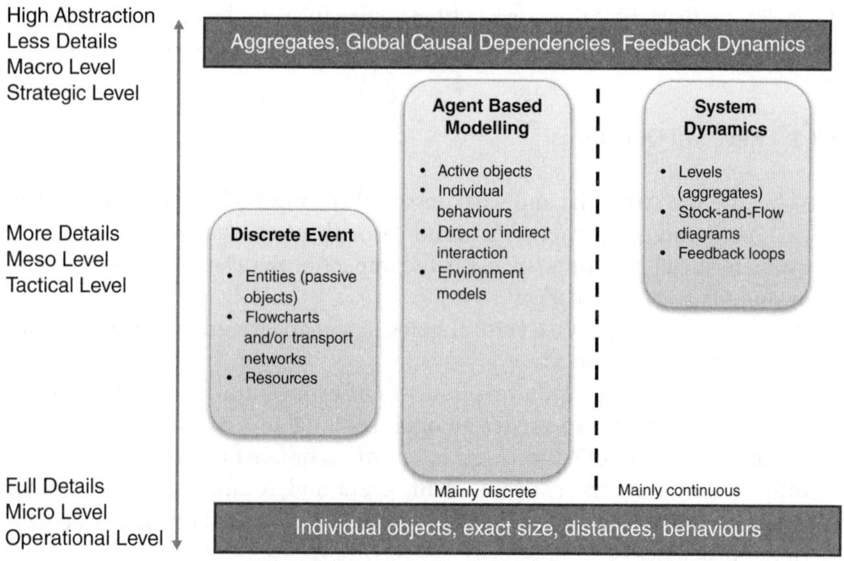

Figure 8.5 Broad comparison between discrete event, agent-based and system dynamics modeling. *Source:* Borshchev and Filipov (2004).

way. The variables are mostly deterministic and time is continuous using differential equations. The main source for technical information about system dynamics is Sterman (2000).

Conceptually hospitals can be considered a simple input–output system. Patients arrive, they go through different treatment paths depending on their health problems, and then leave the hospital. However, neither patients nor treatment paths are similar. Therefore, more specific indications are necessary to model hospitals' processes. Depending on the health problem, patients use services which are performed in a specific unit, e.g. seeing a doctor in Accident and Emergency, or they are complemented by other units, e.g. seeing a doctor in Accident and Emergency and having an X-ray in radiology. This is usually called "patient pathways". Having an inventory of all patient pathways in a hospital and modeling them simultaneously can be a daunting task so simulation models are usually focused on only one pathway. However, a key challenge in modeling processes, as patient pathways, is to represent the interaction between multiple services (units) and activities since the lack of efficiency of a unit can substantially affect the performance of other units.

Data for simulation models varies significantly depending on the modeling technique and the level of detail of the model. Higher levels of detail mean more data. Most data can be obtained from existing information systems, e.g. patient admission or treatment logs by units, but the most valuable data may reside in the head of the staff or from observation of the process.

The modeling methodology employed can have different strengths and weaknesses. Gunal (2012) lists some of them:

- Discrete event simulation is very useful in health services modeling due to the strong queueing structure underpinning the services. Discrete event simulation is flexible in terms of level of detail but its focus is predominantly operational. It has an individual patient (entity) focus so a patient (tests, X-ray, prescriptions, etc.) can be tracked easily through a treatment pathway. Any resource of the hospital can be identified as a server, e.g. doctor, nurses, beds, X-ray equipment. It can deal with stochastic factors such as random emergency patients. A discrete event can immediately highlight waiting times, which is one of the key performance measures of health services. Discrete event software can be visually engaging so it can help to communicate the results to hospital staff.
- Agent-based models start with an assumption that patients (or doctors) are autonomous in their behavior (individual rules defined by historical behavior, explicit goals or traditional rational assumptions) but they interact with the environment (other patients, doctors, etc.). Additionally, agents have different attributes or characteristics (more or less ill). Given the autonomous characteristics of agents, agent-based models do not try to replicate specific health services' processes but they are useful in evaluating the impact of uncontrolled events on processes, e.g. the spread of a disease in a hospital.
- System dynamics models represent patients (entities) as aggregate numbers so they tend to represent health services' processes at a strategic level and over a longer period of time compared with discrete event simulation. System dynamics models tend to focus on the interrelationships between parts of the system and the feedback processes underpinning the performance of the hospital or for a group of patients in a treatment pathway that is strongly interconnected with other pathways. The movement of patients is driven by simple behavioral rules comprising the feedback processes. System dynamics software is also visually engaging, especially to observe the pathways and the feedback processes determining the dynamics in the system.

Table 8.4 lists the most common units in a hospital.

Here are a few actions to perform related to improving health services:

1) Select two units and develop a process map indicating the most important performance metrics for the unit.
2) Develop a conceptual discrete event model for the unit. Find an article describing a similar discrete event model and compare it with your proposal. What was missing? Why?
3) Consider the treatment pathways for an old person who arrives at Accident and Emergency with pain in the abdomen and bleeding. This situation may

Table 8.4 Most common units in a hospital.

Name of unit	Activities
Accident and Emergency	Receive patients brought by ambulance or arriving in person. Patients are assessed in terms of their urgency. Minor injuries or health problems are solved in the unit. More serious issues are directed to other areas
Anesthetics	Provision of anesthesia to patients before surgery. Support the delivery of relief to acute, chronic, critical pain. Support childbirth by giving obstetric anesthesia
Screening	Provides screening services to diverse diseases such as cancer
Cardiology	Receive outpatients for consultations. Treat inpatient with cardiac problems. Perform diagnostic procedures such as electrocardiogram, echocardiogram, and blood pressure tests. Perform minor surgical procedures
Intensive care	Controls and supports patients with serious health problems or in critical condition It has a small number of beds and its staff is comprised of specialists from different disciplines
Diagnostic imaging	Provide imagining services such as radiography (X-ray), mammography (breast scan), ultrasound scan, angiography (X-ray of blood vessels), CT scanning (computer tomography), and MRI scanning (magnetic and radio wave-based scan generating 3D images)
Gastroenterology	Provide services to patients with problems in the stomach, intestines, pancreas and liver
Endoscopy	An imaging diagnostic service employing a small tube with a camera to investigate issues in the esophagus and digestive system. Other specialties are colorectal surgery and inflammatory bowel service
General surgery	Involves operation theatres and surgeons. It includes day surgery, thyroid surgery, kidney transplants (working with nephrologists), colon surgery, laparoscopic cholecystectomy, endoscopy, breast surgery, etc.
Gynecology	Investigate and treat issues related to female urinary tract and reproductive organs to outpatient and inpatients It may also perform screening services
Hematology	Provides services related to blood diseases
Maternity	Has theaters for mothers to give birth. Obstetrics doctors and midwives are part of the unit There are also antenatal care and postnatal support
Neonatal intensive care	Has a set of cots to be used by newborn babies who need intensive care

Table 8.4 (Continued)

Name of unit	Activities
Nephrology	Provides dialysis day unit for patients who need a transplant
Neurology	Treats issues on the nervous systems including the brain and spinal cord. Specialist nurses can support special patient needs such as epilepsy and multiple sclerosis
Oncology	Offers therapy to treat cancers through radiotherapy and chemotherapy
Ophthalmology	Provides different services related to eyes such as outpatient appointments, laser treatments, optometry, ophthalmic imaging
Orthopedics	The unit works with problems related to muscles, joints, bones, ligaments and tendons. Doctors and nurses treat trauma (e.g. bone fractures), surgery to correct torn ligaments and hip replacements and other less complex issues
Pharmacy	Dispenses the drugs for inpatients and outpatients
Urology	Treats problems related to kidney and bladder including screening tests such as cystoscopy

result in cancer in the digestive system. Consider using system dynamics to develop a model that extrapolates the situation of this person to the whole population. What information do you need to include in the model? Find an article describing a similar system dynamics model and compare with your proposal. What was missing? Why?

4) In health services, what is the value added generated by the service? How do you measure this? What proportion of the processes related to health services occur outside the hospital? Why?

5) How do you make sure the improvements detected by a simulation model are aligned with the strategy of the organization?

References

Aguilar-Saven, R.S. (2004). Business process modelling: Review and framework. *International Journal of Production Economics*, 90(2), 129–149.

Albright, C. and Winston, W.L. (2010). Business Analytics: Data Analysis & Decision Making. Cengage Learning.

Baesens, B., Van Vlasselaer, V., and Verbeke, W. (2015). Social network analysis for fraud detection networks. In: Fraud Analytics Using Descriptive, Predictive, and Social Network Techniques: a Guide to Data Science for Fraud Detection, Ch. 5. John Wiley & Sons, Inc.

Boccaletti, S., Latora, V., Moreno, Y., et al. (2006). Complex networks: Structure and dynamics. *Physics Reports*, 424(4), 175–308.

Borshchev, A. and Filippov, A. (2004). From system dynamics and discrete event to practical agent based modeling: reasons, techniques, tools. Proceedings of the 22nd International Conference of the System Dynamics Society, Oxford, UK (25–29 July 2004).

Davenport, T.H. (1993). Process Innovation: Reengineering Work Through Information Technology. Harvard Business Press.

Earl, M.J. (1994). The new and the old of business process redesign. *The Journal of Strategic Information Systems*, 3(1), 5–22.

Freeman, L. C. (1979). Centrality in social networks conceptual clarification. *Social networks*, 3(1), 215–239.

Grant, R.M. (2013). Contemporary Strategy Analysis: Text and Cases, 8th edn. John Wiley & Sons., Ltd.

Greiner, L.E. (1972). Evolution and revolution as organizations grow. *Harvard Business Review*, 50(4), 37–46.

Gunal, M.M. (2012). A guide for building hospital simulation models. *Health Systems*, 1(1), 17–25.

Hammer, M. and Champy, J. (1993). Reengineering the Corporation: A Manifesto for Business. HarperCollins.

Kettinger, W.J., Teng, J.T., and Guha, S. (1997). Business process change: a study of methodologies, techniques, and tools. MIS Quarterly, March, 55–80.

Lechevalier, D., Narayanan, A., and Rachuri, S. (2014). Towards a domain-specific framework for predictive analytics in manufacturing. 2014 IEEE International Conference on Big Data, 987–995). IEEE.

Little, J.D. (2011). OR FORUM – Little's law as viewed on its 50th anniversary. *Operations Research*, 59(3), 536–549.

Little, J.D. and Graves, S.C. (2008). Little's law. In: Building Intuition: Insights from Basic Operations Management Models and Principles, 81–100. Springer.

Macal, C.M. and North, M.J. (2010) Tutorial on agent-based modelling and simulation. *Journal of Simulation*, 4(3), 151–162.

Näslund, D. (2008). Lean, six sigma and lean sigma: fads or real process improvement methods? *Business Process Management Journal*, 14(3), 269–287.

Pojasek, R. (2003). Lean, six sigma, and the systems approach: management initiatives for process improvement. *Environmental Quality Management*, 13(2), 85.

Revere, L., Black, K., and Huq, A. (2004). Integrating six sigma and CQI for improving patient care. *The TQM Magazine*, 16(2), 105.

Robinson, S. (2008). Conceptual modelling for simulation Part I: definition and requirements. *Journal of the Operational Research Society*, 59(3), 278–290.

Senge, P.M. (1990). The leader's new work: building learning organizations. *MIT Sloan Management Review*, 32(1), 7.

Spector, R. (2006). How constraints management enhances lean and six sigma, *Supply Chain Management Review*, 10(1), 42–47.

Sterman, J.D. (2000). Business Dynamics: System Thinking and Modeling for a Complex World. McGraw-Hill.

Walker, W.E. (2009). Does the best practice of rational-style model based policy analysis already include ethical considerations? *Omega*, 37(6), 1051–1062.

Womack, J. (2006). Value stream mapping, Manufacturing Engineering, May, 145–156.

Womack, J. and Jones, D. (1994). From lean production to the lean enterprise. *Harvard Business Review*, 72(2), 93–103.

Futher Reading

Baker, W.E. and Faulkner, R.R. (2002). Inter-organizational networks. In: J. A. C. Baum (Ed.), The Blackwell Companion to Organizations (ed. J.A.C. Baum), 520–540. Blackwell Publishers Ltd.

Berkovitz, J. and Feldman, M. (2006). Entrepreneurial universities and technology transfer. A conceptual framework for understanding knowledge-based economic development. *Journal of Technology Transfer*, 31(1), 175–188.

Borgatti, S.P., Everett, M.G. and Johnson, J.C. (2018). Analyzing Social Networks 2nd Edition. Sage, London

Checkland, P. and Poulter, J., 2010. Soft systems methodology. In: Systems Approaches to Managing Change: A Practical Guide (eds M. Reynolds and S. Howell), 191–242. Springer.

Child, J., Faulkner, D., and Tallman, S. (2005). Cooperative Strategy. Managing Alliances, Networks, and Joint Ventures. Oxford University Press.

Cooper, G.F. and Herskovits, E. (1992) A Bayesian Method for the Induction of Probabilistic Networks from Data. Machine Learning, 9, 309–347.

Davenport, T.H. (1993). Process Innovation: Reengineering Work Through Information Technology. Harvard Business School Press.

Håkansson, H. and Persson, P. (2004). Supply chain management: The logic of supply chains and networks. *The International Journal of Logistics Management*, 15(1), 11–26.

Lambert, B (2018) A Student's Guide to Bayesian Statistics. Sage, London.

Lane, D., Monefeldt, C., and Husemann, E. (2003). Client involvement in simulation model building: hints and insights from a case study in a London hospital. *Health Care Management Science*, 6(2), 105–116.

Lane, D., Monefeldt, C., and Rosenhead, J. (2000). Looking in the wrong place for healthcare improvements: a system dynamics study of an accident and emergency department. *Journal of the Operational Research Society*, 51(5), 518–531.

Malerba, F. and Vonortas, N.S. (2009). Innovation Networks in Industries. Edward Elgar.

Malhotra, Y. (1998). Business process redesign: an overview. *IEEE Engineering Management Review*, 26, 27–31.

Phillips, R.A. (2010). Ethics and network organizations. *Business Ethics Quarterly*, 20(3), 533–544.

Pidd, M. (2004). Computer Simulation in Management Science, 5th edn, John Wiley & Sons, Ltd.

Robinson, S. (2004). Simulation: The Practice of Model Development and Use. John Wiley & Sons, Ltd.

Thorelli, H.B. (1986). Networks: Between markets and hierarchies. *Strategic Management Journal*, 7(1), 37–51.

Tinnilä, M. (1995). Strategic perspective to business process redesign. *Business Process Re-engineering & Management Journal*, 1(1), 44–59.

Van Ackere, A., Larsen, E.R., and Morecroft, J.D. (1993). Systems thinking and business process redesign: an application to the beer game. *European Management Journal*, 11(4), 412–423.

Worren, N., Eger, T., and Hærem, T. (2016). Reconfigure An organization design exercise. *Simulation & Gaming*, 47(6), 851–865.

9

Performance Measurement System

Objectives

1) To define the concept of performance measurement systems
2) To learn tools to support the design of performance measurement systems
3) To identify approaches using analytics to analyze performance measures

Learning outcomes and managerial capabilities developed

1) To apply tools on performance measurement system tasks
2) To be able to design and implement a performance measurement system

---

Chapter 8 discussed the methods used to analyze and design the organizational structure and processes responsible for creating value to customers. This chapter addresses the process of defining organizational performance and control systems that need to be implemented on a daily basis in order to achieve the desired organizational performance. Defining organizational performance is key because "managers measure what they value and they get what they measure" (Figure 9.1), affecting their behavior significantly (Tapinos and Dyson, 2007).

The definition of organizational performance is key in defining the feedback processes responsible for keeping the organization on track to achieve its strategy and vision. Controls are necessary to not only guarantee that standards are achieved but also to guide managerial decisions since it is important that managers are able to know whether an action is achieving its effect. Timeliness of information about performance is critical. Delays affect the reactions of managers to non-desired situations and preclude taking corrective actions. Additionally, learning about performance with a long delay hinders the opportunity to discover the right factors behind the performance observed. Availability of information is crucial for managers in order to test their assumptions about the

Strategic Analytics: Integrating Management Science and Strategy, First Edition. Martin Kunc.
© 2019 John Wiley & Sons Ltd. Published 2019 by John Wiley & Sons Ltd.
Companion website: www.wiley.com/go/kunc/strategic-analytics

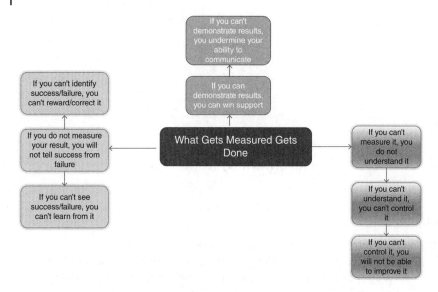

Figure 9.1 What gets measured gets done. *Source:* Tapinos and Dyson (2007: figure 11.1). Reproduced with permission of John Wiley & Sons.

factors driving the organizational performance and help them to forecast future performance together with potential impact of new actions. This is the realm of Big Data analytics in their two variations: descriptive and predictive.

Thus, organizations collect and process data to reduce the uncertainty about their performance and facilitating the learning process by resolving the ambiguities about the drivers of the performance. However, managers can only make sense of the data if there is some guidance about the expected performance through objectives and goals. Moreover, the organization needs a performance measurement culture where responses to deviations are encouraged and open communication is enabled in order to discuss results and solutions. It is important that managers focus their attention on actual management of performance rather than on the measurement process.

While the mission emphasizes the long-term aims of an organization, many times organizations' short-term actions are misaligned with their long-term aims. The mission statement needs to clearly articulate its long-term intentions in order to be able to define useful goals for aligning expectations, underpin planning processes and support performance evaluation. This is the realm of strategic controls. Long-term objectives can be usually established in a few areas, which are critical to the business, such as:

- **Economic sustainability.** The ability of an organization to survive in the long term depends on achieving a sustainable competitive advantage leading to continuous profits.

- **Productivity.** Organizations need to improve their relationship between inputs (resources consumed) and outputs (services or products generated) in order to be able to achieve economic sustainability.
- **Competitive position.** It indicates the success of the organization in the markets where it operates. Some objectives may be expressed quantitatively in terms of sales in monetary terms or volume or market share as well as qualitatively such as customers' quality perceptions with respect to competitors.
- **Employee relations.** Being proactive in satisfying needs and expectations of employees through adequate salaries and career opportunities helps to maintain and increase productivity and reduces turnover (which can drain the pool of knowledge and skills).
- **Product/service positioning.** Organizations need to decide the stance they wish to take in the market. For example, they can lead or follow the market in technology development. They can compete on price or other dimensions.
- **Social responsibility.** Organizations need to consider their objectives with respect to society and the environment by following or leading in terms of contributions to society through diverse objectives in key dimensions: diversity, education, environment.

It is important to remember that long-term objectives define what the organization wants to achieve without defining how to achieve (types of actions), which is the realm of strategies.

Performance management focuses on the link between organizational objectives/strategy and performance measurement systems (Kaplan and Norton, 2008). Ferreira and Otley (2009) propose a set of components for performance management systems:

- *Vision and mission* defines the attention of managers and employees to what is relevant in the organization (see Chapter 6).
- *Key success factors* for the business need to be identified for managers and employees (see Chapter 6).
- *Organizational structure* affects performance management system design and use as structure defines *areas of responsibility* (see Chapter 8).
- *Strategies and plans* are linked to *processes and activities* required for their implementation (see Chapter 8).
- *Performance measures* to capture the development of strategies and plans as well as the performance of key success factors.
- *Appropriate performance targets* for the performance measures should be chosen.
- *Performance evaluation processes* together with *rewards for target achievement* must be implemented.
- *Information infrastructure* (technology, flows and repositories) to support performance management activities (see Chapter 1).

In this chapter we focus on the performance measurement system (performance measures, performance targets and evaluation processes)

9.1 Measuring Financial Performance

Financial performance measures focus on controlling the financial inputs (cash available, expenses) and outputs (revenues, profits) of the organization. Their main focus is on income and expenses, so the organization can achieve economic sustainability. These types of control can always tilt the emphasis towards the achievement of short-term goals, e.g. current profits, to the detriment of the long-term health of the organization, e.g. ability to innovate. Financial measures are usually evaluated in absolute number, percentages or ratios. Table 9.1 provides a list of some financial metrics to evaluate business performance.

In terms of assessing financial performance, the usual analysis suggested in strategic management literature tends to be intuitive and generalist. There are usually two approaches that may or may not be combined.

First, the evaluation of trends in either internal or external longitudinal data is used to judge the performance track of the organization over time in three categories: growth; stable; or decline. The analysis can be applied to either raw data or ratios. Some considerations about the evaluation of trend are necessary:

- Time horizon: how long ago in the past does the data need to be analyzed? There are many factors determining it: external events, industry dynamics, but 5 years on average is suitable for most organizations.
- Noise: there are many specific events that can alter trends such as mergers, organizational restructuring, large investments, financial crisis, political crisis, environmental disasters.

Table 9.1 Financial performance measures.

Type of metric	Name	Formulae
Liquidity indicates the organization's ability to satisfy current (short-term) financial obligations such as salary payments, payments to creditors, banks or government taxes	*Working capital* refers to how much money is left if the organization has to pay all its liabilities. The unit is in currency (absolute number)	*Working capital* = Current assets – Current liabilities
	Current ratio is similar to working capital but it avoids the confusion of absolute numbers. Basically, a number above one is positive and a number below one reflects potential problems	*Current ratio* = Current assets/Current liabilities
	Operating cash flow ratio shows the capacity to generate cash considering the organization's debts. Since it is a ratio any value above one indicates the company is able to pay to debtors	*Operating cash flow ratio* = Operating cash flow/Current liabilities

Table 9.1 (Continued)

Type of metric	Name	Formulae
Activity or efficiency measures an organization's efficiency in the use of resources.	*Sales per employee* measures the productivity of the employees in terms of revenues. The number of employees is an average of the employees in a year. This is an absolute number but it can be compared with the average salaries paid in the company, or compared with competitors, in order to obtain an idea of productivity	*Sales per employee* = Net sales/Average number of employees
	Asset turnover indicates the productivity of the total assets in terms of sales generated. Conceptually it is similar to the previous metric but it is applied with the assets of the organization. The higher the value of the metric, the shorter the time required to pay off the assets' value (measured in sales). It is important to compare this metric with similar competitors	*Asset turnover* = Net sales/Total assets *Fixed asset turnover* = Net sales/Fixed assets (property, plant and equipment)
	Stock turnover ratio shows the number of times the inventory turns into sales. Inventories with low turnover are idle and consequently do not generate cash becoming non-productive assets	*Stock turnover ratio* = Cost of goods sold/ Average inventory
	Return on assets shows the efficiency of the organization to generate earnings from the total assets. It is measured as a percentage and it is usually compared with the interest rate or any other investment option to evaluate the efficiency of the use of the funds	*Return on assets* = Net earnings/Total assets
Financial leverage compares the ability of the organization to pay to its creditors	*Debt ratio* compares the total liabilities with the total assets. A value higher than one indicates that the organization can pay its debtors with its assets	*Debt ratio* = Total liabilities/Total assets
	Debt to equity ratio compares the total liabilities with the equities. A value higher than one indicates the organization can pay its debtors with the owner's equities	*Debt to equity ratio* = Total liabilities/Total equity
	Times interest earned ratio (or interest coverage ratio) shows if the organization is able to pay the interest charges from its operations	*Times interest earned ratio* = Earning before tax and extraordinary items/Interest expenses
	Return on equity ratio shows the performance of a company with respect to the funds of the owners	*Return on equity ratio* = Net earnings/Total equity

(Continued)

Table 9.1 (Continued)

Type of metric	Name	Formulae
Market ratios measure investor sentiment to the company and the cost of issuing stock. The sentiment is usually associated with the relationship between return and the value of an investment in the company's shares	*Earnings per share* shows the return of the company to each shareholder. It has to be compared with other companies in the industry *Price to earnings ratio* is widely employed to determine if the shares are valued correctly with respect to the earnings (the future earnings is used in some versions). The value depends on the perception of the risk of the company and future earnings expectations. A low ratio shows either high risk or low growth.	*Earnings per share* = Net Earnings / Number of shares *Price to earnings ratio* = Market price per share/ Earnings per share

Secondly, the comparison of the data with the organization's competitors using either longitudinal data (trends) or cross-sectional data (comparing one specific data point with a large set of competitors) can indicate the relative performance of the organization. Is the performance better or worse than the competitors'? What events in the competitors have not affected the organization or vice versa?

Food for thought 9.1 The airline industry generates intense attraction in terms of financial analysis for a number of reasons. First, most of the companies are in the stock market so financial information is access easily. Secondly, airline companies tend to have clearly distinguished business models: full service and low cost, as well as geographically segmented in some business models. Thirdly, the business model tends to be fairly standard, so it can be compared without fearing for some hidden concepts. Table 9.2 shows a set of financial information for European low cost airlines.

Table 9.2 Financial ratios for four large European low-cost airlines in 2016.

Company	Price to earnings ratio	Debt to equity ratio	Current ratio	Operating expense ratio	Return on assets (%)
Ryanair	12.18	1.12	1.43	0.78	10.6
Norwegian Airlines	46.31	6.60	0.48	0.98	0.9
easyJet	12.77	0.22	0.72	0.85	11.8
Wizz Air	6.43	0.04	1.70	0.83	18.6

Address the following issues:

- Explain the reasons behind the differences in the four companies in terms of operational efficiency measures use in the airline industry. You can find them on the website of the International Air Transport Association (IATA), which is the trade association for the world's airlines representing some 265 airlines or 83% of total air traffic, or you can also see Chapter 4.
- Find information of the financial ratios in Table 9.2, or additional ratios, for the past 5 years in order to make a trend analysis. Which companies have been performing well, stable or worse? If you extrapolate the past performance of the companies, which company is going to have problems?
- Using simple regression analysis, what is the best predictor of the price of the share in the stock market of the companies?

9.2 Strategic Controls

Strategic controls emphasize the content of strategic actions rather than their short-term results. They are very useful under conditions of uncertainty where some strategic actions may lead to short-term losses but they may ensure the survival of the organization in the long term.

One of the most well-known control systems that balances strategic and financial controls is the balanced scorecard (Kaplan and Norton, 1996a). The balanced scorecard aims to translate a business unit's mission and strategy into tangible objectives and measures (Kaplan and Norton, 1996a). The measures represent a balance between outcome measures – the financial results of the organization – and the measures that will drive future performance – such as customer satisfaction, critical business processes, resource and capabilities. The balanced scorecard highlights the linkages between long-term strategy with tangible (short-term) objectives and actions by dividing the goals and actions into four categories: financial results; customer satisfaction; critical business processes; and resources and capabilities. Each perspective feeds on the following perspective. Resources and capabilities are necessary to perform critical business processes, which are responsible for providing customer satisfaction. Customer satisfaction generates revenues that feed the financial results while resources and capabilities have costs associated with them. Each perspective contains its specific objectives, the measures for the objectives, targets for each measure and a list of actions that will contribute to reaching the targets. The idea behind operationalizing strategy through a set of objectives, measures and targets is to help the organization guide their daily operations. For example, defining specific measures and targets within a time horizon supports the evaluation of the progress made. The use of measurable outcomes permits the company to identify the impact of actions and activities, which can be employed

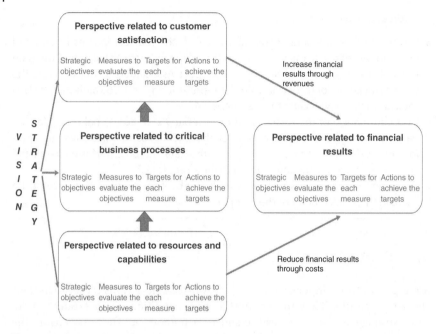

Figure 9.2 A strategic performance measurement system.

to offer feedback and discuss corrections. The actions and activities are aimed at situations that have to be solved immediately to implement the strategy. There is a distinction between actions and activities from operating procedures, also known as business policies, where policies are guidelines for managers to make recurrent decisions. Figure 9.2 presents a basic template for a balanced performance measurement system at strategic level.

9.3 Integrating Management Science into Strategic Management

The balanced scorecard intends to be a feed-forward control system as it links outcome measures and performance (Kunc, 2008). As such, the basis for this section is to discuss approaches that work with balanced scorecards. The first approach is based on focusing on the causal links between the performance measures to design a performance management system. The second approach discusses the use of analytics to data capturing/analysis and the resulting information management in terms of information provision, interpretation, and decision making.

9.3.1 Causal Models to Design Performance Management Systems

The balanced scorecard intends to be a feed-forward control system as it links outcome measures and performance drivers in cause-and-effect relationships but it has received some criticisms related to the interrelationships between measures (Nørreklit, 2000; Marr and Schiuma, 2003). Greater clarity in the linkages between different dimensions of the organizational performance should become an important issue during the process of designing performance measurement systems (Neely et al., 2002). For example, when a performance is different to expectations, managers should know where the problems are coming from so that they can intervene on the part of the organizations that improve the performance at the lowest possible cost. A relevant notion employed in the previous statement is that of interconnectedness between processes, areas and functions in the organization so a manager cannot improve one area, or the whole, without influencing other areas as well. In other words, the balanced scorecard should be robust enough to assist the implementation of strategy through a reduction of the causal ambiguity between actions and results (Kunc, 2008).

To understand how long-term objectives are translated into value through interconnected processes, areas and functions in the organization, Kaplan and Norton developed the idea of mapping causal relationships between strategic objectives and their measures into a strategy map (Kaplan and Norton, 1996a). Later on, Kaplan and Norton emphasized this idea in a book (Kaplan and Norton, 2004). Organizations are increasingly using causal models like strategic maps for the basis of their performance measurement systems (Franco-Santos and Bourne, 2005), so methodologies already established to develop causal models can be more widely employed to help in the design phase of performance measurement systems. The use of systems thinking, as a methodology to overcome some of the criticisms, arises from my experience in teaching strategic control systems in executive MBA and MBA courses.

When managers understand the linkages between performance measures and strategic objectives, they tend to use more strategically linked performance measures for evaluating performance than common financial measures. The use of a performance measurement system becomes more interactive in high-performing businesses as managers communicate and discuss performance both at formal meetings and at every opportunity because there is an instant understanding of what is going on. An adequate causal model helps to understand how objectives can be achieved as well as to evaluate individual's performance based on strategically linked measures rather than common financial measures. In other words, strategic control systems supported with causal maps can enhance organizational learning processes which try to test, validate, and modify the hypotheses embedded in a strategy (Kaplan and Norton, 1996b).

Hypotheses are related to magnitude and speed of response between changes in performance drivers and the associated outcome measures. In a first instance, the evaluation needs to be done subjectively and qualitatively until the organization gets enough data (here the role of Big Data is critical) to conduct periodic strategic reviews. Reviews should aim to understand the past in order to learn about possible futures. In that sense, Kaplan and Norton (1996a: page 269) said: "Whether managers reaffirm the existing strategy but adjust their judgments about the speed and magnitude of the cause-and-effect relationships, or the managers adopt a modified or entirely new strategy, the scorecard will have successfully stimulated a strategic (double-loop) learning process among key executives about the viability and validity of their strategy".

The development of the scorecard should also describe the temporal relationship of the strategy in order to assist managers in understanding how decisions made today will affect future outcomes. However, the temporal link between the variables is not clear in traditional performance measurement frameworks, including balanced scorecard and strategy maps. For example, the learning and growth perspective suggest training and other activities to improve the performance of business processes and, later on, the value added to customers but it does not explicitly portray the temporal horizon before results can be seen.

Finally, a balanced scorecard is an important representation of the dominant logic existing in the top management team, and, as such, it can be considered a key tool for strategic control and learning, although it requires different assumptions and tools to construct it. Tools should consider performance indicators (especially leading indicators) and their relationships as simply representations of the theories in use about the business and they should not restrict or encapsulate managers' presentation of their strategy, such as the four perspectives suggested in the balanced scorecard. To summarize, the development of the balanced scorecard, or other performance measurement systems, should start from what is important to measure for the managers, and what is important to measure is determined by their dominant logic rather than non-familiar templates, despite the fact that templates can help to elicit the areas that are important in an organization.

A wealth of methods for mapping out managerial cognition have been developed by many scholars, from causal mapping to mind mapping. For a review of methods for mapping out managerial cognition see Ackerman and Eden (2004). These tools capture not only the concepts (which can later be transformed into indicators) but also ways in which they are connected together (interrelationships). Cognitive maps with associated performance measurement indicators can be tested using simulation models so managers can be alerted about future organization performance and prevent them from falling into the trap of implementing actions which will make things worse (Akkermans and van Oorschot, 2005). Next, the use of one of the most widely used tools in systems thinking, causal loop diagrams, is presented followed by an explanation of the use of a simulation model using system dynamics. Table 9.3 describes the process used to embed systems thinking into a performance measurement table similar to a strategy map (Kunc, 2008).

Systems thinking   Systems thinking aims to identify the dynamic complexity existing in organizations by looking at multiple cause-and-effect relationships over time (Senge, 1990). Causal relationships described in the balanced scorecard between performance measures follow a linear logic: business processes → customer value, and do not consider the information feedback processes where the outcome performance measures (effects) are used to change processes captured in the leading performance indicators (causes). The information in the balanced scorecard is not neutral to the process of decision-making and can affect the future value of the performance indicators, leading to a circular process: causes → effects → causes. The design of the causal relationships in balanced scorecards, or any performance measurement systems, should consider the feedback processes existing between the information provided in the performance indicators and the likely intervention in the organization to correct deviations. Causal loop diagrams can illustrate the feedback processes existing between performance indicators and related organizational processes. Some of the reasons for using causal loop diagrams are: first, learning the mechanics of drawing these diagrams is fairly simple and can typically be handled quickly; and, secondly, experience with a vast number of managers and students has shown that they enjoy using causal loop diagrams to describe their perspectives about the business.

In this type of performance measurement map, the average number of concepts is 16 within a range of 10–24 concepts. The number of concepts can be considered in line with good practice in designing a balanced scorecard according to Kaplan and Norton (1996a: pages 162–163) but only 50–75% of the concepts may be related to the traditional balanced scorecard areas. More concepts can generate detailed complexity (too many measures) which hinders the process of decision making, especially when individuals weigh each measure differently. Qualitatively, concepts can be a mix between common and unique measures for an organization but it is important to use recognized and specific language accepted in the organization. The performance measures should reflect the business's reality, adequacy and practicality.

Table 9.3 Systems thinking strategic maps.

Step	Activity	Outcome
Identify key concepts in vision	The vision has to be divided into a set of concepts that can reflect its achievement over time. For example, market share In the balanced scorecard, the key concepts are usually related to financial objectives	Two to three key concepts and their expected trajectory over the time horizon the vision wants to be realized
Define the drivers of the key concepts	Each of the concepts need to have at least a driver. For example, what is/are the driver/drivers responsible for the market share? Market share can be driven by quality, price or customer service In the balanced scorecard, the usual drivers of financial performance are related to customer objectives	Each concept will have one or more drivers attached influencing its result. In our case, the concepts can have either a positive impact (quality) or a negative impact (price). The links between concept and drivers are represented using arrows and either a positive or negative sign depending on the impact
Define the organizational processes responsible for the drivers of the key concepts	For each driver, there has to be one, or more, organizational process accountable for it. For example, what process is responsible for the quality? High precision manufacturing determines the quality of the products. The balanced scorecard classifies the processes into an area called "internal processes"	Each driver needs to have one or more processes associated
Define the resources and capabilities supporting organizational processes	Organizational processes employ resources and capabilities existing in the organization. For example, high precision manufacturing is underpinned by high precision machinery (resource), highly skilled operators (resource), just-in-time operating (capabilities), and a sophisticated purchasing function which obtains good quality raw materials (capabilities). The balanced scorecard names the concepts in this area as "learning and growth"	Each business process should have a resource and a capability supporting it. It is possible that one resource or capability can be employed by more than one organizational process

Table 9.3 (Continued)

Step	Activity	Outcome
Define the financial performance	If the key concepts in your vision do not include financial results, you will need to identify them as a consequence of the concepts underpinning the vision. For example, what will be the result if the organization achieves a certain market share: income generated? Additionally, the business processes generate expenses that need to be accounted for in the financial performance The balanced scorecard suggests financial concepts are the initial concepts	Key concepts in the vision and business processes linked to financial concepts to any of the concepts of financial statements: assets, liabilities, income or costs
Identify key external factors	Some of the key concepts in the vision can be subject to external factors which are either threats or opportunities. For example, market share can be affected by social trends in consumption There is no correspondence in the balanced scorecard	External factors affecting key concepts are included using diamond figures
Represent the underlying feedback loop and delays	Each linkage between concepts needs to reflect the time required to observe its result. If the maps are used to evaluate the performance every quarter, then delays need to be indicated if the effect will take effect in more than one quarter Feedback processes can arise when the concepts are interconnected. The feedback processes can be either reinforcing (positive) or balancing (negative). Feedback processes are not included in the balanced scorecard	Each arrow needs to have a line crossing it to represent the delays beyond the normal operational time horizon Feedback processes are represented using the letter R for reinforcing or B for balancing. Feedback processes can only occur when there is a closed circuit of links between concepts
Define the measurements for each concept	Each concept needs to be measured using an indicator, whose information needs to be captured to be able to track the performance of the business toward its vision	One performance measure is located in a column next to each concept
Agree on targets for each measurement	Measures have to be subject to an expectation or target. Initially the targets can be agreed intuitively through negotiation	Numerical value and time to be reached for each concept
List one or two key actions that will drive each concept	Critical actions to improve the current performance are indicated. If there is no need for improvement, then the action will be related to maintaining the current situation	List of actions next to each target

Another interesting observation is the number of feedback loops identified in maps. The concept of feedback loops helps managers to realize the interconnectedness between different performance measures and how changes in one area lead to changes in other areas. Feedback loops aid managers to move from unidirectional causal relationships to bidirectional relationships, and more importantly help them to visualize the dynamic complexity of their business. On average, five to six feedback loops is a satisfactory number as it gives an average number of three to four concepts per feedback loop.

Food for thought 9.2 The fishing industry is not one of the most appealing industries but sustained demand, trade liberalization policies, globalization of food systems, improvement of transportation and logistics, technological innovations as well as changes in distribution and marketing have significantly made consumers aware of fish as a fashionable product (FAO, 2016). Growth in the global supply of fish for human consumption, growing at an average annual rate of 3.2% from 1961 to 2013, was larger than population growth in the past five decades (FAO, 2016). World per capita fish consumption increased from an average of 9.9 kg in the 1960s to 14.4 kg in the 1990s and up to 19.7 kg in 2013, and preliminary estimates for 2014 and 2015 pointed towards further growth beyond 20 kg (FAO, 2016). For example, the trade was US$ 150 billion in 2014, which is 9% of the trade in food commodities, and prices have increased 40% in the last 10 years (FAO, 2016). For fishing companies, there are important factors to consider when they are defining their strategies given the potential constraints in the environment and their impact on the performance of the company. In the face of rising fishing restrictions due to the decline of fish stocks, companies are making use of two different business models. One business model focuses on the development of fish farms, aquaculture, that have become the main suppliers of fish since 2014 (FAO, 2016)(Figure 9.3). Fish farming can be inland aquaculture, with fresh water fish, or marine/coastal aquaculture, with ocean fish such as salmon and mollusks. While the two main producers of salmon are Norway and Chile, which share similar environmental conditions for salmon farming, the larger producers of farmed fish, mostly inland aquaculture practices, are located in Asia, e.g. China and Indonesia. A typical vision for a fish farming company is "To be recognized as an innovative company, efficient and respectful of the environment and the communities where the activity takes place so it can achieve cost leadership and profitability" (www.altamarfoods.com).

The other model is based on the use of fishing vessels to capture different wild species in the ocean. Companies employ either purse seine or trawlers depending on the fish species. Fishing vessels have the capacity to refrigerate the fish, so they

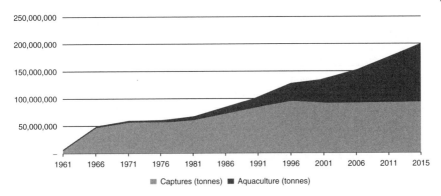

Figure 9.3 World capture fisheries and aquaculture production. *Source:* FAO (2016: Figure 1).

can stay on the ocean fishing for many days. Then, the fish is processed in their own plants onshore for either direct (mackerel, hake) or indirect (anchovy) human consumption. Fish for direct human consumption can be canned or frozen. In recent decades, major innovations in refrigeration, ice-making and transportation fostered the distribution of fresh fish so its share in the total of fish for human consumption increased from 3% in the 1960s to 25% in 2014 in developing countries (FAO, 2016). Fish for indirect human consumption is called fishmeal and it is employed in diverse food supplements for farmed fish, pig feed, poultry feed or fish oil (if the fish is fatty). Basic information about fish meal can be obtained from the FAO website. One typical vision for this type of company is "To be a company recognized as a leader in improving nutrition and health based on innovation, efficiency and respect for the environment." Some of the largest fishing companies are located in Peru, which is one of the largest producers of fishmeal.

The next step is to develop the systems thinking strategy map using the method described in Table 9.3 for the fishing companies. The application for a fishing company is presented in Table 9.4

After following the steps indicated in Table 9.4, the management will be able to visualize a systems thinking strategic map (Table 9.5). First, external key factors (global demand and fisheries biomass) are represented using diamond shapes. Secondly, linkages related to financial information, e.g. the use of profits to determine investment on production technology, staff training on process technologies and expansion of capacity in vessels and plants, use broken lines. Thirdly, operational linkages are reflected with solid lines and those linkages that have some delays embedded include two cross lines, e.g. since fisheries' biomass is unknown and subject to yearly variations, the impact of the current level of biomass on fish

Table 9.4 Systems thinking strategic maps process for a fishing company.

Step	Outcome
Identify key concepts in vision	Efficiency; innovation; and respect for the environment
Define the drivers of the key concepts	Efficiency is driven positively by investing in technology in order to improve the efficiency in fishing fleets and production plants and it is measured by the production costs
	Innovation is driven positively by investment in process technology (including staff training) to increase the quality of the packaged fish or fish meal and it is measured by the price premium
	Respect for the environment is driven positively by quota management systems and it is measured by certifications related to sourcing from sustainable fisheries
Define organizational processes responsible for the drivers	Production costs are driven by fish capture process and fish processing plants
	Premium quality is generated by fish processing processes
	Sourcing from sustainable fisheries is achieved by quota management process
Define the resources and capabilities supporting organizational processes	Resources: fishing vessels and processing plants/production lines. Capabilities: fast capture and with less waste/economies of scale and flexibility
	Resources: fish processing human resources. Capabilities: fish selection and cutting
	Resources: relation with regulators/competitors area and marine biologists in fleet operations. Capabilities: obtaining fishing quotas and bargaining quotas with competitors/forecasting fisheries sustainable yield
Define the financial performance	Fishing fleet and productions costs from processing plants reduces profits
	Premium quality leads to higher market prices and prices influence profits
	Fishing fleet and processing plants generate product volume that influence profits
Identify key external factors	Global market demand affects price
	Fishery biomass determines fishing quotas and production

Table 9.4 (Continued)

Step	Outcome
Represent the underlying feedback loop and delays	Technology leads to efficiency. Efficiency implies volume and production costs. Production costs reduce profits but volume generate sales, which determines profits. Profits are employed to invest in technology. Investment in technology can improve process quality leading to premium products that lead to higher price, which improve profits. Profits are reinvested in the fishing fleet that generates capture for the plants and volume. Fish capture reduces biomass which lead to fishing quotas and lower fish capture
Define the measurements for each concept	The outcome for these steps are presented in the final system thinking strategy map
Agree on targets for each measurement	
List one or two key actions that will drive each concept	

capture can take years to be revealed. Then, the clouds reflect the key concepts in the vision of the company.

Address the following issues:

- Track the linkages between the different concepts and identify the expected impact of one concept on another by evaluating the targets agreed. For example, how much does the fleet need to expand in order to reach the sales target agreed?
- Identify all feedback loops in the systems thinking strategic map
- Develop a similar map to Table 9.5 for an aquaculture-based business model. What are the main differences and similarities?
- The systems thinking strategy map can be converted into a system dynamics model to run diverse "what if" situations and observe the future performance of the business.

Table 9.5 Systems thinking strategic maps of a fishing company.

Systems thinking strategy map

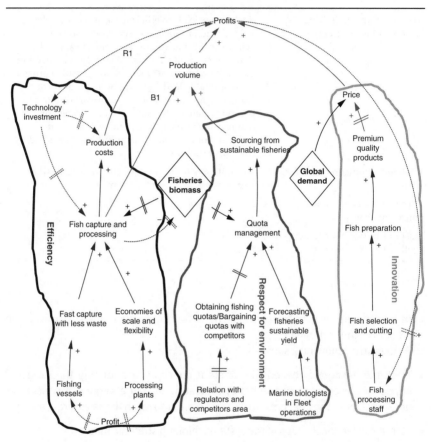

DHC, direct human consumption; IHC, indirect human consumption.

R1 (Reinforcing feedback process 1): Profits promotes Technology Investment that increases Fish capture and processing. Fish capture and processing leads to higher Production volume further augmenting Profits and closing the feedback process.

B1 (Balancing feedback process 1): Profits promotes Technology Investment that increases Fish capture and processing. Fish capture and processing leads to higher Production costs decreasing Profits and closing the feedback process.

Measures	Targets (Annual)	Actions
Return on assets	Industry +2%	No action is on target
DHC and IHC volume and price	Direct 60% sales	More DHC +2%
	Indirect 40% sales	Less IHC −2%
	Global market price +10%	Improve 2%
Operating cost per ton of fish captured and fish processed.	US$ 10 per ton vessel	Sonar and nets
	US$ 3 per ton process	Less energy
Market share of quota available	15% of total quota	No action
	100% tests passed	Improve 5%
Fishmeal quality tests passed/ Customer loyalty in fresh fish	100% sales to returning customers	
Global demand growth	3% annual	Keep as it is
Size of quota over time	Increase 2% annual	
New fisheries attained	One	Explore Africa
Size of quota	90% total sales	No action
Waste in fish preparation due to quality issues	5% of total fresh production	Reduce 2%
Speed to fulfil quota and quality of capture	20 days and 5% waste	Reduce 2 days
	30 days	Reduce 2%
Time to process fish	3% year-on-year	Reduce 5 days
Increase in market share quota	Error +/- 10%	Buy quotas
	Variability less than 5%	New model
Exactness of fisheries' biomass		Train staff to improve quality
Quality of fish fillets		
Size of fleet	20 vessels	Add 1 vessel
Processing capacity	100 000 tons	Expand 1 line
Years of experience	20 years	No action
Number of marine biologist	2	No action
Fish processing staff turnover	Less than 10%	Improve contract

9.3.2 Implementing the Performance Management System: Analyzing, Reviewing, and Reporting Performance Data – the Role of Analytics

A key aspect of business analytics is its relationship with the strategic use of information technology: collecting, analyzing, reviewing and reporting performance data (Hedgebeth, 2007). If analytics is included in performance management systems, they will be able to provide new insights into the dynamics of business and their related performance, which can result in increased management effectiveness. Moreover, the role of analytics is to uncover the causal linkages between performance measures in order to provide a predictive capability to managers. Once the cause-and-effect relationships are known, the management's actions, together with the design of management control (and reward) systems, can be designed using this information. On the one hand, organizational continuous learning is stimulated by evaluating the causal linkages using the data capture. On the other hand, feed-forward loops can be used for predictive purposes.

Performance measurements are usually formulated based on one or more raw pieces of information. Analysis aggregates the individual components to become the foundation for the performance measurement. However, you must analyze individual data components before you can use them to create a performance measure. When data is aggregated, it loses context and, potentially, usefulness. Therefore, aggregated data may be used as part of a report card but it will not determine what needs to be fixed. The following paragraphs discuss some techniques for analyzing, reviewing and reporting performance data.

Initially, analysts have to determine if data is accurate. Accuracy is judged differently for different types of information and can involve cross-checking information between reports, verifying numbers with knowledgeable respondents, or assessing the plausibility, the detail, the documentation and the consistency. An initial check of the data quality can be to plot each variable in the data set as it was collected and examine them for inappropriate data points. Additionally, logical inconsistencies can be discovered by cross checking two or more separate items of information against each other using cross tabulations, contingency tables, and scatter plots. Another evaluation is to identify sampling errors considering the four principles that guide sampling: the population must be clearly identified, the sample has to be of appropriate size, the sample has to be representative, and probability sampling (random or stratified) must be used. Statistical techniques have been developed to test whether the numbers generated from a sample can be generalized to the population from which it was drawn, given the sample size and the variation within the sample. The statistical significance gives us the generalizability of the data. The chi-square and t-test are two statistical methods most frequently used to address the question. When data is primarily qualitative, and for purposes of validation, experts may be asked to combine data and describe the findings in qualitative terms.

One important issue to consider is that data does not have meaning outside its context; data contains noise that distorts key trends. Therefore, before you can detect a trend, you must first filter out the noise. Unfortunately, traditional limited comparisons, such as visual comparisons, can neither filter out the noise nor highlight potential trends so it is important to use statistical methods. It is important for leaders, whether they be leaders of a company or key members of a team, to understand statistical concepts of variation, including statistical distributions. However, the best analysis is the simplest analysis although you have to consider the impact of arbitrary goals on the system behavior because they tend to distort it.

Another key consideration is the reaction to a significant variance: What do you do when actual performance is compared with expected performance and when trend analysis is completed? If the variance between the actual and expected performance is significant, more analysis will determine whether corrective actions are necessary. There are three usual responses: you can choose to ignore it; take an action to change the drivers of the results; or change the goals. If an action is needed, what will be the corrective action and what will be the priority? The key objectives of a corrective action are:

1) To improve the actual performance which is usually achieved by doing more of similar activities and it is located at the level responsible for the performance measure.
2) To eliminate the cause of the actual performance which implies an action to change the activities (drivers) responsible for the actual performance. Dependent upon the cause, this action may involve higher levels of the management team.
3) To maintain or enhance the efficiency and effectiveness. This objective is an essential condition for continuing process improvement.

If the variance is small, the business processes/activities are probably working properly. However, you can consider re-evaluating your goals in order to make them more challenging. Another option is to make changes to the business processes which will imply the need to re-evaluate goals to make sure they are still viable. Goals need to be realistically achievable for either easy or hard goals.

To summarize, there are two categories of analytics tools: (1) to analyze data; and (2) to identify root causes of variance and support improvements. Table 9.6 displays some common tools to analyze data and Table 9.7 presents tools to identify root causes.

9.4 End of Chapter

There is a set of characteristics that need to be considered when defining performance measures. First, they can be financial and non-financial measures. Secondly, they are measured with a predefined frequency which is determined by the business cycle. Thirdly, they are acted upon from the CEO and top

Table 9.6 Analytical tools to describe data: descriptive analytics.

Tool (reference)	Description
Check sheet (McQuarter et al., 1995)	The check sheet is a document employed to collect and categorize measurements. The measurements can be quantitative or qualitative
Descriptive statistics (Wisniewski, 2010)	Descriptive statistics are used to quantitatively describe a set of data and summarize the characteristics of the statistics. Descriptive statistics differentiate from inferential statistics because they only describe the data rather than use the data to learn (infer) about the population that the data represents.Some statistics used to describe a data set are statistics of central tendency and variability or dispersion. Statistics of central tendency are mean, median and mode, while statistics of variability include standard deviation (or variance), minimum and maximum values of the variables, kurtosis and skewness
Contingency tables (Agresti, 2003)	A contingency table (also known as a cross tabulation or crosstab) is a matrix that displays the frequency distribution of multiple variables
	Contingency tables provide a simple picture of the interrelation between two variables in order to understand their interactions. Contingency tables are usually complemented with statistical analysis such as Pearson's chi-squared test
Tree diagrams	The purpose of tree diagrams is to classify data. In this case, the name for a decision tree is decision tree classifiers. In the case of performance measures, it can be employed to recognize patterns across multiple sets of measures (Safavian and Landgrebe, 1990)
Time series (Hamilton, 1994)	A time series is a series of data points arranged in time order. Time series are frequently displayed using line charts. Time series analysis comprises methods to extract characteristics of the data in terms of trend, noise and seasonal variations
Scatter plots (Wisniewski, 2010)	A scatter plot (also called a scatter graph, scatter chart, or scatter diagram) is a type of graph using Cartesian coordinates to display values for typically two variables. The data is displayed considering the value of one variable on the horizontal axis and the value of the other variable on the vertical axis. It is used to discover patterns across variables but they require regression analysis to confirm the observations
Regression analysis (Wisniewski, 2010)	Regression analysis estimates the relationships among variables. There are many regression techniques for modeling and analyzing variables depending on types and objectives of the analysis. If the focus is on the relationship between variables: the outcome variable (dependent variable) is predicted by an equation including one or more predictors (one or more independent variables)

Table 9.7 Analytical tools to identify the root causes of performance.

Tool (reference)	Description
Affinity diagram (Pyzdek and Keller, 2014)	It is a tool used to organize ideas and data. The tool is commonly used to organize large numbers of ideas generated from brainstorming sessions based on their relationships. This tool can help to identify the sources of problems detected in the performance. Once completed, the affinity diagram may be used to create a cause-and-effect diagram
Cause-and-effect diagram (Pyzdek and Keller, 2014)	Cause-and-effect diagrams were created by Kaoru Ishikawa (1968) in order to illustrate the causes of a specific event. Each cause or reason for imperfection is a real (or potential) source of variation. Causes are usually grouped into major categories in order to identify specific sources of variation
Fault tree analysis (Lee et al., 1985)	Fault tree analysis is a deductive analysis in which an undesired performance is analyzed using Boolean logic (AND – OR) to uncover the lower-level events responsible for it. It has been adopted for the identification of risk factors
Root cause analysis (Rooney and Heuvel, 2004)	Root cause analysis is a method of problem solving used for identifying the causes of an unsatisfactory performance. A factor is considered a root cause if management has control to fix it and prevent the unsatisfactory performance from recurring. Causal factors can affect an outcome but they are not a root cause because they do not prevent the recurrence with certainty
	While it is used as a reactive method of identifying causes (since analysis is done after the performance is reported), root cause analysis can be used to forecast or predict probable events even before they occur by using the insights generated
Histogram (Wisniewski, 2010)	It is a graphical representation of the distribution of numerical data which can be employed as an estimate of the probability distribution of a continuous numerical variable
	There are differences between histograms and bar charts. A histogram is used with continuous variables, where categories represent ranges of the variable. A bar chart is a plot of the frequency of categorical variables. One way in which to differentiate between histograms and bar charts is that the bar charts may have gaps between the rectangles
Pareto analysis (Pyzdek and Keller, 2014)	A Pareto chart is a type of chart where individual values are represented in descending order by bars and the cumulative total is represented by an increasing line
	The left vertical axis represents the frequency of occurrence of factors or events responsible for the performance. The right vertical axis is the cumulative percentage of the total number of occurrences. The purpose of the Pareto chart is to highlight the most important factors or events from a set of factors

(Continued)

Table 9.7 (Continued)

Tool (reference)	Description
Gap analysis (Balm, 1996)	A gap analysis is a method of assessing the differences in performance between current results and a benchmark or objectives in order to determine whether the requirements are being met and, if not, what steps should be taken to ensure they are met successfully

management team to the very last employee in the organization. Fourthly, they are employed to direct decisions and actions, e.g. the person responsible understands the linkages between the actions that need to be taken and the corresponding result – cause-and-effect relationship is clear. Fifthly, measures have a responsible actor associated, e.g. CEO, business unit manager, functional manager, employee, or supplier. Sixthly, the measure captures a significant impact for the level of decision. Seventhly, the measure is verified that it does not generate spurious responses, e.g. gaming behavior.

Performance management activities can be greatly enhanced by the extensive use of data and analytical methods to understand the dynamics of business through the control of key performance drivers. Big Data analytics can support capturing and communicating tangible and/or intangible concepts underpinning the systems thinking strategy map. Different analytical methods can be used to identify and verify the causal linkages within the map. Some examples are visual maps (Kaplan and Norton, 2004) or performance tree diagrams (Lynch and Cross, 1991). Analytics systems can use multiple sources such as drilling down accounting data (e.g. from profits to revenue and cost breakdowns) to sophisticated mathematical and statistical methods that can provide insights into the dynamics of performance drivers. Analytics-based performance management uses business analytics systematically to identify, use, and prove the quantitative relationships between the factors, inputs, processes and outputs identified in the systems thinking strategy map. In this way, analytics support value creation in the long run.

Effective use of business analytics in performance management requires many components: data availability, IT infrastructure and analytical competencies. Only organizations that have advanced IT infrastructure such as an enterprise resource planning (ERP) system, data warehouse, data mining systems, or customer relationship management can exploit the use of business analytics successfully in performance management. However, gathering some data for business analytics can be a problem when performance measures are hard to measure, especially intangible values. Since business analytics use past data, past data may not always be a good predictor of current and future performance. Consequently, it is important to identify different maturity levels in the

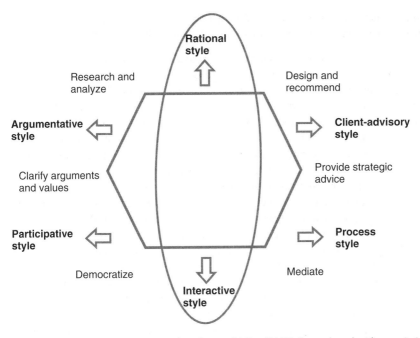

Figure 9.4 Management science styles. *Source:* Walker (2009). Reproduced with permission of Elsevier.

integration of business analytics with performance management systems that are related to the capability of identifying and using cause-and-effect relations for performance optimization and techniques that combine logical reasoning with analytical methods (mathematical, statistical, or econometric models). In this situation, the styles of management science (Figure 9.4) interventions are related to provide rational explanations for the performance observed together with interactive tools allowing decision makers to question the data observed.

9.4.1 Revision Questions

1) What are the differences between input, process and output measures? What organizational factors influence the importance between input, process and output measures?
2) What other management science tools can help the selection of targets for performance measures? Explain the strengths and weaknesses of the tools.
3) List the sources of information for capturing customers' mood. What systems (data capture and analysis) need to be developed in order to have a systematic understanding of customers?
4) What are the conditions needed to employ the information collected from customers on strategy design or strategy change?

9.4.2 Case Study: The Impact of Performance Measurement Systems Adoption in Business Performance: the Shipping Industry Case

The implementation of a performance measurement system (PMS) is a key issue that every organization must continuously pay attention to in order to ensure its survival. However, there is no coherent or unique body of knowledge about the type of PMS that will support organizations. Although there is a prevalent use of the balanced scorecard (as discussed earlier in the chapter), there are also a large number of performance measurement frameworks, e.g. performance prism, gap analysis, balanced scorecard, key performance indicators (Marr and Schiuma, 2003), available that have multiple dimensions and interpretations. The shipping industry is still adopting the PMS primarily due to the absence of a generic framework that takes into account the particularities of this industry (Otheitis and Kunc, 2015). Kunc and Bhandari (2011) suggest the attention of companies between industry key success factors and their particular strategies affect the design and use of a PMS, which preclude the establishment of a generic framework. Measures developed outside the actual strategic context will not be able to drive the results called by the strategy. For example, adopting a PMS due to regulations may mislead the focus of attention of the companies, thus impacting on their performance (Otheitis and Kunc, 2015).

Most of the world's trade is carried by the international shipping industry and without ships the import and export of bulk goods such as oil, gas, grains, iron ore, coal, etc. would not be possible or be very expensive. Commercial ships are extremely sophisticated and can cost up to US$ 200 million. The owner and manager of the ship are not always the same. Owning companies are usually incorporated in countries with favorable tax regimes. Operating companies are located in the main users of maritime transport, e.g. Germany, USA, etc. Merchant ships can be grouped in the following categories: Oil/Chemical/LNG tankers; Ore/Bulk Carriers; Container ships; Other/General cargo (Reefer ships, specialized cargo, fishing, etc.) and Passenger ships (Otheitis and Kunc, 2015). Oil tankers account for 30% of the fleet in tonnage, bulk carriers 40%, container ships 15%, and the rest is the general cargo fleet. The world shipping industry has grown four times in size since 1968. One of the key issues with the industry is the cyclicality of the freight prices which is reinforced by the cycles in the world economy. The industry is heavily regulated by diverse organizations among them the International Maritime Organization (IMO).

Otheitis and Kunc (2015) performed a study on the adoption of a PMS in the shipping industry using a questionnaire distributed to 100 ship management companies. Likert scales were the base for the answers, so the companies could only be classified into groups in terms of responses. Table 9.8 shows the characteristics of the responses obtained.

In terms of the responses, the study split the responses between non-tankers and tankers because tankers are more regulated which affects their adoption of

Table 9.8 Companies involved in the study.

Characteristics of sample companies		Count	% of total
Years in operation	1–10	12	29.3
	11–20	6	14.6
	21–30	7	17.1
	31+	16	39.0
Fleet size	1–10	15	36.6
	11–30	17	41.5
	30+	9	22.0
Ownership	Privately owned	29	70.7
	Public listed	12	29.3
Location of company	Belgium	2	4.9
	Cyprus	2	4.9
	Denmark	2	4.9
	France	1	2.4
	Germany	2	4.9
	Greece	16	39.0
	India	1	2.4
	Netherlands	2	4.9
	Norway	6	14.6
	Singapore	2	4.9
	Sweden	1	2.4
	Turkey	1	2.4
	USA	3	7.3

PMS due to regulatory pressures. The results clearly indicate the importance of regulatory frameworks on forcing companies to adopt a specific PMS as shown in Table 9.9 with the tanker's operating companies. One interesting aspect of the results is the low adoption of the balanced scorecard.

When the PMS is adopted, it seems to be highly valued in terms of the support to strategy, organizational performance and decision making as Table 9.10 shows. In general, all companies agree with the usefulness of PMSs in terms of achieving organizational growth and a competitive advantage, reducing risks as well as satisfying social and environmental responsibilities, and supporting decision making in the implementation of strategies. However, the results highlight the impact of regulations in the use of PMSs for benchmarking and

Table 9.9 Adoption of performance measurement systems in the companies of the study.

		Non tanker		Tanker	
		Number of responses	% of total	Number of responses	% of total
Performance measurement tools	Performance indicators	10	30	4	8
	Key performance indicators	11	33	20	40
	Key results indicators	2	6	5	10
	Balanced scorecard	1	3	3	6
	Gap analysis	3	10	11	22
	Shipping key performance indicators	1	3	6	12
	Performance prism	0	0	0	0
	Other	0	0	1	2
	None	5	15	0	0
	Total responses	**33**	**100**	**50**	**100**
		Number of companies	**% of total**	**Number of companies**	**% of total**
Years using performance measurement tools	Not using	5	25	0	0
	Not more than 5	8	40	5	24
	5–10	6	30	9	43
	More than 10	1	5	7	33
	Total responses	**20**	**100**	**21**	**100**
		Number of companies	**% of total**	**Number of companies**	**% of total**
Years in operation	1–10	9	45	3	14.3
	11–20	4	20	2	9.5
	21–30	3	15	4	19.1
	31+	4	20	12	57.1
	Total responses	**20**	**100**	**21**	**100**

fulfilling their environmental responsibilities. While tankers have adopted PMSs due to regulatory requirements rather than business needs, non-tanker companies that adopted PMSs due to business needs seem to be more satisfied with the use of PMSs in supporting strategic decision making. Therefore, PMSs

Table 9.10 Perceived usefulness of performance management systems on the companies.

	Strongly disagree (%)	Disagree (%)	Neither agree nor disagree (%)	Agree (%)	Strongly agree (%)
Non tanker					
PM has facilitated my organisation's growth	0.0	6.7	26.7	53.3	13.3
PM has protected my organisation from loss and excessive risk	0.0	6.7	20.0	53.3	20.0
PM has helped me benchmark my organisation with respect to the industry	0.0	0.0	33.3	53.3	13.3
PM has helped my organisation gain a competitive advantage over rivals	0.0	13.3	26.7	53.3	6.7
PM is used to enhance my organisation's social and environmental responsibility	6.7	0.0	33.3	53.3	6.7
PM is used for decision making and strategy implementation	6.7	0.0	6.7	73.3	13.3

(Continued)

Table 9.10 (Continued)

	Strongly disagree (%)	Disagree (%)	Neither agree nor disagree (%)	Agree (%)	Strongly agree (%)
Tanker					
PM has facilitated my organisation's growth	0.0	9.5	23.8	47.6	19.0
PM has protected my organisation from loss and excessive risk	0.0	4.8	14.3	52.4	28.6
PM has helped me benchmark my organisation with respect to the industry	0.0	0.0	9.5	42.9	47.6
PM has helped my organisation gain a competitive advantage over rivals	0.0	19.0	14.3	57.1	9.5
PM is used to enhance my organisation's social and environmental responsibility	0.0	9.5	14.3	57.1	19.0
PM is used for decision making and strategy implementation	0.0	4.8	9.5	57.1	28.6

PM, performance management.

imposed by regulators do not seem to be internalized within the organizations.

The behavior observed illustrates the principles in Kunc and Bhandari (2011) regarding the attention of companies towards key success factors in their industries, including regulation and impacts on the use of PMSs. Shipping companies only turned their attention to PMSs when there was a failure, e.g. a major maritime accident such as the Exxon Valdez oil spill in Alaska, which led to new regulations. Thus, institutional conditions can have an influence on the adoption of PMSs.

Another important observation is the lack of adoption of a more suitable PMS, e.g. Performance Prism (Neely et al., 2002). Performance Prism is suitable for organizations with many stakeholders (port authorities, flag regulators, classification societies, local environmental bodies, direct and indirect customers, employees, owners) as a template to capture their requirements.

Here are a few actions to perform related to the study on the adoption of PMSs:

1) Select two industries and identify the PMSs adopted by the key companies in the industry.
2) What are the differences between the companies in the industry? What are the differences between the industries?
3) Are there any factors significantly affecting the adoption of a certain PMS? Or the adoption of a PMS in general?

References

Ackerman, F. and Eden, C. (2004). Using causal mapping – individual and group, traditional and new. In: Systems Modelling Theory and Practice (ed. M. Pidd), 127–145. John Wiley & Sons, Ltd.

Agresti, A. (2003). Categorical Data Analysis, Vol. 482. John Wiley & Sons, Inc.

Akkermans, H.A. and van Oorschot, K.E. (2005). Relevance assumed: a case study of balanced scorecard development using system dynamics. *Journal of the Operational Research Society*, 56, 931–941.

Balm, G.J. (1996). Benchmarking and gap analysis: what is the next milestone? *Benchmarking for Quality Management & Technology*, 3(4), 28–33.

FAO. (2016). The State of World Fisheries and Aquaculture 2016. Contributing to Food Security and Nutrition for All. FAO.

Ferreira, A. and Otley, D. (2009). The design and use of performance management systems: an extended framework for analysis. *Management Accounting Research*, 20(4), 263–282.

Franco-Santos, M. and Bourne, M. (2005). An examination of the literature relating to issues affecting how companies manage through measures. *Production Planning & Control*, 16(2), 114–124.

Hamilton, J.D. (1994). Time Series Analysis, Vol. 2. Princeton University Press.

Hedgebeth, D. (2007). Data-driven decision making for the enterprise: An overview of business intelligence applications. *The Journal of Information and Knowledge Management Systems*, 37(4), 414–420.

Kaplan, R.S. and Norton, D.P. (1996a). The Balanced Scorecard: Translating Strategy into Action. Harvard Business School Publishing.

Kaplan, R.S. and Norton, D.P. (1996b). Strategic learning and the balanced scorecard. Strategy & Leadership, 24(5), 18–24.

Kaplan, R.S. and Norton, D.P. (2004). Strategy Maps: Converting Intangible Assets into Tangible Outcomes. Harvard Business School Publishing.

Kaplan, R.S. and Norton, D.P. (2008). Mastering the management system. *Harvard Business Review*, 86(1), 63–77.

Kunc, M. (2008). Using systems thinking to enhance the value of strategy maps. *Management Decision*, 46, 761–778.

Kunc, M. and Bhandari, R. (2011). Strategic Development processes during economic and financial crisis. *Management Decision*, 8, 1343–1353.

Lee, W.S., Grosh, D.L., Tillman, F.A., and Lie, C.H. (1985). Fault tree analysis, methods, and applications: a review. *IEEE Transactions on Reliability*, 34(3), 194–203.

Lynch, R.L. and Cross, K.F. (1991). Measure Up – The Essential Guide to Measuring Business Performance. John Wiley & Sons, Ltd.

Marr, B. and Schiuma, G. (2003). Business performance measurement – past, present and future. *Management Decision*, 41(8), 680–687.

McQuater, R.E., Scurr, C.H., Dale, B.G., and Hillman, P.G. (1995). Using quality tools and techniques successfully. *The TQM Magazine*, 7(6), 37–42.

Neely, A., Adams, C., and Kennerley, M. (2002). Performance Prism: The Scorecard for Measuring and Managing Business Success. Prentice Hall.

Norreklit, H. (2000). The balance on the Balanced Scorecard – a critical analysis of some of its assumptions. *Management Accounting Research*, 11, 65–88.

Otheitis, N. and Kunc, M. (2015). Performance measurement adoption and business performance: An exploratory study in the shipping industry. *Management Decision*, 53, 139–159.

Pyzdek, T. and Keller, P.A. (2014). The Six Sigma Handbook, 25. McGraw-Hill.

Rooney, J.J. and Heuvel, L.N.V. (2004). Root cause analysis for beginners. *Quality Progress*, 37(7), 45–56.

Saaty, T.L. (1990). How to make a decision: the analytic hierarchy process. *European Journal of Operational Research*, 48(1), 9–26.

Safavian, S.R. and Landgrebe, D. (1991). A survey of decision tree classifier methodology. IEEE Trans. *Systems, Man, & Cybernetics*, 21(3), 660–674.

Senge, P.M. (1990). The Leader's new work: Building learning organizations. *MIT Sloan Management Review*, 32(1), 7.

Tapinos, E. and Dyson, R.G. (2007). Performance measurement. In: Supporting Strategy: Frameworks, Methods and Models (eds F.A. O'Brien and R.G. Dyson), 285–312. John Wiley & Sons, Ltd.

Walker, W.E. (2009). Does the best practice of rational-style model based policy analysis already include ethical considerations? *Omega*, 37(6), 1051–1062.

Wisniewski, M. (2010). Quantitative Methods for Decision-makers. Pearson Education.

Futher Reading

Cheng, E.W. and Li, H. (2001). Analytic hierarchy process: an approach to determine measures for business performance. *Measuring Business Excellence*, 5(3), 30–37.

Suwignjo, P., Bititci, U.S., and Carrie, A.S. (2000). Quantitative models for performance measurement system. *International Journal of Production Economics*, 64(1), 231–241.

Osei-Bryson, K.M., (2004). Evaluation of decision trees: a multi-criteria approach. *Computers & Operations Research*, 31(11), 1933–1945.

Witten, I. H., Frank, E. (2005). Data Mining: Practical machine learning tools and techniques. Morgan Kaufmann.

10

Start-ups

Objectives

1) To understand the challenges facing new companies
2) To define the components of start-ups
3) To identify analytic tools to support the development of start-ups

Learning outcomes and managerial capabilities developed

1) To be able to develop a business plan
2) To develop financial analysis for start-ups under uncertainties

There are two basic trends in the conceptualization of entrepreneurship. The first trend considers the entrepreneur to be the person who creates and develops new businesses to the market, without necessarily bringing in new technology. The second perspective presents the entrepreneur as an innovator, and therefore a relatively inventive person, who can change the economy through innovation.

In this chapter, we look at the first perspective which defines entrepreneurs as people who want to create and run a business. The needs for the creation of a business can be very different, as Harris (2006) suggests:

- Lifestyle business: the founder of the business runs the business primarily with the aim of sustaining a particular level of income and/or to provide a foundation from which to enjoy a particular lifestyle. In this case, it would be unlikely to receive financial support from investors.
- Long-term business: the entrepreneur develops the company and its assets in order to ensure the long-term sustainability of the business. Potentially, some investors may be interested but not many of them will finance the business if there is no exit strategy.

Strategic Analytics: Integrating Management Science and Strategy, First Edition. Martin Kunc.
© 2019 John Wiley & Sons Ltd. Published 2019 by John Wiley & Sons Ltd.
Companion website: www.wiley.com/go/kunc/strategic-analytics

- High growth business: it is usually a small to medium size company that grows either its employees or turnover by an average of more than 20% per year for three or more consecutive years. This business requires large investments and high growth market in order to achieve this growth pace, so it is usually highly sought by investors.
- Entrepreneurs do not create a firm only to obtain profits but also to solve social problems. These entrepreneurs are usually called social entrepreneurs and this activity is known as social entrepreneurship (Johnson et al., 2008). Social entrepreneurship involves creating an organization earning revenues, but it is not-for-profit, in order to obtain resources that are employed to address a social problem (Johnson et al., 2008). Social entrepreneurship implies three aspects: a mission highlighting the achievement of a social objective; specific types of organizational forms such as cooperatives or charities; and a special business model which favors earning revenues in the market in order to be more flexible in solving the social problem (Johnson et al., 2008).

Starting a new business is done by many people but managing a successful start-up is a formidable challenge, especially for those who lack prior business ownership, management skills and experience. A good understanding of the business model, key resources and financial needs can play an important role in the beginning of a business. There are other issues, such as raising financial resources, doing market research and designing a business plan, but the most important issue to consider is the business idea. In order to develop a high-quality business idea, it is necessary to investigate the market and the industry (see Chapters 3, 4 and 5). Then, the critical step is to develop the business plan (Harris, 2006: Reuvid, 2006) defining the competitive advantage, resources and capabilities together with the organizational components (see Chapters 6, 7 and 8). See Table 10.1 for a summary of the components of a business plan for a start-up. The following sections discuss in detail the different components and the support that management science tools can offer each of them.

Before we review the business plan in detail, it is important to know the stages of entrepreneurial growth (Johnson et al., 2008). There are four stages (start-up, growth, maturity and exit), which are intrinsically related to the size of the company. Some of the challenges faced in each stage (Johnson et al., 2008) are:

- **Start-up.** Finding financial resources is critical in this stage for the business to take off. Many sources can be from own savings, friends, bank loans to venture capitalists (when the idea is appropriate).
- **Growth.** Management can be an important constraint since the size of the business is expanding rapidly and the entrepreneur needs to delegate more activities in order to concentrate on managing the business. Therefore, recruiting professional managers can be an option.

Table 10.1 Elements of a business plan.

Element of the business plan	Components
Management	• Description of the business model and its objectives • Skills and experience of the entrepreneur and the management team • Competitive advantage of the business
Market	• Total size and location • Potential market segment • Customers' characteristics • Customers' needs and requirements • Competitors • Value proposition • Marketing mix: price, channels (place) and promotion • Brand development • Market research and other marketing expenses
Product/service and business processes	• Specifications of product/service and customers' needs satisfied • Characteristics • Production process/service delivery • Physical resources required (equipment, installations) • Inbound and outbound logistics • After sale processes

Organization design and Resources	• Organization structure
	• Human resources:
	  - Top management team: responsibilities
	  - Managers existing and future requirements: skills, experience and responsibilities
	  - Staff existing and future requirements: skills and roles
	  - Hiring processes and timing
	• Other resources:
	  - Knowledge: existing patents, future patents, regulation compliance
	  - Technology: software, hardware, networks, communications

Financial management	• Critical assumptions and scenarios behind the cash flow calculations • Breakeven analysis and required investment in terms of initial funding and future requirements to support operating costs or financing business expansion • Projected profit and loss (income statement) based on revenues and operating costs • Key performance indicators • Sources and amount of funding is required together with the implications on ownership and exit strategy for investors and/or entrepreneur team

- **Maturity.** The challenge in this stage is the transition into a continuous source of growth besides the initial business idea, whose sales reach a plateau. Growth can be achieved by new products, diversification and expansion into new markets but it requires management skills closely related to mature organizations in terms of organizational complexity.
- **Exit.** It is important to consider the timing and circumstances in which the entrepreneur and the original funders will exit the start-up by releasing all or part of the capital. Three options are available: selling the company to another company; sell to the current professional managers (management buy-out); or stock trading (initial public offering).

10.1 The Components of a Business Plan for a Start-up

10.1.1 Management

This section discusses strategic aspects of the start-up such as the entrepreneur, the team supporting the entrepreneur, risks and the development of a growth strategy through the business model.

Entrepreneur   Personal characteristics of the entrepreneur are important to the success of a start-up. Three psychological characteristics of entrepreneurs that contribute to their success are: the need for achievement (McClelland, 1965); risk-taking propensity (Stewart Jr and Roth, 2001); and locus of control (Hansemark, 2003).

The need for achievement is a key psychological aspect that distinguishes entrepreneurs from non- entrepreneurs and successful entrepreneurs from non-successful entrepreneurs (Hansemark, 2003). An individual with a high need for achievement is characterized as having a desire to take personal responsibility for decisions, setting goals and trying to achieve them, as well as having the ability to think and plan ahead (Hansemark, 2003). This orientation helps entrepreneurs overcome obstacles and compensate for other weaknesses (Hansemark, 2003).

Taking risks is another important characteristic of entrepreneurs (Stewart Jr and Roth, 2001). Many successful entrepreneurs attribute success in business to their ability to confront uncertainty and take a calculated risk (Stewart Jr and Roth, 2001). Studies demonstrated that entrepreneurs exhibit a stronger risk-taking propensity, as well as a higher tolerance for ambiguity, than non-entrepreneurial individuals do (Stewart Jr and Roth, 2001).

Locus of control has been identified as one of the most dominant entrepreneurial characteristics since entrepreneurs perceive themselves as being in control of their environment (Poon et al., 2006). In entrepreneurs, locus of control is the ability to be self-directed in the pursuit of opportunities (Lumpkin and Dess, 1996).

Team   Many start-up companies are conceived and run by an entrepreneur, who is motivated and talented, without a team supporting him. However, an experienced team, together with the experience and knowledge provided by external advisers, can support the entrepreneur in developing a strong business model that creates value for customers. An experienced team will increase the opportunities of success since they are able to provide useful suggestions for managing the start-up. Moreover, networking plays an important role in start-ups because new businesses need to establish relationships with customers, suppliers, investors and the local communities.

More specifically, an effective team consists of three to six members who bring their expertise and skills together with their network (Sorensen, 2012). The management team can also be supported by boards that not only share similar positive aspects in terms of skills and expertise but also offer investment money and network. There are two types of boards: a board of directors, which has formal legal responsibilities to the firm; and management/scientific advisory boards, which provide their expertise in the industry and act like in-house consultants (Sorensen, 2012). In either case, there should be an open culture to allow challenging views and sharing information openly.

Risk management   Starting and managing a business is risky, entrepreneurs must examine how much risk they are prepared to accept. Identifying the risk factors is a key procedure for start-ups. Normally, the first sets of managerial risks come from the entrepreneur's ability to employ and retain key staff. Losing key staff can adversely impact the potential to run the business in the short and medium term. Management risks should be focused on the legal side of operations such as insurance, taxes and regulatory issues. Subsequently, the strategic risk needs to be considered. Strategic risks are related to market changes that can make the whole business model obsolete from the product/service and market positioning to the business processes. Another risk to consider is the financial risk coming from cash flows and investment requirements. Basically, technical risks refer to risks which originate during either the process of product manufacturing, and its delivery, or the delivery of services. Technical risks could be avoided by working carefully through testing relevant aspects of the production and delivery processes. Commercial risks can be avoided by examining the design of the service/product, by looking at the positioning of the company and the products/services offered to the potential market as well as the reaction of competitors.

Growth strategy and business idea as a competitive advantage of the business The growth strategy which makes a start-up sustainable is one of the key management functions of a new business. In general, growth strategy helps the start-up to become profitable and involves coordinating human resources, marketing, finance and operations to become aligned with the business idea or model (Zott and Amit, 2010). However, entrepreneurs need to establish the boundaries of the business and set up the organizational structure during the start-up process. Business models, which represent the sources of new value creation and potential competitive advantage (Chesbrough and Rosenbloom, 2003), are useful frameworks to establish the boundaries of start-ups. Start-ups require business model experimentation in order to rapidly test the market and validate or reject the business opportunity. A start-up delivers new value in the form of a product or service under conditions of extreme uncertainty. Due to this uncertainty many start-ups fail, and a large number of those that survive end up being acquired by larger companies. However, most of these failures could have been avoided by entrepreneurs with the implementation of a sound business model. There are six steps for developing the business idea (Harris, 2006; Reuvid, 2006):

1) Define the problems the company will solve for the customers.
2) Identify the reasons behind customers' willingness to buy existing products offered by competitors.
3) Understand changes in customer behavior that can affect the willingness.
4) Identify the customers that are most likely to change their behavior and their potential number.
5) Select the type of business that will serve these customers by defining the Unique Selling Point (USP).
6) Determine the trends that can affect the type of business.

To summarize, the building blocks of good business models, which is a key management task in a start-up, are superior value creation, key internal and relational resources, key tasks and processes and value appropriation (Sorensen, 2012). Thus, "A business model is made up of the set of interdependent tasks and processes that an organization performs with its key internal and relational resources and key processes in the pursuit of delivering superior customer value and appropriating value" (Sorensen, 2012: page 158). Some of the key questions to ask about each component are presented in Table 10.2.

Table 10.2 Key questions for a business model.

Building block	Key questions
Superior customer value creation	What do customers value?
	Who are our customers and target segment?
	What value proposition do we offer our customers?
	Do our customers understand our value propositions?
	What are the key issues facing potential customers and their potential solutions?
Key internal and relational resources	What resources and capabilities are necessary and sufficient to deliver superior customer value?
	Who holds those resources?
	Which resources are held in potential partners and alliances?
Key tasks and processes	What tasks and processes are necessary and sufficient to deliver superior customer value?
	Who holds those tasks and processes?
	How do we reach out customers?
	How do we relate to them?
Value appropriation	How do we make money in this business?
	What is the underlying strategy logic that explains how we can deliver value to customers at an appropriate cost?
	What is the revenue model: price × volume? What price should be charged? What volume should be expected?
	What is the cost structure? What are the direct and indirect costs driven by the key resources and activities?

Source: Adapted from Sorensen (2012: table 5.2, page 160).

Food for thought 10.1   Consider two industries, or two separate segments in the same industry, driven by opposite key success factors: size and profitability of companies, configuration (resources and capabilities) of the companies, level of differentiation, strength of the Five Forces, industry life cycle, key products and type of customers. Fill in Table 10.3 with the information.

Then, for each of the two industries you need to consider a business model for a start-up using the key questions indicated in Table 10.2.

Based on the two tasks performed, reflect on the following issues:

- What are the key differences between the two industries? How do the differences affect the way companies compete?
- What industry seems to be easier to enter?
- Based on your business model, what will be your chances of success in each industry?

Table 10.3 Key success factors.

Industry key success factors	Industry A	Industry B
Size and profitability of companies		
Configuration of companies		
Level of differentiation		
Strength of Five Forces		
Industry life cycle		
Key products		
Type of customers		

10.1.2 Market

The analysis of the market involves understanding what will be required from the company and how to lure customers into buying the products/services offered. Harris (2006: page 69) defined "The [marketing] strategies are employed across the entire process of designing your offering to meet the needs of the customers you want to sell to, and the mechanisms by which you promote it and finally deliver it to their satisfaction". The marketing plan is the largest component of the business plan and it is the main piece of information used to describe how to create superior value for the customers. Two key challenges discussed in the marketing plan are identifying and creating demand while configuring the marketing mix to achieve the highest customer satisfaction in a profitable way. Basically, a marketing plan includes a description of the market, the marketing strategy, investments required and the implementation of plans together with the controls (Kotler, 2000). With respect to the description of the market, the basic information is:

- Total size and location of the target market: How many customers are in the industry? Where are most of the customers located? Where do they get their products?
- Potential market segment: What particular group of customers will be interested in the product/service? How many potential customers are in this group?
- Potential customers' characteristics: What are the main characteristics (demographics, income, lifestyles, cultural, etc.) of the customers? What is the behavior (volume of use, purchase occasion, use occasions, brand loyalty, etc.) of the potential customers?
- Potential customers' needs and requirements: What are the needs of the potential customers that are not satisfied? How will the product address these needs? What specific requirements will address the customers' needs?

- Competitors: How many competitors are in the market segment? What are the main competitors? What are their main strengths and weaknesses? What companies may enter into the market if it grows? What are their products' characteristics and prices? What needs are satisfied by the existing products? What needs are not satisfied by the existing products?

The marketing strategy and implementation plans involve:

- Value proposition: How the new product differentiates from existing products: characteristics (features, quality, performance, innovativeness, and consistency), services (delivery, installation, and support), channel (coverage, suitability)? What positioning (image) will the product have in the mind of customers? How will the potential customers perceive the new product characteristics? Does it add value to them? Or is it sufficiently different to existing products? What is your USP?
- Marketing mix: price, channels (place) and promotion. Price variables are retail price, wholesale price, volume and cash discounts, bundling with other products, credit terms, and pricing strategy based on demand, seasonality, etc. Channels variables are distribution channels, coverage (broad, narrow, exclusive), downstream members, inventory, transportation and logistics management. Promotion variables involve USP, push or pull promotion, advertising, selling approach, sales promotions, and usage of different media.
- Brand development plan: What will be the brand name? What is the positioning of the brand in the industry? What will be the communications strategy?
- Market research and other marketing expenses: How often will market research be performed? How are customers' opinions going to be captured? What will be the size of the sales force? What will be the structure of the sales area, e.g. managers, supporting personnel? What IT will be required to support the area? In terms of approaches to face the market, Sorensen (2012) suggests two approaches: responsive; and proactive. A responsive approach focuses on expressed wants of customers using existing information collected through customer surveys, focus groups and concept testing (Sorensen, 2012). A proactive approach concentrates on unrevealed preferences of customers that are discovered through customer-drive toolkits and experiments, which generate new information.

10.1.3   Product/Service and Business Processes

The main elements of this component of the business plans are:

- Specifications of product/service and customers' needs satisfied. Most of the time, the entrepreneur has an idea of a product or service but it is important that the idea is checked with the potential customers in order to verify if the idea is able to satisfy customers' needs. The requirements can be expressed in many different semantic, imprecise and usually qualitative ways. The main challenge is to translate vague, non-technical customer needs into useful design specifications for the product or service. One interesting tool to support this process is called House of Quality (Hauser and Clausing, 1988; Hauser, 1993).

- Characteristics of the product/service. It presents the list of terms used for the definition of the product. For example, new drugs may involve terms such as efficacy, effectiveness, dose to therapeutic effect, dosing device, formulation characteristics, strength/concentration, etc. In general, the characteristics of the products involve price, functionality, materials employed, accessibility, easiness of use, etc. Then, each term has the specification for the characteristics for the product and it is recommended to have the characteristics of competing products.
- Production process/Service delivery. This area will be determined by the boundary of the company in terms of activities performed internally, together with other companies in alliances or simply bought from the market. Some of the tools, such as activity system, value chain, and business process mapping, used to represent the processes were discussed in Chapter 6.
- Physical resources required (equipment, installations). The requirement of physical resources is defined by the level of activities performed internally. A higher number of activities done internally will imply more resources owned or under the control of the company with the consequence of higher investment, debts or capital from investors, and fixed operating costs. Another important aspect affecting the physical resources is their specificity for the process and services defined. More specific products and services generated with proprietary processes require specific resources which reduce the competitors' ability to imitate the company's products and services. However, specific resources also make the company inflexible to changes in the market or the products/services. Potentially, specific resources can be more expensive than simple generic resources. The definition of the production process and service delivery involves key trade-offs.
- Inbound and outbound logistics. Inbound logistics become a key process when production is managed internally due to its implications on working capital, inventory management and scheduling with the production plans. Outbound logistics are critical in generating customer value since they determine the level of service provided and the reliability of the company. Outbound logistics, different to inbound logistics, are also critical even if the production occurs externally in a supplier or through an alliance. Outbound logistics can be an important cost depending on the location of the company's facilities.
- After sale processes. Customers may need support after they buy the product in regards to repairing defective products, explaining its functionality

and following up with additional features. Depending on the capacity of the firm, the activities are run in-house or through a network of firms that cover the markets where the product is sold. The internet has substantially simplified the activities to support customers as it offers a direct channel for customers.

Food for thought 10.2   Complete the business model designed previously with a marketing plan considering the following aspects (see questions for each concept defined previously in Sections 10.1.2 and 10.1.3):

- Product description
- Total size and location of the target market
- Potential market segment
- Potential customers' characteristics
- Potential customers' needs and requirements
- Competitors
- Value proposition
- Marketing mix
- Brand development plan
- Market research and other marketing expenses

Based on the marketing plan, reflect on the following issues:

- What are the main sources of information to identify and calculate the size of the market segment?
- What are the risks to defining the price? Have you evaluated the elasticity of the demand to different price levels? How did you evaluate it: using statistical data or focus groups?
- What criteria did you employ to define your competitors? How close is their value proposition to the value proposition of your product?

10.1.4   Organization Design and Resources

Table 10.1 indicates three key aspects of the business plan: the organization structure, human resources and other resources, not related to marketing, finance and production.

- Organization structure. It involves defining the corporate governance in terms of ownership structure, business form, composition of the board and the role of the board, as well as compensation and equity holdings of managers responsible for the daily operations. Corporate governance becomes a key issue when ownership and management are separated as well as there being conflicting interests between stakeholders (owners, management, employees). The business form defines the legal ownership of the new business. Business form can be sole ownership, private and public limited companies, and general and limited partnerships. Depending on the choice, it will affect the possibilities for the different stakeholders (owners, management and investors) to appropriate the value created for the business. Another aspect of the organizational structure is the formal system of tasks, decision rights, authority relationships and incentive systems to control and coordinate the work of the staff.

- Human resources are a critical resource in a start-up since they are at the center of creating value for customers and are responsible for all tasks and processes due to the low investment in formal processes and supporting systems, e.g. purchasing or invoicing:
  - Top management team: responsibilities. The responsibilities for the top management are a direct consequence of the organizational structure of the company and the allocation of tasks among them. The organizational structure was discussed in detail in Chapter 8. Initially, start-ups do not have rigid or complex structures since almost everybody is doing something, teamwork and informality is pre-eminent. However, once the start-up starts growing, the formalization of structure and responsibilities become critical for the success of the company. Members of the top management team have responsibilities aligned to their skills, such as strategic planning may be developed by the CEO due to their skills in strategy, knowledge of the business model and industry, or a Chief Financial Officer needs to have monitoring and functional expertise in finance.
  - Managers existing and future requirements: skills, experience and responsibilities. Managers responsible for the daily management of the company have functional expertise, and lead their areas of responsibility through goal-setting abilities. For example, a production manager needs to have an adequate professional background connected directly with the production processes, knowledge about the technology and, depending on the level of integration, good negotiating skills with suppliers and strategic partners.
  - Staff existing and future requirements: skills and roles. Skills and roles of the staff are determined by the extent of activities performed internally. In addition to knowledge and skills to perform the basic primary activities, staff need to have some skills to develop businesses, do market research, and understand legal issues and financial aspects.
  - Hiring processes and timing: selecting the new staff is an important activity especially in the initial steps of the company since the initial personnel can become future managers once the business grows. Therefore, it is important to strategically evaluate the different managers and staff categories in order to define the attention of the entrepreneurial team on the hiring process. A final consideration is the timing to hire staff. Kunc (2008) shows the timing for hiring staff/managers is fundamental in avoiding stressful conditions, having enough time to develop skills and

providing training to new staff. Moreover, growth pace can also substantially influence the timing to have the new staff in the company.

- Other resources:
  - Knowledge: existing patents, future patents, regulation compliance. Knowledge, as a resource, needs to be developed carefully. On the one hand, there are important delays between investing in R&D and the transformation into useful knowledge for developing products/services. On the other hand, knowledge can become obsolete if the start-up is in an industry where technology changes rapidly. Therefore, the use of existing patents in product and services is a critical activity in maximizing their value. Additionally, the outcome of R&D, in terms of new patents, need to be managed carefully so the existing products are not cannibalized and there is not a large delay in the release of new products. Knowledge about regulation compliance is key in certain industries, e.g. biotechnology or healthcare. While the existence of advisors can provide the capabilities to deal with regulatory issues, it is important that regulation compliance is part of the daily decisions and business operations in order to avoid future issues.
  - Technology: software, hardware, networks, communications. Nowadays, companies need the IT infrastructure to be set up immediately. Data collection from business operations may not be stored in a sophisticated management accounting system, e.g. ERP (Enterprise Resource Planning), initially but widely available software, e.g. spreadsheets, can store information about the operations to perform analysis and control operations, e.g. tracking and controlling costs. Moreover, the data requirements increase exponentially as the business grows. A growing start-up requires transactional systems, customer databases and analytical tools to evaluate the information that is being generated daily.

Food for thought 10.3 Complete the business model designed previously considering the following aspects (see questions for each concept defined in Section 10.1.4):

- Production processes: product manufacturing (internal or external) and service delivery.
- List the key business processes responsible for delivering value to the customer and complete the list with processes and activities using the "value chain" framework (discussed in Chapter 6). For each process, indicate if it is performed internally or externally.
- For the processes performed internally, identify the key resources (human resources, technology, and knowledge) supporting them.
- Define the organizational structure corresponding to each year for the next five years.

- Prepare a human resources hiring and training strategy aligned with the expected growth in revenues.

Reflect on the following issues:

- What business processes are easier to transfer externally to a supplier? Explain your reasons.
- What criteria should you use to find an external company to perform a business process?
- What factors influence the categories and number of staff in the new company?
- What is the right timing to recruit new staff? What factors affect the timing?

10.2 Financial Management

The purpose of financial management and the finance plan is to inform the investors of the viability of the business. Thus, key components of the financial management of a start-up are:

- Critical assumptions and scenarios behind the cash flow calculations.
- Breakeven analysis and required investment in terms of initial funding and future requirements to support operating costs or financing business expansion.
- Projected profit and loss (income statement) based on revenues and operating costs.
- Key performance indicators.
- Sources and amount of funding is required together with the implications on ownership and exit strategy for investors and/or entrepreneur team.

Critical assumptions and scenarios/cases for cash flow calculations Broadly speaking, the financial health of an organization depends on two concepts: cash inflows and outflows, where inflows need to exceed outflows over time. In order to know the origins of the flows and the reasons for their fluctuations over time, the entrepreneur team present the assumptions behind the cash flows. The assumptions are based on the analysis performed for the other parts of the business plan. The financial management part only reflects in numbers the analysis performed previously.

While short-term considerations for revenues and costs are usually unpredictable due to many factors, long-term projections are easier to calculate than short-term projections because they tend to be more stable. Long-term projections also act as goals or objectives for the business because the entrepreneurial team has enough time to make decisions and correct deviations in order to achieve the projected performance of the business. However, long-term projections will inevitably include different scenarios, or cases, to account for the uncertainty.

Given the uncertainties in future projections, more than one projected cash flow needs to be prepared. The projections will depend on diverse internal, i.e. sales growth rate or capacity expansion, and external, i.e. environmental factors, assumptions. The variations in cash flows are usually described as scenarios that, in this case, are a set of coherent internal and external conditions that change between different futures. Scenarios, as business cases, usually comprise three situations: a base case (everything is working as expected in the future); best case (internal and external conditions contribute positively to a better performance than the base case); and worst case (internal and external conditions affect negatively the performance displayed in the base case). Examples of assumptions and scenario variables are listed in Table 10.4.

While cash flows are not perfect predictions given the uncertainties surrounding the new business, start-ups usually fail when real cash flows do not follow the assumptions. The divergence between the real and predicted cash flow can indicate a lack of understanding of the drivers of the business during the planning process or a lack of control of the drivers in the implementation.

Table 10.4 Cash flow components: critical assumptions and scenarios factors.

Cash flow concepts	Critical assumptions	Scenarios factors
Cash inflows		
• Revenues	Price: fixed or variable, discounts offered	Seasonal variability, competitors' price discounts
	Volume: price elasticity, volume per buyer, repeated sales	Different price elasticity due to diverse economic conditions, effect of discounts on volume, product usage, changes in behavior
• Funding	Payment methods: cash, credit	Length of payments, economic conditions, interest rates
	Frequency, timing, amount	Availability of sources, timing for obtaining funds, interest rates for loans, economic situation
Cash outflows		
• Operating expenses	Outsourced processes	Price, payment frequency, length of contracts, usage volume
	Internal processes:	
	Human resources (productivity, number, type of contract: flexible or full-time, training costs)	Salaries, productivity, availability, hiring timing, training frequency, business volume
	Technology resources (maintenance costs)	Performance, level of integration to processes, type of technology
• Marketing expenses	Frequency of advertising campaigns, timing, amount	Advertising costs, results obtained from advertising, economic conditions
• Investments	Asset acquisition: type, costs and timing	Payment method, economic conditions, technology available, business volume

Breakeven analysis   A breakeven analysis involves finding the level of revenues that cover the total costs. It also shows the amount of cash necessary (funding) until revenues can pay for the total costs. Breakeven analysis only depicts the moment when the start-up becomes self-financing but it does not show the profitability of the start-up, this information is presented in the profit and loss statement. Table 10.5 shows an example considering cash flows on an annual basis. The information shows an initial strong growth in revenues, expenses and the expansion of the assets (manufacturing plant and offices) followed by slower growth rates similar to a mature company. As the market growth declines, the investment in marketing and assets also declines generating a higher cash flow surplus. For the first two years, banks and venture capitalists provide funding to cover the expansion in assets and working capital. In year 5, funding is returned.

Breakeven analysis can discover important inconsistencies in the assumptions: revenues are too low, costs are too high or mix of both. In terms of revenues, some actions to resolve the inconsistencies are:

- Increasing buyers by reevaluating the size of the potential target market segment.
- Increasing buyers by defining additional market segments that can purchase the product.
- Growing the total target market by increasing awareness among people outside the industry.
- Increasing purchases from customers through new applications or promoting more uses of the product.
- Defining a dynamic pricing strategy based on the price sensitivity of the market segments and cost reductions due to economies of scale and efficiency improvement.

Table 10.5 Example of a profit and loss statement.

Cash flow concepts	Year 1	Year 2	Year 3	Year 4	Year 5
Cash inflows	15 000 000	18 000 000	21 600 000	23 000 000	24 000 000
• Revenues					
Cash outflows	10 900 000	12 900 000	18 000 000	18 000 000	18 000 000
• Operating	1 000 000	3 000 000	3 000 000	3 000 000	1 500 000
• Marketing	6 000 000	2 000 000	500 000	500 000	500 000
• Investments in assets					
Net cash flows	**−2 900 000**	**100 000**	**100 000**	**1 500 000**	**4 000 000**
• Net funding	2 900 000	1 000 000	—	—	−3 900 000

Source: Sorenson (2012: table 12.7, page 462). Reproduced with permission of John Wiley & Sons.

In terms of operating costs, some actions to consider are:

- Performing the processes or activities inside vs. outside the company: make or buy.
- Change the drivers of fixed costs: leases, size of the manufacturing facilities, office space, location of facilities, negotiate flexible working contracts, offer pay for performance or stock options to staff and managers.
- Change the drivers of variable costs: negotiating with suppliers, using different production technology.

Sometimes breakeven analysis involves the determination of a breakeven point. The breakeven point defines the minimum amount of products or services that must be produced in order to cover fixed and variable costs. Another approach using breakeven point is to find the minimum price for a given level of production that covers all fixed and variable costs. Figure 10.1 shows an example of a breakeven analysis using different cases for price and variable costs. The results clearly offer a potential risk for the start-up in the worst case because of the high costs and low price. In the base case, a volume of 20 units will cover all costs but only a volume of 13 units is required in the best case. Unfortunately, the worst case demands 50 units to cover all costs since the net difference between price and variable costs is $ 2 so the company needs to sell 50 units in order to cover a fixed cost of $ 100.

Projected profit and loss (income) statement   The income statement provides an accounting overview of the revenues and operating costs before considering other expenses such as interests and taxes. The profit and loss statement captures most, but not all, concepts presented in the calculation of cash flows. Table 10.6 shows an example of a profit and loss statement for a company with R&D activities so its revenue comes from sales of products and patents used in products (royalties) or licensed to other firms (license fees)

Revenues are based on sales forecasts, which are associated with assumptions about reaching a certain target market share of the selected market segment at the price indicated in the market plan. In other words, the expectation is to obtain a certain sales volume, which is growing over time, under a pricing strategy. One key consideration is the expected market share. The information for calculating revenues comes directly from the market section of the business plan:

- Total size and location of the target market: How many customers are in the industry? Where are most of the customers located? Where do they get their products?
- Potential market segment: What particular group of customers will be interested in the product/service? How many potential customers are in this group?

Base Case

Net Income (in thousand)	$ -50	$ -25	$ -	$ 25	$ 50	$ 75	$ 100
Total Revenue (in thousand)	$ 150	$ 225	$ 300	$ 375	$ 450	$ 525	$ 600
Volume (in thousand)	10	15	20	25	30	35	40
Total variable costs (in thousand)	$ 100	$ 150	$ 200	$ 250	$ 300	$ 350	$ 400
Total fixed costs (in thousand)	$ 100	$ 100	$ 100	$ 100	$ 100	$ 100	$ 100
Variable costs	$ 10	$ 10	$ 10	$ 10	$ 10	$ 10	$ 10
Price	$ 15	$ 15	$ 15	$ 15	$ 15	$ 15	$ 15

Best Case

Net Income (in thousand)	$ -20	$ 20	$ 60	$ 100	$ 140	$ 180	$ 220
Total Revenue (in thousand)	$ 170	$ 255	$ 340	$ 425	$ 510	$ 595	$ 680
Volume (in thousand)	10	15	20	25	30	35	40
Total variable costs (in thousand)	$ 90	$ 135	$ 180	$ 225	$ 270	$ 315	$ 360
Total fixed costs (in thousand)	$ 100	$ 100	$ 100	$ 100	$ 100	$ 100	$ 100
Variable costs	$ 9	$ 9	$ 9	$ 9	$ 9	$ 9	$ 9
Price	$ 17	$ 17	$ 17	$ 17	$ 17	$ 17	$ 17

Worst Case

Net Income (in thousand)	$ -80	$ -70	$ -60	$ -50	$ -40	$ -30	$ -20
Total Revenue (in thousand)	$ 130	$ 195	$ 260	$ 325	$ 390	$ 455	$ 520
Volume (in thousand)	10	15	20	25	30	35	40
Total variable costs (in thousand)	$ 110	$ 165	$ 220	$ 275	$ 330	$ 385	$ 440
Total fixed costs (in thousand)	$ 100	$ 100	$ 100	$ 100	$ 100	$ 100	$ 100
Variable costs	$ 11	$ 11	$ 11	$ 11	$ 11	$ 11	$ 11
Price	$ 13	$ 13	$ 13	$ 13	$ 13	$ 13	$ 13

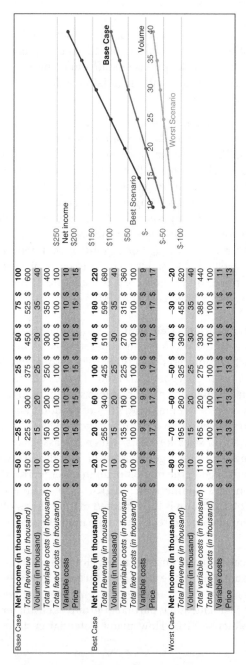

Figure 10.1 Example of a breakeven analysis using three scenarios for price and variable costs.

Table 10.6 Example of a profit and loss statement.

Profit and loss concepts		Amounts
Revenues		**15 000 000**
Direct sales	10 000 000	
Royalties	2 500 000	
License fees	2 500 000	
Costs of goods sold (COGS)		**10 000 000**
Direct materials	5 000 000	
Direct manufacturing labor	3 000 000	
Indirect manufacturing labor	2 500 000	
Gross margin		**5 000 000**
Operating costs		**2 400 000**
Marketing activities	1 000 000	
Marketing and sales salaries	300 000	
IT costs (contracted)	100 000	
Administrative	500 000	
Depreciation and amortization	500 000	
Operating income		**2 600 000**
Other non-operating costs	500 000	
EBIT (Earning before interests and taxes)		**2 100 000**
Interest expenses	300 000	
Earnings before taxes		**1 800 000**
Taxes	360 000	
Net income		**1 440 000**

Source: Sorenson (2012: table 12.7, page 462). Reproduced with permission of John Wiley & Sons.

- Pricing strategy in terms of retail price, wholesale price, volume and cash discounts, bundling with other products, credit terms, and pricing based on demand, seasonality, etc.

Scenarios for revenues can be determined by changes in legislation that affect number of customers, competitors' prices, different price elasticity and prices. It is important to have detail for all factors affecting revenues so their effect on the revenues can be explored through sensitivity analysis.

In terms of projected costs, the "value chain" (see Chapter 6) can help to identify the different costs in the organization but recording and controlling costs using accounting systems is a key activity for the entrepreneurial team. The costs can be broadly classified into direct and indirect costs:

- Direct costs are directly assigned to a specific process or activity due to their intrinsic relationship with them.
- Indirect costs cannot be allocated to a specific process because they originate from resources that are used by multiple processes and activities.

Moreover, costs can vary automatically, "variable costs", or remain fixed, "fixed costs", with respect to diverse levels of activities, e.g. volume of units sold or produced, or cost drivers, e.g. time, size of the plant.

An accounting classification of costs can be related to their association with products/services, i.e. "costs of goods sold", or activities, "operating costs" are related to primary activities, and "overhead or administrative costs" to supporting activities. Finally, there are a set of expenses that cannot be allocated specifically to a product or activity such as interest paid on loans, management expenses, and taxes. These concepts are subtracted at the end of the profit and loss statement.

Scenarios for costs can be determined by location of processes (in-house vs. outsourced), geographical locations (labor, logistics), changes in legislation that affect processes, different technologies with diverse economies of scale. It is important to detail all scenario factors affecting costs, so a sensitivity analysis can be performed.

Key performance indicators Entrepreneurs face an important challenge in deciding how to measure and control their business. Basically, there are a number of indicators that can be used but the most difficult task is choosing a few indicators that are critical (Rockart, 1978). Definitively, critical performance indicators are related to the early financial performance of the business such as:

- Sales growth: percentage of growth in sales (in volume and money) measured with a determined frequency.
- Gross margin: difference between revenues and costs directly attributed to the product/service measured in absolute number or percentage of revenues. It measures the operating profitability.
- Operating expenses: percentage of growth in costs associated with processes not directly related to the products and services measured in absolute number or percentage of revenues. It indicates the costs related to areas such as administration, selling, marketing, IT and other support areas. It is important that the growth rate is below sales growth otherwise the business is not achieving economies of scale.

- Cash burn rate: amount of cash spent per month compared with cash available. It is a measure of the time available to achieve the breakeven point, obtain positive cash flows or negotiate further funding from investors.
- Accounts receivable collection period: time to collect the customers' payments. In a Business to Business start-up, the time can be quite substantial and it is necessary to contemplate it given its impact on the cash flows. When the start-up sells directly to a customer (Business to Consumer), this indicator is irrelevant unless the business sells expensive items which may be paid for over a period of time, such as luxury items, vehicles and houses.

Another approach to measure the performance of the business is the use of a performance measurement system comprised by financial measures and strategic controls (see Chapter 9).

Sources and amount of funding   One of the key factors to a successful start-up is the entrepreneur's ability to gain enough financing until the business reaches its breakeven point. There are three general ways of funding a start-up business: equity; debt; and grants. According to Table 10.7, equity means the investors devote money with the expectation that the company being invested will succeed therefore gain returns in the form of shares. Among those forms of equity, "business angels" is the most common one for start-ups (Harris, 2006). Investment from venture capitalists is considered to be the most suitable selection for high growth business. Sometimes, the equity investment may be more expensive than debt but there is no interest repayment. The grants mean that governments support entrepreneurs to start and manage their business in the form of providing useful strategies, employee training, and financial support among others.

There is another aspect to discuss in this area: exit strategies. Exit strategies are plans for investors to cash out their investments in the start-up. There are two possibilities: sales of shares; or obtaining royalties from product and/or technologies created. Sales of share can be performed by Initial Public Offerings of the capital of the start-up in the stock market. This is a very well-known method for companies which require a large amount of funding for rapid growth, e.g. digital businesses, or investing in the long term, e.g. mining projects. Another option is to integrate the company with another company through a merger or sell the company through an acquisition. A final option is to sell the company to the management team, which is known as Management Buy Out. Exit by royalties imply paying the investor a percentage of the sales from specific products or technologies. Different to exit by shares, the investors do not have to wait until the company is sold or launched in the stock market.

Table 10.7 Sources of funding.

Source	Characteristics	Advantages	Disadvantages
Equity	Exchange of shares of the company for funding from the investors	Venture capitalists and business angels focus not only on the financial aspects but also on the skills of the entrepreneur team, business strategy and exit They can provide experience and advice	Monitoring and active participation on the management of the business Contractual agreements Milestones-based financing
Debt	Request of funds formally or informally		
	Formal debt is receiving a loan from the bank or purchasing assets through credit facility provided by a supplier	No control on the decisions or involvement on the management of the business	Only financial aspects are considered on the decision
	Informal debt occurs when family, friends and relatives provide funding	No contractual arrangement Flexible times	A collateral is required for a bank loan. The asset is the collateral when a supplier provides financing Personal relationships Limited funding
Grants	Money offered by institutions, e.g. government, without the requirement to return it but it has to be used for a specific purpose determined by the institution	It does not need to be reimbursed There is support in managing the business	It is specific It has to go through competing processes It requires massive investment in preparing the applications

Food for thought 10.4   Prepare a projected cash flow for your business based on the information prepared in Food for thought 10.3. The financial information should be presented as in Table 10.5 and Figure 10.1. Remember to make the assumptions for each value and the options determined by the scenarios clear.

Based on the financial information, reflect on the following issues:

- What are the main sources of information to identify the price of the product/ service?
- What actions can you take to improve your breakeven point?
- Depending on the investment requirements, what options seem feasible to explore?

10.3   Integrating Management Science into Strategic Management

This section provides an introduction to a management science tool that can support entrepreneurs in their preparation of a business plan and the strategic trade-offs implied in building their business. The tool, called Monte Carlo simulation, provides an approach to incorporate uncertainty in the financial projections for the new business or to perform risk analysis of the new business. Basically, the method proposed generates a large number of possible combinations of diverse situations in the new business. Then some combinations will occur more often than others giving rise to profiles of potential results for the business, e.g. profits above a certain threshold will occur 30% of the time (frequency of occurrence) or the business will lose money 20% of the time. From this information, an entrepreneur can estimate the probability of the success of the business and the risk associated with the new business.

10.3.1   Monte Carlo Simulation

One of most important issues for entrepreneurs is to deal with uncertainty since developing only one set of expected cash flows means considering only one future out of a large number of possible realizations. Clark et al. (2010) suggest finance textbooks only propose two tools to face uncertainty: sensitivity analysis; and scenario analysis. On the one hand, sensitivity analysis implies changing one variable and evaluating its impact on the cash flow, e.g. the change in variable costs in Figure 10.1. Sensitivity analysis complements cash flow analysis in identifying the extent of the impact of uncertain or risk variables if their values differ from the base case (Ragsdale, 2004). One of the drawbacks is the lack of consideration of interdependencies between variables so modifying one variable at a time is not realistic. Sensitivity analysis does not capture the likelihood of outcomes since it is only one point (Ragsdale, 2004). On the other hand, scenario analysis examines a number of combinations of variables, e.g. price and variable costs in Figure 10.1, through a series of possible situations: worst case, base case, and best case, to determine future cash flows (e.g., sales, costs, growth rates, etc.). Scenarios compensate one of the issues of sensitivity analysis but it only presents a range of outcomes and not their likelihood of occurrence (Ragsdale, 2004).

Monte Carlo simulation is a technique using random or pseudo-random numbers to represent uncertain elements of problems in order to assess risks. Monte Carlo simulation involves calculating a probability distribution of the cash flow based on the range of possible values for critical variables affecting it, e.g. volume. Through random sampling of the distributions of the critical variables, the simulation determines the distribution of all potential cash flows under uncertainty. Therefore, the decision is made observing a distribution of cash flows rather than one value, or a limited combination of values like in sensitivity analysis or scenarios, respectively.

To summarize, Monte Carlo simulation allows managers to understand and visualize risk and uncertainty in cash flow analysis. The primary output is a histogram of values mapping the distribution of possible cash flows as a bell-shaped curve. Furthermore, the curve helps to estimate the probability of success for the initial business. Monte Carlo simulation is usually performed using spreadsheets. The steps to develop Monte Carlo simulation for cash flows are:

1) **Prepare a cash flow considering revenues and costs**. See Section 10.2 for an example.
2) **Identify the components in the cash flow that are strongly impacted by uncertainty.**

   The components in the cash flow are essentially uncertain but they have different degree of uncertainty. Monte Carlo simulation works best using only variables that have a critical impact on cash flows, e.g. a small deviation in the variable can have a significant impact on the start-up survival.

   There are two reasons for only choosing one or two critical variables. First, the analysis of the model is critical. If a large number of probability distributions are employed in a stochastic simulation, it will generate scenarios that can be incoherent due to the difficulty of monitoring relationships for correlated variables. Secondly, defining probability distributions and correlation conditions for many variables is costly in terms of time and involvement of the entrepreneurial team and external experts (if they are required) (Ragsdale, 2004).
3) **Define the variables and their range of uncertainty**.

   Once the variables have been selected, we need to define the probability distributions either subjectively or from historical data. Probability distributions can be either discrete distributions (e.g. binomial or Poisson) or continuous distributions (e.g. the normal or lognormal distribution). It is important to consider the range of feasible outcomes for the variables, so the values generated from the simulation are within reasonable ranges. Another important consideration is the availability of the data. Most of the time data to draw a distribution may not exist. Therefore, there is a judgmental decision to define the probability distribution types reflecting the expected behavior of the critical variables. Winston et al. (1997) suggest considering two types of simplified distributions: continuous; and triangular. First, continuous uniform distribution implies similar probability for all values between the minimum and maximum value. This is useful when there is no knowledge about most probable cases. Secondly, triangular distribution, which approximates the normal bell-shaped distribution, needs information about three values: minimum, maximum and the most probable. The minimum and maximum values have almost zero probability and the most probable value has the highest. Another possibility is to consider the normal distribution, which is assuming the distribution has a bell-shaped curve, where the information required is an average value and its standard deviation.

A final consideration is to identify the existence of interdependence (correlation) or independence (no correlation) in the variables. Considering the variables independent simplifies the simulation and the analysis but conditional sampling is applied to elicit the probability distributions when the variables are interdependent (Goodwin and Wright, 1998). Conditional sampling implies the elicitation of the probability distribution of a certain (dependent) variable given the values of the other variables (independent) (Goodwin and Wright, 1998). For example, the variable costs (dependent variable) depend on the level of production (independent variable). Thus, the simulation generates a value of the independent variables and then automatically assign the value of the dependent variable from the corresponding distribution (Goodwin and Wright, 1998).

4) **Run the simulated cash flow using the variables selected in the previous step.**

In this stage, software generates random numbers within the ranges specified previously and within the set probability distributions and correlation conditions. Widely available software such as Microsoft Excel® can be used in this stage or more specific software such as Crystal Ball @Risk® (Winston et al., 1997). The generation of random numbers is repeated many times until a sufficient number of simulations have been performed, e.g. when the simulated distribution of results changes very little (Winston et al., 1997). The results can be allocated in ranges and their frequency counted to generate histograms that provide a profile of the probable distributions of the cash flows. Then, average and standard deviations of the results can also be calculated.

5) **Analyze the results and assess the effects of uncertainty on the cash flow.**

This step involves the analysis and interpretation of the simulation results. Since the results are presented in the form of a probability distribution of the possible cash flows, the probability distribution includes the entire range of possible outcomes including negative and positive cash flows and their probabilities. Beside graphical formats, the simulation results are also reported as various measures of location, dispersion, skewness, and kurtosis.

Additionally, potential alternatives can be also analyzed through simulation. Then the alternatives are evaluated by inspecting their probability distributions using line graphs (Goodwin and Wright, 1998). Another possibility is to evaluate the highest expected utility employing first-degree stochastic dominance (Goodwin and Wright, 1998). Stochastic dominance exists when the expected utility in an alternative is greater than the other for the whole function (Goodwin and Wright, 1998). Stochastic dominance is observed by plotting the cumulative probability distribution functions of the alternatives (Goodwin and Wright, 1998). In the case of the cash flow, higher cash flows provide higher utility and higher probability to obtain higher cash flows dominates alternatives where the amount has lower probabilities.

Table 10.8 presents an example of Monte Carlo Simulation applied to the cash flow evaluated in Figure 10.1. Since the cash flow has been generated and the component of the cash flow most influential is volume, Table 10.8 starts with step 3.

Table 10.8 Performing Monte Carlo simulation using Microsoft Excel®.

Step	Implementation in the spreadsheet
3. Define the variables and their range of uncertainty	The variable with the highest impact and uncertainty is the volume of sales with a range of 10 (minimum) to 40 (maximum) thousand units Ideally the entrepreneurial team should have some data to determine probabilities to the volume of sales, e.g. historical data from similar products or similar consumers, consumers' surveys. If this data is not available, the entrepreneurial team needs to make a judgement about the probability of the volume of sales. In this case the probabilities indicated are:

Volume (thousand)	Probability
10	0.05
15	0.10
20	0.15
25	0.30
30	0.30
35	0.07
40	0.03

Step	Implementation in the spreadsheet
4. Run the simulated cash flow using the variables selected in the previous step	In order to run the simulated cash flows for the start-up given the probability distribution of sales, we can use Microsoft Excel®. However, any software can generate random numbers between 0 and 1. In Excel, the formula to generate random numbers is = RAND(). The RAND function generates numbers uniformly distributed between 0 and 1

Step	Implementation in the spreadsheet

To generate the distribution of the volume in our example, we need to assign random numbers to the different volumes so that a particular random number can be allocated to a particular volume

Volume (thousand)	Probability	Random numbers
10	0.05	0.000–0.049
15	0.10	0.050–0.149
20	0.15	0.150–0.299
25	0.30	0.300–0.599
30	0.30	0.600–0.899
35	0.07	0.900–0.969
40	0.03	0.970–

The spreadsheet model is presented below. The first column shows the number of trials and the second column contains the random number generated using RAND(). The third column presents the demand corresponding to each random number obtained using the LOOKUP function applied to the table "Cutoffs – Demand". The table shows the cumulative probability for each demand based on the information presented before. Revenues result from the multiplication of the demand by the price in the "base case". Operating margin ($ 5) is obtained by subtracting the price ($ 15) from the variable costs ($ 10) multiplied by the demand. Fixed costs are obtained from Figure 10.1. Net income comes from subtracting fixed costs from the operating margin. The simulation shows the potential cash flows resulting from operations

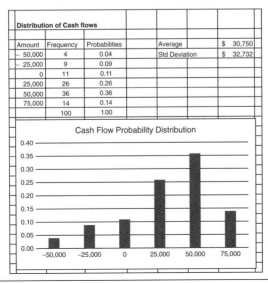

Table 10.8 (Continued)

Step	Implementation in the spreadsheet
5. Analyze the results and assess the effects of uncertainty on the cash flow	The results after 100 simulations is presented below. In this step, the resulting cash flows ("Net income") are organized in different categories (column "Amount") and their frequencies counted (column "Frequency"). Then, the frequency for each category is divided by the total trials to calculate the probabilities (column "Probabilities"). From the distribution of probabilities, there is a 0.24 probability (probability of losing $ 50 000 is 0.04, $ 25 000 is 0.09, and the probability to breakeven is 0.11) the base case only breaks even or loses money. The probability of having positive operating cash flows is 0.76. The average cash flow is $ 30 750 with a 95% confidence of results between $ −34 714 (Mean − 2*Std Deviation) and $ 96 214 (Mean + 2*Std Deviation). The base case seems to show a strong result for the business under uncertainty

Trials	Random Number	Demand	Revenues	Operating Margin	Fixed costs	Net Income		Cutoffs	Demand
1	0.78	30,000	$ 450,000	$ 150,000	$ 100,000	$ 50,000		0.00	10,000
2	0.61	30,000	$ 450,000	$ 150,000	$ 100,000	$ 50,000		0.05	15,000
3	0.65	30,000	$ 450,000	$ 150,000	$ 100,000	$ 50,000		0.15	20,000
4	0.30	20,000	$ 300,000	$ 100,000	$ 100,000	$ -		0.30	25,000
5	0.10	15,000	$ 225,000	$ 75,000	$ 100,000	$ −25,000		0.60	30,000
6	0.84	30,000	$ 450,000	$ 150,000	$ 100,000	$ 50,000		0.90	35,000
7	0.10	15,000	$ 225,000	$ 75,000	$ 100,000	$ −25,000		0.97	40,000
8	0.80	30,000	$ 450,000	$ 150,000	$ 100,000	$ 50,000			
9	0.43	25,000	$ 375,000	$ 125,000	$ 100,000	$ 25,000			
10	0.61	30,000	$ 450,000	$ 150,000	$ 100,000	$ 50,000			
11	0.45	25,000	$ 375,000	$ 125,000	$ 100,000	$ 25,000			
12	0.73	30,000	$ 450,000	$ 150,000	$ 100,000	$ 50,000			
13	0.72	30,000	$ 450,000	$ 150,000	$ 100,000	$ 50,000			
14	0.10	15,000	$ 225,000	$ 75,000	$ 100,000	$ −25,000			
15	0.69	30,000	$ 450,000	$ 150,000	$ 100,000	$ 50,000			
16	0.38	25,000	$ 375,000	$ 125,000	$ 100,000	$ 25,000			
17	0.00	10,000	$ 150,000	$ 50,000	$ 100,000	$ −50,000			
18	0.94	35,000	$ 525,000	$ 175,000	$ 100,000	$ 75,000			
19	0.87	30,000	$ 450,000	$ 150,000	$ 100,000	$ 50,000			
20	0.69	30,000	$ 450,000	$ 150,000	$ 100,000	$ 50,000			
21	0.93	35,000	$ 525,000	$ 175,000	$ 100,000	$ 75,000			
22	0.39	25,000	$ 375,000	$ 125,000	$ 100,000	$ 25,000			
23	0.17	20,000	$ 300,000	$ 100,000	$ 100,000	$ -			
24	0.22	20,000	$ 300,000	$ 100,000	$ 100,000	$ -			
25	0.72	30,000	$ 450,000	$ 150,000	$ 100,000	$ 50,000			

10.4 End of Chapter

Entrepreneurs are optimistic and risk-taker decision makers. Entrepreneurs would not be able to face the uncertainty in starting a new business without these characteristics. This chapter intends to provide frameworks and tools to make more robust decisions under the uncertainties faced in their new business. The business plan is an important check list to clarify assumptions and identify blind spots in the new business. Thoroughly thinking about the business model and its components is critical for the survival of new firms. Products, Resources and Capabilities are key elements of any business and, more importantly, of a new business. The numerical tools provided (cash flows, scenarios, sensitivity analysis and Monte Carlo simulation) are elements to facilitate discussion and learn about the assumptions employed to launch the new business. Let us suppose the entrepreneurial team sees that there is an optimistic bias in the forecast of unit sales. Then, it is a simple matter of changing the worst case and/or the best case estimates and determining the resulting decrease in the probability of success in the new business. Suppose the entrepreneurial team believes that prices and volume are negatively correlated – e.g. higher prices may imply lower sales volume. Alternatively, variable and fixed costs can move up or down together implying a positive correlation. Simulation permits the specifying of such correlations and the quantifying of their effects on the probability of success or failure. A final comment on the usefulness of numerical analysis is to identify implausible assumptions. Monte Carlo simulation can be a useful tool for detecting the inherent optimistic bias of entrepreneurs and the entrepreneurial teams.

Therefore, analytics, as a use of management science tools, can clarify arguments and values, support the design of the new business by analyzing the assumptions behind the future performance of the start-up and provide strategic advice, as indicated in Figure 10.2.

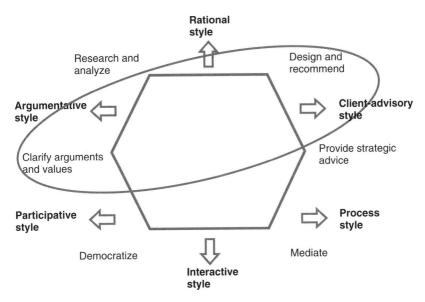

Figure 10.2 Management science styles. *Source:* Walker (2009). Reproduced with permission from Elsevier.

10.4.1 Revision Questions

1) What will be the most important differences in the business plan between the different types of entrepreneurs' intentions: Lifestyle business, Long term business and High growth business?
2) Recently, scholars have suggested that the most important resource for entrepreneurs is their networks. Explain the benefits and issues of networks.
3) What sources can entrepreneurs employ to obtain probabilities for the components of the cash flow? Explain the strengths and weaknesses of each source.
4) What other management science tools can entrepreneurs employ? Explain the strengths and weaknesses of each tool.

10.4.2 Case Study: Designing the Next Boutique Winery

In a review of the Chilean wine industry, Kunc (2007) found that small- to medium-sized wineries follow basic recipes to drive success in the wine industry. They have a strong emphasis on finding the right partner in the distribution channel, constant quality that is driven by improved viticulture practices, and the importance of a competitive price (Kunc, 2007). Winery managers suggest finding the right distributor and forming a relationship with them is key to future survival and growth, so gaining access to distribution channels in export markets has been a key determinant of success in the wine trade. Supply dependability is fostered by the introduction of technology at plant level, so wineries can deliver products that constantly conform to the international standards of quality and volume. Strategies related to product (type of wine, portfolio of wines and medals won) can be considered secondary factors determining the success of the small- to medium-sized wineries in some regions and for some wineries' managers (Kunc, 2007).

From the perspective of the wineries' owners and winemakers, the goal for establishing a winery is to produce the best wine, from excellent vineyards, using excellent vine management techniques and excellent wine making methods, such as employing barrels for the varietal wine so it ages for the appropriate time (californiawinesandwineries.com, 2016). However, each of the components of a new winery has multiple options, which makes choosing the right options a complex problem. For example:

- Vineyards. Location is key for wine owners. Options are sloped hillsides, volcanic soil, loam topsoil, rocky, vineyard layout: north to south or east to west, etc., which provide a certain effect for each varietal for uniqueness and taste consideration, also known as "terroir".
- Vine management. Options are in-house or consultant viticulturist, organic vs. use of agrochemicals, dry vs. irrigated, etc.
- Wine making: barrels for aging. Options for red wine are French, Hungarian, American oak, new vs. old barrels. Options for white wine are oak, stainless steel or cement egg.

- Wine making: time in barrels. Options are integration with oak, balance of acid and tame the tannins, which lead to 12–14 months, 36 months and more. Financial considerations to wait for time in barrels.
- Wine making: blending or block. Options are percentages of each grape, which can change year to year, to make an established style, only one grape but separating by block, blending all blocks or mix approach.

Specialists in the wine industry suggest a boutique winery is a winery that produces high quality, artisan or authentic wine by using the following in their business (californiawinesandwineries.com, 2016):

- One or a few specific wines produced in small quantities, high quality and with a personal touch, independent of their overall production size.
- Manual, artisan-based, wine making methods developed by oenologists, wine makers, who aim for highest quality. They are inspired by the developments of the vines and the harvest.
- The wine production process is mostly performed in-house or under strict control from vineyard to blending to bottling.
- Selective in vineyard management from pruning techniques and selecting vines block by block or row by row to be harvested. Grape yield (production of grapes by vines) is extensively controlled.
- Focus on varietals where their vineyard/soil has strengths so there is no experimentation or using sub-standard grapes/harvest to obtain profits.
- The business is a way of life rather than a value extraction model.
- Distribution channels are selective and imply a strong commitment with the consumers.

Here are a few actions to perform related to helping develop a new boutique winery:

1) Using multi-criteria decision analysis (Belton and Stewart, 2002) help the entrepreneur to choose the best possible place for their new boutique winery between Chile and Spain. Multi-criteria decision analysis is employed to facilitate the selection of choices among alternatives by dividing the decision into small parts, analyzing each part and integrating them. The basic five components of the method are:
   - Define the goal of the decision and decision alternatives.
   - Identify the decision maker and the components of their decisions.
   - Define the evaluation criteria: scoring (evaluating the expected performance of each alternative against the criteria) and weighting (assigning weights for each criterion considering their relative importance).
   - Generate outcomes related to the alternative/preference combinations.
   - Perform sensitivity analysis with respect to preferences or weights and evaluate the advantages/disadvantages of your options.
   See Table 10.9 for an example.

Table 10.9 Steps for performing a multi-criteria decision analysis for a winery.

Step	Implementation
1. Define the goal of the decision and the decision maker	Goal: select the location for the new boutique winery Decision alternatives: location (Chile or Spain) Decision makers: owner, wine maker (oenologist), future sales manager
2. Identify the components of decision	Components of decision: • Vineyards location: hillside or flat. • Vineyards size: small (10 hectares) or medium (20 hectares). • Vine management: only global grapes (Cabernet Sauvignon, Merlot, Pinot Noir) or global and local grapes (Cabernet Sauvignon, Tempranillo, Garnacha). • Harvest management: block by block or whole area by grape. • Wine making: manual or mechanized. • Wine storage: stainless steel-bottling or stainless steel-barrels-aging-bottling. • Wine aging cask: French or American oak. • Wine aging time: 18 months or 24–36 months. • Wine bottling: blending or block/brand or varietal.

3. Define the evaluation criteria: scoring (evaluating the expected performance of each alternative against the criteria) and weighting (assigning weights for each criterion considering its relative importance)	Two common rating scales that that are used in multi-criteria decision analysis are (1) relative scale, and (2) ordinal scale
	
	Relative scale: each alternative is rated relative to the others in satisfying a particular component by assigning the highest number to the best alternative and the lowest number to the worst alternative
	
	Ordinal scale: using any scale (5 or 10 points) assign each alternative a value for how well it satisfies a particular component where the highest number is the best and the lowest the worst.
	
	Using ordinal scale (0–10 points), some of the components can be scored as:
	
	             Vineyards location / Vineyards size
	Chile 9 5
	Spain 7 8
	
	Weights reflect the personal preferences of the decision makers. The overall score is calculated assigning the relative importance to each criterion. Weights reflect the intrinsic worth and discrimination of each criterion. In our case study, an example for weights of location and size within the vineyards is:
	
	                           Weight
	Vineyards location 0.40
	Vineyards size 0.60
	
	Therefore, the score for the example is Chile 6.6 (score * weight) and Spain 7.6

Table 10.9 (Continued)

Step	Implementation
4. Generate outcomes related to the alternative/ component combinations for different decision makers and compare or agree on one unified combination through a workshop	Specific interests of the decision makers can be used to assign the evaluation criteria (scoring and weights). Therefore, three evaluations can be performed for each decision maker to compare their selections: • Owner is interested in quality volume but not niche wines. • Wine maker prefers special editions based on specific characteristics. • Future sales managers aim to have very good quality of standard grapes and a large portfolio of wines to access distributors in foreign markets. Another option is to agree on a unified evaluation through a discussion of the evaluation criteria
5. Perform sensitivity analysis with respect to scoring or weights and evaluate the advantages/ disadvantages of options	The objective of this step is to check the robustness of the preferred option to changes or issues in the information for each component and the weights employed Another aspect is to evaluate from the experience of the decision makers the advantages/disadvantages of the choice in either reasonableness or missing criteria/components

2) Find probability distributions for grape yield by searching the Internet and develop a cash flow considering three types of grapes (Cabernet Sauvignon, Merlot and Pinot Noir) in the two potential sites for the boutique winery (Chile and Spain). You should consider the appropriate distribution of the area planted by each grape within the chosen size of winery (hectares) given their risk profile. Use the Monte Carlo simulation.

References

Belton, V. and Stewart, T. (2002). Multiple Criteria Decision Analysis: An Integrated Approach. Kluwer.

Californiawinesandwineries.com (2016). *What is a Boutique Winery?* https://californiawinesandwineries.com/2016/02/04/what-is-a-boutique-winery/comment-page-1/ (accessed 9 February 2017).

Chesbrough, H. and Rosenbloom, R. (2003). The dual-edged role of the business model in leveraging corporate technology investments. In: Taking Technical Risks: How Innovators, Managers, and Investors Manage Risk in High-Tech Innovations (eds L.M. Branscomb and P.E. Auerswald), 57–68. The MIT Press.

Clark, V., Reed, M., and Stephan, J. (2010). Using Monte Carlo simulation for a capital budgeting project. *Management Accounting Quarterly*, 12(1), 20–41.

Goodwin, P. and Wright, G. (1998) Decision Analysis for Management Judgement, 2nd edn. John Wiley & Sons, Ltd.

Hansemark, O.C. (2003). Need for achievement, locus of control and the prediction of business start-ups: A longitudinal study. *Journal of Economic Psychology*, 24(3), 301–319.

Harris, T. (2006). Start-up: a Practical Guide to Starting and Running a New Business. Springer Science & Business Media.

Hauser, J.R. 1993. How Puritan-Bennett used the house of quality. *Sloan Management Review*, 34(3), 61–70.

Hauser, J.R. and Clausing, D. (1988). The house of quality. *Harvard Business Review*, 66(3), 63–72.

Johnson, G., Scholes, K., and Whittington, R. (2008). Exploring Corporate Strategy: Text & Cases. Pearson Education.

Kotler, P. (2000). Marketing Management, 10th edn. Prentice-Hall.

Kunc, M. (2007). A Survey of Managerial Practices in the Chilean Wine Industry. *Journal of Wine Research*, 18, 113–119.

Kunc, M. (2008). Using systems thinking to enhance the value of strategy maps. *Management Decision*, 46, 761–778.

Lumpkin, G.T. and Dess, G.G. (1996). Clarifying the entrepreneurial orientation construct and linking it to performance. *Academy of Management Review*, 21(1), 135–172.

McClelland, D.C. (1965). N achievement and entrepreneurship: A longitudinal study. *Journal of Personality and Social Psychology*, 1(4), 389–392.

Poon, J.M., Ainuddin, R.A., and Junit, S.O.H (2006). Effects of self-concept traits and entrepreneurial orientation on firm performance. *International Small Business Journal*, 24(1), 61–82.

Ragsdale, C.T 2004 Spreadsheet Modelling and Decision Analysis. Southwestern.

Reuvid, J. (2006). Start Up & Run Your Own Business: The First Steps, Funding & Going for Growth. Kogan Page Publishers.

Rockart, J. (1978). Chief executives define their own data needs. *Harvard Business Review*, 57(2), 81–93.

Sorensen, H.E. (2012). Business Development: a Market-oriented Perspective. John Wiley & Sons, Ltd.

Stewart Jr, W.H. and Roth, P.L. (2001). Risk propensity differences between entrepreneurs and managers: a meta-analytic review. *Journal of Applied Psychology*, 86(1), 145.

Walker, W.E. (2009). Does the best practice of rational-style model based policy analysis already include ethical considerations? *Omega*, 37(6), 1051–1062.

Winston, W.L., Albright, S.C., and Broadie, M. (1997). Management Science: Spreadsheet Modeling and Applications. Duxbury.

Zott, C. and Amit, R. (2010). Business model design: an activity system perspective. *Long Range Planning*, 43(2), 216–226.

Futher Reading

Afuah, A. (2004). Business Models, 1st edn. McGraw-Hill/Irwin.

Anderson, J.C., Narus, J.A., and Van Rossum, W. (2006). Customer value propositions in business markets. *Harvard Business Review*, 84(3), 90–99.

Benninga, S. (2001) Financial Modeling, 2nd edn. The MIT Press.

Bratley, P., Bennett, L.F. and Linus, E.S. (1987) A Guide to Simulation, 2nd edn. Springer-Verlag.

Daily, C.M., McDougall, P.P., Covin, J.G., and Dalton, D.R. (2002). Governance and strategic leadership in entrepreneurial firms. *Journal of Management*, 28(3), 387–398.

French, N. and Gabrielli, L. (2004). The uncertainty of valuation. *Journal of Property Investment and Finance*, 22(6), 484–500.

Kang, S. and Tucker, C.S. (2016). Automated mapping of product features mined from online customer reviews to engineering product characteristics. ASME 2016 International Design Engineering Technical Conferences and Computers and Information in Engineering Conference, Volume 1B: 36th Computers and Information in Engineering Conference, Charlotte, NC, USA (21–24 August 2016). ASME.

Shafer, S.M., Smith, H.J., and Linder, J.C. (2005). The power of business models. *Business Horizons*, 48(3), 199–207.

Teece, D. (2010). Business models, business strategy and innovation. *Long Range Planning*, 43(2), 172–194.

Vijayasarathy, L.R. (2002). Product characteristics and Internet shopping intentions. *Internet Research*, 12(5), 411–426.

Zeithmal, V.A. (1988). Consumer perceptions of price, quality and value: A means-end model and synthesis of evidence. *Journal of Marketing*, 52, 2–22.

11

Maturity

Objectives

1) To identify strategic actions that sustain profitability
2) To understand the issues faced by mature organizations
3) To identify analytic tools to support mature organizations

Learning outcomes and managerial capabilities developed

1) To be able to use analytic tools to support the improvement of organizational performance
2) To learn the critical aspects of implementing strategies in mature organizations

---

Chapter 10 presented the first stage, called the birth or start-up, of any company in their life cycle (Miller and Friesen, 1984; Hoy, 2006). Companies in their start-up stage concentrate on growing fast until they reach a mature phase where growth does not stop but instead the growth and performance of the company tends to become stable and low over time. The set of strategies that companies tend to adopt when they are reaching maturity are driven by long-term objectives such as:

- **Economic sustainability.** The ability of a company to survive in the long term depends on achieving stable profits.
- **Productivity.** Companies need to improve their relationship between inputs (resources consumed) and outputs (services or products generated) in order to be able to achieve economic sustainability.
- **Competitive position.** This indicates the stance of the company in the markets where it operates in terms of products and strategies. Competitive position may be expressed quantitatively in terms of sales in monetary terms or volume or market share as well as qualitatively such as customers' quality perceptions with respect to competitors.

Strategic Analytics: Integrating Management Science and Strategy, First Edition. Martin Kunc.
© 2019 John Wiley & Sons Ltd. Published 2019 by John Wiley & Sons Ltd.
Companion website: www.wiley.com/go/kunc/strategic-analytics

- **Position in the value system.** Companies are components of larger (industry-level) value chains so the extent to which they control either more or less components of the value system depends on the strategies related to vertical and horizontal integration, diversification and strategic alliances. Companies can retain a large or small proportion of the value created for customers depending on their position in the value system.
- **Product/service positioning.** Companies need to decide the position they wish to have in the market. For example, they can lead or follow the market in technology development. They can compete on price or other dimensions.
- **Social responsibility.** Companies need to consider their objectives with respect to society and the environment by following or leading in terms of contributions to society.

An important factor that affects the effectiveness of the strategies adopted by mature companies is the industry life cycle. Chapter 5 discusses the industry life cycle extensively, so this chapter does not discuss the same topic again. However, it is clear that changes in the industry and the markets need to be accounted for. Some changes are listed in Table 11.1.

Table 11.1 Key changes occurring in the industry during the industry life cycle.

Emerging industry	Transition to mature industry	Mature and declining industry
Technologies are related to pioneers so they are fragmented	Technology becomes widespread	Technology is being replaced partially or totally
Technology is uncertain due to fragmentation	Technology becomes standard together with product	Technology is mature and easily available
Competitors are not clearly identified and are growing due to low barriers	Battle for market share unfolds as growth in demand declines	Battle for market share and survival
Customers are still undefined and unclear so initial investment in customer's education	Customers more knowledgeable so they become more demanding	Customers are focused on price due to standardization of products.
	Focus on value for money for demanding buyers	Focus on value for money for remaining demand
High initial costs but declining with experience	Lower costs and established suppliers	Lower number of suppliers
Lack of adequate suppliers		
Strong uncertainty due to unknown demand and technology	High uncertainty due to competition.	Low operational uncertainty but high uncertainty in future developments that may replace the industry

The following sections develop a set of strategies that mature companies can implement. However, it is necessary to have a guide to select the strategies. Pearce and Robinson (2000) propose a strategy selection matrix which considers two dimensions related to the objectives followed by the top management team and the focus on the resources to implement the strategy (Figure 11.1). The approach used to guide the selection of the strategy is to consider the objective of the strategy (overcome weaknesses or maximize strengths) and the focus of the actions in order to achieve the strategic objective (internal or external resources). Kunc and Morecroft (2010) suggested the selection of the strategies is a combination of managerial dominant logic (as a process of resource conceptualization to implement the strategy that intends to overcome weaknesses and maximize strengths) and resource management (in terms of selecting the best way to achieve the targets defined for the external and internal resources conceptualized).

The strategies in quadrants II and III in Figure 11.1, except Concentrated growth and Market and product development, are considered in Chapter 12. Strategies in quadrant I (Figure 11.1) are inspired by the identification of weaknesses in the portfolio of resources that can only be solved by acquiring the resources externally in other parts of the value chain (vertical integration) or industries (unrelated diversification). Strategies in quadrant II are mostly related to situations where the financial, operational and competitive situation of the company is extremely weak, which usually occurs when the company reaches a maturity stage. In quadrant II, the strategies aim to either recover the

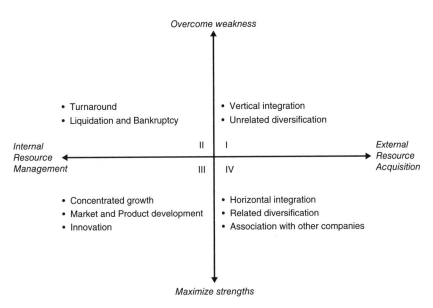

Figure 11.1 Strategy selection matrix. *Source:* Adapted from Pearce and Robinson (2000).

firm from its poor situation (turnaround) or liquidate it (liquidation and bankruptcy). In quadrant III, strategies involve using the strengths already existing in the company in order to obtain more market share using the existing product (concentrated growth) or partially modifying the product (product development) or looking for additional markets (market development). Another strategic option in this quadrant (innovation) is to play with the strengths in developing and launching new products in the market as a continuous process of regenerating the company. Finally, quadrant IV (Figure 11.1) contains the strategies in which the company tries to maximize existing strengths through acquiring external resources that can complement the existing strengths. For example, acquiring a competitor will add more market share and expand the economies of scale within the same business model (horizontal integration). Another option is to buy a company that is not a competitor but can complement the existing portfolio of resources, so the company can extract synergies and expand in a more robust path (related diversification). The final strategy in quadrant IV is to associate with other firms (joint venture, alliances, consortia) in order to share and obtain the resources missing in the company while employing the existing strengths.

11.1 Strategies for Mature Organizations

11.1.1 Concentrated Growth, and Market and Product Development

Concentrated growth means the strategic emphasis of the firm is on increasing market share in its main markets by investing its main products (Pearce and Robinson, 2000). This strategy is also called market penetration. The strategy is based on understanding the market needs, knowing the consumers' behavior in terms of prices and features, and running effective promotion activities. One of the key rationale for this strategy is the use of existing capabilities and resources in the firm while avoiding potential issues related to launching products without enough experience. Additionally, this strategy implies the use of less funds and lower risks than strategies related to completely new products or markets. Concentrating in its own markets, the firm intends to increase productivity by exploiting the learning curve, fully occupying its market segments and exploiting the technology behind its main products. Thus, the firm tries to reach its maturity in organizational terms by concentrating on its key markets and the resources and capabilities that it dominates.

The key conditions facilitating this strategy are:

- Industry is mature so the product is fairly standard with stable, but growing, demand and barriers to entry are fairly high (see Chapter 5 for a description of a mature industry and Table 11.1 for changes in the industry).

- There are still few market segments to fill so the expansion of market share does not come from battling competitors. Simultaneously, the market segments are clearly defined by barriers (e.g. customer taste or channels) preventing multiple competitors from entering simultaneously.
- The materials for the products and production technologies are stable in terms of availability and price.
- Demand tends to be stable over time determined by slow growth in the market favoring the investment in capacity and helping to develop pricing policies.
- The company has competitive advantages in their production (economies of scale) and distribution capabilities (market reach).
- The external environment (political, economic, social and technological forces) does not show signs of future major changes.

Market development is a strategy which implies only marketing current products with minor modifications to customers in related market areas. Customers may already be using products that are similar, but not identical, to the current product. To reach the new customers, the firm must find a new channel of distributions and advertise/promote the modified product. Market development involves identifying new uses for current products in different demographically or geographically defined markets. However, the opportunities do not imply major growth for the whole industry.

In contrast to market development, product development occurs when the current product is changed substantially or a new product, which is related to the current product, is created and sold to existing customers. This strategy aims to extend the life cycle of current products or exploit the competitive advantage of some aspects related to the current product, e.g. quality or brand reputation. The strategy intends to further develop existing markets by expanding the current product line.

A summary of the strategic options under the concentrated growth, and market and product development are listed in Table 11.2.

One important strategy coming from concentrating growth and market development is internationalization. Internationalization strategies can be divided into three basic strategies: *global; locally responsive;* and *transnational* (Barlett and Goshal, 1989). The basic dimensions considered in internationalization strategies are the costs involved to reach the international markets, which are driven by the impact of economies of scale and the need for being locally responsive (which is influenced by the demands of the local buyers). See Table 11.3 for examples of internationalization strategies. *Global strategy* involves products that are standardized in most of their dimensions: characteristics, configurations and brands. The products are produced in a few strategic locations and shipped worldwide. The objective is to achieve economies of scale in most dimensions of the value chain, recover development costs in high volumes and have a presence in all key markets. One of the key successful

Table 11.2 Strategic options for concentrated growth, and market andproduct development.

Type of strategy	Strategic options
Concentrated growth	Increasing current customers' purchases by: • Augmenting size • Affecting rate of obsolescence • Informing them of other uses of the product • Promoting increased use giving price incentives Attracting competitors' customers by: • Differentiation through brand reputation • Promoting aggressively • Reducing price Attracting new customers by: • Facilitating trial use by sampling • Matching price to similar products used by new customers • Advertising new uses
Market development	Opening additional geographic markets through: • Regional expansion • National development • Entering international markets by exports or direct investments Attracting other market segments by: • Adding new product versions • Using other distribution channels • Using other media channels to advertise the product
Product development	Developing new product features through: • Adapting to developments • Modifying characteristics • Amplifying propositions • Reducing size • Substituting ingredients or materials • Rearranging into other forms • Combining with other ingredients or materials Offering different variations in terms of quality Developing new models and sizes (product proliferation)

Source: Adapted from Pearce and Robinson (2000).

factors in the strategy is the existence of homogeneous buyers, who are willing to buy standard products, in many countries. *Locally responsive strategy* implies the adaptation of products to each local market, which are not only produced but also most of the activities in the value chain are performed in the same country. This strategy generates more costs for the company due to the duplication of costs globally and locally. Finally, *transnational strategy* consists of the customization of some aspects of the products while achieving cost advantages by producing some parts at regional or global level. In this case, the companies are part of a global network of affiliates that exploit their local advantages while achieving economies of scale in some dimensions, e.g. financial resources, cost advantages, technology.

Table 11.3 Examples of international strategies.

Internationalization strategy	Economies of scale	Local responsive
Global	High emphasis on economies of scale to reduce costs in large fixed costs activities	Due to the high level of standardization, it is not responsive to local needs
	Example: car industry (Toyota, VW, GM)	
Transnational	Focus on economies of scale aims to minimize costs for large investments	Standard products are adapted to local needs
	Example: drink industry (Anheuser-Busch InBev, Coca Cola)	
Locally responsive	There is no attempt to achieve economies of scale at a global level as the product/service is particular for each market	Products are designed for local needs
	Example: food industry (Sadia (Brazil), Wyke Farms (UK), Morinaga Seika Kabushikigaisha (Japan))	

Food for thought 11.1 The car manufacturing industry is one of the most well-known global industries. The car manufacturing industry requires global sales to be able to sustain new product development as well as to exploit the economies of scale required to produce cars at a competitive price. The largest manufacturing companies originated around the 1900s but became consolidated through a series of mergers and acquisitions every time the business cycle led to a decline in profitability and sales. France has two large car manufacturers: Renault and PSA (Peugeot and Citroen). There are two issues to discuss from this industry in terms of market and product development. The case of PSA (www.peugeot.com) illustrates these two issues.

First, the location of manufacturing plants is very important in order to enter into new markets and develop markets in the automotive industry. Often companies leave markets when the economy or the participation in the market is not strong enough to keep competing in the market. For example, Peugeot left India in 1997 and returned in 2011 building a new manufacturing facility supported by the local government and the increasing attractiveness of the location due to the establishment of additional car manufacturers (Autocarindia, 2011). PSA has three types of car manufacturing plant arrangements: manufacturing plants owned by the company which are mostly in France, Spain and South America; manufacturing plants originated from joint ventures with local companies such as in China, Czech Republic, Italy, Russia and Vietnam; and production plants that are contracted out with local companies in Austria, Czech Republic, Iran, Japan, Malaysia, Netherlands and Turkey. The configuration of the plants reflects the distribution of sales where 43% of the sales occur outside Europe (Peugeot, 2017).

Secondly, there is a wide range of car types (e.g. compact, family, sport) and companies tend to specialize in certain types. Therefore, there is always an opportunity to keep developing new types to penetrate new market segments. Peugeot has never been recognized as a company selling sport utility vehicles (SUVs) since this is mainly a vehicle for the North American market. However, the market for SUVs has been growing steadily for a number of years. In 2007, Peugeot started producing a SUV called Peugeot 4007 based on a similar model produced by Mitsubishi. The car was initially manufactured and sold in Japan but failed to reach the minimum threshold in order to be produced in other areas, e.g. Europe, and it was discontinued in 2012. Then, Peugeot developed different versions such as the 3008 (2008) which won numerous awards as car of the year in various years. The SUV is now a strong component of the product portfolio of Peugeot. Another product development is the development of electric vehicles (EVs) as more consumers are adopting EVs. In 2017, Peugeot presented a new EV with a range of 170 km.

Address the following issues:

- What are the key characteristics of the car industry that lead companies to become global producers? Expand the concept of international strategies to answer this question.
- How do car manufacturing companies, which are not global, survive? What are the resources, capabilities and key value propositions in order to survive?
- What are the reasons influencing Peugeot to have three types of car manufacturing plant arrangements? What is more valuable for a car manufacturing company: to own the car manufacturing plant or to design and license unique car models?

11.1.2 Integration

Integration is the concept employed to identify the level of ownership in the activities comprising a company. The higher the ownership, the higher the level of integration. There are two types of integration: horizontal and vertical. Integration, like any strategy, has been subject to changes in trends. Until the 1990s, integration was beneficial because it improves coordination and reduces risks in terms of the issues raised by the Five Forces framework. In the last 25 years, the trend has switched to more "disintegration" of the companies through outsourcing as it improves flexibility and helps companies to focus on their core competences. The development of better coordinating mechanisms facilitates this process.

There are different positions in *horizontal integration* strategies. One position in horizontal integration involves the acquisition of competitors in the same markets. The main benefits of this strategy are to eliminate competition and to have access to more markets, so the firm can expand operations through larger market shares and obtain economies of scale. Another position is the acquisition of firms in similar stages in the value chain where the objective is to achieve interrelationship effects by sharing resources or skills in activities that have relatedness in order to achieve synergy, create value and achieve competitive advantage by economies of scope. Some conditions determining the success of this position (Ensign, 1998) are:

- Integration must take place between activities that have a significant portion of total operating costs or assets.
- Sharing must reduce the cost of performing shared activities through economies of scale and capacity utilization.
- The integration can help the company to move down the learning curve faster by higher capacity utilization.

Vertical integration involves acquiring either, or both, suppliers and customers. A company may acquire a supplier to have control over the inputs used for its production. This integration is called backward vertical integration because the firm moves upstream (back) in the supply chain. A company can acquire firms located downstream in the supply chain, which are usually customers, to control the access to markets. This integration is called forward vertical integration. Most of the rationale for vertical integration can be associated with issues defined by Five Forces analysis (see Chapter 3) related to the bargaining power of either suppliers or customers. One of the indicators of the level of vertical integration is the ratio of internal value added, measured by the total operating, to its revenue. Some of the benefits and costs of vertical integration (Grant, 2013) are:

- The integration of production processes in one location can obtain technical economies from the physical integration of business processes.
- When there are market contracts between suppliers in the value chain and the industry conditions favored opportunism (few suppliers, lack of information, specific investments and high switching costs), there will be a chance that transaction costs will be higher than the management costs of an integrated company. Thus, integration can reduce transaction costs.

- The minimum efficient scale of one stage is much higher than the demand for the following stage in the value chain. Then, the downstream company will face more supply than required which needs to be sold in the market. Therefore, an acquisition can help to achieve similar scales across the value chain of the acquiring company.
- An organizational unit which only serves one customer may not have an incentive, and the possibility, to develop its organizational capabilities at the same level as an organizational unit facing market competition and multiple customers. Thus, a vertical acquisition can foster distinctive organizational capabilities.
- Certain industries require flexible organizations to be able to adjust to unpredicted changes in demand so that market transactions can be more adequate than integration. However, a vertical acquisition can reduce the flexibility of the company.

Food for thought 11.2   Tesla Motors Inc. (www.tesla.com) is an electric vehicle car manufacturer based in Palo Alto, California. The company was founded in 2003 by Elon Musk, Martin Eberhard, JB Straubel and Marc Tarpenning. The corporate mission for Tesla is "to lead the surge of the global transition towards sustainably-sourced renewable energy". The main business for Tesla is designing, manufacturing and trading high-performance electric vehicles as well as licensing its own powertrain components (Schwartz and Xia, 2013). There are many powertrain technologies competing in the automotive industry such as hybrid electric vehicles (still has a petrol-based engine that feeds a small electric engine for short distances), range extended electric vehicles (mostly electric with a small petrol-based engine to extend the range of the vehicle), fuel cell electric vehicles (uses hydrogen for generating electricity to supply its electric engine) and battery electric vehicles (the engine runs on batteries and can only be charged from the grid). Tesla produces vehicles for the battery electric vehicle (BEV) segment. In 2008, Tesla launched its first highway-capable BEV which can last up to 250 miles.

Currently, Tesla has diversified into three business segments – automotive sales, electric vehicle components supplier and Tesla energy (standalone home and commercial energy storage devices) (Reeves, 2015). In 2016, Tesla acquired SolarCity. SolarCity provides solar energy services to businesses, government, and non-profit organizations. The company also offers the installation of solar panels, solar roof and batteries (Tesla's powerwall) for homeowners. Tesla has a joint venture with Panasonic (www.panasonic.com) (a Japanese company recognized for expertise in batteries) to build Gigafactory in Nevada (Schwartz and Xia, 2013) and to build solar cells in Buffalo (Forbes, 2016).

Address the following issues:

- Does it make sense for Tesla to acquire a solar panel company? What type of integration can be associated with this acquisition?

- Review the supply chain in renewable energy from the generation to its use. Then, what other organizations can be acquired by Tesla? What is the rationale for the acquisitions?
- Regarding the joint venture with Panasonic for building batteries and solar cells, will Panasonic consider acquiring Tesla? What will be the rationale for Panasonic?

11.1.3 Diversification

Diversification strategies imply a change from the traditional business of the company. However, it represents a difficult choice for a company since it can cause destruction of value to the company if it is performed in the wrong way and turbulent market conditions can make decision making more volatile, which is not a viable context when a top management team needs to understand multiple businesses. Diversification can also help to access new growth opportunities and reduce the risks inherent to the main business as well as being an attractive move if the industry conditions are adequate, costs of entry are low and it generates competitive advantages (economies of scope and the corporate provides value added through its management skills).

Diversification can be obtained by either acquiring another company or creating a new company and separating from the main business (spin-off). If the target of the diversification has a business somehow related to the firm, this diversification is called *related diversification*. Some of the benefits sought through related diversification are related to: increase in the growth rate of the firm; use of the surplus in funds originated by the main business in businesses that can either provide synergies or reduce risks; expanding the product portfolio with complementary or new products; and acquiring resources and capabilities not existing in the firm.

If diversification is employed to build a portfolio of businesses due to their investment value, this diversification is called *conglomerate or unrelated diversification*. Unrelated diversification does not intend to create synergies with or expand the current business. The main objectives of the strategy are concerned with financial measures: revenue stabilization, cash availability, debt and leverage opportunities.

Some questions can be considered to evaluate diversification strategies:

1) **Are there opportunities for sharing resources and capabilities?** Opportunities can be identified in resources and capabilities related to market, operations or management areas. For example, market-related opportunities are sharing sales force, after sales services, brand, distribution channels, etc. Operations-related opportunities arise from procurement capabilities, manufacturing resources, logistics services, technologies for processing and

product development. Management opportunities occur when there is the possibility to share dynamic capabilities, managerial resources, etc.

2) **How do you manage the portfolio of businesses that are being added?** The role of the corporate is to balance the cash flow, growth opportunities and use of resources/capabilities across all the businesses that comprise the portfolio of a multi-business company. Different consulting firms, e.g. Boston Consulting Group or McKinsey, have developed tools to support this process, which can have limitations and do not cover all dimensions that can be considered to control a multi-business company.

Tools for managing business portfolio. One of the tools developed by the Boston Consulting Group is called the BCG Growth-Share Matrix. The matrix organizes the business across two dimensions: market share, as a proxy for the generation of cash flows due to its strong competitive positioning (market share of the company divided by market share of largest competitor), and market growth rate, as a measure for the use of cash flows (percentage of increase in market sales or volume in the last two years). The business with high market growth rate and strong cash generation due to its large market share is considered a *star business* given its strong future performance but is subject to high levels of investment as a requirement to sustain the competitive position. *Cash cow business* generates more cash than it is required to invest in it because it has a strong competitive position in a mature market, which does not require high investments. These businesses are milked to support other growing businesses. *Dog businesses* are in a difficult position since they are not in attractive markets and their competitive position is weak, so they are ready to be divested or liquidated once they are harvested. *Unknown businesses* are located in high growth markets but their competitive positioning is weak. This business consumes more cash than it generates due to the growth in the market (Figure 11.2).

Another matrix to evaluate the portfolio of business was proposed by McKinsey and General Electric. The matrix is called the Industry Attractiveness-Business Strength Matrix. The two dimensions considered are the level of Industry Attractiveness as measured by a set of criteria such as competitive rivalry, bargaining power of suppliers and customers, threat of substitutes and new entrants (the criteria are closely connected with the Five Forces framework discussed in Chapter 5) together with economic, financial and sociopolitical factors (the factors partially reflect the analysis of macro factors presented in Chapter 4). In terms of Business Strength, the criteria involve aspects related to the value chain and generic strategies (see Chapter 6) such as cost position and differentiation levels together with resources (see Chapter 7) such as financial, human and intangible. There are three categories for each dimension (high, medium, low) where each business is allocated based on subjective evaluations. Then strategies are proposed for each of the nine quadrants in terms of investment (financial and management attention) in the development of the resources to support the growth of the business (Figure 11.3).

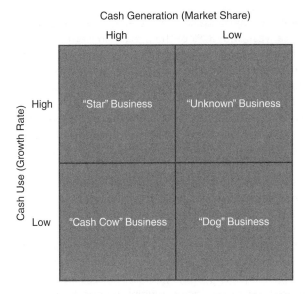

Figure 11.2 The BCG Growth-Share Matrix. *Source:* Adapted from Proctor and Hassard (1990).

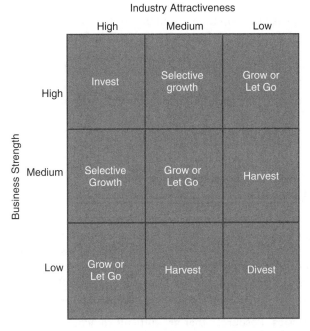

Figure 11.3 The McKinsey/GE Industry Attractiveness-Business Strength Matrix. Source: Adapted from Pearce and Robinson (2000).

Food for thought 11.3   Honda (www.honda.com) achieved global sales of 4 million vehicles in the 2006 fiscal year, with 37% of them made in North America. Globally, Honda revenues (US$ 94 billion) correspond to 55% of automobile sales and 45% for motorcycles, power products, and financial services operations (Meyer, 2008). In 2006, Honda obtained 5 out of 10 number-one reports in Consumer Reports (Meyer, 2008). One of the interesting aspects about Honda is that the company started as a producer of motorcycles in 1949 and only in the late 1970s started its production of cars (Pascale, 1996). Moreover, Honda did not abandon the motorcycle industry as it maintains a leading position globally. One of the key concepts behind its success is the development of engines.

Honda develops engines centrally in a state-of-the-art R&D Center in Tochigi, Japan, where hundreds of engineers work on a range of engine technologies and create specific engine designs for all products. Honda owned more than 10 900 patents in Japan and 18 500 abroad as of 2007. Their main focus is to create engines that are more powerful, e.g. greater horsepower per liter of combustion chamber, energy efficient, e.g. include all technologies (conventional, hybrid, zero-emission, and fuel-cell), and reduce engine emissions (Meyer, 2008). The broader business objective is to create engines that can be used across multiple product lines including sedan, SUVs, motorcycles and boats.

Address the following issues:

- Using the matrices in Figures 11.2 and 11.3, map out the position of Honda's main products.
- What type of diversification is Honda following?
- What are the core resources and capabilities responsible for driving the diversification?
- Recently Honda has become a leader in robots and humanoids. Explain this latest movement in terms of diversification and what core resources and capabilities are being leveraged in this new product.

11.1.4   Associations with Other Companies: Joint Venture, Strategic Alliances and Consortia

When organizations do not have the necessary resources, scale or funds to develop a strategy, organizations can associate in order to aggregate, share or exchange valuable resources. From a resource-based perspective, associations usually occur when resources cannot be acquired through market exchanges or mergers and acquisitions (Das and Teng, 2000). Das and Teng (2000) propose three dimensions to evaluate the formation and performance of alliances:

1) **Resource characteristics.** Resources that are difficult to acquire, attract, imitate or substitute, e.g. non-mobile, non-imitable and non-substitutable,

motivate the formation of associations. Since rival organizations cannot obtain but still need them, there is an incentive to obtain their benefits. For example, the impact of reputation for a new product in a target market can be achieved by establishing an alliance with a highly reputed organization in the target market.

2) **Type of resources.** While there are a number of ways to define types of resources, this framework proposes two types: property-based resources, such as property rights of patents, designs or trademarks, contracts, which are inimitable; and knowledge-based resources, e.g. technology as the know-how and skills to develop patents and designs, which are not only inimitable but also non-substitutable.

3) **Inter-partner resource alignments.** The alignment between the resources in an association will impact upon the performance of the alliance. In this sense, resources can be supplementary or complementary depending on their level of similarity and utilization in the alliance. When resources are similar, in terms of type and amount committed in the alliance then resources are supplementary. The usual cases are financial resources and manufacturing capacity. When resources are different between partners, in terms of type and amount, and they are employed to achieve the objective of the association, then resources are complementary. Some cases are R&D and marketing, e.g. new product launch, or manufacturing and access to a market, e.g. market entry in a new country.

While there are a multitude of forms of associations, this section reviews three of the most common types: joint ventures; strategic alliances; and consortia.

Joint ventures are organizations created and operated for the benefits of the owning organizations. They usually have specific objectives, imply cooperative behaviors between the owning organizations and reduce risks for the owning organizations. Joint ventures can be employed to develop assets which may be too costly for one organization, e.g. joint plants, in order to foster relationships in the supply chain, and enter into new markets. Using the dimensions suggested by Das and Teng (2000), joint ventures are better suited for associations where one of the partners provides property-based resources and the other partner offers knowledge-based resources. Equity joint ventures help to avoid unintended transfer of skills and knowledge for the property-based partner but there may be transfer of tacit knowledge from the partner offering the knowledge-based resources. Potential problems with joint ventures are limited control, share profits and uncontrolled transfer of capabilities to partners.

Strategic alliances are partnerships created for a defined period of time with a specific objective where partners share or combine their capabilities and resources to achieve it. Most of the time the aim of alliances is to learn from the other company and then the partners develop their own capabilities and resources internally. Therefore, it is very important to define the right conditions for alliances. Sometimes alliances only involve licensing agreements where one company transfers the property rights of products or technologies to the partner. In other circumstances, strategic alliances are associated with outsourcing strategies where a company hires another company to perform some of their activities. Some of the reasons for outsourcing are related to focusing on the core business, accessing global standards in certain processes, sharing risks and freeing resources. Alliances can be unilateral contract-based, e.g. a clear transfer of property rights sharing property-based resources such as a licensing agreement, or bilateral contract-based, e.g. a joined production of property rights using knowledge-based resources as in joint R&D projects (Das and Teng, 2000).

Consortia are sets of companies strongly interconnected through interlocking relationships. Interlocking relationships occur through shared ownerships, board of directors and other governance mechanisms attaching the strategic destiny of the firms participating in the consortia. This form of association is common in Asian countries such as Japan (keiretsu), South Korea (chaebols), and developing countries where a large business tends to buy participation in other firms in the industry and the supply chain in order to overcome market imperfections (e.g. lack of trustful suppliers) forming business groups (Latin America).

Food for thought 11.4 Volvo (www.volvo.com) has made a joint venture with the leading ride-sharing company Uber (www.uber.com) in order to produce the next generation self-driving autonomous cars. Volvo and Uber are investing US$ 300 million in the project to develop fully autonomous driverless cars (Volvo, 2016). The vehicles will be produced by Volvo and then Uber will incorporate them into its fleet. Then the vehicle developed will be used by each of the partners in their specific strategies. For example, Uber can add cars from other manufacturers to the fleet and Volvo will be able to sell the car as part of their autonomous driving strategy.

Volvo is planning to use its technology for car manufacturing called Scalable Product Architecture (SPA) (Volvo, 2016). SPA, which was developed as part of its transformation program started in 2010, has been generated to address new drive technologies, and for the generation of electrification and connectivity advances (Volvo, 2016). The added value from the joint venture with Uber will be safety, redundancy and new features for autonomous vehicles on the road. The joint project will involve teams of engineers from both companies working together.

Address the following issues:

- What does the joint venture add to each company in terms of resources and capabilities? Which company will gain more from the joint venture or will the benefits be similar?

- What are the advantages of a joint venture for companies with such different businesses? And the disadvantages?
- What will be the next steps (strategic options) for Volvo after the joint venture? What will be the next steps (strategic options) for Uber? You can use scenarios to answer these questions.
- What company will suffer most from failures, e.g. driverless car accidents, in the joint venture?

11.2 Integrating Management Science into Strategic Management

In mature organizations, one of the main strategic decisions is related to optimizing a certain aspect of the business, e.g. maximizing profits given the restrictions on capacity, because there are less opportunities to grow and profitability is declining. Certain management science tools are more suitable for mature organizations because the business model is relatively stable. When the business model is stable, the management team has more knowledge about the profit function, processes and resources required, as well as abundant information from the information systems. One of the tools for optimization is linear programming. This modeling approach provides rational choices for decision makers because:

- The different courses of actions (multiple options) are known so the problem is selecting the best option.
- There is enough knowledge and information to predict the consequences of actions in terms of the limitations (resources) existing in the business.
- There is a criterion for determining the preferred actions associated with either minimizing or maximizing (optimal choice) a certain performance measure in the organization (profits).

Targett (1996) suggests the solution to linear programming problems offers four insights. First, the solution can show whether the resources (constraints) are tight or "slack" (Targett, 1996). A constraint is tight when all the capacity of a resource is used for the optimal solution. A constraint is slack when not all the capacity of a resource is employed so there is spare capacity but it is not optimal to use since it does not improve the profits. This is a key piece of information for strategic decisions regarding either capacity expansion to eliminate bottlenecks or product expansion to exploit the capacity of the resource not fully utilized. The next insight provides guidance on capacity expansion.

Secondly, "dual values", or shadow prices, are derived from the constraints and indicate the impact on the objective function of a change on them (Targett, 1996). In some way, they measure the real value of the resources to the decision maker so they may help to indicate the maximum price to be paid for an additional unit of a resource. When dual values are equal to zero, then no extra value can be generated from expanding the resource. It is important to consider that expanding one of the resources based on its dual value will affect the resulting option, e.g. production allocation.

Thirdly, dual values are marginal values since their impact is only measured within small increments and not guaranteed to hold over larger changes in the resources. Any information obtained from the solution of the linear programming problem is the maximum value for which the dual values remain valid. This information is called "right-hand side ranges" (Targett, 1996). At the extremes of the range, the dual value is equal to zero.

Fourthly, "coefficient ranges" are insights related to the objective function (Targett, 1996). They provide similar information to right-hand side ranges so they indicate the validity of changes in the coefficients, e.g. the prices of the products, of the objective function. The coefficients of the objective function reflect the slopes of the line defining the objective function. Therefore, this information helps decision makers to evaluate the sensitivity of the profits to changes in the function responsible for them.

This section covers a selection of the methods within the context of supporting strategic decision making related to market expansion and optimization of existing resources under stable markets. Optimization is a critical component of prescriptive analytics due to the possibility of having a large amount of data to develop the models and test their results with historical data. See Section 11.5.3.

11.2.1   Linear Optimization

Basically, a linear programming approach has three parts: decision variables (the variables defined as part of the courses of actions); the objective function (the criteria to distinguish between bad or good decisions related to maximizing or minimizing a certain performance measure); and constraints or limitations that restrict the options available for the decision variables (Targett. 1996). The constraints define the solution area for the optimization so any solution must satisfy the constraints that act as bounds on the solution area. Typical constraints are related to the resources available, e.g. productive and service capacity and raw material availability, and size of the market demand, e.g. minimum or maximum historical demand.

Linear programming solutions are highly sensitive to changes in the assumptions, e.g. the objective function or constraints. Therefore, linear programming may be used in an exploratory mode to investigate desired courses of actions, although this does not happen in reality. The power of linear programming resides in searching through many alternatives for a problem defined by constraints and finding an optimal solution. Consequently, linear programming is used for automatizing decision-making processes involving the allocation of resources in an efficient way. When the model becomes too complicated due to the implementation of numerous constraints, the possible solutions expand enormously leading to issues related to finding the optimal solution overall or within a certain time frame. In this situation, the search process looking for solutions in the solution area resembles exploratory behaviors trying to find not the optimal solution but the best possible solution within a reasonable period of time. This second management science tool is called heuristics. Heuristics complement linear programming.

Food for thought 11.5 A company produces two key products that share the same manufacturing capacity. The company can sell most of the products immediately or store them for a while. The production process involves using two resources: skilled workers and machines. Unfortunately, both resources are inflexible in the medium term due to regulations and the costs involved in changing the manufacturing capacity. Skilled workers can work for 600 minutes per day and machines produce for 800 minutes per day. The skilled worker's time for product A is 6 minutes and for product B is 3 minutes. Machines' time for product A is 2 minutes and for B is 5 minutes. The critical strategic decision is to optimize the use of the resources across the two products while maximizing the profits. The profit per unit of product A is 16 and for product B is 12.

Decision variables: There are two decisions to make: volume for product A (x) and volume for product B (y).

Objective function: Since the main objective of the analysis is to maximize the profitability of the firm by selling products A and B, the function that describes the objective of the analysis is

$$\text{Maximize } 16 * x + 12 * y$$

In other words, the profits will be equal to the volumes for products A and B multiplied by their respective profit per unit produced.

Constraints: Given the limitations in the resources comprising the manufacturing capacity, the profits will be limited to the best use of resources available within the time required to produce each of the products. In mathematical terms, the use of the resources in the two products does not have to be used completely so there may be some capacity not employed at the optimal production level.

$$\text{Skilled workers capacity} \rightarrow 6 * x + 3 * y \leq 600 \text{ minutes}$$
$$\text{Machines capacity} \rightarrow 2 * x + 5 * y \leq 800 \text{ minutes}$$

The linear programming formulation is presented below and two final constraints are included to denote the impossibility of negative production:

$$\text{Maximize } 16*x + 12*y$$
$$\text{Subject to}$$
$$6*x + 3*y \leq 600 \text{ minutes}$$
$$2*x + 5*y \leq 800 \text{ minutes}$$
$$x \geq 0$$
$$y \geq 0$$

This problem can be solved using simple algebra, e.g. the method of simultaneous equations. The method of simultaneous equations requires you to combine the equations of the constraints, after transforming the inequalities into equalities, so that there is only one variable. Then, the volume of the production for products A and B is calculated to satisfy the optimal production and employed to calculate the profits. The answer to the problem is:

- The optimal production will be 25 units of product A and 150 units of product B with profits equal to 2200.
- The dual value for skilled workers capacity is 2.33 and for machines capacity is 1.
- The maximum right-hand side range for skilled workers is 480–2400 and for machines is 200–1000.
- The coefficient range for product A is 4.8–24 and for product B is 8–40.

Address the following issues:

- Which resource is more critical? Why is it more critical?
- What will you consider to expand the resources? Which resource will be prioritized? Look at additional articles to support your answer.
- Try to develop additional linear programming models for some of the strategies mentioned in Sections 11.1, 11.2 and 11.3. What will be the components? What insights do you expect to obtain?

11.2.2 Extensions in Linear Programming

The extensions in the basic linear programming algorithm consider different issues faced when applying the algorithm on real situations such as the results should only be integers, equations can have non-linear terms, or if there is not enough data (Targett, 1996).

Integer programming When the amount of resources or investments required has to be an integer, e.g. one truck or an investment in a certain asset, then the linear programming algorithm uses a different solution, which is more complex and takes longer to calculate. Sometimes the solution can be approximated with a linear programming algorithm and the results interpreted considering the integer and then the fraction as an extra capacity that can be rented.

Applications of integer programming are in different areas. For example, integer programming is employed to minimize logistic costs during the selection of suppliers in a low-cost strategy (Ghodsypour and O'Brien, 2001). Another example is to support the design of a remanufacturing strategy due to environmental, economic, government and social pressures. In this case, the algorithm calculates optimal values of production and transportation quantities of manufactured and remanufactured products as well as defining location problems of collection and distribution facilities (Demirel and Gökçen, 2008).

Non-linear programming   In this case, the equations have squared, cubed or logarithmic components. For example, any objective function related to a demand function includes squared price or unit costs follow a quadratic function related to the number of items produced due to economies of scale.

A key application of non-linear programming is the strategic issue of determining the number of different segments, using price as a variable, and size of the segments in hotels so as to maximize occupancy and revenues (Ladany, 1996). The model starts with a non-linear demand function and resource constraints in capacity together with the limitation that capacity is perishable, e.g. a room not sold is lost. This type of model is the basis of revenue management models (See Chapter 4).

Programming under uncertainty   Basic linear programming is based on the assumption that data for all equations is known. The coefficients and constants in the problem formulation are fixed and deterministic. However, many problems include data that is estimated or forecasted, e.g. demand. Targett (1996) suggests three approaches to managing uncertain data in programming situations:

1) *Sensitivity analysis.* It involves changing the data that is uncertain over a range of values and solving the linear programming problem again many times to see the sensitivity of the optimal solution. This is similar to the use of dual values, right-hand ranges and coefficient ranges.
2) *Stochastic programming.* The algorithm includes the information as probabilities for the different components of the model (mostly constraints). Then there is a transformation of the formulation into a linear programming problem, such as using the means of the normal distribution of the variables.
3) *Chance-constrained programming.* When some constraints cannot or do not have to use up all the time but only a certain percentage of the time, then linear programming offers a solution that is related to the chance or probability of an occurrence.

A critical decision for oil companies exploring offshore fields is to define the investment in a new oilfield through the commission of oil platforms that can cost between US$ 200 million and US$ 650 million. An example of an application of stochastic programming is this decision where there is uncertainty in the initial maximum oil flowrate and recoverable oil volume (Tarhan et al., 2009).

11.2.3 Making the Integration of Organizations Reality Through Internet of Things and Analytics

The Internet of Things (IoT) comprises devices (and/or sensors) that are interconnected and exchange data continuously. These devices may be in products manufactured by a company, installed by another company to provide a service and used by a customer during the service. In other words, the IoT makes reality the integration of manufacturers, service provides and customers in the value chain. The applications of the IoT can be found in different areas: maintenance, pricing, inventory management and payment systems. Networks of connected devices are defining the relationships between organizations, their customers and suppliers in a similar way as joint venture, alliances and integration processes.

Jernigan et al. (2016) found in their survey that 66% of companies were working on IoT projects that collect data from and send to customers, suppliers and even competitors. Data sharing can also be performed with competitors and data sharing increases with the experience and capability to extract value from the data (Jernigan et al., 2016). However, most of the data originates from customers.

One of the downsides of the IoT is the additional costs of running the real network. Jernigan et al. (2016) suggested that the IoT requires investments to acquire the products and operating costs related to maintaining the network. The economic principles behind the IoT are different than software since the growth of the network can lead to diseconomies of scale due to its complexity and operations. For example, the number of potential connections increases with the square of the number of nodes and the addition of new nodes may imply new data formats and processes further complicating the management of the network (Jernigan et al., 2016). Other potential issues are the response from customers to being observed and keeping the data safe and trustworthy (Jernigan et al., 2016).

To obtain value from the IoT, Jernigan et al. (2016) proposed a series of aspects for consideration. First, analytics capabilities are fundamental to obtain insights from the data especially data that may be unstructured and very large, e.g. GE collects more than 50 million data variables from 10 mission sensors (Jernigan et al., 2016: page 12). Secondly, IoT projects are more complex than traditional IT projects. Devices can have different origins, being located in distant locations and not under the control of the organization, and being mobile. Thirdly, sharing data and preparing all actors in the network (customers, suppliers, competitors) is critical to maintain a sustainable relationship through their IoT devices. However, the possibility of optimizing resources (e.g. manufacturing and service) and outputs (e.g. product and service configurations) in real time can generate invaluable profits for mature organizations with a stable customer base.

11.3   End of Chapter

Mature organizations slow their growth rate and the performance of the company tends to become stable over time. More complexity in products, processes and systems tend to make the management of mature organizations more difficult. Since the set of strategies are driven by long-terms objectives such as economic sustainability and productivity, mature companies need to find management science tools that optimize the use of the existing resources within the competitive positioning selected. Linear programming, and its extensions, is a highly suitable tool to address the strategic goals of economic sustainability and productivity. A profitable and productive mature organization can sustain performance for many years. The linear programming approach is an important way to think logically in terms of the elements of the business that are controlled (decision variables) and the limitations to achieve the objectives for the decisions in terms of resource constraints, customer satisfaction, or any aspect of the business that needs to be satisfied.

The logical way of thinking in linear programming is an excellent complement to the selection process of strategies indicated at the beginning of the chapter. More specifically, the approach to guiding the selection of strategies has to consider the objective of the strategy (overcome weaknesses or maximize strengths) and the focus of the actions in order to achieve the strategic objective (internal or external resources), as shown in Figure 11.1. For example, strategies inspired by the identification of weaknesses in the portfolio of resources are informed by the resource limitations exhibited in linear programming problems. Then the price for acquiring the resources externally can be explored through some of the insights generated from solving the linear programming problem, e.g. dual values or right-hand ranges. Strategies involving expanding the portfolio of products can be optimized through linear programming as the Case study (Section 11.6.2) will show.

Definitively, the use of one method from the management science field is not enough and more methods can be integrated in strategic management. Linear programming is an important addition to the dynamic resource management issues discussed in Chapter 6. While resource mapping can identify the resources responsible for supporting the business model of the firm, resource mapping may not be able to calculate the optimal use of the resources. However, system dynamics modeling, which comes after resource mapping, can inform the progression of the market over time to evaluate the timing for expanding resources.

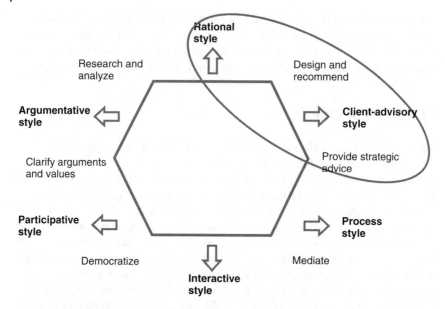

Figure 11.4 Management science styles. Source: Walker (2009). Reproduced with permission of Elsevier.

Therefore, the management tools in this situation provide support to rational decisions through the design and recommendation of strategies or supporting the implementation of strategies, as shown in Figure 11.4.

11.3.1 Revision Questions

1) Different consulting firms have developed tools to support managing multi-business companies, e.g. BCG Growth-Share Matrix and McKinsey/GE Industry Attractiveness-Business Strength Matrix (see Section 11.3). Like any framework, they have limitations and do not cover all the dimensions that can be considered to control a multi-business company. Propose two additional frameworks by defining the dimensions and range of values for the dimensions together with a broad classification for cases.
2) Identify applications in linear programming that have been employed in strategic decisions in the automobile industry.
3) How can strategic alliances be evaluated using multi-criteria decision making? Review the methodology used in Chapter 3.

11.3.2 Case Study: Choosing the Right Set of Capabilities – Development Projects to Achieve Multiple Organization Goals

Many organizations develop multiple projects simultaneously to achieve their organization goals, which may be more than simply maximizing profits. Two steps are necessary to evaluate the adoption of the competing projects under different organization goals. First, the set of organization goals that need to be satisfied with the projects must be identified. Secondly, it is necessary to collect various metrics, e.g. costs, return on investment, complexity, associated with the projects. Metrics can be related to soft, e.g. complexity, and hard variables, e.g. costs. All the information is employed to calculate a variation of linear programming called "goal programming'" (Lee, 1972; Romero, 2014). Basically, goal programming follows similar principles as linear programming but the main difference is that there is more than one objective, or goal, because satisfying multiple conflictive goals is impossible. The task of the solution is to get as close as possible to each objective. Thus, goal programming follows the principle of satisficing (Simon, 2001). A variation of goal programming includes the relative preferences of the decision makers between goals (weighted goal programming) so the decision makers can evaluate the trade-offs between goals using different weight sets. A summary of the steps in a goal programming problem (Ragsdale, 2004) is as follows:

1) Identify the decision variables.
2) Identify hard constraints and formulate as if it were a linear programming problem.
3) Define the goals together with their target values.
4) Define constraints using the decision variables that achieve the goals.
5) Transform the constraints into goal constraints including deviational variables.
6) Determine undesirable deviations from the goals using deviational variables.
7) Formulate the objective that penalizes the undesirable deviations.
8) Solve the problem and evaluate the solution.

In this case, a company has six projects as part of its strategic intent to improve its operational capabilities through the investment in specific resources and processes (Table 11.4).

The objectives, or goals, are:

1) Achieve a return on investment equal or higher than US\$ 360 million.
2) Increase productivity equal or higher than 10.
3) Achieve a technological risk lower than 10.

The company has the following constraints:

1) Limit the total costs of projects to US\$ 150 million.
2) Limit required workforce to 150 technicians.

A goal programming model is developed using an Excel spreadsheet following instructions suggested in Winston and Albright (2009) and the steps indicated previously. First, the spreadsheet is developed. The spreadsheet includes

Table 11.4 Metrics for six projects related to building operational capabilities.

				Project		
	Project 1: Build a testing laboratory	Project 2: Buy a 3D design system	Project 3: Implement flexible manufacturing systems for new products	Project 4: Install a high speed Wi-Fi service	Project 5: Develop simulation software to support product design	Project 6: Implement Lean program
Return on investment (million US$)	250	10	145	5	25	17
Project costs (in million US$)	125	8	100	3	18	10
Productivity improvement (0=none, 5=high)	3	4	3	2	4	3
Technological risk (0=none, 5=high)	3	1	4	0	3	2
Workforce requirements (full time equivalent)	120	2	15	2	25	15

the inputs, which are the data regarding each project, decision variables and constraints divided into hard constraints and goals. After formatting the spreadsheet with the basic information (title, sections: metrics, decision variables, constraints and goals), then the data for each project is entered in the range allocated (B5:G9). The data comes from Table 11.4. Then, the decision variables correspond to the selection of some of the six projects. The decision variables are 0–1 variables, 1 is project selected and 0 is project not-selected, located in range B14:G14. The next section corresponds to the constraints such as total costs and total workforce requirements and they are located in range D18:D19. The range of cells B18:B19 contains the result of the decisions made with respect to the constraints, e.g. projects selected multiplied by project costs and projects selected multiplied by workforce requirements. To implement the result, you need to enter the following formula in cell B18, where the first part is the decisions made and the second component is the information of the costs: "=SUMPRODUCT($B$14:$G$14,B6:G6)". Now, the same process is performed in cell B19: "=SUMPRODUCT($B$14:$G$14,B9:G9)".

Finally, the achievement of goals is considered in the final section following a similar procedure as the constraints. In cell B24, the formula "=SUMPRODUCT($B$14:$G$14,B5:G5)" is entered. In cell B25, the formula "=SUMPRODUCT($B$14:$G$14,B7:G7)". Finally, the formula "=SUMPRODUCT($B$14:$G$14,B8:G8)" is included in cell B26. The values for the goals and constraints are entered opposite the results in column D. Figure 11.5 shows the spreadsheet.

The final stage is to evaluate the feasibility of the problem. Thus, we need to verify that there is a solution that satisfies goals and constraints. For that purpose, we use an add-in in excel called "Solver". At this point, the problem is treated as simple linear programming without a specific objective to maximize since we are testing the feasibility of the problem. Then, we choose the set of decisions using the box called "By Changing Variable cells" and entering the range of cells, as shown in Figure 11.6. Finally, we enter the constraints in the box named "Subject to the Constraints:". The first line indicates the results of the decisions have to be binary variables (0–1 variables) since a project is either selected or not selected. This is performed using the icon "Add" (Figure 11.6) and choosing the cells with the results, cells in column B, defining the type of relationship, e.g. bin (binary), <=, >=, and entering the constraints, cells in column D. Finally, the solving method is chosen as "Simplex LP".

The solution found by Solver indicates there is no feasible solution, as Figure 11.7 shows. Consequently, there is not a selection of projects that can satisfy all of the requirements simultaneously. Moreover, the results do not satisfy the binary requirement because of their infeasibility.

Since it is impossible to satisfy all requirements in an optimal way, we need to find a solution that is good enough to try to achieve as many of the goals as possible. In order to implement this approximation, we transform the goals

	A	B	C	D	E	F	G
1	**Implementing New Product Development Capabilities**						
2							
3	Metrics to evaluate each project			Projects			
4		Project 1	Project 2	Project 3	Project 4	Project 5	Project 6
5	Return on Investment	250	10	145	5	25	17
6	Project Cost	125	8	100	3	18	10
7	Productivity Improvement	3	4	3	2	4	3
8	Technological Risk	3	1	4	0	3	2
9	Workforce Requirements	120	2	15	2	25	15
10							
11							
12			Decision variables				
13		Project 1	Project 2	Project 3	Project 4	Project 5	Project 6
14	Project selected	1	0	0	1	0	1
15							
16			Constraints				
17		Total		Budget			
18	Project Costs	138	<=	150			
19	Required workforce	137	<=	150			
20							
21							
22		Achievement of goals					
23		Achievement		Goals			
24	Return on investment	272	>=	360			
25	Productivity Improvement	8	>=	10			
26	Technological risk	5	<=	10			

Figure 11.5 Spreadsheet with linear programming formulation.

into a set of differences that become decision variables as well. In other words, the decisions are not only to select projects but also to reduce the differences between the results obtained and the stated goals.

To implement the next step in the spreadsheet, we need to modify the original linear programming solution. First, the achievement of goals section will compute the deviation from each goal in terms of values under and over the goals. The range of cells C24:C26 will contain the results from the optimization process so these cells can have any value initially. Then, cells E24–E26 will calculate the balance of the achievement of the goals by adding to the achievement column (column B), the under achievement of the goal (column C) and subtracting the over achievement of the goal (column D). In other words, the formula is E24=B24+C24–D24 and then copy in E25 and E26. Secondly, the new decision variables related to the deviations from goals are implemented. The new section, starting in row 28, contains the deviations under the goals which will be minimized as part of the linear programming solution. The value for cells B30–B32 are directly related to the values in column C (under goals) so you need to implement the formula "=C24" in cell B30 and then copy it to B31:B32. Finally,

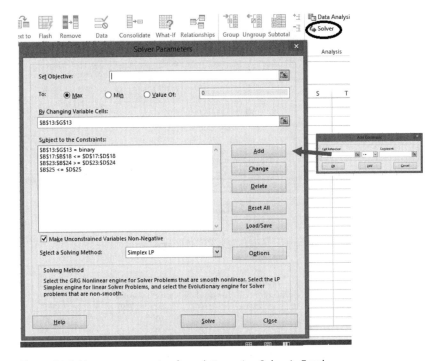

Figure 11.6 Linear programming formulation using Solver in Excel.

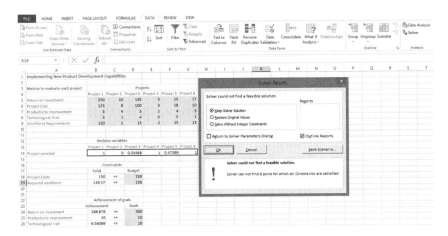

Figure 11.7 Solver results from the problem.

	M		B	L	D	E	F	G
1	Implementing New Product Development Capabilities							
2								
3	Metrics to evaluate each pr			Projects				
4		Project 1	Project 2	Project 3	Project 4	Project 5	Project 6
5	Return on Investment	250	10	145	5	25	17
6	Project Cost	125	8	100	3	18	10
7	Productivity Improvement	3	4	3	2	4	3
8	Technological Risk	3	1	4	0	3	2
9	Workforce Requirements	120	2	15	2	25	15
10								
11								
12			Decision variables					
13		Project 1	Project 2	Project 3	Project 4	Project 5	Project 6
14	Project selected	1	0	0	0	0	0
15								
16			Constraints					
17		Total			Budget			
18	Project Costs	125	<=		150			
19	Required workforce	120	<=		150			
20								
21								
22			Achievement of goals					
23		Achievemer	Under goal	Over goal	Balance			Goals
24	Return on investment	250	0	0	250	=		360
25	Productivity Improvement	3	0	0	3	=		10
26	Technological risk	3	0	0	3	=		10
27								
28	Deviations from goals (amount below goals, or 0 if currently meeting goal)							
29			Deviation under		Already obtained			
30	Return on investment		0	<=	360			
31	Productivity Improvement		0	<=	10			
32	Technological risk		0	<=	10			
33								

Figure 11.8 Spreadsheet with the goal programming formulation.

a column to keep track of the deviations obtained is copied. The initial value is equal to the value of the goals. See Figure 11.8 for the new spreadsheet.

The last step is to run the solution using Solver again. See Figure 11.9 for the configuration of the Solver. First, there is now an objective, the deviation from the goal (cell B:30), that has to be minimized (so the choice "Min" is selected) by changing a set of cells containing the projects (B14:G14) and the cells containing the deviation under goal (C24:C26) and above the goal (D24:D26). Secondly, there are additional constraints to the original constraints. The first line indicates the project selection has to be either 0 or 1. The second line is related to the constraints in costs and workforce requirements. The third line indicates all deviations need to be lower than the value already achieved. These constraints are useful during each of the iterations to minimize the deviations with respect to the goals. The final line indicates the balance needs to be equal to the goal.

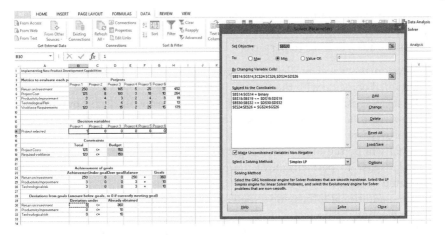

Figure 11.9 Configuration of the Solver.

The first iteration involves minimizing the deviation for the first goal, return on investment, and is presented in Figure 11.10. Solver approximates the solution within the tolerance defined by the user. In my case, I use a large tolerance so the results are slightly above the constraints. There are interesting insights from the solution. The return on investment is below its goal by almost 20% but the productivity improvement goal is achieved with very low technical risk (total risk is 7 which is below the maximum of 10). The results of the second and third iterations, which imply minimizing the deviations for the second and third goal, do not improve the first results so they are not presented here. This poses some interesting questions for the decision makers about trade-offs with respect to the

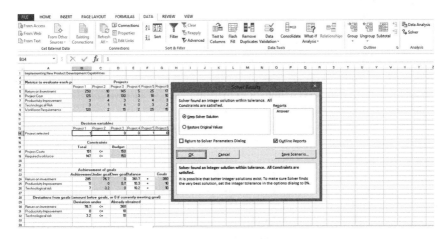

Figure 11.10 First iteration by minimizing the deviation for return on investment.

goals defined. For example, the goal for return on investment needs refinement by either decreasing it or relaxing the budget and workforce constraints.

Here are a few actions to perform:

1) Develop the Excel model as described previously and verify the results obtained coincide with the figures.
2) Perform sensitivity analysis related to tolerance to risk (e.g. how much is prepared to lose), aggressiveness in return on investments and productivity improvements.
3) What will be the minimum budget to perform all of the projects? Does it make sense to perform all of the projects? Respond considering aspects related to risks.
4) What additional information/metrics will you consider to make a decision on selecting the projects?
5) Evaluate the article by Sampath et al. (2015) using the lessons learned from the Case study, e.g. what is different? What is similar? What are the reasons for choosing multiple stages and models?
6) Consider the expansion of the Case study with the use of another methodology such as System Dynamics. For an example and further ideas, see Wang et al. (2017) and Chapter 12.

References

Autocarindia. (2011). *Peugeot marks re-entry into India*. http://www.autocarindia.com/auto-news/peugeot-marks-re-entry-into-india-278944.aspx (accessed 12 March 2017).

Barlett, C.A. and Goshal, S. (1989). Managing Across Borders: The Transnational Solution, 2nd edn. Century Business.

Das, T.K. and Teng, B.-S. (2000). A Resource-based Theory of Strategic Alliances. *Journal of Management*, 26, 31–61.

Demirel, N.Ö. and Gökçen, H. (2008). A mixed integer programming model for remanufacturing in reverse logistics environment. *The International Journal of Advanced Manufacturing Technology*, 39(11–12), 1197–1206.

Ensign, P.C. (1998). Interrelationships and horizontal strategy to achieve synergy and competitive advantage in the diversified firm. *Management Decision*, 36(10), 657–668.

Forbes. (2016). *Why Tesla is partnering with Panasonic on solar tech*. http://fortune.com/2016/10/17/tesla-panasonic-solar/ (accessed 12 March 2017).

Ghodsypour, S.H. and O'Brien, C. (2001). The total cost of logistics in supplier selection, under conditions of multiple sourcing, multiple criteria and capacity constraint. *International Journal of Production Economics*, 73(1), 15–27.

Grant, R.M. (2013). Contemporary Strategy Analysis: Text and Cases, 8th edn. John Wiley & Sons, Ltd.

Hoy, F. (2006). The complicating factor of life cycles in corporate venturing. Entrepreneurship: Theory and Practice, November, 831–836.

Jernigan, S., Ransbotham, S., and Kiron, D. (2016). Data sharing an analytics drive success with IoT. MIT Sloan Management Review, September, 1–16.

Kunc, M. and Morecroft, J. (2010). Managerial decision-making and firm performance under a resource-based paradigm. *Strategic Management Journal*, 31(11), 1164–1182.

Ladany, S.P. (1996). Optimal market segmentation of hotel rooms – the nonlinear case. *Omega*, 24(1), 29–36.

Lee, S.M. (1972). Goal Programming for Decision Analysis. Auerbach.

Meyer, M.H. (2008). Perspective: How Honda Innovates. *Journal of Product Innovation Management*, 25, 261–271.

Miller, D. and Friesen, P. (1984). A longitudinal study of the corporate life cycle. *Management Science*, 30(10), 1161–1183.

Pascale, R.R. (1996). The Honda effect. *California Management Review*, 38(4), 80–90.

Pearce, J.A. and Robinson, R.B. (2000). Strategic Management: Formulation, Implementation, and Control, 7th edn. Irwin/McGraw-Hill.

Peugeot. (2017). *The PSA Group benefits from the strong growth of the European market, focused on its pricing power strategy.* http://media.groupe-psa.com/en/press-releases/finance/psa-group-benefits-strong-growth-european-market (accessed 14 March 2018).

Proctor, R. A., & Hassard, J. S. (1990). Towards a new model for product portfolio analysis. *Management Decision*, 28(3).

Ragsdale, C.T. (2004). Spreadsheet Modeling and Decision Analysis. Thomson South-Western.

Reeves, B. (2015). *Tesla Motors – Electrifying the Future.* https://rctom.hbs.org/submission/tesla-motors-electrifying-the-future/ (accessed 12 March 2017).

Romero, C. (2014). Handbook of Critical Issues in Goal Programming. Elsevier.

Sampath, S., Gel, E.S., Fowler, J.W., and Kempf, K.G. (2015). A decision-making framework for project portfolio planning at Intel Corporation. *Interfaces*, 45(5), 391–408.

Schwartz, C. and Xia, C. (2013). *Tesla Motors Inc.* https://www.uoinvestmentgroup.org/research-reports/ (accessed 12 March 2017).

Simon, H.A. (2001). The Sciences of the Artificial, 3rd edn. The MIT Press.

Targett, D. (1996). Analytical Decision Making. Pitman Publishing.

Tarhan, B., Grossmann, I.E., and Goel, V. (2009). Stochastic programming approach for the planning of offshore oil or gas field infrastructure under decision-dependent uncertainty. *Industrial & Engineering Chemistry Research*, 48(6), 3078–3097.

Volvo. (2016). *Volvo Cars and Uber join forces to develop autonomous driving cars.* https://www.media.volvocars.com/global/en-gb/media/pressreleases/194795/ volvo-cars-and-uber-join-forces-to-develop-autonomous-driving-cars (accessed 12 March 2017).

Walker, W.E. (2009). Does the best practice of rational-style model based policy analysis already include ethical considerations? *Omega*, 37(6), 1051–1062.

Wang, L., Kunc, M., and Bai, S.J. (2017). Realizing value from project implementation under uncertainty: An exploratory study using system dynamics. *International Journal of Project Management*, 35(3), 341–352.

Winston, W.L. and Albright, S.C. (2009). Practical Management Science. South-Western Learning.

Futher Reading

Birkinshaw, J., Goshal, S., Markides, C., et al. (eds) (2003). The Future of the Multinational Company. John Wiley & Sons, Ltd.

Bronthers, K.D., Bronthers, L.E., and Wilkinson, T.J. (1995). Strategic Alliances: Choose your partners, Long Range Planning, June, 68–82.

Esquejo, N., Miller, K., Norwood, K., et al. (2015). Statistical and optimization techniques for laundry portfolio optimization at Procter & Gamble. *Interfaces*, 45(5), 444–461.

Ghemawat, P. (2003). Semiglobalizacion and international business strategy. *Journal of International Business Studies*, 34, 138–152.

Gomes, E., Barnes, B.R., and Mahmood, T. (2016). A 22 year review of strategic alliance research in the leading management journals. *International Business Review*, 25(1), 15–27.

Kukolis, S. and Jungemann, M. (1995). Strategic planning for a joint venture. Long Range Planning, June, 46–63.

Leontiades, M. (1990). The case for nonspecialized diversification. *Planning Review*, January–February, 26–33.

Lu, J.W. and Bearmish, P.W. (2004). International diversification and firm performance: the s-curve hypothesis. *Academy of Management Journal*, 47, 598–609.

Maier, A. (1999). Learning from Honda. *Journal of Management Studies*, 36, 25–44.

Mintzberg, H., Pascale, R.T., Goold, M., and Rumelt, R.P. (1996). The "Honda effect" revisited. *California Management Review*, 38(4), 78–117.

Pérez, J. A. H., Geldes, C., Kunc, M. H., & Flores, A. (2018). New approach to the innovation process in emerging economies: The manufacturing sector case in Chile and Peru. Technovation.

Pérez, J. A. H., Kunc, M. H., Durst, S., Flores, A., & Geldes, C. (2018). Impact of competition from unregistered firms on R&D investment by industrial sectors in emerging economies. Technological Forecasting and Social Change.

Porter, M.E. (1990). The Competitive Advantage of Nations. Macmillan Business.

Prahalad, C.K. and Doz, Y. (1987). The Multinational Mission: Balancing Local Demands and Global Vision. Free Press.

Sampath, S., Gel, E.S., Fowler, J.W., and Kempf, K.G. (2015). A decision-making framework for project portfolio planning at Intel Corporation. *Interfaces*, 45(5), 391–408.

Schoenberg, R., Collier, N., and Bowman, C. (2013). Strategies for business turnaround and recovery: a review and synthesis. *European Business Review*, 25(3), 243–262.

Sturgeon, T.J., Memedovic, O., Van Biesebroeck, J., and Gereffi, G. (2008). Globalisation of the automotive industry: main features and trends. *International Journal of Technological Learning, Innovation and Development*, 2(1–2), 7–24.

12

Regeneration

Objectives

1) To understand the issues faced by declining companies
2) To identify strategic actions to regenerate companies
3) To identify analytic tools to support regeneration processes

Learning outcomes and managerial capabilities developed

1) To be able to use analytic tools to support regeneration actions
2) To learn the critical aspects of implementing strategies in declining companies

---

Companies evolve through a life cycle which involves four stages: birth; growth; maturity; and decline (Miller and Friesen, 1984; Hoy, 2006). There are two possibilities for companies at the terminal stage: either they fail to respond to the decline and go into liquidation and bankruptcy; or they turn around their decline process and regenerate. There are usually two situations that can unfold when companies need to regenerate: they either respond rigidly towards their decline or innovate and change. The first response leads to a downward spiral that can take a company to bankruptcy or liquidation. The second response implies a turnaround in its performance. These responses are important because they can determine the fate of a company – survival or death. This chapter discusses the conditions under which each of the situations is likely to emerge, developing signals to understand them and specifying propositions about them.

In developing a strategic framework for regeneration, it is important to distinguish between flexible and inflexible organizations as factors in turnaround

Strategic Analytics: Integrating Management Science and Strategy, First Edition. Martin Kunc.
© 2019 John Wiley & Sons Ltd. Published 2019 by John Wiley & Sons Ltd.
Companion website: www.wiley.com/go/kunc/strategic-analytics

success or failure. There are four elements comprising strategic changes: diagnosing the situations; identifying levers of change; defining change agents; and preparing the strategic change program (Johnson et al., 2008).

The first element is the process of *diagnosing the situation* by considering the types of change required as well as context and cultural issues to be considered (Johnson et al., 2008). Types of change refer to the nature (incremental or radical) and extent of changes (realigning or transformative) to be introduced into the organization. Typically, small or incremental changes that imply a realignment of the organization are usually associated with strategy adaptation, which is usually observed in mature organizations. When the changes are incremental and transform the organization, managers attempt to evolve the organization, i.e. strategy evolution. If the nature of the changes is radical and the extent implies a realignment, then they are known as turnaround strategies. When the nature of changes is extensive and the extent is transformative, the organization goes through a revolution or innovation. Context involves the factors that can affect the strategic changes such as the size of the organization, time available for change, existence of strengths, managerial capabilities to implement the changes and organizational readiness for change. Culture defines the tacit dimension in organizations that can derail or support strategic change. Culture comprises symbols, stories, rituals and routines that define the dominant paradigm in the organization.

Secondly, *levers of change* available for the managers, such as changes in organizational structure, processes and control systems, need to be identified and will depend on the types of changes, context and cultural issues (Johnson et al., 2008). In other words, levers for change are a reflection of the emphasis to be employed in the process of change. On the one hand, the emphasis can be in "hard" aspects of organizations such as organizational structure, processes and control systems including the disposal of assets and cost cutting actions. The objective is to increase economic value in the organization. On the other hand, if the emphasis is on "soft" aspects of the organization such as culture, learning, participation in change and experimentation, the aim will be to develop organizational capabilities. Traditional changes in organizational structure, process and control system were discussed in Chapters 8 and 9. Depending on the context and culture factors, the changes can be implemented through redesigning operations in a top-down approach, challenging assumptions about the current operations in order to obtain change, facilitating changes in operations in a bottom-up way or emerging opportunities. Changes in soft aspects of the organization are implemented by changing symbols such as objects, events, rituals, routines, language and behaviors.

Thirdly, the identification of the *change agents* in terms of roles, styles and political importance, is required and it will be based on the types of changes, context and cultural issues (Johnson et al., 2008). Change agents are individuals or groups which are directly related to the process of strategic change. There are three roles for agents (Johnson et al., 2008):

- Strategic leadership is responsible for influencing the organization to move in the direction of the change. It may not be a person in the top management team but amember of the organization that can mobilize the organization. Two possible types are: charismatic leaders, who provide a vision and energy for the people to achieve it; and transactional, who design systems for the organizational activities and control its performance.
- Middle managers are responsible for implementing the strategy by allocating resources, controlling the process, interpreting the changes required, adapting the strategic change program to events and providing information as well as advice to the top management team on the performance of the change.
- Outsiders are actors that are participants in the strategic change process but are not part of the organization before the change is started. Some examples are new top management team, new managers, consultants, and external stakeholders.

There are five styles for change, which depend on the context and culture (Johnson et al,. 2008). The first is *educational* and it intends to internalize the logic of change through explaining it and achieving understanding in the organization. The second style is related to promoting *participation* by defining an agenda and assigning the process to different groups in order to generate ownership and improve the quality of decisions. The main issue with the first two styles is the long time that they can take and solutions may not be innovative. The third style involves delegating the process of change (*intervention)* to other members of the organization while the control is retained by the agent. The last two styles, *direction* and *coercion*, imply using the authority to set direction and the process of change together with the use of power to manage change in a fast way. It is useful in a situation of crisis to bring transformational change. While it provides speed and sense of direction, it may not be accepted and the direction can be erroneous.

Politics refers to the management of the power structures in the organization (Johnson et al., 2008). Three activities are associated with the political mechanisms to manage power structures. First, building a power base aims to control resources and acquire expertise through association with an elite in the organization using alliances or team building. The key objective is to build legitimation for the change. Secondly, overcoming resistance aims to reduce the resistance to change through breaking or dividing the elites or associating them with change agents or outsiders. Thirdly, the agent of change intends to achieve obedience by allocating resources to elites supporting change using rewards, reassurance and symbolic confirmation.

The final element is establishing the type of *strategic change program* in terms of innovation based or turnaround focused that is most suitable given the input of the previous three elements (Johnson et al., 2008).

12.1 Strategies for Regenerating Organizations

12.1.1 Innovation

For companies operating in competitive markets and being threatened with failure, innovation is often a necessity in order to survive in the market. In contrast to strategies based on pure innovation activities, which intend to obtain high profits from the initial stages of the product life cycle when customers rush to buy new or significantly improved products, innovation in this stage of the organizational life is critical. Innovation is necessary in order to avoid competing in the areas of production and marketing associated with the end of the product life cycle. Thus, this type of innovation strategy differs from product/market development strategies with also involve innovation. It also differs from companies employing pure innovation strategy that aims to make existing products obsolete and continuously develop new product life cycles. Companies using pure innovation strategy are "moving targets" for their competitors since they are not established for long in a market, in contrast to companies that need regeneration. Companies needing regeneration have remained inert after their initial innovations until competitors closed the gap in terms of products or technologies. However, a pure innovation strategy is also highly risky because it requires strong investment in R&D and market research in order to transform an invention into a profitable innovation. Thus, companies in pure innovation strategies may also face critical situations which require regeneration. There are multiple innovation strategies and some of them are discussed in the following.

- The attitude of companies towards the source of innovations determines two positions: push or pull. Some companies prefer selling to the market the result of their R&D activities. This is usually known as *technology push innovation strategy*. The intention is to impose on the market their own technologies but the strategy will not work when the organizational decline is due to the obsolescence of the current technology and the company is intrinsically associated with a technology that is disappearing. A company can choose to perform all processes within the organization in isolation or involve external actors, e.g. universities, other companies, government institutes, etc. The second approach is called "open" innovation (Chesbrough, 2003). Open innovation permits the existence of knowledge flows to and from the company in order to source external ideas and improve internal ideas by sharing them. Investment in R&D is necessary in order to be part of a wider network of knowledge resources existing externally.

Other companies let the market suggest the next ideas for innovations, a *market pull innovation strategy*. Basically, the company observes the uses of products in the market and considers the suggestions of lead users. One potential problem is to listen to only loyal users without accounting for the decline in customers and the reasons for their abandoning the products. Another problem is to implement the ideas from users in terms of costs and required capabilities.

- In terms of types of innovations, innovations can change products, processes or business models. *Product innovation* implies an emphasis on changing the characteristics of the product or service. The innovation in the product characteristics aims to close the gap with existing competitors or to surpass them. The implications for each objective are very different in terms of investment, risks and rewards. The innovation can be performed internally, using in-house R&D, or externally by acquiring a company or creating a strategic alliance with other companies. An important consideration when the intention is to surpass the current product is to foresee the level of market and technology saturation for the current product. *Process innovation* changes the activities related to the production and distribution of the product/service to improve either costs or reliability (delivery, quality, etc.). The innovation in processes can also close the gap with existing competitors or to beat them. Some considerations are related to adopting a system's perspective where the process is evaluated in terms of impacts on equipment, designs, human resources and partners in the supply chain.

  Business model innovation involves changes to all dimensions related to the business (see Section 6.3 in Chapter 6 for tools to represent business models). Changes do not need to be associated with new technologies but by the way in which the company delivers value to customers. Key issues are associated with the complexity of the business models (new and existing), managerial capabilities to manage the redesigned business, size of the existing business and fragmentation in terms of value creation propositions.

- Some companies prefer waiting for innovations rather than being the first in the market: *follower or late-mover* vs. *innovator or first-mover*. Some contextual factors affect the effectiveness of these strategies: ability to copy/replicate the innovation; the need for complementary resources not owned by any firm in the industry; and stability in the technology.

  Being a *follower* offers some advantages. First, the company can imitate the full innovation with less costs if the technology and resources required to implement the innovation are widely available. Secondly, learning from the pioneer can help the follower to implement the innovation more effectively and efficiently. *First-mover* gives a set of advantages for companies. First, experience builds faster than competitors which is useful to manage the new product and process better than competitors. Secondly, size is reached faster leading to economies of scale. Thirdly, the company will secure strategic resources at low cost. Fourthly, a reputation for innovativeness helps to reduce customer switching due to its dominance in the market.

- Finally, the impact of the innovation can determine two categories of innovations: *incremental;* or *radical.* Incremental innovation does not depart significantly from the existing products, services, processes and businesses. Incremental innovation enhances the existing technologies and resources. Radical innovation affects significantly the existing conditions in the companies and industries by removing technologies and resources while providing customers with enhanced value.

Food for thought 12.1 (based on Dogson et al. 2006) P&G is one of the largest multinational companies in the area of consumer goods. It has nearly 100 000 employees and is present in almost every country in the world. P&G has a large R&D area with more than 6000 scientists and 29 000 patents. In 1999, P&G implemented a strategy to grow through innovation developing connections between its R&D area and the outside world. The connections led to innovations in emulsifiers and surfactants which are part of shampoos and dishwashing liquids. To put into effect an open innovation strategy, P&G implemented:

- Fifty percent of the innovations need to be generated with external partners.
- A new organizational unit responsible for licensing P&G technologies to obtain returns on the investment in R&D and searching complementary technologies from external sources.
- Activities to showcase technologies developed internally and by external suppliers.
- Purchasing of entrepreneurial companies and use of funding to support internal start-ups.
- Changes in organizational culture to embrace openness and collaboration and communication tools to facilitate the interconnections.
- Rapid prototyping technologies to develop and test new products.

Address the following issues:

- What conditions may facilitate the adoption of an open innovation strategy: industry, products, resources, size of the firm?
- Can you find evidence of situations where open innovation was not successful?

12.1.2 Turnaround

Turnaround strategies usually follow a process of organization decline. Organization decline tentatively proceeds in four stages (Weitzel and Jonsson, 1989). In the first stage, which is called *blinded*, the company fails to anticipate and detect deficiencies in the strategy and its implementation, leading to its decline in performance. In the second stage, called *inaction*, management fails to decide on corrective actions, delaying responses, leading to further decline, and higher organizational stress. In the third stage, *faulty action*, stress is high and the dominant coalitions in the company compete for diminishing resources leading to initiating and implementing faulty actions which deepen its decline. In the fourth stage, known as *crisis*, defective actions lead to the critical point of either major revitalization or certain failure as key stakeholders withdraw their support for the company and the management.

While the decline can take some time to materialize, it is important to verify that the sources of the decline are internal rather than external. External sources can be the macro environment (see Chapter 3) or industry-specific (see Chapter 4). External sources will affect all organizations in the industry similarly, so the financial performance deteriorates equally for all of them and there are no significant changes in market share. Robbins and Pearce (1992) found companies that attributed their decline to external sources were less likely to reduce their assets (retrenchment) in their turnaround process, affecting their survival. On the other hand, companies, which considered the decline mostly due to their own inefficiencies, reduced their assets as part of their turnaround strategy (Robbins and Pearce, 1992). Figure 12.1 shows a model of the turnaround process based on Robbins and Pearce (1992).

At the core of turnaround strategies is not only returning the organization into profitability but also focusing on the core activities. The application of this strategy implies a belief that the company can be recovered and there are no substantial external (see Chapter 3) or internal issues (see Chapters 6, 7 and 8) affecting its survival. Moreover, there is an urgency to implement the change because once poor performance sets in, it becomes self-reinforcing as it depletes companies' resources, which in turn further deteriorate performance, eventually leading to their failure (Hambrick and D'Aveni, 1988). Common types of successful turnaround "gestalts" are: "asset/cost surgery" and "selective product/market pruning" (Hambrick and Schecter, 1983).

Basically, an asset/cost surgery strategy involves executing two activities, most commonly, by new management teams:

- *Cost reduction by making the use of resources more efficient, increasing the effectiveness of certain expenses or eliminating sources of costs.* One of the key objectives of this strategy is to stabilize the financial performance of the firm by returning to profitability and positive cash flows. Profitability is obtained eliminating costs and leaving market segments which are not profitable. Positive cash flows can be obtained by disposing of assets which are not essential to the business and eliminating products which are not generating positive cash flow. It is important to understand the driving forces for the situation and to not confuse them with short-term effects, e.g. economic

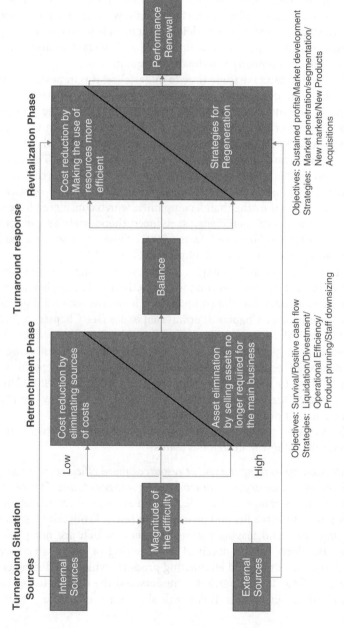

Turnaround Situation Sources

Turnaround response

Internal Sources

Magnitude of the difficulty

External Sources

Retrenchment Phase

Low

Cost reduction by eliminating sources of costs

Asset elimination by selling assets no longer required for the main business

High

Balance

Revitalization Phase

Cost reduction by Making the use of resources more efficient

Strategies for Regeneration

Performance Renewal

Objectives: Survival/Positive cash flow
Strategies: Liquidation/Divestment/
Operational Efficiency/
Product pruning/Staff downsizing

Objectives: Sustained profits/Market development
Strategies: Market penetration/segmentation/
New markets/New Products
Acquisitions

Figure 12.1 A model of the turnaround process. Source: Adapted from Robbins and Pearce (1992: figures 1 and 2, page 291).

recession. Decline determined by external forces needs to produce innovations to face changes in the markets. When the decline is associated with internal factors, the usual focus is on achieving efficiencies.

- *Asset elimination (retrenchment) involves selling fixed assets that are no longer required for the main business.* Another activity related with turnaround strategy is the divestiture of components of the company to other companies, also known as asset retrenchment. Sometimes the actions aimed at turning around the failing business do not produce the desired effect, so the only option is to find a buyer for the part of the business that is not core to the strategy. The sale is performed through a selective process of finding buyers who are willing to pay a premium above the value of the assets. Therefore, the objective is to sell the business as a functioning entity and not as a set of assets. Sometimes asset retrenchment is implemented together with actions to improve cost efficiencies. It may not only involve generating cash flow from the disposal but also disposing of aging assets and replacing with new assets.

Selective product/market pruning involves increasing revenues by identifying profitable options for the organization. In other words, it implies a return to the core activities for the organization. More specifically, it involves:

- Selecting the key market segments in terms of profitability, volume and competitive strength. See Chapters 6, 7 and 8.
- Focusing marketing activities in the key market segments.
- Changing pricing in order to maximize revenues from market segments, even those markets that are going to be abandoned.
- Researching the needs of customers in key market segments.
- Exploiting additional opportunities for revenues from key market segments.
- Abandoning market segments which are not recoverable after the implementation of the previous activities.

Turnaround strategies are successful if the organization has the capacity for transformation and not reverting to the previous operational situation, which may imply managing the turnaround process correctly (Schoenberg et al., 2013). Managing turnaround involves some processual considerations (Schoenberg et al., 2013):

- *Replacing the organization leadership.* This may occur early in the turnaround process. Most studies suggest the new leaders (both CEOs and top management team) come from outside the organization. Changes reflect either pressures from shareholders or other stakeholders or if the current leadership does not find the right solution to the existing problems. Sometimes the decline is not related to the intrinsic issues in the organization but general problems in the industry or macro-environment so the changes in leadership are counterproductive.

- *Change in culture.* The organization needs to leave the operating routines that led it to crisis, so culture has to change and employees, who cannot adapt, leave the organization. Signaling and information dissemination is part of the change in culture. Changes in the organization do not only imply modifying the systems and structures but also the behavior of the employees.

Food for thought 12.2 (adapted from Schoenberg et al., 2013)   Harley-Davidson is an American manufacturer of heavyweight motorcycles. The company went through a strong downturn period between 2007 and 2009 with sales falling 40%.

In 2009, a new CEO was appointed who came from outside the company and made changes in the top management team, specifically bringing in external appointments and promoting some key internal people. The company initially reduced production (−26%) and the number of employees (−22%) in order to follow the decline in sales. Then, they implemented improvement techniques such as lean product development which reduced the time to market, enhanced customer insights and managed more product development initiatives. Simultaneously, production was made flexible to respond to seasonal and product changes. The cost of the turnaround was calculated as US$ 500 million by 2013.

Harley-Davidson also owned two motorcycle companies: one in the USA and the other in Italy, which produced sports motorcycles. Both companies were acquired as part of diversification strategies in 1997 and 2008, respectively. Some of their own motorcycle models were also discontinued and new more modern models were introduced that highlighted their core product proposition: American engineering, heritage and vintage style. The company focused in new markets such as Asia and Latin America.

Profits recovered together with sales between 2009 and 2011.

Address the following issues:

- Why did Harley-Davidson decide to focus in Asia and Latin America? Check for evidence using PESTE analysis (see chapter 3).
- What happened with the culture in the case of Harley-Davidson? Find evidence of changes in the culture.

12.1.3 Ambidextrous Strategies

In general, companies need to combine the two previous strategies. First, companies need "adaptability" which is the ability to exploit new opportunities and adapt to changes in turbulent markets. In other words, companies need to be innovative and proactive in order to regenerate. Secondly, companies also have to exploit the value of their strategic resources through their business models while keeping costs low. In other words, companies need to be able to achieve "alignment" (Birkinshaw and Gibson, 2004). Successful companies manage both adaptability and alignment in the long term, which is called "ambidexterity". The problem is how difficult it is to achieve an adequate balance as innovation and turnaround strategies seem to be contradictory. Innovation implies building for the future at the expense of the current operations. Turnaround involves streamlining the short-term performance of the company by losing the long-term perspective of investing in facing the threats and opportunities the future will bring. Evidence suggests that companies are not good at managing the tension between both dimensions of ambidexterity (Birkinshaw and Gibson, 2004; O'Reilly and Tushman, 2004). There are two approaches in the literature recommended to deal with these challenges.

First, companies try to keep the core business focus on alignment and certain business units, e.g. new product based, or departments, e.g. R&D, are responsible for exploring opportunities and bringing adaptability. This is usually known as "structural ambidexterity" where separate organizational entities are responsible for each approach and are firmly integrated at top management level (O'Reilly and Tushman, 2004). Ambidextrous companies have two types of business units: alignment- and adaptability-oriented (O'Reilly and Tushman, 2004). On the one hand, alignment-oriented business units focus on costs and profits through efficient operations and incremental innovations. Therefore, their structure is formal with focus on operational competencies and rewards for profitability and productivity. The leadership is top-down and formal with a culture fomenting efficiency, low risk and quality. On the other hand, adaptability-oriented business units are interested in growth through innovation. Therefore, the leadership is visionary and informal fostering speed, flexibility, risk taking and breakthrough innovations. The competencies are related to entrepreneurial activities supported by a project-based structured aimed to develop new products and experimenting.

However, the structural approach may lead to isolation and lack of coordination in the companies (Birkinshaw and Gibson, 2004). Some forms of mixed structures, e.g. embedding personnel from core business into new business development, have been tried but their results are still not satisfactory (Birkinshaw and Gibson, 2004). To solve these issues, Birkinshaw and Gibson (2004) suggest employing "contextual ambidexterity" which involves:

- Systems and structures are flexible in order to allow employees to divide their attention between adaptation-oriented and alignment-oriented activities.
- Decisions about alignment and adaptability are made by employees on the day-by-day operations.
- The top management team is not in charge of making trade-offs between alignment and adaptability but it is responsible for providing a context (performance management systems and social structures) to facilitate the trade-offs.

- Employees tend to be generalist and are comfortable having multiple roles.
- Also developing "structural ambidexterity", which involves the structural separation between alignment and adaptability activities (O'Reilly and Tushman, 2004), to complement the contextual approach.

Food for thought 12.3 Google has become a synonym of the twenty-first century. Google is not only a search engine with advertisements but a broad umbrella of companies providing multiple services in the digital world. Recently, Google decided to create a new holding company called Alphabet.

Here, the challenge is to distill the meaning of ambidextrous from the letter by one of the founders of Google and the CEO of Alphabet, Larry Page. The letter was retrieved from Google's website (https://abc.xyz/investor/founders-letters/2015/index.html).

Larry's Alphabet Letter

G is for Google.

As Sergey and I wrote in the original founders letter 11 years ago, "Google is not a conventional company. We do not intend to become one." As part of that, we also said that you could expect us to make "smaller bets in areas that might seem very speculative or even strange when compared to our current businesses." From the start, we've always strived to do more, and to do important and meaningful things with the resources we have.

We did a lot of things that seemed crazy at the time. Many of those crazy things now have over a billion users, like Google Maps, YouTube, Chrome, and Android. And we haven't stopped there. We are still trying to do things other people think are crazy but we are super excited about.

We've long believed that over time companies tend to get comfortable doing the same thing, just making incremental changes. But in the technology industry, where revolutionary ideas drive the next big growth areas, you need to be a bit uncomfortable to stay relevant.

Our company is operating well today, but we think we can make it cleaner and more accountable. So we are creating a new company, called Alphabet. I am really excited to be running Alphabet as CEO with help from my capable partner, Sergey, as President.

What is Alphabet? Alphabet is mostly a collection of companies. The largest of which, of course, is Google. This newer Google is a bit slimmed down, with the companies that are pretty far afield of our main internet products contained in Alphabet instead. What do we mean by far afield? Good examples are our health efforts: Life Sciences (that works on the glucose-sensing contact lens), and

Calico (focused on longevity). Fundamentally, we believe this allows us more management scale, as we can run things independently that aren't very related.

Alphabet is about businesses prospering through strong leaders and independence. In general, our model is to have a strong CEO who runs each business, with Sergey and me in service to them as needed. We will rigorously handle capital allocation and work to make sure each business is executing well. We'll also make sure we have a great CEO for each business, and we'll determine their compensation. In addition, with this new structure we plan to implement segment reporting for our Q4 results, where Google financials will be provided separately than those for the rest of Alphabet businesses as a whole.

This new structure will allow us to keep tremendous focus on the extraordinary opportunities we have inside of Google. A key part of this is Sundar Pichai. Sundar has been saying the things I would have said (and sometimes better!) for quite some time now, and I've been tremendously enjoying our work together. He has really stepped up since October of last year, when he took on product and engineering responsibility for our internet businesses. Sergey and I have been super excited about his progress and dedication to the company. And it is clear to us and our board that it is time for Sundar to be CEO of Google. I feel very fortunate to have someone as talented as he is to run the slightly slimmed down Google and this frees up time for me to continue to scale our aspirations. I have been spending quite a bit of time with Sundar, helping him and the company in any way I can, and I will of course continue to do that. Google itself is also making all sorts of new products, and I know Sundar will always be focused on innovation—continuing to stretch boundaries. I know he deeply cares that we can continue to make big strides on our core mission to organize the world's information. Recent launches like Google Photos and Google Now using machine learning are amazing progress. Google also has some services that are run with their own identity, like YouTube. Susan is doing a great job as CEO, running a strong brand and driving incredible growth.

Sergey and I are seriously in the business of starting new things. Alphabet will also include our X lab, which incubates new efforts like Wing, our drone delivery effort. We are also stoked about growing our investment arms, Ventures and Capital, as part of this new structure.

Alphabet Inc. will replace Google Inc. as the publicly-traded entity and all shares of Google will automatically convert into the same number of shares of Alphabet, with all of the same rights. Google will become a wholly-owned subsidiary of Alphabet. Our two classes of shares will continue to trade on Nasdaq as GOOGL and GOOG.

For Sergey and me this is a very exciting new chapter in the life of Google— the birth of Alphabet. We liked the name Alphabet because it means a collection of letters that represent language, one of humanity's most important innovations, and is the core of how we index with Google search! We also like that it means alpha-bet (Alpha is investment return above benchmark), which we strive for! I should add that we are not intending for this to be a big consumer brand with related products—the whole point is that Alphabet companies should have independence and develop their own brands.

We are excited about...

Getting more ambitious things done.

Taking the long-term view.

Empowering great entrepreneurs and companies to flourish.

Investing at the scale of the opportunities and resources we see.

Improving the transparency and oversight of what we're doing.

Making Google even better through greater focus.

And hopefully... as a result of all this, improving the lives of as many people as we can.

What could be better? No wonder we are excited to get to work with everyone in the Alphabet family. Don't worry, we're still getting used to the name too!

12.2   Integrating Management Science into Strategic Management

12.2.1   New Product Development: the Use of Text Analytics

Unstructured text analytics is used for finding pieces of information from text, e.g. news from competitors in newspapers or websites. Natural Language Processing (NLP)is an old method but the increasing performance of computers, massive storage and capture of text in a digital way have foster its development recently. NLP uses machine learning and statistical algorithms to generate results from thousands of documents (Markham et al., 2015). However, the complexity of language implies that the results are still ambiguous and mostly based on probabilities in order to assess the usefulness of a potential source of information. NLP results may be similar to an Internet search engine query but there are four differences (Markham et al, 2015, page 35). First, NLP performs searches using all expressions in all dictionaries simultaneously so it is an integrated method rather than using one term at the time as on the Internet. Secondly, data sources are selected by the users, so the results are constrained to specific sources, which is not possible on the Internet. Thirdly, the expressions employed for the search can be defined as parts of speech to reduce ambiguity. Fourthly, there is a context defined for the search.

Markham et al. (2015: page 32) suggest NLP can be employed for:

- *Morphological segmentation*, e.g. identification of work forms.
- *Parsing* in order to understand sentence structures.

- *Disambiguation* is used to differentiate similar terms and phrases and identify irregular usage.
- *Sentiment analysis* involves the determination of the emotional content of a text.
- *Discourse analysis* tries to clarify discussions based on following discussions through a set of sentences.

Markham et al. (2015: page 33) propose that the unstructured text analysis process involves:

1) *Define specific questions to guide the search and evaluate the answers obtained from the analysis.* In the case of a new product, the questions should be aimed at opinions about the functionality of existing products that may be replaced with the new product.
2) *Identify sources of information that could provide the best set of text data for answering the question.* For example, trade magazines can be useful to find product reviews and websites are also important sources to obtain opinions about products.
3) *Create dictionaries, which are groups of search terms, and rules, which are relationships between terms.* The dictionary and rules should be defined by the engineers or other people in charge of the functionalities for the new product. Another set of dictionaries and rules can be defined by the marketing department.
4) *Gather data through different tools such as R and Hadoop and conduct the text analysis using NLP.*
5) *Evaluate the data for sufficiency, applicability and veracity before a decision is made based on the answers obtained.* Essentially the team needs to ask themselves if the results make sense in terms of sources of information, relevance and usefulness.
6) *Score the answers obtained from the text analysis.*

Therefore, text analytics can be used for market-led innovation as the company can find opportunities in the market from opinions expressed from their own and competitors' customers.

Text analytics can also help to prevent organizational decline by understanding the sentiment existing in the market about their products and reputation.

12.2.2 Implementing Turnaround Strategies Using Data Envelopment Analysis: Identifying Operational Units for Either Improving or Pruning

One of the key issues in turnaround strategies is identifying the operational units that need to be either improved or pruned. Traditional approaches can involve accounting analysis, benchmarking, process mapping or econometric approaches. However, many of those approaches are laborious or require strong assumptions. In this subsection, a highly popular approach called Data Envelopment Analysis (DEA) is explained. DEA has become very popular with over 3000 publications by over 2000 authors (Tavares, 2002) after its introduction by Charnes et al. (1978).

DEA is a popular method for comparing the efficiency performance of decision-making units (DMUs) because it is a flexible method to measure the efficient use of resources (inputs) in order to generate products or services (outputs). DEA models calculate the relative performance of a DMU with respect to other DMUs rather than a comparison of the absolute performance with respect to a defined standard (Targett, 1996). DMUs can be branches, business units of an organization, entire organizations or regions (e.g. Han et al., 2016). A key assumption is that all DMUs exist in the same environment and convert the same set of inputs into the same set of outputs (Targett, 1996). DEA is more suitable for services where the capacity is difficult to quantify and it is difficult to define its qualitative components, e.g. skills.

DEA can also be used as a multiple-criteria evaluation methodology where DMUs are alternatives, and the inputs and outputs are two sets of performance criteria where inputs are minimized and outputs are maximized (Cook et al., 2014).

DEA has been applied to many industries: banking (Cook et al., 2000; Cook and Hababou, 2001; Weill, 2004); hospitals (O'Neill et al., 2008); fast food restaurants (Banker and Morey, 1986); and sports (Einolf, 2004).

Data   There are a set of characteristics to consider when selecting data for DEA models. First, a performance measure is a suitable input if the measure will have to be minimized by the DMU, e.g. a cost or a resource. Secondly, measures should be different, so they do not double count specific aspects of the DMU. Thirdly, DEA models do not require or assume any functional relationship between the inputs and outputs since DEA models are non-parametric methods. Fourthly, a rule of thumb indicates the number of DMUs has to be at least twice the number of inputs and outputs combined for a DEA model (Cook et al., 2014). Dyson et al. (2001) provide a thorough discussion on the process to select data for performing DEA analysis without making mistakes.

Formulation   DEA models assign a score of one to a DMU only when comparisons with other relevant DMUs do not provide evidence of inefficiency in the use of any input or output. DEA assigns an efficiency score less than one to (relatively) inefficient units indicating a linear combination of other units from the sample can produce the same vector of outputs using a smaller vector of inputs. The score reflects the distance from the estimated production frontier to the DMU under consideration.

A common formulation for DEA models considers the efficiency of DMUs as a ratio of the inputs to the outputs, constrained to be equal or lower than 1. Then a linear programming model (see Chapter 11) finds the costs of the inputs and the prices of the outputs that maximize the ratio for a specific DMU

(Winston and Albright, 2009). Both costs and prices are calculated by the linear programming model and they are not related to financial information. A basic formulation is presented below.

Objective function: Maximize the efficiency of a DMU. The efficiency of a DMU is equal to the value of the DMU's output divided by the value of the DMU's input (Wilson and Albright, 2009):

$$Efficiency\,DMU\,1 = \frac{Total\,output\,values\,for\,DMU\,1}{Total\,input\,costs\,for\,DMU\,1}$$

The values for output and inputs are calculated by multiplying the data for each output (*O*) and input (*I*) by different weights, price and costs, respectively, given to each output (*WP*) and input (*WC*), e.g.

$$Total\,input\,costs\,for\,DMU\,1 = WC_1 * I_{11} + WC_2 * I_{21} + \ldots + WC_n * I_{n1}$$

$$Total\,output\,values\,for\,DMU\,1 = WP_1 * O_{11} + WP_2 * O_{21} + \ldots + WP_n * I_{n1}$$

Decision variables: The decision variables for the linear programming are the weights (*W*) of inputs and outputs.

Constraints: Efficiency for a DMU cannot be larger than 1 since no DMU can be more than 100% efficient. Consequently, total input costs must be greater than or equal to total output value. All weights cannot be negative.

The linear programming model runs for every DMU. The calculation can be performed using Excel in a similar way to the Case study in Chapter 11 (Section 11.6.2). In this case, each DMU has to be done manually. See Figure 12.2 for a screen shot of a simple Excel model for DEA. In the example, the ratio between input costs and output prices is presented as a constraint where the input costs cannot be larger than output values so any efficiency measure is equal to or lower than one. Another constraint is total input costs should be equal to one as an approach to scale input prices (Winston and Albright, 2009). Therefore, the efficiency of the DMU is equal to the value of the outputs (Winston and Albright, 2009). The solver optimization is run five times for each DMU and the results are shown at the bottom of Figure 12.2. The model is available in the companion website. There is software that calculates DEA easily and some packages are embedded in Excel, e.g. www.deafrontier.net., while others run in different platforms including open source, e.g. opensourcedea.org.

Interpretation   It involves two dimensions: technical and managerial.

Technical. In this basic implementation of DEA, the results of a DEA model indicate that a DMU is inefficient when its efficiency value is below one. In other words, there is no output price (weight) combinations that can help the

Efficiency evaluation using DEA						
	Input 1	Input 2	Input3	Input 4	Output 1	Output 2
DMU 1	250	10	145	5	25	17
DMU 2	125	8	100	3	18	10
DMU 3	3	4	3	2	4	3
DMU 4	3	1	4	0	3	2
DMU 5	120	2	15	2	25	15

	Decision variables					
	Input 1	Input 2	Input3	Input 4	Output 1	Output 2
Input costs/Output prices	0.002340426	0.041489362	0	0	0	0.024255

	Constraints			
	Input costs		Output values	
DMU 1	1	>=	0.4123404	
DMU 2	0.624468085	>=	0.2425532	
DMU 3	0.172978723	>=	0.072766	
DMU 4	0.048510638	>=	0.0485106	
DMU 5	0.363829787	>=	0.3638298	

DMU 1 Total input costs	1	=	1
DMU 1 Total output value	0.412340426		

	Output Values	
DMU 1	0.412	inefficient
DMU 2	0.441	inefficient
DMU 3	1.000	efficient
DMU 4	1.000	efficient
DMU 5	1.000	efficient

Figure 12.2 Example of a DEA model implemented in Excel. DMU 1 and 2 are inefficient.

DMU to match the total input costs. There are additional interpretations related to comparing the weights for DMUs. For example, the ratio of the weights between two inputs can be considered a marginal rate of substitution of one input for another input (Winston and Albright, 2009). Another interpretation is how much the inefficient DMU has to reduce its inputs or increase its outputs to become as efficient as the most efficient DMUs. Basic DEA models evaluate the relative efficiency of DMUs but do not generate a ranking of units in terms of efficiency (Figure 12.2), which is an important weakness that has been solved in more advanced DEA models. The DEA field has developed many suitable sources with useful information (Cooper et al., 2011), in order to interpret results.

Managerial. First, the flexibility of the method allows the combination of multiple measures for inputs, e.g. number of employees, direct costs, rents, age in the market, local competitors, customers, and outputs, e.g. sales, transactions, profits. Therefore, DEA models can easily integrate with reporting systems, e.g. performance measurement systems and enterprise resource planning, existing in the company and the type of information that is employed in strategic analysis. Secondly, the result shows in a simple way the organizational units that are not using the inputs/resources allocated to them efficiently. Thirdly, the next step can involve a detailed analysis of the inputs and outputs of inefficient units to understand the reasons for their low performance compared with other units. The DEA model only offers a first screening of the units that can be either improved or eliminated during turnaround strategies.

A DEA model can substantially reduce the time in the preparation of turnaround strategies for companies with a large number of organizational units, e.g. branches, shops, restaurants, schools, hospitals, clinics, etc.

12.3 End of Chapter

This chapter has addressed two strategies that seem to be contradictory: innovation and turnaround. However, they are both necessary in order to regenerate a company that may be under risk of collapsing. There is no question that skills and focus differ substantially between both strategies but the common theme is strategic change. Strategic change can occur as preparation to a new stage of the company, when innovation is the driver, or it can occur as avoidance of the decline of the company, when turnaround is the driver. Another common theme is the use of limited resources in the best possible way through models that optimize the allocation of resources or models that highlight when they are being wasted in inefficient organizational units.

Developing the "right" new products is critical to the firm's success and is often cited as the key to a sustained competitive advantage. Managers often set ambitious goals for future revenue generated from new products pressured by statements such as "innovate or die". Any company that engages in new product development faces the important problem of allocating resources between innovation initiatives in a portfolio. However, it is also critical that the new product is designed in the right way. Therefore, the use of analytic tools such as text analysis can provide important clues about the situation of the market and opinions on the existing products.

Most managers and management researchers view organizational decline as reversible given the right actions. Specific turnaround strategies have been proposed to enhance the company's chances of surviving through a threatening performance decline. Turnaround strategies are a set of consequential, long-term decisions and actions targeted to reverse a perceived crisis that threatens survival. Organizational turnaround often involves retrenchment actions. Retrenchment is a process to consolidate the current strategic and financial position in order to sustain the company while organizational changes become realized. Retrenchment implies a reduction in the essential elements of a company that can generate a profitable operation. In this case, the role of DEA can be fundamental for a successful turnaround by eliminating units that are objectively performing badly rather than engaging in political discussions with the managers of the units. In this chapter, the management styles are appropriate to support rational approaches to design new organizations for those that are failing while management science tools can facilitate interactive processes when the focus is on innovating and new ideas need to be generated (Figure 12.3).

12.3.1   Revision Questions

1) What type of innovations can be best managed through a portfolio of new product development and its quantitative selection method?
2) What tools will be mostly used in an ambidextrous organization? Provide evidence for your answer through the activities that the ambidextrous organization performs.
3) In an organization under a turnaround process, who will be the best champion to promote the use of DEA techniques to perform the organizational retrenchment? Justify your answer.

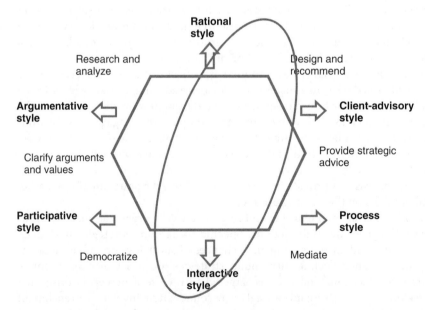

Figure 12.3 Management science styles. *Source:* Walker (2009). Reproduced with permission of Elsevier.

12.3.2 Case Study: Managing Strategic Change Successfully: the Role of Benefits Realization Management

Organizational change requires the development of projects, e.g. IT projects, process improvement, new products, etc. However, organizations fail in implementing their strategies even though they employ project, program and portfolio management techniques to support organizational change. Benefits Realization Management (BRM) is a set of processes structured to close the gap between strategy planning and execution by ensuring the implementation of the most valuable initiatives. Good business strategies are those that deliver stakeholder value. Business strategies set targets of future value, which are met by achieving strategic objectives. Since these objectives are measurable, the difference between the current situation and the target future situation sets the value gap, which is fulfilled by a portfolio of initiatives defined by the organization in their strategic plan. Strategic initiatives usually fill the value gap by enabling new capabilities – or promoting changes – through the outputs delivered by a set of projects (Figure 12.4). These strategic improvements in the business are called "benefits". Benefits are increments in the business value from not only a shareholder's perspective but also customers', suppliers', or even societal perspectives. Benefits lead to the successful execution of business strategy so strategies, e.g. innovation or turnaround, strongly depend on the projects delivering the expected benefits. Careful management of each

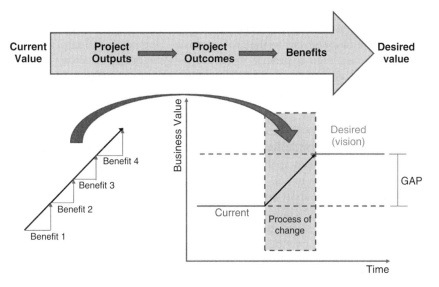

Figure 12.4 Benefits realized through projects fill the gap between current and desired situation (Serra and Kunc, 2015).

project ensures the delivery of outputs, enables outcomes, and then supports the realization of further benefits to realize the expected value defined in the strategy.

A set of key BRM practices has been suggested in Serra and Kunc (2015):

1) Expected outcomes (changes provided by project outputs) are clearly defined.
2) The value created to the organization by project outcomes has to be clearly measurable.
3) The strategic objectives that project outcomes are expected to achieve has been clearly defined.
4) A business case needs to be approved at the beginning of the project. The business case describes all outputs, outcomes and benefits expected from the project.
5) Project outputs and outcomes are frequently reviewed to ensure their alignment with expectations.
6) Stakeholders are aware of the results of project reviews and their needs are frequently assessed with a view to make changes in the project if necessary.
7) Actual project outcomes adhere to the expected outcomes planned in the business case.
8) There are activities aiming to ensure the integration of project outputs to the regular business routine (training, support, monitoring, and outcomes evaluation) as part of the project's scope.
9) After project closure, the organization keeps monitoring project outcomes to ensure the achievement of all benefits expected in the business case.
10) From the first delivery to the project closure, the organization performs a pre-planned, regular process to ensure the integration of project outputs into the regular business routine (including outcomes evaluation).
11) Project benefits management is applied throughout the company.
12) Project benefits management is applied at the project level.

However, one aspect not developed in Serra and Kunc (2015) is how to manage a project under conditions of the uncertainty and delays and disruptions. These aspects have been analyzed through a simulation model in Wang et al. (2017). Uncertainties in the environment generate changes to the system. Strategic change may arise at organizational level and then be interpreted as a variation in the project's strategic targets. Meanwhile, the tactical uncertainty may cause disruptions and delays on project progress even without strategic changes. Thus, there may be situations where the strategic objective for the project cannot be achieved or the project is of little value to new strategic objectives. Remedial actions (i.e. adjustments to schedule priority or investment in additional funds or both) are required to mitigate the deviation. Thus, the objective of the simulation study is to understand behavioral remedial

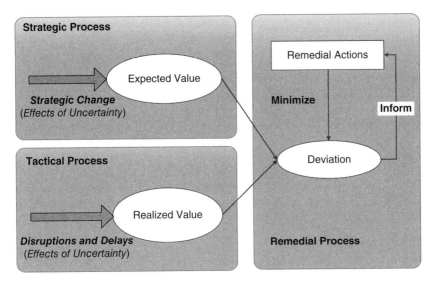

Figure 12.5 Project implementation processes at strategic and tactical levels.

actions for on-going projects taken to minimize the deviation between realized value and expected value (Figure 12.5).

According to the previous discussion, the project implementation process consists of three subsystems: Goal (Strategic process); Project Implementation (Tactical process); and Investment (Resource Allocation process). The model is illustrated in Figure 12.6. The output of the Goal subsystem is expected value, which is defined during the project design and tries to align the project with the strategy of the firm but it can be modified if there is a change in strategy. The Project Implementation subsystem includes the tactical activities to achieve the realized value of a project. Project Implementation consumes funds from the Investment subsystem. The deviation between the output of the Project Implementation subsystem and the Goal subsystem requires an adjustment in the investment funds to narrow the existing gap, which is part of the Remedial process. The three subsystems dynamically interact with each other and affect the value realized in a project.

Here are a few questions that you can answer using the simulation model:

1) What is the best function reaction to observe gaps between realized and expected value?
2) What impact is more significant on the final performance: high level of delays and disruptions or a substantial change in the strategic goal?
3) What is the impact of delays on reporting the gaps between realized and expected value?

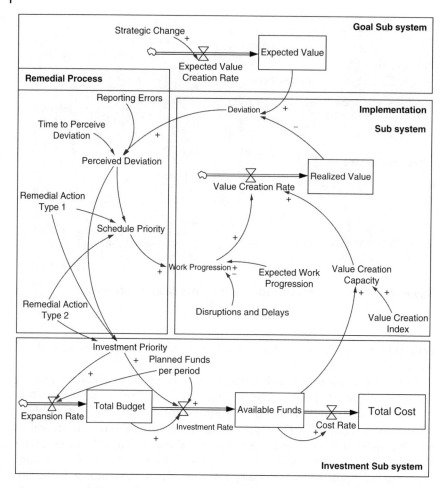

Figure 12.6 Structure of the simulation model to evaluate remedial actions to correct deviations in projects.

References

Banker, R.D. and Morey, R.C. (1986). Efficiency analysis for exogenously fixed inputs and outputs. *Operations Research*, 34(4), 513–521.

Birkinshaw, J. and Gibson, C. (2004). Building ambidexterity into an organization. *MIT Sloan Management Review*, 45(4), 47–51.

Charnes, A., Cooper, W., and Rhodes, E. (1978). Measuring the efficiency of Decision Making Units. *European Journal of Operational Research*, 2(6), 429–444.

Chesbrough, H.W. (2003). The era of open innovation. *MIT Sloan Management Review*, 44(3), 35–41.

Cook, W.D. and Hababou, M. (2001). Sales performance measurement in bank branches. *Omega*, 29, 299–307.

Cook, W.D., Hababou, M., and Tuenter, H.J.H. (2000). Multicomponent efficiency measurement and shared inputs in Data Envelopment Analysis: An application to sales and service performance in bank branches. *Journal of Productivity Analysis*, 14, 209–224.

Cook, W.D., Tone, K., and Zhu, J. (2014). Data envelopment analysis: Prior to choosing a model. *Omega*, 44, 1–4.

Cooper, W.W., Seiford, L.M., and Zhu, J. (eds) (2011). Handbook on Data Envelopment Analysis, Vol. 164. Springer Science & Business Media.

Dogson, M., Gann, D., and Salter, A. (2006). The role of technology in the shift towards open innovation: the case of Procter & Gamble. *R&D Management*, 36(3), 333–346.

Dyson, R.G., Allen, R., Camanho, A.S., et al. (2001). Pitfalls and protocols in DEA. *European Journal of Operational Research*, 132(2), 245–259.

Einolf, K.W. (2004). Is winning everything? A Data Envelopment Analysis of Major League Baseball and the National Football League. *Journal of Sports Economics*, 5(2), 127–151.

Hambrick, D.C. and D'Aveni, R.A. (1988). Large corporate failures as downward spirals. *Administrative Science Quarterly*, 33, 1–23.

Hambrick, D.C. and Schecter, S.M. (1983). Turnaround strategies for mature industrial-product business units. *Academy of Management Journal*, 26(2), 231–248.

Han, U., Asmild, M., and Kunc, M. (2016). Regional R&D efficiency in Korea from static and dynamic perspectives. *Regional Studies*, 50(7), 1170–1184.

Hoy, F. (2006). The complicating factor of life cycles in corporate venturing. Entrepreneurship: Theory and Practice, November, 831–836.

Johnson, G., Scholes, K., and Whittington, R. (2008). Exploring Corporate Strategy, 8th edn. Pearson Education Ltd.

Markham, S.K., Kowolenko, M., and Michaelis, T.L. (2015). Unstructured text analytics to support new product development decisions. *Research Technology Management*, March–April: 30–38.

Miller, D and Friesen, P. (1984). A longitudinal study of the corporate life cycle. *Management Science*, 30(10), 1161–1183.

O'Neill, L., Rauner, M., Heidenberger, K., and Kraus, M. (2008). A cross-national comparison and taxonomy of DEA-based hospital efficiency studies. *Socio-Economic Planning Sciences*, 42(3), 158–189.

O'Reilly, C.A. and Tushman, M.L. (2004). The ambidextrous organization. *Harvard Business Review*, 82(4), 74–83.

Robbins, D.K. and Pearce II, J.A. (1992). Turnaround: retrenchment and recovery. *Strategic Management Journal*, 13, 287–309.

Serra, C.E.M. and Kunc, M. (2015). Benefits Realisation Management and its influence on project success and on the execution of business strategies. *International Journal of Project Management*, 33(1), 53–66.

Schoenberg, R., Collier, N. and Bowman, C. (2013). Strategies for business turnaround and recovery: a review and synthesis. *European Business Review*, 25(3), 243–262.

Targett, D. (1996). Analytical Decision Making. Pitman Publishing.

Tavares, G. (2002). A Bibliography of Data Envelopment Analysis (1978–2001). Rutcor Research Report. Rutgers University.

Walker, W.E. (2009). Does the best practice of rational-style model based policy analysis already include ethical considerations? *Omega*, 37(6), 1051–1062.

Wang, L., Kunc, M., and Bai, S.J. (2017). Realizing value from project implementation under uncertainty: An exploratory study using system dynamics. *International Journal of Project Management*, 35(3), 341–352.

Weill, L. (2004). Measuring cost efficiency in European banking: A comparison of frontier techniques. *Journal of Productivity Analysis*, 21, 133–152.

Weitzel, W. and Jonsson, E. (1989). Decline in organizations: a literature integration and extension. *Administrative Science Quarterly*, 34, 91–109.

Winston, W.L. and Albright, S.C. (2009). Practical Management Science, 3rd edn. South-Western Cengage Learning.

Futher Reading

Archer, N.P. and Ghasemzadeh, F. (1999). An integrated framework for project portfolio selection. *International Journal of Project Management*, 17(4), 207–216.

Balogun, J. and Hope Hailey, V. (2007). Exploring Strategic Change, 3rd edn. Prentice Hall.

Balogun, J. and Johnson, G. (2004). Organizational restructuring and middle manager sensemaking, *Academy of Management Journal*, 47(4):523–549.

Barker III, V.L. and Duhaime, I.M. (1997). Strategic change in the turnaround process: Theory and empirical evidence. *Strategic Management Journal*, 18(1), 13–38.

Beer, M. and Nohria, N. (2000). Cracking the code of change. Harvard Business Review, May–June, 133–141.

Deal, T. and Kennedy, A. (1984). Corporate Cultures: The Rights and Rituals of Corporate Life. Addison-Wesley.

Harris, L.C. and Ogbonna, E. (2002). The unintended consequences of culture interventions: a study of unexpected outcomes. *British Journal of Management*, 13(1): 31–49.

Higgins, J.M. and McCallaster, C. (2004). If you want strategic change don't forget your cultural artefacts, *Journal of Change Management*, 4(1): 63–73.

Kanter, R.M. (2003). Leadership and the psychology of turnarounds. *Harvard Business Review*, 81, 58–67.

Kets de Vries, M.F.R. (1994). The leadership mystique, *Academy of Management Executive*, 8(3), 73–89.

Kotter, J. (1995). Leading change: why transformation efforts fail. *Harvard Business Review*, March–April, 59–67.

Lovett, D. and Slatter, S. (1999). Corporate Turnaround. Penguin Books.

McKinley, W., Latham, S., and Braun, M. (2014). Organizational decline and innovation: Turnarounds and downward spirals. *Academy of Management Review*, 39(1), 88–110.

Miller, S., Wilson, D., and Hickson, D. (2004). Beyond planning strategies for successfully implementing strategic change. *Long Range Planning*, 37(3), 201–218.

Mintzberg, H. (1983). Power In and Around Organization. Prentice Hall.

Pratt, M.G. and Rafaelli, E. (1997). Organizational dress as a symbol of multi-layered social idealities. *Academy of Management Journal*, 40(4), 862–898.

Rasheed, H.S. (2005). Turnaround strategies for declining small business: The effects of performance and resources. *Journal of Developmental Entrepreneurship*, 10(03), 239–252.

Tangpong, C., Abebe, M., and Li, Z. (2015). A temporal approach to retrenchment and successful turnaround in declining firms. *Journal of Management Studies*, 52(5), 647–677.

Trahms, C.A., Ndofor, H.A., and Sirmon, D.G. (2013). Organizational decline and turnaround: A review and agenda for future research. *Journal of Management*, 39(5), 1277–1307.

Wang, X., Zhang, X., Liu, X., et al. (2012). Branch reconfiguration practice through operations research in Industrial and Commercial Bank of China. *Interfaces*, 42(1), 33–44.

Yukl, G.A. (2005). Leadership in Organizations, 6th edn. Prentice Hall.

Zimmerman, F.M. (1991). The Turnaround Experience: Real-world Lessons in Revitalizing Corporations. McGraw-Hill.

Index

Strategic Analytics: Integrating Management Science and Strategy, First Edition. Martin Kunc.
© 2019 John Wiley & Sons Ltd. Published 2019 by John Wiley & Sons Ltd.
Companion website: www.wiley.com/go/kunc/strategic-analytics